MOCK TRIALS

PREPARING, PRESENTING, AND *WINNING* YOUR CASE

THIRD EDITION

Mock Trials

Preparing, Presenting, and *Winning* Your Case

Third Edition

Jill Koster
Attorney at Law

Steven Lubet
Williams Memorial Professor of Law Emeritus
Northwestern University Pritzker School of Law
Chicago, Illinois

© 2024 by the National Institute for Trial Advocacy

All rights reserved. No part of this work may be reproduced or transmitted in any form or by any means, electronic or mechanical, including photocopying and recording, or by any information storage or retrieval system without the prior written approval of the National Institute for Trial Advocacy unless such copying is expressly permitted by federal copyright law.

Law students who purchase this NITA publication as part of their class materials and attendees of NITA-sponsored CLE programs are granted a limited license to reproduce, enlarge, and electronically or physically display, in their classrooms or other educational settings, any exhibits or text contained in the printed publication or online at the proprietary website. However, sharing one legally purchased copy of the publication among several members of a class team is prohibited under this license. Each individual is required to purchase their own copy of this publication. See 17 U.S.C. § 106.

Address inquiries to:

Reprint Permission
National Institute for Trial Advocacy
325 W. South Boulder RD., Ste. 1
Louisville, CO 80027-1130
Phone: (800) 225-6482
Email: publications@nita.org

ISBN 979-8-88669-057-6
FBA 2057
eISBN 979-8-88669-058-3
eFBA 2058

Printed in the United States of America

Library of Congress Cataloging-in-Publication Data

Names: Lubet, Steven, author. | Koster, Jill, author.
Title: Mock trials / Steven Lubet, Williams Memorial Professor of Law, Northwestern University School of Law, Chicago, Illinois; Jill Koster, Attorney at Law.
Description: Third Edition. | Louisville : NITA, The National institute for Trial Advocacy, 2024. | Includes index.
Identifiers: LCCN 2023030655 (print) | LCCN 2023030656 (ebook) | ISBN 9798886690576 (paperback) | ISBN 9798886690583 (ebook)
Subjects: LCSH: Moot courts--United States. | Trial practice--United States.
Classification: LCC KF281 .L83 2024 (print) | LCC KF281 (ebook) | DDC 347.73/75--dc23
LC record available at https://lccn.loc.gov/2023030655
LC ebook record available at https://lccn.loc.gov/2023030656

Official co-publisher of NITA.
aspenpublishing.com/NITA

*To my nephews and nieces:
Michael Trumbull, Joshua Harris, Hunter Harris, Kristina Justus,
Elizabeth James, and Taylor Harris*

J.K.

To Shoshana Noa

S.L.

Contents

Acknowledgments .... **xxv**

About the Authors .... **xxvii**

Chapter One: Trial Basics **1**
    I. **Understanding the Law** **1**
        A. Civil Cases 2
            1. Cause of Action 2
            2. The Burden of Proof 2
            3. Damages 3
        B. Criminal Cases 3
            1. The Burden of Proof 3
            2. Aggravating and Mitigating Factors and
                Affirmative Defenses 4
        C. Case Law 4
    II. **The Order of a Trial** **5**
    III. **The Format of a Courtroom** **6**
    IV. **The Anatomy of a Case File** **7**

Chapter Two: Case Preparation **9**
    I. **Organize Your Trial Binder** **9**
    II. **Read and Outline the Case** **10**
        A. Grasp the Applicable Statutes and Case Law 10
        B. Determine Which Witnesses are Helpful to Each Side 10
        C. For Each Witness, Identify the Key Favorable and
            Unfavorable Facts 12
        D. Consider the Admissibility of All Facts 13
        E. Compile a Summary of Key Facts that Will Likely be
            Established at Trial 15

Contents

    III. Analyze the Facts to Develop a Story, Theory, and Theme.................. 16
        A. Consider the Possibilities 17
        B. Prepare Your Case Theory and Theme 18
            1. Develop a Theory 18
            2. Develop a Theme 19
            3. Return to Your Story 20
    IV. Get the Most from Your Work... 21
        A. Planning Closing Argument and Opening Statement 21
        B. Planning Direct Examinations 22
        C. Planning Cross-Examinations 23
        D. Planning Objections and Responses 23

Chapter Three: Communication Techniques 25
    I. The Importance of Effective Communication 25
        A. Confidence 25
        B. Integrity 26
    II. Nonverbal Communication Techniques... 26
        A. Stay in Role at All Times 27
        B. Be Careful Not to Upstage Your Witnesses 27
        C. Make Eye Contact with the Witnesses and Factfinder...................... 28
        D. Use Body Movement to Explain and Emphasize Points................... 29
        E. Minimize Reliance on Notes 31
    III. Verbal Communication Techniques 33
        A. Show Respect to the Judge 33
        B. Use Powerful Speech 33
            1. Take the Lead Out 34
            2. Say What You Mean and Mean What You Say...................... 34
        C. With Descriptive Language and Legalese, Be Mindful of Your Audience 35
            1. When the Factfinder Is a Jury.. 35
            2. When the Factfinder Is a Judge 36
        D. Use Primacy and Recency 36

	E.	Use Repetition and Duration to Emphasize Your Most Important Points 36
	F.	Use Reflective Questioning to Illustrate Time, Distance, and Intensity 38
	G.	Use Nouns and Verbs in Place of Adjectives 39
	H.	Use Apposition to Compare Related Facts 40
	I.	Use Headlines for Emphasis and Transition 40
	J.	Use Enumeration When Addressing Related Points 41
	K.	Do Not Be Overly Thankful 42
	L.	Resist the Temptation to Respond to Witnesses' Answers 42
IV.	**Communicating with Pictures and Demonstrations** **43**
	A.	Use the Exhibits 43
	B.	Create Visual Aids 44
	C.	Conduct Demonstrations 44

Chapter Four: Pretrial Matters 45

I.	**Preliminary (A.K.A. "Housekeeping") Matters—Establishing the Courtroom Rules** **45**
	A. Should I Treat the Trial as a Jury Trial or Bench Trial? 46
	B. Should I Assume Objections are Being Argued at Sidebar? 47
	C. Does the Court Have Rules About Moving Around the Courtroom? 50
	D. Should I Seek Permission Prior to Each Instance of Approaching a Testifying Witness? 51
	E. (In Jury Trials) Is the Court Willing to Read Stipulations Aloud? 51
II.	**Additional Housekeeping Matters** **52**
	A. Provide Pretrial Notice if Required 52
	B. Inform the Court that You Plan to Use Demonstrative Evidence 52
	C. Cover Any Other Plans You Have that are Remotely Controversial 54
III.	**Motions in Limine** **55**

Contents

Chapter Five: Playing an Effective Witness 57

I. The Importance of Effective Witnesses 57

II. Key Qualities of Effective Witnesses 58
  - A. Be Prepared 58
    1. Take Note of Any Conflicts with Another Witness's Anticipated Testimony 58
    2. If While Testifying You Forget an Important Fact, Say So 59
    3. Describe Key Facts Using the Same Words that Appear in the Witness's Statement/Affidavit/Transcript 60
  - B. Be Believable, Credible, and Confident 61
  - C. Be Interesting 63

III. Techniques for Handling Direct and Cross-Examination 65
  - A. Listen Critically to Each Question and Pause Before Answering 65
  - B. On Cross-Examination, Listen for Clues Within Objections 66
    1. Vague 68
    2. Compound 69
    3. Calls for Speculation 69
    4. Relevance 70
    5. (Calls for) Hearsay or Double Hearsay 70
  - C. Address Internal Assumptions, Premises, or Predicates Separately 72
  - D. Be Succinct If Possible but Explain If Needed 72
  - E. Ask to See Any Document Referenced 73
  - F. Do Not Fight Necessary Admissions 74
  - G. Do Not Take on the Role of Advocate 74
  - H. Be the Same Person on Cross as Direct 75
  - I. Make Only Reasonable Inferences from the Case File 76

Chapter Six: Evidence Made Simple 79

I. Relevance 79

II. Unfair Prejudice 80

III.	Lack of Personal Knowledge and Speculation 80
IV.	Hearsay.. 81
V.	**Improper Character Evidence Generally**.. 84
	A. Conviction of Crime 84
	B. Character for Untruthfulness 85

Chapter Seven: Direct Examination... 87

I. **The Role of Direct Examination**... 87
   A. Set Forth Your Theory of the Case 87
   B. Introduce the Undisputed Facts 87
   C. Enhance the Likelihood of Disputed Facts................................ 88
   D. Lay Foundation for Introducing Exhibits.................................. 88
   E. Reflect upon Witness Credibility.. 88
   F. Hold the Factfinder's Attention.. 88

II. **The Rules of Direct Examination**.. 89
   A. Ask Only Nonleading Questions.. 89
   B. Avoid Questions That Elicit "Narrative" Responses.................. 90
   C. Obey the Nonopinion Rule.. 91
   D. Refresh the Witness's Recollection When Necessary 92
   E. Have the Appropriate Witnesses Identify the Defendant
      (Prosecution Only) 94
   F. Use Stipulations When Helpful.. 95

III. **Planning Direct Examinations** 98
   A. Content 98
      1. What to Include 98
      2. What to Exclude... 100
   B. Organization 101
      1. Start Strong and End Strong 101
         a. The Overall Examination 101
         b. The Sub-Examinations 102
      2. Use Topical Organization 102
      3. Get to the Point... 103

Contents

    4. Tell the Story 103
    5. Do Not Interrupt the Action 104
    6. Affirm Before Refuting 105
    7. Draw the Sting 105
    8. End with a Clincher 106
    9. Ignore Any Rule When Necessary 106
  IV. **The Ethics of Direct Examination** **107**
    A. Asking Objectionable Questions 107
    B. Eliciting Unreasonable Inferences 108

Chapter Eight: Foundations and Exhibits 111

 I. **Evidentiary Foundations Generally** **111**
   A. The Requirement of Foundation 111
   B. Components of Foundation 112
    1. Relevance 112
    2. Authenticity 113
    3. Specific Admissibility 114
   C. Establishing Foundations 114
    1. Using a Single Witness 114
    2. Using Multiple Witnesses 115
    3. Cross-Examination 115
    4. Conditional Admissibility 116
 II. **Foundations for Testimonial Evidence** **117**
   A. Personal Knowledge 117
   B. Conversations 117
    1. Conversations that Occur in Person 118
    2. Conversations that Occur Over the Telephone 118
   C. Prior Identification 119
   D. Habit and Routine 120
   E. Character and Reputation 121
    1. Other Crimes or Past Misconduct 121
    2. Reputation for Untruthfulness 124

	F.	Foundations for Hearsay Statements 125
		1. Party Admissions 125
		2. Present Sense Impression 126
		3. Excited Utterance 127
		4. State of Mind 128
		5. Dying Declaration 129
III.	**Exhibits Generally** **130**
	A.	The Role of Exhibits 130
	B.	Types of Exhibits 131
		1. Real or Tangible Evidence 131
		2. Demonstrative Evidence 131
		3. Documentary Evidence 131
	C.	Offering Exhibits at Trial 132
		1. Mark the Exhibit for Identification 132
		2. Identify the Exhibit for Opposing Counsel 133
		3. Show the Exhibit to the Witness 133
		4. Have the Witness Identify the Exhibit 133
		5. Complete the Foundation for the Exhibit 134
		6. Offer the Exhibit into Evidence 134
		7. Publish and Use the Exhibit 134
		a. Publishing an Exhibit 134
		b. Using an Exhibit 135
IV.	**Specific Foundations for Exhibits** **137**
	A.	Real Evidence/Tangible Objects 137
		1. Establishing Authenticity 138
		2. Showing the Chain of Custody 139
	B.	Photographs 141
	C.	Demonstrative Evidence 141
		1. Maps, Charts, and Diagrams 142
		2. Illustrative Aids 142
	D.	Documentary Evidence 143
		1. Authentication 143

Contents

		a.	Handwriting and Signature	143
		b.	Circumstantial Evidence of Authorship or Origin	144
		c.	Mailing or Transmission	145
	E.	Hearsay Exceptions		145
		1.	Business Records	145
		2.	Public Records	146
		3.	Party Admissions	147

Chapter Nine: Cross-Examination **149**

I. **The Purpose of Cross-Examination** **149**
    A. Repair or Minimize Damage Done on Direct 149
    B. Enhance Your Case 150
    C. Detract from Your Opponent's Case 150
    D. Lay the Foundation for Introducing Exhibits 150
    E. Discredit the Witness or Another Witness 150
    F. Stay in Control 150

II. **The Rules of Cross-Examination** **151**
    A. Ask Only Leading Questions 152
    B. Get In and Get Out 152
    C. Ask Only Questions to Which You Already Know the Answers ... 153
    D. Do Not Invite Objections or Argue with Witnesses 153
        1. Ask Short Questions 154
        2. Ask Fair Questions 155
    E. Do Not Ask the Ultimate Question 155
    F. Insist on a Responsive Answer 157
        1. Correct the Problem Yourself 157
        2. Enlist the Judge's Help, if Necessary 158

III. **Planning Cross-Examination** **159**
    A. Content 159
        1. Determining the Usable Universe 160
        2. Preparing Your Questions 161

		B.	Organization 162

		B.	Organization 162

Contents

    B. Organization 162
        1. General Tips for Organizing Cross-Examinations 163
           a. Do Not Worry About Starting Strong 163
           b. Use Topical Organization 163
           c. Give the Details First...165
           d. Scatter the Circumstantial Evidence 165
           e. Save a Zinger for the End 165
        2. A Classic Format for Cross-Examination 167
           a. Friendly Information 167
           b. Affirmative Information 167
           c. Uncontrovertible Information..167
           d. Challenging Information 167
           e. Hostile Information 168
           f. Zinger.. 168
IV. **The Ethics of Cross-Examination**... 168

Chapter Ten: Impeachment 171
I. **The Role of Impeachment**... 171
II. **The Rules of Impeachment**... 172
    A. Impeach Only on Significant Matters 172
    B. Impeach Only on Actual Inconsistencies....................................173
    C. Be Sure of Success Before Beginning...174
    D. Do Not Impeach Favorable Information 174
    E. Consider the Impact of Multiple Impeachment.........................175
    F. Consider the Timing of Impeachment 175
III. **The Types of Impeachment** 177
    A. Prior Inconsistent Statements 177
        1. Recommit the Witness 178
        2. Accredit the Witness's Prior Opportunity to Tell the Full Story...178
        3. Confront the Witness with the Prior Statement........................ 180
    B. Impeachment by Omission...182

Contents

        1. Recommit the Witness 184
        2. Accredit the Witness's Prior Opportunity to Tell the Full Story.. 184
        3. Confront the Witness 185
    C. Character and Case-Specific Motive Impeachment 187
        1. Impeachment Based on the Witness's Character or Characteristics.. 187
            a. Conviction of a Crime 188
            b. Past Untruthfulness and Other Bad Acts............................ 188
            c. Impaired Perception or Recollection 188
        2. Case-Specific Motive Impeachment..189

Chapter Eleven: Redirect and Recross-Examinations 191

  I. **Redirect Examination** 191
    A. The Purpose of Redirect Examination 191
    B. The Rules of Redirect 191
        1. Follow the Same Rules as Direct Examination 191
        2. Stay Within the Scope of the Cross-Examination......................191
    C. Planning Redirect Examination 192
    D. Waiving Redirect Examination 192
    E. Conducting Redirect Examination..193
  II. **Recross-Examination** 194

Chapter Twelve: Expert Testimony 197

  I. **The Purpose of Expert Testimony** 197
  II. **The Standards for Expert Testimony**.. 197
    A. Areas of Expertise..198
    B. Scope of Opinion 198
    C. Bases for Opinion..198
  III. **Direct Examination of Experts** 199
    A. Planning Expert Testimony...199
        1. Determine the Expert's Theory 199
        2. Encourage Using Plain Language... 200

    3. Help to Avoid Narratives 201
        a. Prompt the Witness to Give Internal Summaries 202
        b. Use Visual Aids 203
    B. Organizing Expert Testimony 204
        1. Introduce the Witness and Foreshadow the Testimony 204
        2. Elicit the Expert's Qualifications 205
            a. Fulfill the Technical Requirements 205
            b. Be Persuasive When Qualifying 206
            c. Tender the Witness (If Allowed) 207
        3. Elicit the Expert's Opinion and Theory 207
            a. Have the Expert State Opinions Up Front 207
            b. Elicit the Expert's Theory 208
        4. Elicit the Explanation and Support for the Expert's
           Opinion 209
            a. Have the Expert Explain the Data 209
            b. Be Clear About What Assumptions Were Made 210
        5. Use Theory Differentiation If Your Case Involves
           Dueling Experts 210
        6. Send Expert Out with a Bang 212
IV. **Cross-Examining Experts** 212
    A. Challenge the Witness's Credentials 212
        1. Voir Dire on Credentials 212
        2. Cross-Examine on Credentials 214
            a. Limit the Scope of the Witness's Expertise 214
            b. Stress Missing Credentials 215
            c. Contrast Your Expert's Credentials 215
    B. Obtain Favorable Information 217
        1. Affirm Your Own Expert 217
        2. Elicit Areas of Agreement 217
        3. Criticize the Opposing Party's Conduct 218
    C. Challenge the Witness's Impartiality 218
        1. Question Fees 219

Contents

        2. Question the Expert's Relationship with the Participants 219
        3. Question the Expert's Positional Bias 219
    D. Point Out Omissions 219
    E. Substitute Information 221
        1. Change Assumptions 221
        2. Maximize Any Uncertainty 221
    F. Challenge Technique or Theory 222

Chapter Thirteen: Objections 225

  I. **The Purpose of Objections** 225
    A. Nonsubstantive Objections 226
    B. Substantive Objections 226
  II. **The Rules of Objecting** 226
    A. Consider Objections Carefully 226
    B. Direct All Arguments to the Judge 227
    C. In Jury Trials, Request Sidebars 228
    D. Raise Objections Appropriately 228
        1. Stand Up 228
        2. Object and State Your Grounds 229
        3. Pause for the Judge to Consider the Objection 229
        4. If Appropriate, Respond to the Court 230
        5. Special Considerations 230
            a. Repeated Objections 230
            b. Requests for Voir Dire of the Witness 232
    E. Time Objections Appropriately 233
    F. Respond to Objections Appropriately 235
        1. Wait for the Judge's Cue to Respond 235
        2. If Appropriate, Request to Be Heard 235
        3. Respond Specifically 236
            a. Inform the Court of Limited Admissibility 237
            b. Inform the Court of a Conditional Offer 237
        4. Cure the Objection Whenever Possible 238

		G.	Follow Up on the Judge's Ruling 239
			1. Objection Overruled 239
			a. Proponent's Job 239
			b. Opponent's Job 240
			2. Objection Sustained 241
			a. Proponent's Job 241
			b. Opponent's Job 243
		H.	Reevaluate Your Theory 244
	III.	**Ethics and Objections** **245**	
		A.	Asking Objectionable Questions 245
		B.	Making Improper Objections 246
		C.	Making "Tactical" Objections 246
	IV.	**A Short List of Common Objections** **247**	
		A.	Nonsubstantive Objections 247
			1. Leading Question (On Direct Examination Only) 247
			2. Compound Question 247
			3. Vague Question 248
			4. Argumentative Question 248
			5. Narratives 248
			6. Asked and Answered 249
			7. Assumes Facts Not in Evidence 249
			8. Nonresponsive Answers (On Cross-Examination Only) 250
		B.	Substantive Objections 250
			1. Hearsay 250
			a. Statements that Are Not Hearsay 251
			b. Exceptions to the Hearsay Rule 251
			2. Irrelevant 252
			3. Unfair Prejudice 253
			4. Improper Character Evidence Generally 253
			a. Conviction of Crime 253
			b. Untruthfulness 254
			c. Reputation 254

Contents

        5. Speculation or Lack of Personal Knowledge 255
        6. Improper Lay Opinion 255
        7. Authenticity 256
        8. Lack of Foundation 256

Chapter Fourteen: Opening Statement 259

  I. The Purpose of the Opening Statement 259
      A. Grab the Opening Moment 259
      B. Explain the Anticipated Evidence 260
      C. Advocate for Your Client 260
  II. The Rules of Opening Statement 261
      A. Do Not Argue 262
        1. Defining Argument 262
        2. Other Considerations 263
      B. Do Not Comment on the Law 263
      C. Weave Your Theory and Theme into Your Trial Story 264
        1. State Your Theory Clearly 264
        2. Introduce Your Theme 265
      D. Order and Contrast the Facts Persuasively 266
  III. Planning Your Opening Statement 268
      A. Content 268
        1. Include Only Provable Facts 268
        2. Include the Necessary Facts 268
          a. The Physical Scene 269
          b. Action and Key Events 269
          c. Transactions and Agreements 269
        3. Include a Brief Reference to the Other Side's Case 270
          a. Plaintiff/Prosecution Opening 270
          b. Defendant's Opening 271
      B. Organization 272
        1. Begin with Your Theme and Theory 272
        2. Introduce Yourself and Your Client 273

		3.	Tell the Full Story 274
			a. Avoid the Witness-By-Witness Approach 274
			b. Use Chronology Wisely 275
		4.	Highlight the Legal Issues 276
		5.	Request a Verdict 277
IV.	Objections 277		
	A.	Raising Objections 277	
	B.	Responding to Objections 278	

Chapter Fifteen: Closing Argument 279

I.	The Purpose of the Closing Argument 279		
II.	The Principles of Closing Argument 281		
	A.	Use Your Theory and Theme 281	
	B.	Argue, Argue, Argue! 282	
		1.	Make Inferences and Conclusions 282
		2.	Cluster Circumstantial Evidence and Accumulate Details 282
		3.	Use Analogies, Allusions, and Stories 283
			a. Analogies 283
			b. Allusions 284
			c. Stories 284
		4.	Emphasize the Undisputed Facts 285
		5.	Refute the Opposing Witnesses' Testimony 285
		6.	Tie Up Your Cross-Examinations 286
		7.	Argue Witness Credibility and Motive 287
		8.	Assert the Weight that Should Be Given to Evidence 288
		9.	Comment on the Opposing Witness's Demeanor 288
		10.	Confront Your Weaknesses 288
		11.	Comment on Promises Kept and Broken 289
		12.	Argue Damages, Where Applicable 290
		13.	Apply the Law 290
	C.	Avoid Making Impermissible Arguments 291	
		1.	Do Not Comment on Privilege 291

2. Do Not Misuse Evidence 291
3. Do Not Interject Your Personal Beliefs Regarding the Facts or Issues in the Case 293
4. Do Not Make Appeals to the Factfinder's Personal Interest..... 293
5. Do Not Make Appeals to Emotion, Sympathy, or Passion........ 294
6. Do Not Misstate the Evidence... 294
7. Do Not Misstate the Law or Discourage the Jury from Following It 295

III. **Planning Closing Arguments**.. **296**
   A. Content 296
      1. Tell a Persuasive Story 296
         a. Known Facts—What Happened? 296
         b. Reasons—Why Did It Happen? 297
         c. Credible Witnesses—Who Should Be Believed? 297
         d. Supportive Details—How can We Be Sure? 297
         e. Common Sense—Is It Plausible? 298
      2. Use the Format of Closings to Your Advantage 298
         a. Plaintiff/Prosecution Argument in Chief........................... 299
         b. Defendant's Argument... 299
         c. Plaintiff/Prosecution Rebuttal 301
   B. Organization 304
      1. Use Topical Organization 304
         a. Issues 304
         b. Elements 304
         c. Jury Instructions... 305
      2. Alternative Organization Methods 305
         a. Chronological Organization 305
         b. Witness Listing... 306
      3. Whatever Your Format, Follow These Guidelines..................... 306
         a. Start Strong and End Strong.. 306
         b. Argue Your Affirmative Case First 308
         c. Embrace or Displace the Burden of Proof.......................... 308

		d.	Address Witness Credibility Throughout 309
		e.	Argue Damages 310
IV.	**Objections** **311**
	A.	Raising Objections 311
	B.	Responding to Objections 311
	C.	Asking for a Cautionary Instruction...311

Appendix..**313**

Index **315**

ACKNOWLEDGMENTS

I have been blessed with wonderful mentors over the years and would like to thank them for their guidance and support: Georgia Brousseau, Roger Duncan, Steven Lubet, and Judge Robert Gettleman.

Jill Koster—St. Thomas, U.S. Virgin Islands

I am grateful for the insights and other assistance of Ann Miller, Richard Levin, Adam Riback, Joseph Ben-Or, Donald Beskind, Sheila Block, Anthony Bocchino, Robert Burns, James Duane, James Epstein, Thomas Geraghty, Jonathan Misheiker, Linda Lipton, Fred Lubet, Melissa Montemyor, Alex Rose, James Seckinger, Ashley Smith, and Jill Koster.

Steven Lubet—Evanston, Illinois

About the Authors

JILL KOSTER is a lecturer on trial skills with the National White Collar Crime Center. Previously she served the United States Department of Justice, most recently as Criminal Chief of the United States Attorney's Office in the District of the Virgin Islands. Ms. Koster also previously litigated for Bartlit Beck, a highly regarded civil boutique trial firm in Chicago and Denver, and clerked for a federal district court judge in Chicago. Ms. Koster graduated with honors from Northwestern University School of Law and has nearly thirty-five years of experience competing in and coaching mock trial as well as teaching trial advocacy skills to law students and practicing attorneys.

STEVEN LUBET is the Williams Memorial Professor at the Northwestern University Pritzker School of Law, and the former director of the law school's award-winning Bartlit Center for Trial Advocacy. He is an author of several best-selling NITA books and case files, including *Modern Trial Advocacy*, and popular books such as *Murder in Tombstone: The Forgotten Trial of Wyatt Earp* and *Lawyers' Poker: Fifty-Two Lessons that Lawyers Can Learn from Card Players*, as well as three books on abolitionist lawyers in the decade before the Civil War. Professor Lubet is a nationally recognized expert in trial advocacy and legal ethics, having written seventeen books and over four hundred articles and essays on all aspects of law practice.

Chapter One

Trial Basics

Mock trial lands its participants feet-first in a courtroom experience that even many licensed attorneys never experience—conducting a full trial. Even though the stakes are fictional, the hard work and adrenaline are genuine. Your teammates and your coaches take this experience seriously, and they expect you to do the same.

The fact remains, though, that you are not a practicing attorney. You may not even be a college graduate. You may, in fact, feel overwhelmed by the mock trial experience. This book is designed to allay those fears and lay the foundation you need for success.

Before you prepare your case, there are basic legal concepts you must grasp to fulfill your role as an attorney in a mock trial. You should have a basic understanding of how our legal system operates; you must understand the order of a mock trial and be able to visualize the setup of a courtroom; and you must be familiar with the contents of the mock trial case file.

I. Understanding the Law

There are two kinds of cases: civil and criminal. Both case types involve laws, also referred to as ordinances and statutes, enacted by the legislative bodies of the local, state, and federal governments.

When an individual, business, or government agency violates a law, a civil or criminal case (depending on the law involved) may be brought. Most cases are settled or dropped after being filed. A small number of cases, however, result in trials.

At trial, the parties on each side of a case argue two things: the law and the facts. The judge decides all issues or questions of law; it is the judge's job to determine which laws apply to the case and how they should be applied. In jury trials, the jurors decide the issues of fact contested by the parties. In bench trials, the presiding judge performs this function, listening to the evidence and deciding what to believe. When serving in this capacity, the judge or jury is referred to as the "finder of fact," "factfinder," or "trier of fact" of the case. While deliberating, the factfinder must rely upon the testimony of witnesses and the evidence presented; the lawyers' arguments are considered only to the extent they explain the witnesses' testimony and the evidence.

Chapter One

A. Civil Cases

Civil lawsuits may be brought for breach of contract, personal injuries, defamation, or violations of civil rights. The participants may be individuals, businesses, or government agencies. The two parties in a civil case are referred to as the plaintiff and the defendant; the plaintiff is the person bringing the lawsuit and the defendant is the person being sued.

The goal of civil litigation is to determine whether the defendant violated the law and what the appropriate consequence of that violation should be.

1. Cause of Action

The legal basis for a civil lawsuit is called a cause of action. Each cause of action consists of elements that the plaintiff must prove in order to prevail. For example, the elements of a cause of action for negligence are duty, breach of duty, proximate cause, and damages.

A plaintiff bringing a civil lawsuit against a defendant files a court document called a complaint that identifies the cause(s) of action and alleges the specific acts of the defendant that violated the law. So, a plaintiff suing a defendant for negligence would allege that the defendant had a duty, that the defendant breached the duty, that this breach was the proximate cause of the plaintiff's injuries, and that the plaintiff sustained damages as a result.

Causes of action are often divided into separate counts. For example, the complaint in an automobile accident case might include one count for personal injury and another for property damage. In a contract case, the plaintiff might bring one count claiming that certain goods were not delivered on time and another claiming that the goods were damaged when they were finally received.

2. The Burden of Proof

A plaintiff can prevail in a civil case only by proving each element of their claim by a "preponderance of the evidence." Translated literally, preponderance of the evidence means a majority of the evidence. This does not mean that the plaintiff must merely present more evidence or more witnesses than the defendant; it means that the evidence presented must establish more likely than not that the defendant is "liable," as opposed to "not liable." There is no finding of guilt in civil actions.

A party found liable in a civil case may be ordered to correct the action if reversible, alter the current course of action if ongoing, or pay money to the plaintiff for damages. With each of these remedies, the goal is to make the plaintiff "whole" again: to return the plaintiff to their pre-injured state, if possible, or to compensate the plaintiff fairly for their loss due to the defendant's actions.

3. Damages

Payment of damages can be awarded for a plaintiff's financial loss (including lawyers' fees, if appropriate), as well as for physical or mental suffering resulting from the defendant's conduct. There are two types of damages in civil cases: compensatory and punitive. Compensatory damages cover the *actual* loss and suffering of the plaintiff. Punitive damages are awarded above and beyond compensatory damages to *punish* the defendant for their wrongdoing and to ensure that the conduct will not be repeated.

B.   Criminal Cases

Criminal cases are brought by the government against individuals or businesses accused of violating local, state, or federal criminal laws. The parties in criminal cases are the prosecution and the defense. The prosecution is the local, state, or federal government (depending on the law violated), which is represented by a local, state, or federal prosecutor. The defendant is the accused individual or business, who is represented by private counsel or by a government defense attorney (typically called a public defender) if the defendant lacks the financial resources to pay for an attorney.

Laws defining crimes list the criminal elements the government must prove to convict the defendant. These elements usually include a physical act and a mental state. Most statutes also set forth the range of sentences available if the defendant is convicted.

1.   The Burden of Proof

Our criminal justice system is based on the premise that allowing a guilty person to go free is better than putting an innocent person behind bars. For this reason, the defendant is presumed innocent and the prosecution carries a heavy burden of proof during criminal trials. (Note: there is no finding of innocent in criminal trials; only guilty or not guilty.)

To prevail in a criminal case, the prosecution must prove each element of the crime beyond a reasonable doubt. Despite its frequent use, "reasonable doubt" remains difficult to define. As the U.S. Supreme Court explained, reasonable doubt is doubt based on reason that arises from evidence or the lack of evidence. Thus, a defendant can be found guilty even if a *possible* doubt remains in the minds of the jurors. Conversely, the defendant can be found not guilty even if the jurors believe that the defendant *probably* committed the crime but they are not convinced beyond a reasonable doubt. A defendant found guilty in a criminal case may be sentenced by the presiding judge to serve time in jail, fulfill conditions of supervised release, pay a fine, perform community service, or any combination thereof.

Be aware that under some criminal statutes, the burden of proving particular elements of the crime or a defense to the crime shifts between the parties.

2. Aggravating and Mitigating Factors and Affirmative Defenses

Some criminal statutes raise or lower the severity of the crime charged (or the punishment) on the basis of certain aggravating or mitigating factors, when proven at trial. Aggravating factors are circumstances that make the crime or the punishment worse. Mitigating factors are circumstances that tend to decrease the severity of the crime or punishment. For example, a criminal statute outlining the charge of murder might include aggravating or mitigating factors addressing the state of mind of the defendant, the age of the victim, or the method used to commit the crime. Likewise, some criminal statutes set forth affirmative defenses to the crime. An affirmative defense, once proven, legally exonerates the defendant of the crime charged. For example, a frequently used affirmative defense in murder cases is self-defense.

C. Case Law

Many court decisions are recorded and collected for future reference by the public. When a judge interprets and applies a law, the decision is referred to as case law. Case law that is binding on a particular court is also referred to as precedent.

In addition to understanding the statutes in your case, also look to the case law to determine how those laws have been interpreted and applied by courts. In mock trials, relevant case law is sometimes provided to the participants along with the case materials. Just like a legislative enactment, case law is binding on the parties insofar as it is used to determine the *meaning* of a law. When basing an argument on case law, it is important that you argue how the facts of your case are more similar to, rather than different from, the original case.

	CIVIL CASES	**CRIMINAL CASES**
Examples:	Personal Injury, Civil Rights	Burglary, Murder
Titles of Parties:	Plaintiff and Defendant	Prosecution and Defense
Burden of Proof:	Preponderance of the Evidence	Beyond a Reasonable Doubt
Possible Verdicts:	Liable or Not Liable	Guilty or Not Guilty
Common Remedy:	Payment of Damages	Prison Sentence

II. The Order of a Trial

Trials proceed as follows:

A. Opening Statements

    1. Plaintiff/Prosecution

    2. Defendant/Defense

B. Witness Testimony (the number of witnesses may vary)

    1. Plaintiff/Prosecution Case-in-chief

        a. Direct examination of Witness 1 by Plaintiff/Prosecution

        b. Cross-examination of Witness 1 by Defendant/Defense

        c. Redirect and then recross of Witness 1*

        d. Direct examination of Witness 2 by Plaintiff/Prosecution

        e. Cross-examination of Witness 2 by Defendant/Defense

        f. Redirect and then recross of Witness 2*

        g. Direct examination of Witness 3 by Plaintiff/Prosecution

        h. Cross-examination of Witness 3 by Defendant/Defense

        i. Redirect and then recross of Witness 3*

    2. Defendant/Defense Case-in-chief

        a. Direct examination of Witness 4 by Defendant/Defense

        b. Cross-examination of Witness 4 by Plaintiff/Prosecution

        c. Redirect and then recross of Witness 4*

        d. Direct examination of Witness 5 by Defendant/Defense

        e. Cross-examination of Witness 5 by Plaintiff/Prosecution

        f. Redirect and then recross of Witness 5*

        g. Direct examination of Witness 6 by Defendant/Defense

---

* At the judge's discretion, if requested.

Chapter One

        h. Cross-examination of Witness 6 by Plaintiff/Prosecution

        i. Redirect and then recross of Witness 6*

    C. Closing Arguments

        1. Plaintiff/Prosecution (some portion or all)

        2. Defendant/Defense

        3. Rebuttal by Plaintiff/Prosecution (if time remains)

    D. Jury Deliberations (if a jury is the factfinder)

    E. Verdict Announcement

The above order assumes each party calls three witnesses, which is typical in a mock trial. In real trials, the number of witnesses each side calls to testify will vary and need not be equal. In most criminal cases, the defendant has no burden of proof and therefore the defendant may not call any witnesses to testify.

III. The Format of a Courtroom

Mock trials attempt to mirror actual trials in every way possible, including the setup of the courtroom. At the front of each courtroom, there are places set aside for the presiding judge, the clerk, and the parties. Likewise, the jurors are separated from those observing the trial. Jurors sit along one side of the courtroom, with the plaintiff/prosecution seated closer to the jury and the defendant/defense seated farther away. The diagram below illustrates the setup of a typical courtroom.

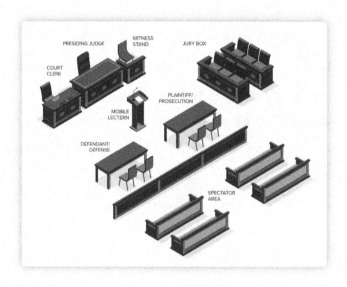

IV. The Anatomy of a Case File

For the most part, mock trial case files include the same basic components.

Case Summary. Most mock trial case files begin with a short summary of the case. Use the case summary to determine the main arguments the drafter of the case anticipates each side making during the trial. If available, read the case summary carefully and often as you prepare for trial.

Stipulations. Some mock trial case files also include a list of stipulations. In a real case, a stipulation is an agreement between the parties about the facts or the law. In mock trials, stipulations set out uncontestable facts or required legal rulings. Stipulations may set forth important facts not included elsewhere in the case file or they may set forth testimony or exhibits to be automatically admitted into evidence. You are bound by the stipulations listed in your case file; you cannot ignore or contest them, no matter how damaging they are to your case. Thus, you should be constantly aware of stipulations as you prepare for trial.

Witness Statements. In mock trials, witness statements make up the bulk of the case file; they include the facts, favorable and unfavorable, that each witness may testify to during trial. In most instances, witness statements represent the summarized prior sworn testimony of the witnesses and are referred to as affidavits. Witness statements may also be in the form of a deposition transcript. A deposition is a formal meeting that includes the counsel for both parties and a testifying witness. During a deposition, the witness is asked questions under oath by each side and the testimony is recorded by a court reporter. Sometimes case files include unsworn statements, or even summaries, such as an account of a witness's statement in a police report. Unsworn prior statements of witnesses are treated differently from prior sworn testimony, as we discuss in Chapter Ten, Section III.

Whatever their form, witness statements include (or sometimes notably fail to include) the facts that the parties for both sides will attempt to establish at trial.

Exhibits. Mock trial exhibits are usually documents, though they can also reference tangible items that you can bring to your trial to enter as evidence. For instance, your case might include a picture of the alleged murder weapon or it could simply list the weapon as an exhibit and indicate that a close facsimile of the weapon fitting the description provided in the case file is an acceptable exhibit at trial. Some competitions, however, do not allow the use of physical exhibits, no matter how closely they match the photographs or testimony in the file.

Statutes and Case Law. Your case file should also contain the statutes and case law that are applicable to your case. As discussed above, the statutes and case law in your case file provide an outline of the legal arguments both sides may make at trial. Although you are only likely to discuss the law during your opening statement (sparingly) and closing argument, they are an integral part of your trial preparation.

Jury Instructions and Verdict Forms. Jury instructions, which provide summaries of the relevant statutes and case law (among other things), may also be included in your case file. When provided, use the jury instructions as a guide to understanding the provided statutes and case law. The same goes for jury verdict forms, when included.

Rules of Evidence, Procedure, and Ethics. Last but certainly not least are the rules of evidence, procedure, and ethics to be used in your trial. As with the statutes and case law, these rules will guide your trial preparation.

The rules of evidence used in most mock trial competitions are the Federal Rules of Evidence or a simplified version of those rules. For that reason, we base our discussion of all evidentiary issues in this book on the Federal Rules. If your competition uses rules other than the Federal Rules, follow those rules instead.

Our advice has likewise been guided by the Federal Rules of Criminal Procedure, the Federal Rules of Civil Procedure, and the ethical standards adopted by the Model Rules of Professional Conduct. As before, follow the specific rules of procedure and ethics adopted by your competition, even if they differ somewhat from the Federal Rules or Model Rules.

Chapter Two

Case Preparation

Trial lawyers spend their entire careers figuring out the method of preparing a case for trial that works best for them. Each trial lawyer has their own strengths and weaknesses, as well as their own work habits, methods, and standards. Just because a method works for one trial lawyer does not mean it will work for their co-counsel. Simply put, there is no single way to prepare a case for trial; there are nearly as many possible permutations as there are trial lawyers.

If you are reading this book, you are likely relatively new to the world of trials and therefore unlikely to know what method of preparation works best for you. To give you a head start, in this chapter we provide a thorough method of preparing a mock trial case. We suggest that you begin by following this method, although you will no doubt find ways to adapt or improve upon it as your work proceeds. If so, we encourage you always to do what works best for you.

Your ability to effectively use this method (or any other method of preparing for trial, for that matter) relies completely on your knowledge and understanding of the rules of evidence, procedure, and ethics that govern your mock trial. We discuss the most important rules of evidence, procedure, and ethics throughout later chapters of this book. For that reason, you would be wise to read this book in its entirety before you begin preparing for your mock trial. If that is not possible, we recommend at the very least that you read through the rules of evidence, procedure, and ethics provided by the organizer of your mock trial before proceeding further. When you are ready to begin the work of preparing for trial, we recommend you start here.

I. Organize Your Trial Binder

Your very first task after receiving a mock trial case file is preparing your trial binder. Start by making a copy of the case file and placing both copies in a three-ring binder.[1] You can write on one copy, but be sure to keep one clean copy of every exhibit and every witness statement for your use at trial.

---

1. Most mock trial case files are distributed with the intention that participants will make additional copies. Note, however, that copyrighted materials may not be duplicated without permission.

Next, insert tabs or otherwise separate each witness affidavit, each item of evidence, and the statutes or relevant case law included in your case file. Also, designate a place in the binder where you will keep copies of your opening statement, direct examination(s), cross-examination(s), and/or closing argument. You may want to also include twenty-five to fifty sheets of blank paper in your binder in a section titled "Notes."

Other useful things to keep in your binder include an enlarged list of objections you can refer to during the trial and a copy of the rules of evidence, procedure, and ethics you will be required to follow.[2]

II. Read and Outline the Case

Using the method we suggest below will take time, and it may not be for everyone. We guarantee, however, that if you follow this method, your efforts will be rewarded in the end.

A. Grasp the Applicable Statutes and Case Law

To be able to read and outline your case intelligently, you must begin with a strong understanding of the causes of action or crimes that are alleged against the defendant. Thus, start by reading and rereading the civil complaint or criminal indictment included in your case file. Next, read any law that applies to your case and has been provided in your case file. In addition to understanding the statutes, you must understand the case law included to see how courts have interpreted the statutes at issue in the case.

Then, make a list of the elements that each side will need to prove to prevail at trial—the jury instructions are an excellent source for a concise list of these elements. Knowing these elements will help you determine which facts in the case file are important and favorable to your case and which facts are important and favorable to your opponent's case. Keep your list of elements and notes on the law next to you and refer to it often as you continue your preparation.

B. Determine Which Witnesses Are Helpful to Each Side

Some mock trial case files provide witness statements for more witnesses than are allowed by the competition rules to be called to testify at trial. This forces participants to determine which witnesses will best help them prove or refute the legal elements at issue in the case. If the witnesses to be called by each side are not specified in your case file, you must consider carefully which witnesses you will call to testify during your case-in-chief.

---

2. See the Appendix for a list of objections for your trial binder.

Other mock trial case files simply include a list of the witnesses who must testify for each side. In these instances, each side is limited to calling only those witnesses.

Either way, next read through your entire case file. Do this in one sitting, if possible, and avoid highlighting or underlining any text, making any notes in the margins, or taking any notes about what you are reading as you go. Think of the case file as a bedtime story you might read to a child and just read it without thinking too much or worrying about your trial preparation. Once you have read through the entire case file once, you will have a much better grasp of which facts, and therefore which witnesses, are most important to each side of the case.

If your mock trial case file dictates which witnesses will be called by each side, then you can move on to the next step of preparing for trial (see Section C below). If your mock trial case file leaves open the question of which witnesses you may call, read through the entire case file a second time. This time, highlight the facts that are most important to each side as we describe in detail in the next section. This may seem like a waste of your time, but we assure you it is not. Until you understand the entire universe of possible testimony and evidence in a mock trial, you cannot appreciate the significance, or lack of significance, of any specific part. So, use this second read-through to examine the case file more critically. Evaluate the possible testimony and evidence as you go and rank the witnesses that are most helpful to each side.

Witnesses are typically important for their personal knowledge of certain facts or evidence. Although two witnesses may be aware that an event occurred, maybe only one actually saw or heard the event take place. A witness with direct knowledge is likely to be more believable and trustworthy than a person who simply heard about the event after the fact. For example, in a personal injury case, a witness who watched as the plaintiff was hurt would be more compelling than a person who merely heard about the incident later.

Keep in mind that the value of a witness is not always based on a particular event they witnessed. Some witnesses, for example, are important because they know the plaintiff's or defendant's reputation for truthfulness in the community. Another witness may know the record-keeping practices of a business in a case where the admissibility of documentary evidence is at issue.

Expert witnesses, in contrast, are valuable because their education, training, or experience can be used to explain important evidence to the factfinder. In a personal injury case, for example, the testimony of a physician might be crucial to justify the damages claimed by the plaintiff as a result of the injury.

As you read back through the case file to figure out which witnesses are most helpful to each side, ask yourself: Which witness(es) must I call in order to prove or refute the elements at issue in this case? If, in answering that question, you identify fewer witnesses than you are allowed to call, next ask: Which other witness(es) best

Chapter Two

support the credibility or believability of the witnesses I must call to prove or refute elements at issue in this case? The answers to these questions should direct you to the witnesses that will best enable you to succeed at trial.

To figure out the witnesses your opponent is likely to call, put yourself in their shoes and ask the same questions about the elements they must prove or refute to prevail.

Some mock trial competitions are designed so that participants remain unsure of exactly which witnesses will be called until virtually the last minute. While teams can decide and rank in order of preference the witnesses they would most *like* to call, they cannot be sure of the exact combination of witnesses they will have in each trial until just before each round begins. In these competitions, the teams meet immediately before each round and pick witnesses in a pre-determined order. In a criminal case with three witnesses per side, the order might be as follows: prosecution picks its first witness, the defendant then picks its first two witnesses, followed by the prosecution's choice of second witness, the defendant's final witness, and then the final prosecution witness.

This competition format complicates every stage of trial preparation—it makes determining the final content of everything you say and do at trial difficult. There are no magic words of advice we can give you for solving this problem; the best we can do is encourage you to be flexible, prepare diligently, practice as many witness combinations as possible, and learn the facts of your case inside and out so that you can prove your case and demonstrate your superior skill at trial regardless of which witnesses are called.

C.   *For Each Witness, Identify the Key Favorable and Unfavorable Facts*

Next, distinguish between the important favorable and unfavorable facts included in each witness's statement. As you read back through your case file the second time, attempt to pick out the facts that, if proven, could affect the outcome of the case. Use highlighters of different colors to indicate the facts favorable to one side versus the other. Be aware that some facts may be favorable to both sides or neither side.

Not all of the facts in a witness's statement will be important, or material, to the case. Facts that do not tend to support or refute the elements of a charge or a defense at issue in the case need not be identified as favorable or unfavorable. In other words, the point of this exercise is not to highlight every word in a witness's statement one color or the other (or both). Rather, the goal is to pick out the important facts that could affect the outcome of the legal dispute in the case—the facts that really matter—and to identify the party to which they matter most.

Advanced students will also read between the lines and identify important favorable and unfavorable facts omitted from each witness's statement. Sometimes what is left unsaid by a witness is even more powerful than what is said. To identify these facts, ask yourself if there is anything you would still like to know after reading through a witness's statement. Are important details absent? Is an explanation mysteriously missing for a curious action taken by the witness or another person? Did the witness refer to something in the statement but then never explain it in depth?

As you identify the important favorable and unfavorable facts in (or missing from) each witness's statement, make a list of those facts on a separate piece of paper or in a file on your computer. (Using a computer to complete this step and the ones that follow will save you considerable time.) The best way to do this is to write each witness's name on the top of a page and create two columns below. Use one column to list the favorable facts for the plaintiff/prosecution; write the facts favorable to the defendant/defense on the other side. When listing each fact, cite to where you found it in the witness's statement by noting the page and line number. This will save you valuable time later and during trial. The following is a sample of how your page might look for a witness in a criminal case.

(Witness's Name)	
Favorable to Prosecution	**Favorable to Defense**
• Fact 1 (page 10, lines 3–4) • Fact 2 (page 12, line 6) • Fact 3 (page 22, lines 6–7)	• Fact A (page 4, line 3) • Fact B (page 11, line 5) • Fact C (page 15, lines 11–12)

Repeat this process for each of the potential witnesses identified in your case file.

Once you have finished this process, review your earlier analysis of the witnesses most helpful to each side in the case. Sometimes the process of identifying and listing the important facts or evidence a witness can offer may cause you to rethink your earlier witness rankings.

If after reading through the case file twice you still are not sure which witnesses each side should or will likely call, move on to the next trial preparation step described below and, if necessary, the step after that. The further along you get in the process of preparing for trial, the easier it should become to decide which witnesses to call.

D. Consider the Admissibility of All Facts

Now that you have made lists of the key testimony each witness can offer that is helpful to one side or the other, determine if any of that testimony is likely to be excluded from the trial.

Chapter Two

Like real trials, mock trials adhere to rules of evidence. These rules, usually a simplified form of the Federal Rules of Evidence, control the testimony and exhibits allowed at trial. If a piece of evidence is allowed under the rules, it is said to be admissible; evidence that is not allowed under the rules is inadmissible.

The presiding judge determines the admissibility of the evidence at trial; the judge hears objections and argument from counsel and rules upon those objections. If an objection is sustained, that means the judge believes it was correctly raised and that admission of the testimony or evidence violates the rules. If an objection is overruled by the judge, they have determined that the testimony or evidence is allowed under the rules.

One of the aspects that makes preparing for trial difficult is that you do not yet know for sure which evidence will be deemed admissible and which will be deemed inadmissible. Unfortunately, there is no way around that uncertainty; effectively preparing for trial involves making your best guess as to how the presiding judge is likely to rule on all possible evidentiary objections. Therefore, evaluate each witness's testimony for possible evidentiary problems. You cannot assume that any fact is automatically admissible; you must be able to state a positive theory of relevance (and be able to overcome any possible objection) for each fact that you intend to offer during your case-in-chief.

When examining the facts in your witnesses' statements, place yourself in the mindset of your opponent and ask, "What can I attempt to exclude using the rules of evidence?" Likewise, with each adverse witness, consider whether any part of the testimony might be excludable. For every statement that the witness might make, imagine all reasonable evidentiary objections.

Chapter Six explains the most commonly used substantive rules of evidence in mock trials. At the end of Chapter Six, you will find a general checklist you can use when considering the admissibility of each fact in a witness's statement.

As you go through your list of favorable and unfavorable facts for each witness, indicate those that are likely to be barred by the rules of evidence and make a note explaining why. For instance, if you determined that "Fact 2" on the prosecution side of your page is likely to be deemed inadmissible hearsay, your page might now read:

(Witness's Name)	
Favorable to Prosecution	**Favorable to Defense**
• Fact 1 (page 10, lines 3–4) • Fact 2 (page 12, line 6, HEARSAY) • Fact 3 (page 22, lines 6–7)	• Fact A (page 4, line 3) • Fact B (page 11, line 5) • Fact C (page 15, lines 11–12)

Be aware that rules of evidence are seldom clear-cut and that you and your adversary will often disagree about their applicability to a particular fact. That is why lawyers spend so much time arguing over objections. The test to determine the admissibility of facts at this stage is whether you can state a reasonable theory of admissibility. If a fact is arguably admissible, you may attempt to use it during trial—but be prepared to state your grounds if you meet an objection.

Next, go through this same process with the exhibits in your case file; determine what facts each exhibit establishes, outlining them as you did the facts in the witness statements, and then determine the admissibility of each fact.

Be sensitive to the possibility that, as you go through this step, the list of witnesses you will likely call (or most likely call) may change. There may be a witness whose affidavit is full of information that appears at first blush to help you but, upon reflection, is likely to be deemed largely inadmissible. That witness, no matter how tempting the things they could but probably won't be allowed to say on the stand, should be replaced by any other whose likely admissible testimony helps your case more.

E. Compile a Summary of Key Facts That Will Likely Be Established at Trial

You are now ready to compile a summary of the facts you and your opposing counsel will likely be able to establish at trial. Taking only the definitely or arguably admissible facts from each witness outline and each exhibit outline, use a separate document to compile a full list of the facts you and your opposing counsel will likely attempt to establish. (If you use a computer, this step is accomplished with ease by copying and pasting.) Remember to cite the witness statement or exhibit where each fact is found. If more than one witness or exhibit establishes the same fact, write the fact once on your summary sheet but cite each of the separate sources. Your case summary sheet might look like this example:

Case Summary	
Favorable to Prosecution	**Favorable to Defense**
• Fact 1 (Dr. Drew, page 6, line 4) • Fact 2 (A. Corolla, page 2, line 9) • Fact 3 (Dr. Drew, page 6, lines 21–23)	• Fact A (Defendant, page 13, lines 6–10) • Fact B (Exhibit B, H. Stern, page 1, line 18) • Fact C (A. Corolla, page 7, lines 11–12)

This final step to outlining your case is so important it is worth double-checking. Look over your summary of the arguably admissible facts in the case file and compare it carefully to the summary of the applicable law you created earlier. Match every fact in your summary to an element that you or your opponent will attempt to prove at trial. Otherwise, it is not a material fact; remove it from your summary. The only exceptions to this rule are facts that bolster or detract from the credibility of a witness, since a witness's credibility is always at issue during trials.

Congratulations! You are now ready to craft the story you will tell at trial.

III. Analyze the Facts to Develop a Story, Theory, and Theme

Trials resolve factual disputes. These disagreements commonly involve the existence or occurrence of events or actions, but they may also turn on questions of sequence, interpretation, characterization, or intent. Thus, trials answer questions such as: What happened? Did it happen on purpose? Why did it happen? Who made it happen? Was it justified?

Each party to a trial has the opportunity to tell their story—albeit through the stilted devices of opening and closing statements, direct and cross-examination, and the introduction of evidence. The party who succeeds in telling the most persuasive story should win.

The steps outlined above have armed you with the ingredients for laying out your story. Your case summary lists the most important facts that may be admitted at trial. From these facts, shape the story each side is likely to tell at trial.

A persuasive trial story has all, or most, of these characteristics:

1) it is told about people who have reasons for the way they act;
2) it accounts for or explains all of the known or undeniable facts;
3) it is told by credible witnesses;
4) it is supported by details;
5) it accords with common sense and contains no implausible elements; and
6) it is organized in a way that makes each succeeding fact increasingly more likely.

Once you know your story, you have done half the storytelling work. Now, craft the version of the story the opposing side will tell. Be just as diligent and persuasive as you were with your version of the facts, because that's what you can expect your counterparts to do. Unless you know the "counterstory," you cannot begin to respond to it.

Devising a persuasive story you can effectively use at trial is a creative process, since many facts in the case file will be subject to interpretation. To imagine the most persuasive trial story, imagine a series of alternative scenarios, and assess each for its clarity, simplicity, and believability, as well as for its legal consequences.

Case Preparation

A. Consider the Possibilities

Assume that you represent a plaintiff who was injured in an automobile accident. Your client knows only that when traffic slowed to allow a firetruck to pass, another car slammed into her car from behind. You are suing the driver of that automobile for their negligence in failing to take due care while operating their car. To tell a persuasive story at trial, determine *why* the other driver failed to slow and stop with the rest of traffic.

While it is not legally *essential* to establish a reason why the defendant failed to stop, consider the questions raised by the absence of a compelling reason. The plaintiff claims that traffic slowed for a firetruck, but the defendant—also part of traffic—did not slow. Could it be that there was no firetruck? Perhaps there was a firetruck, but it was not sounding its siren or alerting traffic to stop. Is it possible that your client did not slow, but rather slammed on her brakes? As you can see, the very absence of a reason for the other driver's actions could make your client's testimony less believable.

The skilled advocate will therefore look for a reason or cause for the defendant's actions. Was the defendant drunk? In a hurry? Distracted? Choose from among these potential reasons by considering each one in the context of your story. Imagine how the story will be told if you claim that the defendant was drunk. Does such a story account for all of the known, admissible facts? When the police came to the scene, was the defendant arrested? Did any credible, disinterested witnesses see the defendant drinking or smell liquor on their breath? If not, drunkenness does not provide a persuasive reason for the defendant's actions.

Assume that your case file shows that at 8:20 in the morning the defendant was driving south on Craycroft Road on his way to work downtown. Rush hour was in full swing and the defendant had an important meeting scheduled for 8:30 a.m. sharp. You also learn that after parking their car near work, the defendant had two more blocks to walk to reach their office. From the point where the accident occurred, it would likely take the defendant another twenty to thirty-five minutes to drive to the parking lot, park, and then walk to their office. Furthermore, your case file reveals that immediately following the collision the defendant used their cell phone to call their office.

How can these basic facts be assembled into a persuasive trial story? A strong trial story would paint the defendant as being in such a hurry that they did not notice the firetruck until it was too late. This story accounts for the known facts, since it explains why traffic might slow while the defendant did not. This story is also plausible and believable; it is in complete harmony with everyone's everyday observations. Furthermore, you already have details on hand that support this story.

Always remember that lawyers are bound to the truth—you are not free to pick stories simply on the basis of their persuasive value. Your trial story must be supported by facts that you know, believe, or have a good-faith basis to believe, are true. In other words, the story has to be based on facts included in your mock trial case file that are not contradicted by the weight of the evidence in the case as a whole.

Returning to our firetruck case, assume that the defendant has denied that he was in a hurry. The defendant has the right to make this denial, but as the plaintiff's lawyer, you have no duty to accept it. Assume also that no witness will testify that the defendant was in a hurry. Despite this, your case file includes numerous facts about the defendant's conduct that day, the location of the defendant's home relative to his office, and his work schedule that support a belief that the defendant *was* in a hurry on the morning of the accident. The following story emerges, based strictly on facts that you have no reason to doubt.

The defendant lives sixteen miles from their office. The defendant usually takes a commuter train to work, but on the day of the accident he drove. The accident occurred on a major thoroughfare approximately eleven miles from the defendant's office. The time of the accident was 8:20 a.m., and the defendant had scheduled an important, and potentially lucrative, meeting with a new client for 8:30 a.m. that day. The parking lot nearest to the defendant's office is over two blocks away. The first thing that the defendant did following the accident was call his office to say that he would be late for this meeting.

Your conclusion is that the defendant was in a hurry. Driving on a familiar stretch of road, thinking about this appointment, maybe even starting to count the money, the defendant failed to pay sufficient attention to the traffic. You are entitled to ask the factfinder to draw this inference because you reasonably believe its entire basis to be true. As long as the story you tell the factfinder is not built on a false foundation, you have met your ethical obligations.

Using the above example as a guide, put together the strongest stories that can be told by each side based on the facts included in your mock trial case file.

B. Prepare Your Case Theory and Theme

You are now ready to turn your story into your case theory and theme—the very heart of your case. Your case theory and theme will pervade every aspect of your case, from your opening statement all the way through to your closing argument.

When choosing what facts to accentuate throughout the trial, you will rely on your theory and theme for direction.

1. Develop a Theory

Your theory adapts your story to the legal issues in the case; it explains why your client must win based on the combined facts and law. A successful case theory is expressed in a short paragraph (at most) and contains these elements:

It is logical. A winning theory has internal logical force. It is based upon a foundation of undisputed or otherwise provable facts, all of which lead in a single direction. The facts upon which your theory is based should reinforce (and never contradict) each other. Indeed, they should support each other, each fact or premise making the next more likely to be true, in an orderly and inevitable fashion.

It speaks to the legal elements of your case. Your trial persuasion must lead to a *legal* conclusion. Your theory must not only establish that your client is good or worthy (or that the other side is bad and unworthy), but also that the law entitles your client to relief. Your theory therefore must be directed to proving every legal element that is necessary to justify a verdict on your client's behalf.

It is simple. A good theory makes maximum use of undisputed facts. It relies as little as possible on evidence that may be hotly controverted, implausible, inadmissible, or otherwise difficult to prove.

It is easy to believe. Even "true" theories may be difficult to believe because they contradict everyday experience, or because they require harsh judgments. Strive to eliminate all implausible elements from your theory. Similarly, try to avoid arguments that depend upon proof of deception, falsification, ill motive, or personal attack. An airtight theory is able to encompass the entirety of the other side's case and still result in your victory by sheer logical force.

To develop your story into your case theory, answer these three questions: 1) What happened? 2) Why did it happen? 3) Why does that mean that my client should win? If your answer is longer than one paragraph, your theory may be logical and true, but it is probably too complicated.

An example theory for the plaintiff in the firetruck case outlined above is: "The defendant was in a hurry to get to work because he was late for an important meeting. Because the defendant was preoccupied, he didn't notice the firetruck until it was too late to stop. As a result, the defendant rear-ended my client, causing serious injuries."

2. Develop a Theme

Whereas a case theory gives the logical and legal basis for a particular verdict, a case theme provides the moral justification for it. A theme is a rhetorical or forensic device with no independent legal weight; it adds persuasive force to your case theory. The most compelling themes appeal to shared values, civic virtues, or common motivations.

Themes should be succinctly expressed, preferably in a short sentence or phrase. Repeat it at virtually every phase of the trial. A case theme is like a slogan in a television commercial; the simpler and more memorable it is, the better.

Using the firetruck case once again, examples of strong themes for the plaintiff would be, "too busy to be careful" or "too late to be safe."

Chapter Two

3. Return to Your Story

Going back to the story you devised earlier, be sure that each detail you include supports the theory and theme you have selected for trial. Also, be sure that your organization is persuasive. For instance, it is important that each fact make every succeeding element increasingly more likely. Considering the firetruck case, ask yourself which aspect should come first: the presence of the firetruck or the fact that the defendant was in a hurry? Since the presence of the firetruck does not make it more likely that the defendant was in a hurry, that probably is not the most effective starting point. On the other hand, the defendant's haste does make it more likely that he would fail to notice the firetruck.

	Checklist	
	HAVE YOU PREPARED YOUR CASE?	
☑	**Did you organize your trial binder?**	Are there two copies of the case in your trial binder?
		Have you organized the witness statements and exhibits?
		Have you included copies of the rules of evidence, procedure, and ethics for reference during trial?
☑	**Did you read and outline the case?**	Do you understand the applicable statutes and case law?
		Do you know which witnesses are helpful to each side?
		Did you identify the favorable and unfavorable facts each witness adds to the case?
		Do you have witness and exhibit summaries of these facts?
		Did you determine the admissibility of all key facts listed in your summaries?
		Do you have a case summary compiling all the arguably admissible facts from each witness and exhibit summary?
☑	**Did you analyze the case and devise a trial story?**	Did you consider every possible story and pick the one best supported by the facts likely to come out at trial?
		Is your story ethical? Is it based on truth?

Checklist	
HAVE YOU PREPARED YOUR CASE?	
☑ **Did you prepare your case theory and theme?**	Is your theory a short explanation of what happened, explaining to the factfinder why your side should prevail?
	Does your theme add moral force to your theory?
	Did you go back to work your theme and theory into your story?

IV. Get the Most from Your Work

Now that you have invested the time and energy preparing the foundation of your case, you might as well benefit from your work.

Your goal at trial is to persuade the trier of fact that your theory is correct and to constantly invoke the moral leverage of your theme. To accomplish this, you have four basic tools: 1) jury address, which consists of opening statement and final argument; 2) testimony on direct examination, and to a lesser extent on cross-examination; 3) introduction of exhibits, including real and documentary evidence; and 4) absolutely everything else that you do in the courtroom.

The skills involved in each of these aspects of a trial will be discussed at length in later chapters. What follows here is an outline of the general steps you should take to get the most from your case preparation. With each of these areas, you should read the applicable chapter that follows for more detailed instruction of what to include and how to organize your work.

A. Planning Closing Argument and Opening Statement

Good trial preparation begins at the end. Plan your final argument first, because that aspect of the trial is the most similar to storytelling. Closing arguments are the single time at trial for you to suggest conclusions, articulate inferences, and otherwise present your theory to the trier of fact as an uninterrupted whole.

In other words, during final argument you are most freely allowed to say what you want to say, so long as what you say was at least arguably supported by the evidence adduced during the trial. By determining the content of your final argument first, you will know what evidence and testimony you must present to the factfinder during the rest of your case. Remember, if it does not come out at trial, you cannot argue it during your summation.

When outlining your closing argument, return to the very first step of your trial preparation: the list of legal elements that you determined each side must

Chapter Two

prove or refute in order to prevail. As you go through each of those elements, list the admissible facts you anticipate introducing at trial through the testimony of witnesses to prove up those elements. Ask yourself these two questions: What do I want to say at the end of the case? What evidence must I introduce or elicit in order to be able to say it? The answers to these questions will focus the content of your case summary. If you can effectively present, emphasize, and repeat these facts throughout the trial using your theory and theme, you will succeed in telling a persuasive story.

Similarly, outline your opening statement by linking together the absolutely admissible facts that you listed in your closing argument outline. Weave them into a descriptive story about what happened in the case. The key to a good opening statement is telling a story that the trier of fact will care about: grab their attention with the most important facts while using your theory and theme to explain why your client should prevail.

B. Planning Direct Examinations

Direct examinations should include only the admissible facts, or at least arguably admissible facts, each witness may offer. If you followed our method, you already have this information mapped out. Elicit the favorable facts in an order that effectively tells the witness's story. Once you assemble the positive information for each of your witnesses, consider all possible problems and weaknesses. Are there inconsistencies or gaps in the witness's testimony? Does the witness have damaging information that is likely to be probed on cross-examination? Use your list of unfavorable facts for each witness to answer these questions. As we explain in detail in Chapter Seven, Section III(B)(7), sometimes revealing unfavorable facts before your opponent can softens the blow of their impact.

Structure your direct examination to avoid or minimize these problems. Perhaps you can resolve the inconsistencies in the witness's testimony by reevaluating your theory. Perhaps a different witness can fill in the gaps of the witness's testimony. Perhaps you can defuse the potentially damaging facts by burying them in the middle of your direct examination.

Once you have outlined your direct examinations, arrange your witnesses in the order most advantageous to your case. While there are no hard and fast rules for determining witness order, the following three principles should help you decide:

- **Retention.** You want your evidence not only to be heard, but also to be retained. Following the principles of primacy and recency discussed in Chapter Three, Section III(D), call your most important witness first and your next most important witness last. Your goal should be to start and end strong, as long as doing so results in a logical progression of testimony.

- **Progression.** The "first and last" principle must occasionally give way to the need for logical progression. Some witnesses provide the foundation for the testimony of others. Thus, it may be necessary to call a "predicate" witness early in the trial as a matter of both logical development and legal admissibility. To the extent possible, you may also wish to arrange your witnesses so that accounts of key events are given in chronological order.

- **Impact.** You may also order your witnesses to maximize their dramatic impact. For example, you might wish to begin a wrongful death case by calling one of the grieving parents of the deceased child. Conversely, bury a necessary witness who is also somewhat unsavory or impeachable in the middle of your case-in-chief. A common exception to the impact principle in real trials is the practice of calling a criminal defendant as the last witness for the defense.

C. Planning Cross-Examinations

Cross-examination is inherently more difficult to plan than direct. Although it is impossible to safeguard yourself against every surprise that may arise at trial, the following steps will help keep them to a minimum.

You have already identified the facts favorable to your side for each witness you will cross-examine. From those, catalog the facts with which the witness will be most likely to agree. You will want to elicit this information early on in your cross-examination, while the witness is most cooperative. Next, list the facts that hurt the other side, and which will likely be left out of your opponent's direct examination. Finally, list your "attack facts," the ones that challenge the witness's credibility or directly contradict the witness.

D. Planning Objections and Responses

Identify and prepare for the objections that may be raised at trial. This is an excellent second check on the credibility of your witnesses and your evidence—if you were opposing counsel, to what would you object? How will you respond to every possible objection raised by opposing counsel? Is that tempting but dangerous piece of evidence worth the risk to your credibility? Sometimes the answer is yes, but consider what your opponent will say and how the judge is likely to rule.

If you followed our method, all you need to do now is decide the objections you will raise. Go through a process of elimination to choose your battles wisely. You will not want to make every possible objection, but you will want to be prepared. The decision to object must be made in reference to your theory of the case. The principal contribution that an objection can make to your theory of the case is to prevent the admission of truly damaging evidence. Hence the maxim, "Do not object to anything that doesn't hurt you." Unless the exclusion of the evidence advances your theory, there is probably no need to raise an objection. Never object to information that you intend to elicit from the same or another witness.

For each objection you decide to make, plan and practice your argument and prepare for every likely counterargument.

Chapter Three

Communication Techniques

I. The Importance of Effective Communication

Every movement and sound you make in a courtroom communicates a message to the factfinder. Perhaps jurors will determine that you are prepared, professional, and intelligent. Perhaps they will listen intently to your every word and ponder your arguments. But what if they do not? What if the judge or jury perceives you to be tired, bored, unconvinced, uninteresting, and, ultimately, not persuasive? It is up to you to make sure that your message is heard by communicating effectively at trial.

To begin, imbue every message you send during trial with confidence and integrity, the key attributes of a good litigator.

A. Confidence

Think of yourself as a walking billboard with a different message appearing each time you move and speak. What message appears when you talk softly in a courtroom? "I'm sorry, I'm nervous." How about when you mumble? "I'm sorry, I'm not very sure about what I'm saying." How about when you slouch in your seat or walk tentatively from one side of the courtroom to the other? "I'm sorry, I probably don't belong here." You get the point. When you act and speak without confidence, you are apologizing to everyone around you. Do not apologize in the courtroom; there is no reason for it, no one enjoys watching it, and it only interferes with your ability to persuade the factfinder.

Demonstrate confidence during trial by knowing and operating within the rules of evidence, procedure, and ethics; by understanding how the judge wants the trial to proceed; and by demonstrating your mastery of the facts of the case. Confident lawyers enter the courtroom knowing what they want to accomplish, why they want to accomplish it, and how they intend to do it; they have prepared their examinations, are ready to call and cross-examine witnesses, and can argue evidentiary objections at any time. Confident lawyers are also well organized and well prepared; they know where their exhibits can be found, how they are to be numbered, and which witnesses will introduce them. And, finally, confident lawyers follow the rules of the trial; they understand which documents can be used to impeach

Chapter Three

which witnesses, they have chosen their objections ahead of time, and know how to explain their objections to the court.

As you can see, competence leads to confidence—and confidence is apparent to the factfinder. Unpreparedness, incompetence, and disorganization lead to insecurity, which is also obvious and can be damning at trial.

B.   Integrity

The word "integrity" comes from the Latin *integritas*, meaning wholeness or soundness, complete in itself. Thus, our concept of integrity has come to mean unsullied, unbroken, and undivided moral principle. In other words, it is a quality of the whole and honest lawyer.

The most important thing you can do to demonstrate integrity in the courtroom is to follow the court's ethical and procedural rules. Good lawyers, lawyers with integrity, do not break these rules or even attempt to dance around them. Likewise, honest lawyers do not overstate their case, do not promise evidence that they cannot deliver, and do not make arguments that they cannot support.

Demonstrating integrity also requires that you treat everyone in the courtroom with respect. This includes your opponent, the witnesses, and especially the judge. You do not have to *like* them, their words, or their actions, but you should respect them by not interrupting them without good cause and by giving them your full attention when it is requested. Do not use bullying tactics to intimidate your opponent or their witnesses. Do not attempt to distract the factfinder during your opponent's case. And do not try to disrupt opposing counsel's legitimate presentation or to use facial expressions, grimaces, or gestures to "argue" your case while other arguments or examinations are proceeding. Each time you fail to show respect to others at trial, your credibility weakens, and with it your persuasiveness.

You also demonstrate integrity by learning to lose gracefully. Without likening a trial to a war, remember that you can lose a few battles and still prevail. So, when a witness does not testify exactly the way you predicted or an exhibit is not allowed into evidence, do not take it out on others or display your frustration—let go and move ahead. Being a good loser has the added benefit of not highlighting your loss for the trier of fact.

A final word about integrity: it cannot be faked. It is not a face or costume that you put on and take off. If you are truly committed to trying a case with integrity, it will show; if you are not, the trier of fact will see that as well.

II.   Nonverbal Communication Techniques

There are two kinds of communication: nonverbal and verbal. Nonverbal communication refers to vocal variation, body movement, facial expression, and the use of space, among other factors. All forms of communication that do not include the spoken or written word fit into the category of nonverbal communication.

You have undoubtedly heard the expression "Actions speak louder than words." This sentiment holds true in trials as well; nonverbal messages are more believable than verbal messages. Therefore, be constantly conscious of the nonverbal messages you send during a trial.

The following are nonverbal techniques that, if followed, will make you a more persuasive advocate.

A. Stay in Role at All Times

During trial, assume that the trier of fact is watching your every move and facial expression.

Make a positive first impression by paying particular attention to your physical appearance, including your grooming and dress. Your posture and voice also influence how others perceive you. As a litigator, you are a professional advocate who has agreed to represent your client to the best of your ability; slouching and mumbling will not do. Each time you stand, stand fully erect. Each time you speak, speak loud enough so that every person in the courtroom can hear you. In short, demonstrate the *purpose* and *intent* of each action and sound you make during trial so that your poise befits your professional role.

This leads to an important corollary: be cautious that your posture and voice do not overstep the bounds of your professional role. Yes, you should appear comfortable and confident during trial, but do not allow your comfort or confidence to translate into informal or arrogant behavior. It is never appropriate to lean back at counsel table with your hands behind your head and, especially, not with your feet elevated. Also, do not lean on the counsel table, chin in hand, or lay your head on the table. The same goes for the other solid structures in the courtroom; do not use them as a crutch, seat, or leaning post. At all times, remember that you are in the courtroom in a professional capacity and that the factfinder is watching.

B. Be Careful Not to Upstage Your Witnesses

All actors know the rules about upstaging another performer. The same rules apply in the courtroom. As your client's advocate, never detract attention as your witnesses testify; the opposite holds true for the opposing witnesses whose testimony you hope to diminish. The following diagram illustrates where you should stand during the various stages of a trial, assuming the presiding judge does not place restrictions on movement in the courtroom:

Stand at the back of the jury box—at the "X"—during direct examinations to encourage your witnesses to make eye contact with the jurors and to speak loudly

Chapter Three

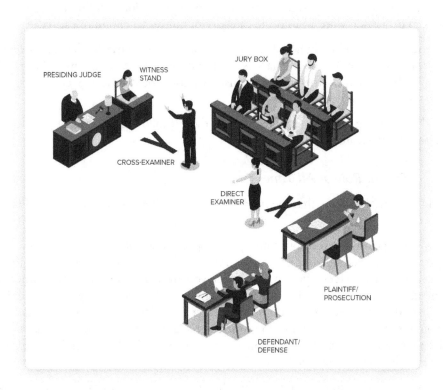

enough that every juror can hear their testimony. Stand in the middle of the courtroom—at the "Y"—during cross-examinations to better control opposing witnesses and to draw attention to yourself, upstaging the adverse witness.

During opening statements and closing arguments, begin where the "Y" is marked and move about the courtroom to signal transitions and to emphasize important points. As you move, never turn your back directly to the jury for more than a second or two; if you must, apologize briefly and appropriately.

C.   Make Eye Contact with the Witnesses and Factfinder

Actors also understand the value of eye contact. You have undoubtedly learned that the best way to convince someone that you are sincere and honest is to look them in the eyes when you are speaking. A trial is no different. A lawyer who looks at jurors while addressing them is more likely to be believed than one who does not.

A particularly powerful use of eye contact during witness questioning is to look at the factfinder and pause for a moment when one of your witnesses gives important testimony during a direct examination, as if to say, "Did you hear that?" Or, shoot them a knowing glance when you make a particularly damning point on cross-examination, as if to say, "Can you believe this guy?" Of course, as with any trial technique, overuse will backfire.

Eye contact is much more than a useful tool of persuasion; it is also a great way to make sure the jurors are listening to, and understanding, your case. In other words, do not just look at the jurors occasionally—make it your habit to watch them throughout the trial. Just as the jurors will be evaluating your actions and reactions throughout the trial, study theirs to determine whether they are following and understanding the testimony.

This advice is not meant to be taken too literally, however. Jurors do not know you personally and will respond with discomfort if they notice you staring intently at them too often or for too long. Moreover, if you are going to act as if the jury is on your side, be absolutely sure it actually is. By all means make eye contact with jurors from the beginning of your trial and check in with them frequently to see how they react to important pieces of testimony and evidence, but focus the vast majority of your energy on doing the best job possible of presenting your case.

D. Use Body Movement to Explain and Emphasize Points

Like your eyes, your body can be a valuable tool of persuasion throughout a trial. Use your fingers to signal numbered points in your argument by lifting them one at a time as you argue. Hold out each of your hands with your palm facing up when comparing two arguments and asking the factfinder to weigh one more heavily than another. Move from one place in the courtroom to another during your argument to signal a transition or to differentiate between items in a list.

For instance, going back to our firetruck case, assume that as the plaintiff's attorney you want to argue in closing that the defendant's negligence is demonstrated by three facts established at trial: 1) the defendant was in a hurry that morning; 2) the defendant's mind was focused completely on the business meeting to which he was heading; and 3) the defendant did not notice the firetruck and pull over, unlike the other drivers on the road. While you could make all of these points while standing in the same position, your argument will be stronger and more memorable if you use movement in the courtroom to signal your transitions from point to point. Starting where the "1" is in the diagram below, argue all the facts brought out at trial that prove the defendant was rushed that morning. When you are ready to move on to your next point, move to the place marked with a "2" and give a transition such as, "The second way we know the defendant was negligent was because the defendant's mind was completely focused on their business meeting while driving to work that morning." And so on.

A strong cross-examination technique is to walk closer and closer to a witness during each series of questions. So, referring to the diagram on the following page, begin a line of questioning where the "3" is shown, moving slowly to the "2" and ultimately to the "1" as you go through your series of questions to arrive at your most

Chapter Three

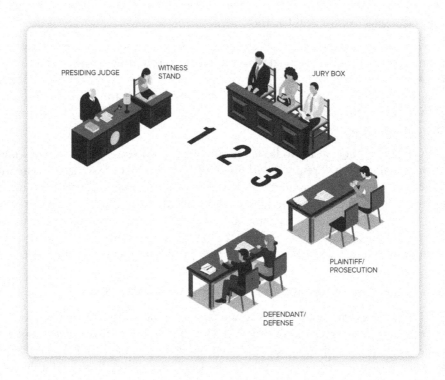

important point. After making that point, turn and walk back to the "3" to begin a new topic.

Likewise, signal a new line of questioning during direct examination by pausing for a moment and then moving purposefully a few steps in any direction; the silence and movement will reinforce each other, making it clear that one topic has ended and another is about to begin. In the same way, emphasize an important point by stepping closer to the trier of fact and lowering your voice slightly during opening statements and closing arguments.

Do not make important points while you are moving—your audience might pay more attention to your motion than to your words. Instead, use a transition sentence while you are moving toward the factfinder, then stop, pause a moment, and deliver your crucial point while standing perfectly still. The contrast will emphasize the issue even more.

Three cautions about movement: First, never invade a witness's or the jurors' personal space. As a rule, avoid getting closer than about four feet to any other person in the courtroom while presenting. Second, be sure your movements in the courtroom are deliberate, since that is the best way to concentrate the factfinder's attention. Pacing is an example of ineffective movement during trial, since it distracts the factfinder from your verbal presentation. Third, pick your moments. Emphasizing every point you make through the use of movement is the same as emphasizing nothing. If you are constantly moving, the judge or jury might think you need a bathroom break or they might daydream about gluing your feet to the floor. These techniques—just like the use of eye contact—are meant to be used judiciously. Abandon these techniques if you sense that they are distracting the judge or the jurors.

E.   Minimize Reliance on Notes

When it comes to the use of notes at trial, students participating in mock trials can learn a great deal from studying and understanding the actions of actual trial attorneys.

Trial attorneys nearly always refer to their notes when questioning witnesses and addressing the finder of fact. They do this because they have an obligation to their client to try the case to the best of their ability.

If a lawyer forgets to elicit a crucial fact during the testimony or to make a persuasive argument in closing, real and serious consequences may result. Most obviously, an innocent defendant could be wrongfully convicted or a guilty defendant could be erroneously set free. Good lawyers therefore take concrete steps to ensure that they do not forget anything important at trial.

On the other hand, experienced trial attorneys recognize that overusing notes *detracts* from their ability to persuade the factfinder.

Relying on notes reduces an attorney's ability to make eye contact with the witnesses and with the finder of fact. As we discussed in the previous section, eye contact is essential to persuasion. When a lawyer reads every question they ask a witness on direct, the examination looks more like a recitation and less like a conversation. Also, relying on notes inhibits an attorney from effectively moving in the courtroom to explain and emphasize important points. In short, if more than a minute or two of a lawyer's presentation at trial is read directly from notes, the lawyer will appear stilted, less confident and, ultimately, less persuasive.

Like actual trials, mock trials present an unfortunate dilemma when it comes to the use of notes. Students need to use notes; although there are no real-life consequences, if a student inadvertently leaves out important information in a mock trial, doing so could affect the factfinder's verdict (if given) or the scores awarded by the judges. Unfortunately, in many mock trials, students are actually *marked down* for using notes. This may be because students who use notes in mock trials are perceived as less persuasive since they cannot make eye contact as often or move around as much as a result. But it may also be simply because students who use notes appear less prepared for trial than their empty-handed counterparts. The

Chapter Three

truth is, the better prepared all of the participants in a mock trial are, the harder it is for judges to differentiate between their performances to pick a winner. So, all other things being equal, judges may give higher scores to students who rely less on their notes or do not use them at all.

What is the answer to this conundrum?

Some students memorize their examinations and arguments. While this certainly takes away the need for notes, it brings up other possible problems. First, memorizing the content of examinations and arguments can be more damaging to your persuasiveness than using notes. There is nothing worse than realizing that you have just made an argument during your closing about facts that did not come out during trial. This sort of mistake will stick out like a sore thumb to everyone in the room, most notably the judges. Also, a memorized statement may seem stilted, since it went straight from paper to prose. Another problem with memorizing the content of your examinations and arguments is that you will be less prepared for and able to deal with interruptions that may occur at trial. A student who memorizes direct examination questions, for example, runs the risk of panicking if asked to rephrase a question or elicit the testimony in a different manner.

The better alternative to rote memorization is to come to the same conclusion that trial attorneys inevitably reach: notes are a necessity, but reliance on them is not. Yes, it is possible for an exceptional attorney to try an entire case without using notes and without missing an important point—but attorneys are human, after all, and even attempting such a feat may be reckless. Thus, to avoid leaving out important information but also to avoid relying on their notes to the detriment of their persuasive ability, trial attorneys have developed a few solutions that allow them to meet their obligations to their clients.

The first thing all trial attorneys learn is not to write detailed notes. For instance, if each question in a direct examination appears in a lawyer's notes in this form, "Please tell us, Dr. Harris, what sort of clinical training you have," the lawyer will be tempted to read each question in that form at trial. The better way for counsel to remember to ask the doctor about clinical training is to simply write "Clinical Training?" in their notes. This form provides direction at a quick glance and forces counsel to ad-lib the question, which will make it seem more conversational and sincere.

Another solution is simply practice. As you might have learned through participation in music or sports, practice makes permanent. Attorneys who practice their direct and cross-examinations and their opening statement and closing argument enough will only need to resort to notes occasionally to check to make sure they have covered every necessary topic. These attorneys are better off leaving their notes at counsel table and referring back to them only when necessary or when they are about to finish and want to make sure every important point was covered.

Smart trial attorneys also make use of their co-counsel, if available. The attorney gives a copy of each examination and argument to their co-counsel. Then, when the attorney loses their place or has finished the examination, it only takes a minute to walk to counsel table to ask about the next topic or to ask whether anything was left out. Short interruptions such as these, if noticed at all, are easily forgiven by the trier of fact.

If you are participating in a highly competitive mock trial, particularly those that involve months of preparation, use these same approaches. Keep whatever notes as simply written as possible and work to keep your notes away from your direct gaze as you perform your examinations and arguments until you become comfortable doing so. Most importantly, practice working with the case so much and so often that the facts become ingrained in your mind. The combination of these efforts will keep you relatively note-free but still afford you flexibility in dealing with interruptions and surprises at trial.

Summary

NONVERBAL TECHNIQUES

- Stay in your role at all times
- Do not upstage your witnesses
- Make eye contact with witnesses and the finder of fact
- Use body movement to explain and emphasize points
- Minimize your reliance on notes

III. Verbal Communication Techniques

While closely monitoring your nonverbal communication at trial, be sure you are also getting the most mileage out of your verbal communication. Verbal communication refers to all spoken and written language. Follow the steps outlined below to become a more persuasive speaker.

A. Show Respect to the Judge

Regardless of whether the factfinder in your mock trial is a judge or jury, *always* address the presiding judge with deference (regardless of whether they are a real-life judge). Address the judge as "Your Honor" and always stand when you do so unless directed otherwise. Likewise, honor every ruling the judge makes and do not attempt to argue with the court.

B. Use Powerful Speech

Intuitively, you already know that powerful speech is more persuasive than powerless speech. Powerful speech is free of vocal pauses, qualifiers, intensifiers, and

Chapter Three

dull adjectives. As with any skill, learn to speak more persuasively by training yourself to use only powerful speech. The following techniques will help get you started.

1. Take the Lead Out

Vocal pauses or fillers, such as "um" and "uh," are sounds speakers use to avoid silence. Students who have sat through their fair share of lectures know that these sounds can be annoying and even downright distracting.

Silence, as opposed to vocal pauses, adds drama to your speech and slows its rate: you gain time to process your thoughts, and grant the listener time to absorb the point you or the witness is making. The trick to replacing vocal pauses with silence is simple. First, become aware of your use of vocal pauses. Then, practice isolating your vocal pauses and consciously eliminate them from your speech. Eventually you will notice how effective and dramatic long pauses can be. What seems like an eternity of silence to you while speaking will sound like a natural pause to the listener.

2. Say What You Mean and Mean What You Say

Another technique is to say what you mean and mean what you say. Qualifiers and intensifiers are used in speech to soften or strengthen the meaning of language. In ordinary conversation, people tend to qualify or temper their ideas as a matter of politeness or convention and exaggerate or intensify their ideas to signify emphasis. Examples of qualifiers are "probably," "sometimes," "perhaps," "maybe," and "sort of." Examples of intensifiers are "really," "very," "highly," and "especially." During casual exchanges, qualifiers and intensifiers hardly raise an eyebrow.

Trials are different. Trials are about persuasion. Trials are about certainty. Trials are about asking the factfinder to reject the other party's claims and to enter a verdict in your client's favor. Whenever you use qualifiers or intensifiers in your speech during trial, your credibility decreases and the trier of fact is less likely to be persuaded by your words. The following excerpts from closing arguments are illustrative:

> COUNSEL: The prosecution has probably not met its burden of proof in this case and therefore you should think twice before finding the defendant guilty.

Or,

> COUNSEL: It is crystal clear that the prosecution has definitely not met its burden of proof in this case and therefore you absolutely must find the defendant not guilty.

Neither of these statements is particularly effective; the former is imbued with uncertainty and the latter is suspect of exaggeration. Do not use qualifiers at trial; if you appear uncertain that your side should prevail, you cannot expect the factfinder to be certain either. Likewise, if you are so confident in your argument that you want to add an intensifier, fight the temptation and let the argument speak for itself: "Because the prosecution has not met its burden of proof, the defendant is not guilty," or "We have proven every element of the crime beyond a reasonable doubt and therefore we ask that you return a verdict of guilty."

Using powerful speech also applies to witness testimony. For example, coach expert witnesses to testify in straightforward, unequivocal terms, avoiding language that unintentionally qualifies or hedges their opinions.

Here is an example of how the use of powerful language can strengthen the testimony of an expert witness. First, consider a "weak" answer.

> ANSWER: My best estimate at this time is that the restaurant chain would probably have earned approximately $3.2 million.

In fact, the witness has conducted an exhaustive study and is completely certain, within the bounds of professional competence, that $3.2 million is the correct figure. That certainty can be better expressed through more powerful language.

> ANSWER: I have calculated lost profits at $3.2 million.

Or,

> ANSWER: The result of my study is a determination of lost profits in the amount of $3.2 million.

Of course, if the expert's conclusions really are tentative or provisional, do not attempt to have the witness testify otherwise.

C. With Descriptive Language and Legalese, Be Mindful of Your Audience

1. When the Factfinder Is a Jury

When the factfinder in your mock trial is a jury, use descriptive language to keep their attention and interest. Be creative; use language to bring the established facts to life and help the jurors to visualize the scene. As we discussed in Chapter Two, the story you tell at trial can make or break your case. Keep that story interesting—the best explanation for the events in the case is worthless if the factfinder has stopped listening.

Unlike jurors, judges are not as easily swayed by drama and emotion. Real-life judges hear enough cases to develop a level of immunity to gruesome crimes; they are no longer shocked by events that might horrify the members of a jury. Thus, while you can and should use descriptive language when presenting your case to a judge, be mindful not to get too wrapped up in drama or emotion.

Chapter Three

Avoid complex legal terms in jury trials. Most jurors are laypersons who have only been exposed to the law through the media or social interaction with attorneys. Laypersons are often skeptical and mistrustful of lawyers they do not know. All of these effects are minimized through the use of simple language. By talking *to* the members of the jury and not *above* them, you will succeed in explaining the law and earning their trust—improving your persuasiveness.

2. When the Factfinder Is a Judge

Though you may use legalese when addressing a judge, still explain legal terms simply to demonstrate that you understand them. Be careful not to adopt the same tone you might use when talking to a younger sibling or cousin; it is safe to assume that the judge understands these concepts.

D. Use Primacy and Recency

Primacy and recency refer to the widely accepted phenomenon that people remember best those things that they hear first and last. Therefore, put your strongest arguments first and last so the jurors will remember them. This applies to every stage of a trial, including discrete subparts within your witness examinations and arguments. Without confusing the trier of fact or neglecting to lay foundation, always try to put your two strongest points at the beginning and end to maximize their impact. In our intersection case, for example, the presence of the firetruck may well be the most important part of the plaintiff's testimony. Introduce it early in your direct examination and allude to it again at the end.

Of course, primacy does not necessarily refer to the very first words out of your mouth. Your direct examinations, for example, will start with a preamble where you ask the witness to introduce themself and generally warm up before you really begin. Primacy applies to the substantive beginning of the argument or witness examination, not to the introduction.

If primacy and recency describe the points remembered best, then it follows that the midpoints—the "interment"—will be remembered least. In every trial, there will be information that you must mention but that is embarrassing or potentially counterproductive to your theory. The principle of interment tells you that the safest approach, therefore, is to bury this material deep in the middle of an examination or argument.

E. Use Repetition and Duration to Emphasize Your Most Important Points

Repetition and duration are related concepts; they are used to emphasize the significance of certain information.

The more times you repeat a fact, the more likely it is to be believed, remembered, and understood by the factfinder. Thus, repeat your most important points again and again throughout the testimony to ensure that they are retained. Repeating information can be tricky at trial since asking the same witness the same question twice will draw the "asked and answered" objection. To avoid an objection, fashion several slightly different questions, each stressing the same point.

How do you decide which facts are sufficiently important to bear repetition? To answer this question, consider your theory and theme and repeat only those facts that are crucial to your theory and those that best evoke your moral theme.

In our firetruck case, the gist of the plaintiff's theory is that she stopped for a passing firetruck while the defendant did not. Her single most important fact is the observable presence of the firetruck. Thus, insert the word "firetruck" at every reasonable point during the examination. At the close of her testimony, you want to have created the image that the firetruck dominated the scenery. How many different ways can the witness describe the firetruck? In how many locations can she place it? How many times can she use it as a reference point for other testimony?

Similarly, the more time you spend on a topic, the more important it will seem. In our example, the most important point for the plaintiff is the presence and noticeability of the fire engine. The plaintiff's initial observation of the truck could be established in a single question and answer, but the importance of the subject dictates greater duration for this part of the direct examination.

QUESTION: What did you see as you drove south on Craycroft Road?
ANSWER: I saw a firetruck.
QUESTION: Describe it, please.
ANSWER: It was your basic firetruck. It was red, and it had firefighters riding on it. It had lights and a bell.
QUESTION: Were the lights flashing?
ANSWER: Yes, and it was sounding its siren.
QUESTION: How far away were you when you first noticed the firetruck?
ANSWER: I would say almost a block away.

Repetition and duration can easily be overdone and misused. Dwelling on something does not require beating it into the ground. Even the most crucial, compelling, climactic evidence can be trivialized by extended overtreatment. Likewise, if too many facts are repeated, repetition will lose its impact. So use repetition and duration, but always use them with restraint. Remember, emphasizing everything is the equivalent of emphasizing nothing.

Chapter Three

F. Use Reflective Questioning to Illustrate Time, Distance, and Intensity

One technique for creating a mental image in the jurors' minds is called reflective questioning, an approach that uses the pacing of language to evoke time, distance, or intensity. The timing or duration of an event, for example, is often crucial in a trial; one side claims that things happened quickly and the other asserts that they were drawn out. It is possible to pace your questions to support your particular theory. Speaking rapidly makes events seem faster, closer together, more intense, and more disorganized. Speaking slowly makes things seem slower, further apart, more reasoned, and more relaxed. Reflect the story that you want to tell by varying your pace as you proceed with your argument or questioning.

Assume that you represent the defendant in our firetruck case. Their defense is that the fire engine appeared only a moment before the collision and there wasn't enough time to stop the car. Your goal during the defendant's direct examination must be to re-create that scene by collapsing the time available to react to the firetruck. You do this by asking only a few, fast-paced questions.

QUESTION: When did the firetruck first become visible?
ANSWER: It approached the intersection just as I did.
QUESTION: What was the very first action that you took?
ANSWER: I slammed on my brakes.
QUESTION: How much time did that take?
ANSWER: Less than a second.

This direct examination proceeds quickly, emphasizing both shortness of time and immediacy of response. This result will be enhanced if you fire off the questions, and if the witness answers them quickly in response.

In contrast, the plaintiff will claim that there was ample time for the defendant to stop. Draw her direct examination out to demonstrate how much time there was:

QUESTION: Where was the firetruck when you first saw it?
ANSWER: It was about a quarter of a block away from the intersection.
QUESTION: How far away from you was it?
ANSWER: About a hundred yards.
QUESTION: How many other cars were between you and the firetruck?
ANSWER: Three or four.
QUESTION: What did they do as the firetruck approached?
ANSWER: They all slowed to a stop.
QUESTION: How long did it take those other cars to stop?
ANSWER: Normal stopping time—a few seconds.

QUESTION:	What was the first thing that you did?
ANSWER:	I started to pull over toward the side of the road.
QUESTION:	How long did that take?
ANSWER:	Five seconds or so.
QUESTION:	What did you do after that?
ANSWER:	I brought my car to a stop.
QUESTION:	How long did that take?
ANSWER:	Well, I applied my brakes right away, and it took a few seconds for the car to stop.
QUESTION:	Then what happened?
ANSWER:	That's when the other car rear-ended me.
QUESTION:	How much time elapsed between the moment when you first saw the firetruck and the time that the defendant's car hit yours?
ANSWER:	At least ten or fifteen seconds.

There is every reason not to hurry through this part of the examination. The length, detail, and pace of your questions demonstrate the validity of your theory: the defendant had plenty of time to stop.

G. Use Nouns and Verbs in Place of Adjectives

The most evocative words used in trials are nouns and verbs. This may seem counterintuitive; many lawyers think that adjectives are the best words for conjuring a mental image. But adjectives tend to convey judgments, which can make them seem argumentative and, thus, undependable to the factfinder. Nouns and verbs, however, do not suggest a belief about something but rather describe the thing itself.

Suppose, for example, that someone told you that a certain automobile was "ugly." The adjective "ugly" conveys an aesthetic judgment. Depending upon the speaker and the circumstances, you might agree with the characterization, or you might not. Adding an intensifying adverb does not help. "The car was *really* ugly." Even with inflection, adjectives and adverbs tend to lack intrinsically descriptive power. They convey opinions but not the bases for those opinions.

Now suppose that the same person told you that the automobile's paint had peeled off the doors and its hood was so rusted that you could see right through to the engine in several places. The windshield was covered by a spiderweb of fracture lines. The tailpipe dragged on the ground. One fender was missing, and another was replaced by a mismatched part from a different model. The hubcaps were gone, and the trunk was held down with bungee cords. These nouns and verbs (helped out by an occasional participle) tell the whole story—that car was ugly!

Chapter Three

H.   Use Apposition to Compare Related Facts

Apposition refers to placement or juxtaposition of important facts in a manner that emphasizes their relationship. Again, looking at the intersection case, a strictly chronological direct examination might have the plaintiff begin by explaining where she was headed on the morning of the accident. Assume now that she was going to an art exhibit that would not open for another hour. The importance and value of this seemingly innocuous fact can be heightened tremendously by apposing it to the conduct of the defendant immediately following the accident. Imagine the impact of contrasting the plaintiff's unhurried trip with the following information about the defendant.

QUESTION: Where were you going on the morning of the accident?

ANSWER: I was going to the Art Institute.

QUESTION: Were you in any hurry to get there?

ANSWER: It wasn't going to open for an hour, so I was in no hurry at all.

QUESTION: What did you do immediately after the accident?

ANSWER: I asked the defendant if he was all right.

QUESTION: What did the defendant do immediately following the accident?

ANSWER: He jumped out of his car and started talking on his cell phone. He shouted that he would talk to me later, but first he had to cancel an important appointment.

I.   Use Headlines for Emphasis and Transition

Believe it or not, trials are just plain dull to most observers. Argument is seldom gripping, and most witness examinations tend to drag on. Burdened by this millstone of tedium, your task as an attorney is twofold. First, make it all as interesting as possible. Second, develop means to let the factfinder know when something interesting (and truly important) is about to happen. Fulfill this responsibility by using headlines, transitions, and signals.

News sites set their headlines in bold fonts, drawing the readers' attention to the story below. A lawyer's headline serves the same purpose. It alerts the factfinder that significant information is about to follow. Although lawyers lack the advantage of distinctive typeface, the phrasing of headlines can perform the same function. In direct examination, a relatively modest headline might take this form:

COUNSEL: Let's talk about your training now, Dr. Harris.

A much bolder headline during an opening statement could be:

COUNSEL: This case is about broken promises. Let me tell you about the first one.

And the equivalent of a screaming banner might come in final argument:

COUNSEL: The defendant is a murderer—and here is the fact that proves it.

A transition is a headline that signals the end of one subject and the beginning of another. Transitions are particularly helpful when moving from a boring or technical area into something more substantive. For example:

COUNSEL: As I told you during the opening statement, the real heart of this case is damages. I want to show you now just how inflated the plaintiff's claim really is.

Or, during a direct examination:

COUNSEL: Doctor, now that we have talked about what qualifies you to testify as an expert, let's discuss the expert opinions you reached in this case.

J. Use Enumeration When Addressing Related Points

Finally, enumeration might be your most effective technique. Think about your classes: As soon as the lecturer announces that there are "three reasons" or "four rules" or "six characteristics," every person in the room takes notes. If you want the factfinder to concentrate, begin a numbered list. Take, for example, this portion of a closing argument:

COUNSEL: There were three different moments at which the defendant could have avoided this accident. Let me explain them to you.

Or, this portion of an expert's direct examination in a civil case involving the calculation of lost profits:

QUESTION: Dr. Harris, what is your opinion of Dr. Gupta's study?
ANSWER: There are three basic problems with Dr. Gupta's study.
QUESTION: What are those problems?
ANSWER: First, she projected profits on the basis of only two factors. Second, she failed to consider location, which should have been the most important element. Third, she doesn't seem to recognize that population growth can be extremely uneven.

Counsel can now ask the witness to explain each of the three points in detail. Note that the introduction of each point will reinitiate primacy and therefore heighten the factfinder's attention. It is also the case that the more times a point is repeated during a trial, the more likely the factfinder is to accept it.

Enumerating is particularly effective when used in conjunction with a visual aid. Do not simply tell the factfinder that the defendant violated three rules of the road. Write the numbered headlines down in bold letters and display them for the jury (assuming you are permitted to do so by your competition rules and the presiding judge).

K.   Do Not Be Overly Thankful

We see this all too often. Students feel compelled to thank the presiding judge and the witnesses constantly during mock trials. While it is natural to thank someone for doing something they did not have to do, you should not thank the participants of a trial for simply doing their job. Judges rule on objections—that is their job. Do not thank a judge for ruling on an objection. Witnesses answer questions—that is their job. Do not thank a witness for answering a question.

Be polite at all times during a mock trial, but do not be overly thankful. After a while, your thankfulness will be distracting to everyone in the courtroom.

L.   Resist the Temptation to Respond to Witnesses' Answers

Another mistake beginners often make during trials is responding to witnesses' answers, whether on direct or cross-examination. This example is not at all uncommon:

> QUESTION: What did you do next?
> ANSWER: I opened the door to see if anyone was inside.
> QUESTION: That makes sense. Then what did you do?

Technically the lawyer's response in this example is an impermissible comment on the evidence and it merits an objection that, "Counsel is testifying." This example is even more common:

> QUESTION: Isn't it true that you then opened the door to see if anyone was inside?
> ANSWER: Yes, that's right.
> QUESTION: OK. But you did that without a search warrant for the premises, true?

Like the previous example, this lawyer's use of the word "OK" is not proper.

The bottom line is that even though you want to make it seem like you are having a conversation with the witness who is testifying at trial, your opinions, beliefs, and reactions to the witness's answers are not relevant. Do your best to keep them to yourself.

> **Summary**
> **VERBAL TECHNIQUES**
> - Always refer to the presiding judge as "Your Honor"
> - Maximize your use of descriptive language and minimize legalese in jury trials
> - Use primacy and recency
> - Use repetition and duration to emphasize important points
> - Use reflective questioning to illustrate the passage of time
> - Use nouns and verbs rather than adjectives
> - Use apposition to compare related facts
> - Use headlines for emphasis and transitions
> - Use enumeration when addressing related points
> - Do not be overly thankful
> - Do not reply to witnesses' answers

IV. Communicating with Pictures and Demonstrations

The saying "A picture is worth a thousand words" is true. Even the best speakers cannot convey detailed information as well as a picture, or, for that matter, a diagram, a chart, or even a list. Therefore, whenever you can, use visual aids when presenting your case.

A. Use the Exhibits

Can the testimony in each of your direct examinations be illustrated with an exhibit? If a witness will testify about a pivotal document, have it enlarged or publish it to the factfinder so they can look at it during the witness's testimony. If the witness will testify about the events at the scene of the crime and a map of the scene has been provided in your case file, enlarge it (if allowed by the rules of your mock trial) so the witness can use it to explain what happened.

Then, return to these exhibits in your closing argument. Any item that has been admitted in evidence may be read out loud, displayed, or (if allowed) enlarged for use during closing argument. Underline key passages in important documents or array various documents side by side. This last technique is particularly useful to demonstrate relational concepts such as contradiction or continuity.

You may also use exhibits in your opening statement, but only if you are *sure* they are admissible and, even then, it is wise to notify opposing counsel and bring any objections to the attention of the presiding judge before your presentation begins. The best time to do this is when addressing pretrial matters with the court. See

Chapter Four, Section II(C) for detailed instructions on raising this and other matters before your mock trial begins.

B.   Create Visual Aids

Depending on the rules of your mock trial, you may be allowed to create visual aids to help explain the evidence to the trier of fact. During witness testimony, use these "demonstrative" aids to help explain the witnesses' testimony. For instance, if a witness will testify about a series of transactions, create a demonstrative exhibit in the form of a timeline to illustrate the progression of events to the jurors.

As with exhibits, return to these aids during your closing argument to summarize the most important testimony elicited during the trial. Depending upon the rules of your competition, you may also be allowed create entirely new visual aids that lay out your arguments for the jury in closing. Be creative—the factfinder will appreciate anything that spices up your argument. Whatever you do, be sure to incorporate your theory and theme, literally or in spirit.

C.   Conduct Demonstrations

The facts of a case come alive when the factfinder sees and hears exactly what the witness experienced. Ask witnesses to demonstrate crucial events or to recreate important sounds by asking, for example: "Please show the jury exactly how the defendant raised their hand before they struck you." "Please clap your hands together to show us how loud the sound was." "Please repeat the plaintiff's words in exactly their tone of voice."

In addition to being more interesting than regular testimony, demonstrations provide *truer* depictions of events. Without a demonstration of how an event occurred, each person in the courtroom could interpret the witness's testimony differently.

Visual and verbal demonstrations need to be reflected in the written record of a trial; although most mock trials are not transcribed by court reporters, the judges will appreciate your recognition of the custom. As a lawyer would in a real trial, ask to have the record reflect what just transpired in the courtroom. Using our prior examples, you might do that by saying: "Let the record reflect that the witness just raised his hand up over his head and clenched his fingers together into a fist" or "Let the record reflect that the witness's tone went higher at the end of the sentence as if asking a question." Your characterization of the testimony must be accurate, however, or you can expect to draw an objection from opposing counsel.

Chapter Four

Pretrial Matters

This chapter addresses pretrial matters that often play a role in mock trials. As with other subjects covered in this textbook, look to your mock trial competition organizer, any published rules or procedures, and your coach to determine whether you will encounter these pretrial matters in your mock trial.

I. Preliminary (A.K.A. "Housekeeping") Matters—Establishing the Courtroom Rules

Prior to the start of a mock trial, there is sometimes an opportunity for the lawyer participants to address the presiding judge. If such an opportunity is not built into the schedule of your mock trial, consider attempting to create such an opportunity by asking the court if you can be heard on a few preliminary, or "housekeeping," matters prior to opening statements.

Use the key words "preliminary" or "housekeeping" to signal to the court that you are inquiring about nonsubstantive matters, as opposed to seeking rulings on substantive matters such as motions in limine, which will be discussed in Section II of this chapter. Here is an example of how your inquiry of the court on preliminary matters might be initiated:

> COUNSEL: Your Honor, before we begin, may we raise a few preliminary matters with the court?
>
> COURT: What do you have in mind?
>
> COUNSEL: We have a few nonsubstantive questions for the court if you will permit us, Your Honor.
>
> COURT: Okay, let's hear them.

Without knowing exactly where you are going at this point, the judge has given you the opening you need to ask any of the following questions to which you do not already know the answer. And for the reasons we explain below, it might be a good idea to ask the questions even if you think you already know what the judge is going to say. When it comes to trials, each judge does things differently, so it is better to ask and be absolutely sure you know what to do rather than to guess incorrectly.

Chapter Four

A. Should I Treat the Trial as a Jury Trial or Bench Trial?

As we explained in Chapter One, Section I, there are two kinds of trials: jury trials and bench trials. In jury trials, the finder of fact is a group of citizens drawn from the local community and individually selected to serve. In bench trials, the factfinder is the presiding judge.

In mock trials, it is rare for jurors to serve as factfinders. A small number of mock trials, however, do involve people playing the role of jurors. In those instances, the jury tends to be made up of younger students who receive course credit or citizens who receive monetary compensation for their service. Mock trial juries are not subject to the laborious process of jury selection employed in real trials during which the presiding judge and the lawyers for each side are permitted to ask questions, often of a highly personal nature. Instead, all those who appear for mock trial "jury duty" are typically enlisted to serve regardless of qualification.

Sometimes mock trial juries deliberate after the trial and decide which side of the case they think should prevail. More often than not, however, the jurors just listen and provide either written or oral feedback to the judges and/or participants afterwards. It is ultimately the presiding and/or scoring judges who decide the winner of a mock trial.

But the absence of an audience in the form of a jury does not dictate whether a mock trial *is treated* as a jury trial, as opposed to a bench trial. Instead, the competition organizer or the presiding judge makes that call. As we will discuss in greater detail in subsequent chapters, the judge versus jury trial distinction can and should affect the communication style you adopt in the courtroom, where you position yourself during direct and cross-examination, where and how you argue objections, and more broadly, the evidence you present and how you go about urging the factfinder to apply that evidence to the law. Indeed, whether the trial is meant to be a jury trial or a bench trial can and should affect every aspect of a lawyer's representation of their client at trial.

Instead of wondering why you would ask this question at the start of a mock trial, the better question is why, if given the opportunity, you *wouldn't*. Of course, you need not raise the question if the materials you were provided make clear whether to treat the trial as a jury trial or a bench trial. But if the materials do not provide an answer, ask the question of your presiding judge.

COUNSEL:	Although no jury is present for this trial, we would like to know if you would prefer us to treat this as a jury trial?
COURT:	If there's no jury here why would we treat it as a jury trial?
COUNSEL:	We would do that, Your Honor, to demonstrate that we understand the differences between jury trials

	and bench trials and to show that we are capable of trying this case in front of either factfinder.
COURT:	I see. Very impressive, counsel. Let me ask you this: Do you have a preference?
COUNSEL:	We do, Your Honor. Our preference is to treat this as a jury trial.
COURT:	Very well, then. That is what we shall do.

Not every judge is going to ask you for your preference, of course. But if one does, ask that the trial be treated as a jury trial. Doing so will put you in the best possible position to demonstrate your superior trial advocacy skills.

B. Should I Assume Objections Are Being Argued at Sidebar?

When the factfinder is a jury, evidentiary objections of a sensitive nature or those that require reciting more than a generic legal ground (e.g., "Objection, lack of foundation"), are most often argued outside the hearing of the jury. When those arguments take place in the courtroom with the jurors still seated, they occur in front of or at the side of the judge's bench—hence the use of the term "sidebar"—and usually in hushed voices or whispers so the jury does not hear what is being said.

The need for sidebar conferences is simple: in the process of arguing why certain evidence should come in or be excluded, a party is likely to divulge what the evidence is and why the evidence supports that side's theory of the case. You may have heard the phrase: "You cannot un-ring the bell." In trials, this refers to how difficult, if not impossible, the task is to get a jury *not* to consider evidence they have—rightly or wrongly—already heard.

The simple solution is for the presiding judge not to let the jurors hear about the evidence or listen to the arguments for admission or exclusion until deciding that the evidence is, in fact, admissible. Accordingly, sensitive objections and extended evidentiary arguments should be heard at sidebar, and proper trial etiquette calls for the party seeking to admit or exclude such evidence to request a sidebar from the court as soon as the matter appears ripe for determination.

Say, for example, in a murder case where the defendant is claiming self-defense, there is evidence that several days before the murder the defendant went target shooting and placed a picture of the victim at the center of the target. The defense will want to exclude that evidence on the ground that its probative value is substantially outweighed by the danger of unfair prejudice it creates. Just because there was no love lost between the defendant and the victim, defense counsel will argue, does not make it any more or less likely that the defendant was justified in using force to protect themselves when the victim attacked. Whatever scant probative value that evidence has, the defense will continue arguing, is substantially outweighed by the

Chapter Four

danger of unfair prejudice that will result when the jury hears that the defendant used a photo of the victim during target practice.

Putting ourselves briefly in the place of the jurors, we can see why these arguments should be made at sidebar; if the judge excluded the evidence *after* the jury heard about the target practice incident, it would be difficult for the jurors to erase from their minds the mental image of the defendant aiming a gun at the victim's face and shooting that gun over and over again during target practice. At the first mention of a shooting range incident, therefore, counsel should object and, if allowed, respectfully request a sidebar conference to argue the admissibility of this evidence.

Thus far, we have explained why the presiding judge and parties would *want* to hold certain discussions outside the presence of the jury. The next question is, of course, why you should ask in a mock trial if you can assume objections *are* being heard at sidebar. This is called asking for a "constructive sidebar"—where the lawyer participants act as if they are being heard at sidebar when in reality they are being heard in open court—so they do not have to walk to the side of the judge's bench and argue objections in a hushed tone.

First, asking for constructive sidebars is efficient. Asking for a sidebar takes time, as does waiting for all counsel to walk up to the judge's bench. During actual trials, this process is further delayed by waiting for the court reporter to move to a position closer to the bench so they can hear what is being said between the attorneys to make an accurate record of the proceedings.

More importantly, a constructive sidebar allows everyone else in the courtroom to hear your evidentiary arguments. You absolutely want any scoring judges who are not the presiding judge to hear your evidentiary arguments. Your teammates playing the roles of witnesses will also want to hear evidentiary arguments and rulings so they can learn from the experience. And finally, your instructor or coach will want to hear the evidentiary arguments so they can offer feedback on your performance after the trial is over and help you fine-tune your arguments going forward.

You may be wondering why, if you want everyone in the courtroom to hear all of the evidentiary arguments made, you would *want* the trial to be treated as a jury trial at all. Remember, treating the trial as a jury trial showcases your superior trial advocacy skills. It provides you with the opportunity to demonstrate that you are capable of pinpointing which arguments should be made outside the presence of the jury. And demonstrating superior trial advocacy skills is the point of mock trials. Asking this next question gives you another opportunity to do just that.

> COUNSEL   Judge, since we are going to treat this mock trial as a jury trial, we have an additional question for the court.
> COURT: What is that?

COUNSEL:	When we are arguing evidentiary matters to the court, should the parties always assume we are being heard at sidebar or would you prefer that we ask you for a constructive sidebar in each instance where we believe a sidebar would be appropriate?
COURT:	I see why you're asking. Sidebars take time and I don't like wasting time, but on the other hand if both sides assume they're being heard at sidebar, it defeats some of the purpose of treating this as a jury trial. Once again, I am interested to know if you have a preference, counsel?
COUNSEL	Our preference would be that both parties be required to ask, where we deem doing so appropriate, whether we can assume we are then being heard at sidebar. Given that the scoring judges and our teammates and coaches cannot hear what is said at the sidebar, however, we think it is best if there are no actual proceedings at sidebar.
COURT:	That sounds perfectly reasonable and logical to me, counsel. Any objection from opposing counsel?
OPPONENT:	That is our preference as well, Your Honor.
COURT:	So ordered.

Once again, your judge might not ask or even care about your preference in the matter, but if given the opportunity to weigh in, suggest the action that will best demonstrate your knowledge and good judgment of which evidentiary matters are sensitive enough to merit a sidebar conference outside the hearing of the jury.

If the presiding judge in your trial decides that you should ask each time you think an evidentiary argument should be made at sidebar, tailor your objection style accordingly.

COUNSEL:	Objection to the admissibility of this testimony, Your Honor. May we assume we are being heard at sidebar?
COURT:	Yes. Now state the legal basis for your objection, counsel.
COUNSEL:	We object to lack of foundation and the probative value of this testimony being substantially outweighed by its prejudicial effect, Your Honor. We also move to strike the first part of the witness's answer and ask that the court instruct the jury to disregard it.

Chapter Four

> COURT: The objection is sustained and the motion to strike is granted. (Turning to the jury) Members of the jury, I instruct you to disregard the testimony you just heard; you should not consider it when deliberating in this case.

(See Chapter Thirteen, Section II(E) to learn more about making motions to strike inadmissible testimony.)

C. Does the Court Have Rules About Moving Around the Courtroom?

One of the many important functions of a presiding judge is maintaining control over their courtroom. The last two words of that sentence are paramount. In the eyes of the judge, the courtroom is theirs and they have near-absolute say over what transpires there. Judges are also naturally protective of witnesses and of jurors. For these reasons, if a lawyer attempts to walk up to a witness while the witness is testifying, the lawyer is likely to draw the presiding judge's attention, and not necessarily in a good way.

Proper etiquette in a courtroom is to ask the presiding judge's permission before getting within arm's reach of a witness. If you intend to get that close to a witness, first ask: "Permission to approach the witness, Your Honor?" or "May I approach the witness, Your Honor?" This gives a heads up not only to the court but also to the witness. By obtaining the court's permission to approach in advance, your action is less likely to be perceived as hostile to the witness. It is never, ever, proper to take a hostile physical stance or make any physical movement that could be perceived as hostile toward a testifying witness.

But even beyond asking for permission to approach witnesses, be aware that some judges do not like it when lawyers move around in their courtrooms. They may find it distracting. Or think it is disrespectful. Many are concerned with the record; while your voice can be heard clearly when standing by the podium microphone or sitting or standing in front of the microphone at the counsel table, moving away from those areas while still talking can result in a lower-quality recording that makes the court reporter's job more difficult. (Court reporters audio-record the proceedings so they can go back and listen while reviewing their draft transcripts, which become the final record of what was said.) For any of these reasons and possibly others, many judges adopt what is known as a "podium rule": other than walking between counsel table and the lectern, you must ask permission to move about the courtroom.

Chapter Three, Section II(D) catalogs some techniques that depend upon your ability to move freely about the courtroom during trial. If you intend to employ one or more of those methods, ask the presiding judge this question prior to trial to confirm in advance that you will be allowed to do so. Nothing can throw an effective cross-examination off kilter quite like an incredulous interruption from the presiding judge telling an attorney, "Get back behind the lectern, counsel!"

D. Should I Seek Permission Prior to Each Instance of Approaching a Testifying Witness?

A minority of judges do not have rules about counsel moving around their courtrooms and, in fact, become annoyed if counsel asks permission to approach a witness prior to each instance of walking within arm's reach. If this describes your judge, you are likely to find it out the second time you ask permission to approach the same witness. The judge will say something along the lines of "Counsel, after I give you permission to approach a witness once, you do not need to keep asking me if you may approach that witness."

Asking this question during your pretrial housekeeping matters will allow you to follow the court's preferences throughout your trial and save you from possibly being caught off guard later.

On the other hand, if you are in the habit of always asking if you may approach the witness and are likely to do so in each instance whether the court wants you to or not, it is probably better not to ask this question before the trial begins so as not to highlight your difficulty overcoming the habit.

E. (In Jury Trials) Is the Court Willing to Read Stipulations Aloud?

As we discussed in Chapter One, Section IV, mock trial case files often include stipulations between the parties. A stipulation is an agreement reached between the parties, such as agreeing that a certain fact or piece of evidence is true or that if called to testify a certain witness would testify to a certain fact or piece of evidence. If there are stipulations in your mock trial case file that help your case, plan ahead to use them in the most effective manner possible at trial. Ask the presiding judge if *they* are willing to be the one to read the stipulations aloud to the jury at trial. Of course, this is not a question you need to ask in a bench trial.

Why ask the judge to read the stipulations? The answer is simple. The presiding judge is the ultimate authority figure in the courtroom. Whether or not they sit on a raised bench (most do) and wear a black robe (most do), jurors perceive the judge to be the most credible person present during a trial. No matter how likeable and trustworthy a lawyer seems, jurors instinctively know that lawyers are paid to represent their clients and therefore their every action in the courtroom is taken with that objective in mind (an accurate assessment indeed).

Thus, if you want a stipulation read to the jury during trial to help prove some aspect or element material to your case, there is no better candidate to do the reading than the judge. So ask, politely, if the judge is willing to read stipulations to the jurors and, if so, provide the judge with a list of the stipulations you intend to

Chapter Four

offer and the approximate point in time at which you plan to offer each. Number the stipulations as they are numbered in the mock trial case file and add a prefatory note prior to each stipulation identifying the witness's testimony during which you will seek to have it read. An example might be: "Stipulation #2, to be read during the direct examination of Special Agent Carrie Landau." Giving a heads-up of when you plan to ask for each stipulation to be read may increase the presiding judge's willingness to participate in the trial in this way.

If the judge prefers not to read stipulations into the record, when the time comes for the stipulation to be read, you stand, face the jury, preface the stipulation by saying, "The parties have stipulated and agreed that . . . ," and once done reading the stipulation exactly as it appears in your case file, turn to defense counsel and ask, "So stipulated, counsel?" so that opposing counsel is forced to acknowledge in front of the jurors that the stipulation is indeed agreed upon by both parties. ("Yes, so stipulated," is the proper response.)

II. Additional Housekeeping Matters

A.   *Provide Pretrial Notice If Required*

Some evidentiary rules adopted for mock trial competitions require one side or the other to provide notice of their intent to pursue a particular defense or seek to admit certain kinds of evidence. If you intend to do one of those things and your notice obligations have not already been met (e.g., through a court filing included in your mock trial case file), now is the time to inform the court and opposing counsel of your intention.

B.   *Inform the Court That You Plan to Use Demonstrative Evidence*

Mock trial competitions have different rules when it comes to creating and using demonstrative evidence, and different judges react differently to the use of this kind of evidence during trial. If your mock trial rules and procedures allow for the creation and use of demonstratives or are silent about them, then by all means use demonstrative evidence whenever possible at trial. Note, however, that some competitions prohibit the use of exhibits beyond those found in the case file (in which case, of course, you must follow the rules).

Demonstrative evidence is evidence that you will not seek to admit into evidence as an exhibit but that will assist a witness in explaining or illustrating a fact at issue in the case. Demonstrative evidence can take the form of models, graphs, diagrams, charts, drawings, or any other objects that explain or illustrate issues in the case. In Chapter Eight, Section III(B)(2), we discuss demonstrative evidence and the foundation that must be laid to use this kind of evidence during mock trials.

Even if demonstrative evidence is or appears to be permissible in your mock trial, inform the judge and opposing counsel prior to trial of your intention to use this kind of evidence.

It is usually safe to assume that the judge presiding over your mock trial has read the witness statements and the documentary evidence included in your case file. If the case file did not include the demonstrative evidence you intend to use at trial, however, the judge may react poorly to your use of that evidence, concerned that you are trying to do something improper or sneaky. Discussing your intention to use this evidence before the trial helps to put the court at ease. It also provides opposing counsel with the opportunity to object to the exhibit before trial rather than by interrupting the flow of your direct examination to take issue with the exhibit.

Here's an example of how you might go about informing a court of your intention to use a demonstrative exhibit during trial:

COUNSEL: Next, we would like to inform the court and opposing counsel that we intend to use a demonstrative exhibit during the testimony of Special Agent Eric Field. For the record, I am providing a copy of the demonstrative exhibit, which we have marked Government Exhibit 10, to the court and counsel. As you can see, Government Exhibit 10 is an approximate diagram of the defendant's residence as perceived by Special Agent Field when he executed the lawfully obtained warrant to search the home on October 9th. This diagram will be used to plot the locations of the weapons and drugs found in the defendant's bedroom and in other parts of his house. Special Agent Field's testimony about this diagram will support the government's theory that the defendant was a knowing participant in a conspiracy to distribute heroin and that he knowingly possessed a weapon at the time of the search despite being a convicted felon.

COURT: Are you expecting some kind of ruling from the court now about the admissibility of this exhibit?

COUNSEL: Not at all, Your Honor. We are merely informing the court and defense counsel of our intention to use this diagram at trial so as not to take anyone off guard when the time comes.

COURT: Very well. We're on notice.

There are a few more points worth making about demonstrative evidence.

Chapter Four

First, be sure no aspect of your demonstrative will be contradicted by an uncontroverted fact. Even pretrial notice will not save your credibility if you use a demonstrative exhibit that will be proven inaccurate at trial.

Next, be sure your demonstrative does not violate the most important mock trial rule: the prohibition on making unreasonable inferences from the facts and information included in your case file. We discuss the ethical prohibition on eliciting unreasonable inferences in greater detail in Chapter Seven, Section IV(B). For now, think of it this way: the facts included in your case file were included for good reason, as were the facts not included in the case file.

Say your mock trial is a criminal case in which the government must prove the defendant knowingly possessed a weapon, and the case file makes clear that the weapon was found in a drawer of the nightstand next to where the defendant was found sleeping in his bedroom. A reasonable inference from those facts is that the defendant was sleeping on a bed. It would also be reasonable to infer that the nightstand in which the gun was found was located right next to the defendant's bed. Those inferences are consistent with the facts to be proven at trial and with people's everyday experience.

It would be an unreasonable inference, however, to draw a diagram and label the nightstand as being exactly one inch away from the bed where the defendant slept. Is it possible the nightstand was an inch away from the bed? Yes. But if the drafters wanted a witness to testify to the exact distance between the bed and the nightstand, they would have included that fact in the case file. If they chose not to include that fact in the case file, which is arguably material to the charge on trial, you should not include that exact measurement in your demonstrative exhibit. Instead, draw a bed with a nightstand next to it and have your witness testify consistent with the information provided in the case file.

One last point about reasonable inferences versus unreasonable inferences: when in doubt whether an inference is reasonable, err on the side of caution and leave it out. Mock trials are not competitions to see which side can make up better facts in order to prevail at trial. Practicing lawyers caught making up or suggesting facts to witnesses are likely to be disciplined or even disbarred. Dishonesty is not a quality becoming of lawyers, and any hint displayed by counsel in a mock trial is a surefire way to draw the ire of a presiding judge. Good lawyers are good not because they change the facts to suit their case and win, but rather because they change their case to suit the facts and still win.

C. *Cover Any Other Plans You Have That Are Remotely Controversial*

Contrary to popular belief, there should be few true surprises during trials. For the most part, whether a case is criminal or civil in nature, the lawyers for each side have a pretty good idea of who the witnesses will be and what evidence and testimony they'll offer. In real cases, this is a function of the discovery process. Discovery refers to each side's legal obligation to hand over to opposing counsel the evidence they have collected and which they intend to use at trial. That is oversimplifying discovery-related rules a bit, but it gives you the general idea. And it is certainly true of mock trials, where *all* of the material facts to be presented have been included somewhere in each case file.

As a result, the element of surprise will be even less at play in a mock trial than it is in real trials, which is to say that it should not be a factor at all. For this reason, if you plan to do or say anything during a mock trial that you think will be remotely controversial, we recommend giving the presiding judge a heads up about it before your trial begins. It is better to know in advance that something you intend to do will not be allowed so you can adapt your strategy accordingly. Not only will you present your case more smoothly that way, but the presiding judge will respect you for being upfront and honest about your intentions in advance, not to mention ably adapting in response to any adverse ruling they may make.

III. Motions in Limine

Before an actual trial begins, the parties are given the opportunity to raise evidentiary issues with the court to seek a ruling, in advance of trial, that certain evidence will or will not be admitted at trial. The term "motion in limine" translates literally to a motion "at the threshold," meaning before the trial begins. It is sometimes thought that a motion in limine may be used only to "limit" or exclude evidence, but that is incorrect. A motion "at the threshold" may seek to admit evidence as well as to keep it out.

In every trial, there is bound to be evidence of debatable admissibility. That is particularly true in mock trials. The individuals who draft mock trial case files purposefully include facts and evidence that probably should not be deemed admissible, as well as facts and evidence that probably—but not clearly—should be admitted. If all of the evidence in the case file was clearly admissible, the only challenge would be in figuring out how best to present it. To the contrary, mock trials are much more complex; not only do participants have to figure out what facts and evidence they want to present, but they have to figure out the best arguments for admission, how to elicit the evidence as persuasively as possible and, if they get an adverse ruling, how to elegantly recover and not signal to the jurors or judge any hint of defeat.

When allowed in a mock trial, motions in limine can be an immensely useful tool for assisting an attorney in determining, prior to trial, which facts and evidence will be admitted. Most mock trial competitions that allow motions in limine insist that they be made and argued orally rather than in writing. We discussed case law briefly in Chapter One, Section I(C). Whenever case law supporting a motion in limine is provided in your mock trial case file, we encourage you to cite it during your argument.

Keep arguments in support of motions in limine as simple as possible. The more complex a legal issue seems, the less likely the court is to definitively rule on the matter prior to trial. Here is an example of a motion in limine a criminal prosecutor might make to prevent defense counsel from attempting to elicit testimony setting forth statements made by the defendant prior to trial:

> COUNSEL: Your Honor, the government moves in limine to exclude from evidence any statements made by the defendant prior to trial that are not being offered against him at trial by the government. Those statements are hearsay under the rules of evidence and are not admissible for any purpose.

When responding to opposing counsel's motions in limine, point out the facts or evidence that complicate the applicable legal analysis, and urge the court to reserve ruling until the evidence can be evaluated in context during the trial. A response to the prosecutor's motion in limine set forth above might be:

> COUNSEL: We believe there may be instances in which the defendant's statements may be admissible in this case when offered by the defense. For example, if on cross-examination the government suggests that certain statements were recently fabricated, prior consistent statements of the defendant could be offered to rebut those claims. We ask the court to reserve ruling on the admissibility of statements of the defendant until an attempt is made to elicit such statements at trial.

Unless the presiding judge clearly states otherwise, assume that rulings on motions in limine are conditional, which means they are conditioned upon the evidence developing in the way represented to the court when the motion was argued. If the evidence develops differently, or if in the context of the trial you believe a new basis for including or excluding the evidence has arisen, you may raise the legal issue with the court again and seek a different outcome. In doing so, at sidebar or a constructive sidebar, acknowledge the prior ruling but point out the facts or circumstances that you believe have changed since the issue was initially argued so the presiding judge understands that you are not simply seeking a second bite at the apple. If the judge disagrees that the ruling should change, adapt your case presentation to the ruling and move on with your case.

Chapter Five

Playing an Effective Witness

This chapter, new to the third edition of this book, provides guidance to participants who play the role of witnesses in mock trials. Often thought to be of secondary importance to those filling the attorney roles, we aim to convince you that having effective witnesses on your side can be just as critical.

I. The Importance of Effective Witnesses

Just as in real trials, effective witnesses can make an appreciable difference in mock trials, both in terms of the spectators' enjoyment and the team's overall performance. By "effective," we mean witnesses who are comfortable with the facts of the case; credible, likeable and confident; interesting to listen to and watch; adept at navigating direct and cross-examination; and both straightforward and fair.

Effective witnesses can help their teams succeed in several ways. High scores for a witness's performance provide a direct and positive contribution to the overall team effort. Witnesses can also contribute indirectly by helping the attorneys who question them look prepared and effective. In this way, it is possible for a single witness to change the outcome of an otherwise close mock trial.

But just as effective witnesses can help their team succeed, the opposite is true of ineffective witnesses. A witness who gives vague or unnecessarily long answers on direct examination, for example, can hurt their team's scores. That is true even if the questions asked are worded simply and formulated to elicit relevant, admissible information. The danger posed by a loquacious or rambling witness is that those assigning scores may penalize the lawyer asking the questions for not crafting a more concise direct examination. As is true in real trials, it is up to the lawyer who calls a meandering witness to rein in their testimony and guide the witness to the information that matters most (more on that below).

In essence, bad witnesses make lawyers look worse on direct and good witnesses make them look better. And on cross, bad witnesses make decent lawyers look better.

Next, we will dig deeper into how you can be an effective witness.

Chapter Five

II. Key Qualities of Effective Witnesses

A. *Be Prepared*

One of the surest ways a witness can hurt the score of their team is by not being sufficiently familiar with the facts of the case.

There is no real trick to familiarizing oneself with the facts of a case. Simply do the work of reading the facts over (and over and over, if necessary), until you remember the facts that matter. There is no shame in not remembering everything you read the first time you read it; simply keep reading the material over (and over and over, if necessary) until you do.

If your competition rules allow witnesses to familiarize themselves with the entire case file, take advantage of that opportunity and do not limit yourself to just the witness statement or the transcript of the witness's prior testimony. To really understand the witness and how they fit in to the larger narrative, you must read the entire case file over (and over and over, if necessary) until a clear picture emerges of the role you will play in the trial. (This is one advantage mock trial witnesses have over witnesses in real trials. In real trials witnesses do not, or at least should not, know in advance what the other witnesses will say.)

1. Take Note of Any Conflicts with Another Witness's Anticipated Testimony

As you read through the case file, take note if another witness's testimony contradicts the testimony of the witness you have been assigned to play. That is not cause to change or alter the account you will provide while acting as the witness—indeed, as we explain further below, doing so would be unethical and potentially disastrous for your team. But knowledge is still power. Understanding that another witness will contradict what you say when you testify will help you better prepare for direct and cross-examination on the matter(s) about which the two witnesses disagree.

Imagine for a moment that the disagreement between two witnesses is about something each observed with their senses—a thing or event they each saw, heard, smelled, tasted, or touched. In that situation, you might assume that whichever witness had the best opportunity or ability to observe would be deemed the most reliable and believable by the factfinder. That is probably true, but it is not a given because the credibility and bias of every witness is "at issue" in a trial. It is therefore possible that the witness with perfect vision and the best vantage point to observe an event could be shown to be less credible or to have an inherent interest in the outcome of the case, leaving the jurors to rely instead on the testimony of the unbiased eyewitness to the event despite their inferior vision or vantage.

If, based on the facts written in the case file, the witness you will play had a good opportunity and ability to observe an event, especially in comparison to another witness who offers conflicting testimony, that is certainly something you can expect to be questioned about during your direct examination. You can also expect the opposing team to test your opportunity and ability to observe during cross-examination, as well as to exploit any weaknesses in your credibility or potential bias.

Most disagreements between witnesses' varying accounts are not straightforward. Two people can observe the same event and perceive it slightly, or even quite, differently. That is why even eyewitness identifications can be suspect in certain circumstances. As you read through the case file, look for even slight inconsistencies between the accounts of different witnesses and take note when a particular account is supported or contradicted by evidence such as an exhibit. Each inconsistency is likely to be raised and addressed on direct and cross-examination; becoming intimately familiar with them in advance will inure to your benefit.

2. If While Testifying You Forget an Important Fact, Say So

Let's say you forget an important fact while testifying. By way of example, imagine the witness you play observed a mugging and provided the police with a detailed description of the assailant at or near the time of the event. And yet, despite reading that description over (and over and over) to prepare for the trial, your nerves get the best of you and your brain blocks out the color of the sweatshirt the assailant was wearing—a fact you know is written in your witness statement. What should you do?

You have two options: 1) admit that you do not remember the color of the assailant's sweatshirt; or 2) guess the answer. Although forgetting a fact is an unfortunate occurrence during a trial, guessing the answer is much riskier; always avoid guessing.

When a witness states that they do not remember a fact (and in a mock trial this refers to a fact written somewhere in the case file—e.g., in the witness's statement or in a transcript of prior testimony by the witness), the attorney questioning the witness can go through a serious of steps to remind the witness what they said on a prior occasion. That process is called "refreshing a witness's recollection," and admittedly it can be time-consuming and awkward if the attorney asking the questions does not know exactly where to find the answers in the witness's prior statement. (We provide step-by-step guidance on how to refresh a witness's recollection in Chapter Seven, Section II(D).) In addition to taking up valuable time, the exercise can throw the examining attorney off their stride. This is because no lawyer *expects* a witness not to remember an important fact while testifying, so when it happens it can lead to scrambling, which can make the attorney appear less prepared for trial than they could have been. On the other hand, as we explain in Chapter Seven, when an attorney smoothly and adeptly refreshes a witness's recollection, it can have a positive effect on the attorney's score because they appear more skilled and prepared than if they had not been required to go through that process. As long as the attorney has practiced refreshing recollection and is familiar enough with the witness's prior statement to quickly pinpoint the forgotten fact, the mere fact that the exercise became necessary need not detract from the attorney's performance.

As unfortunate as it might seem to forget a fact while testifying, admitting that you can't recall the fact is far preferable to *guessing* an answer you no longer recall with certainty. That is because guessing risks getting the answer wrong, and when a witness testifies differently in court than they did in the past, they invite the attorney cross-examining them to impeach them with their prior inconsistent statement. (We provide step-by-step guidance on how to impeach a witness by prior inconsistent statement in Chapter Ten, Section III(A).)

Impeachment is, essentially, the act of proving that a witness changed their testimony in some meaningful way. In addition to impeaching by prior inconsistent statement, witnesses can be impeached "by omission." Impeachment by omission is the act of proving that a witness has added new facts in their current testimony—facts that were omitted previously. When done well, either form of impeachment tends to result in the loss of at least some of the witness's credibility. Simply put, witnesses who are shown to be, or are suspected of, lying or embellishing their prior testimony are not deemed reliable or credible. In a real trial, jurors might (rightfully) disregard everything a witness has said once they have been impeached. And if the jury suspects that the lawyer questioning the witness had something to do with the changing story, the credibility of the attorney can suffer as well. Beware that if the situation is grave enough, the opposing attorney can exploit these developments in their closing argument to urge the factfinder to side with them.

The same is true in a mock trial. The impeachment of a witness is likely to hurt not only the witness's scores, but also possibly those of the attorney who conducted the witness's direct examination. For these reasons, it is never a good idea to guess an answer while testifying and it is *always* wrong to purposefully change or embellish a witness's prior account when testifying under oath.

3. Describe Key Facts Using the Same Words That Appear in the Witness's Statement/Affidavit/Transcript

Sometimes zealous attorneys accuse witnesses of changing or embellishing their prior testimony when in fact all the witness has done is use different words to describe the same facts or events. Does the fact that a witness has used different words necessarily mean they have changed or embellished their story? No, it does not. But depending on the words used or added, it certainly could.

When it comes to changes or additions to a witness's testimony, the conclusions reached are very much in the eye of the beholder. An ultra-competitive and suspicious opposing counsel could make it seem like a witness or team was trying to gain an unfair advantage even when they were not. And to the extent the change in wording tended—even if only slightly—to make the witness's testimony more credible or impactful, that assertion or accusation might seem reasonable to judges or competition organizers. How such a development impacts a team's standing overall will depend on whether competition organizers feel a procedural or ethical rule was violated. But even if the impeachment does not rise to the level of a rule violation, it can hurt a team's performance if the scoring judges thought the change or embellishment was intentional and the impeachment was called for and well executed.

For all these reasons, we urge you to use the same words the witness used in the past to describe the same event or condition. Why risk being impeached if your aim is to give at trial the same general account the witness gave previously? Instead, commit to memory the precise words used by the witness in the past and repeat those words while testifying to avoid even a suggestion that you have attempted to alter or embellish the witness's prior account.

This is especially worthwhile when it comes to the key aspects of a witness's testimony; the more important the fact, the more likely the opposing team is to impeach by prior inconsistent statement or by omission if different or new words are used to testify to that fact.

The bottom line is that it is far better to repeat exactly what the witness said in the past while testifying than it is to attempt to revise the witness's testimony even in a slight, non-substantive manner. And if, while testifying, you cannot remember with certainty something you know is written in your witness statement, it is far better to just say so rather than to attempt to guess the forgotten information.

B. Be Believable, Credible, and Confident

Witnesses are believable and credible when their words and actions are consistent and their testimony is not contradicted by any (or at least not many) of the facts presented at trial.

As we have discussed, some mock trial case files have contradictions among witnesses baked into them. It is not unheard of for two witnesses to the same event to give conflicting accounts. That is true in real life and most mock trials are based, at least loosely, on real cases. Accordingly, entire real and mock trials can be focused on parsing out conflicting witness accounts and determining which witness's version is true (or at least more likely to be true).

If the witness you have been assigned to play will give testimony that conflicts with the testimony of another witness or with other evidence that will be presented in the case, there is really nothing you can do about it except aim to be the most credible version of the witness as is possible. You do that by having a full command of the facts in your witness statement, a good understanding of the entire case file, and by using the same words while testifying as the witness used previously.

Confidence, too, flows naturally from being prepared and well-practiced. If, prior to a mock trial, you are concerned that you are lacking in confidence when playing the witness role, the remedy is to practice playing the role of the witness

Chapter Five

over (and over and over, if necessary) until you build up the confidence you need to remember the key facts and give convincing testimony when the pressure is on.

There is no rule that says you can only practice your testimony at your team practices. If you need additional time to prepare, write out the questions you are likely to be asked and ask a sibling or a roommate or friend to pretend to be the lawyer asking you questions on direct or cross-examination.

One word of caution, however: while it is important to memorize the key words used in the witness's prior statement or transcript, and to practice your direct until you build up the confidence necessary to deliver the testimony in a convincing manner, it is nonetheless important that your words not sound overly rehearsed when you testify.

This is a common mistake made in mock trials. Well-intentioned and diligent students sometimes memorize and practice lines only to recite them at trial in a monotone manner that sounds akin to reading them. Actors can struggle with the same phenomenon when reciting memorized lines as well.

The key to making the witness you are playing believable is to make the testimony sound natural and native to you, the individual reciting it. You do that by embodying the witness and bringing them to life in the same way actors portray the characters they play. They *become* the character, and you should do that, too, when playing the role of a witness in a mock trial. Reimagine yourself as the witness and stay "in character" throughout the time you are present in the courtroom. (But do not use facial expressions or head movements when not testifying in an effort to signal to those present whether you agree with the testimony given by another witness.)

Your goal should be for those observing the trial to remember and picture you when reminded of the testimony you gave in the trial. Following our advice below to make your witness the most interesting version of themselves possible will help in this regard. But you should avoid sounding like you have memorized every answer you give, even if you have. Instead, recite the specific words used in the key portions of your testimony while injecting a sense of spontaneity or humanity as you testify, so the overall effect is that you sound well-prepared and yet still believable.

What do we mean by injecting spontaneity and humanity? We mean to let a little of the witness's personality shine through in your answers. Another way to do that is to have a real and human reaction to something that happens during your testimony. That could be a reaction to a specific word or phrase used in a question you are asked. Or a comment about something you yourself do in the courtroom, such as making a self-deprecating joke if you nearly trip while walking into the courtroom, or if you accidentally bump into the microphone. It can be anything, really, so long as it is "in character" (i.e., consistent with the witness persona you have adopted and are displaying while testifying).

Finally, a word about confidence in this context. Confidence is a feeling you have about who you are. Some people are born confident. Others struggle daily to feel that way. Most people fall somewhere in-between. Regardless of where you personally fall on the confidence spectrum, when you are playing a witness role in a mock trial, try to inject some manner of confidence into the character you are playing. Like many things in life, *acting* confident even if you are not feeling confident can convince your audience that you *are* confident.

Confident witnesses are more likely to be believed than those who are perceived to be unsure of what they are saying. So fake it until you make it—act confident while practicing to testify and hopefully by the time you do testify, you will feel confident too.

C.   Be Interesting

There is a reason most people do not like being summoned for jury duty: trials are (or at least can be) boring. They also take jurors away from things they would rather be doing, such as working or spending time with family and friends. Although televised trials sometimes garner a public following, most trials that take place in local, state, and federal courthouses do not, and the reason is largely because they're not very interesting.

Young trial lawyers tend to find every case they try inherently interesting. And surely there are interesting aspects to most trials. But as lawyers age and gain experience, they come to understand that while a case may be inherently interesting to them, those forced to sit through and watch it are unlikely to feel the same way. So, experienced trial lawyers listen for what is interesting—about a case generally and about individual witnesses specifically—and accentuate those points during the trial to pique the jury's interest.

Remember, too, that participating in a trial is a different experience than watching one. Trials are challenging for the participants: there are a million different ways to try a given case, and no one has ever tried a case perfectly. Even the best trial lawyers and witnesses make mistakes; the key is to learn from them and trust one's instincts going forward to avoid making the same mistakes again. When disaster can strike at any moment, and thus it is important never to let one's guard down, trial participants rarely get bored, even when things are going smoothly.

But as we mentioned, watching a trial is different than participating in one. And in mock trials, just as in real trials, it is the observers who decide the outcome of the trial. Accordingly, it is in the best interests of the participants to make each trial as interesting as it can possibly be for those watching.

Simply put, boring witnesses garner less appreciation, which in a mock trial translates into lower scores. Even worse than being boring is being unlikeable; even

Chapter Five

when we recognize unlikeable people to be smart and effective, we still tend not to want to reward them. The same is true in trials with boring or unlikeable witnesses. The more interesting the witnesses are, and the more likeable, the higher their scores and the greater the direct benefit they add to their team.

Some witnesses are interesting because of what they have to say. The same is true of characters in television shows and movies. Actors—even great actors—seek out roles based in part on what their character will have to say; the more interesting the lines, the more likely it is that a well-regarded actor will want to play the role. In other words, having good material can go a long way.

If you have been assigned the role of a witness who has interesting things to say in the context of your trial, consider yourself lucky. Just by giving that compelling testimony, you are likely to be perceived as interesting. Typically, heightened interest in a witness's testimony reflects favorably on the scores the witness is awarded. Why? It's human nature; we all love to be entertained.

But not all witnesses have interesting things to say. Some are just bit players in the drama, filling in a few necessary facts to complete the larger narrative of one side's case. The real challenge is in making those witnesses interesting too.

When considering how to make the witness interesting to those observing the trial, look first to what the witness will say for clues on how to bring the witness to life. Does the witness have an interesting background you can emphasize? Has the witness acquired specialized knowledge through formal education or experience that can be accentuated to add interest? Has the witness had a notable career or some unique life experience that can be highlighted?

From their background, education, and experience, you might be able to figure out other ways to make the witness memorable. Would the witness's educational level (whether low or high) impact the witness's language or demeanor in the courtroom setting? Does the word usage in the witness's statement suggest a personality trait or peculiarity of some kind that can be emphasized while testifying? Or maybe they have a verbal tick or a nonverbal habit of movement that makes them ever so slightly more compelling or memorable to watch?

Also consider how the witness would likely carry themselves while walking into, out of, and around the courtroom. An older witness who sustained a bodily injury fighting in a war might watch their feet and walk with a limp, for example. A highly regarded and sought-after scientific expert, on the other hand, might glide on and off the witness stand with their head held high and nose slightly turned up toward spectators.

Would a particular style of dress fit the witness more readily than others? A clothing designer would surely dress differently than a construction worker. A doctor and an architect might dress differently too. As long as your mock trial rules allow for participants to wear costumes specific to witness roles, consider taking advantage of that opportunity to add even a minor point of interest for those spectating.

There are an infinite number of ways to make a witness interesting—you are limited only by your imagination.

Having said all of that, when it comes to bringing witnesses to life, we add two important caveats. First, stop short of trying to make any witness the focal point of the trial or of a side's entire case. Although an interesting witness is better than a boring one, the way the role is played must remain believable. And if the witness's testimony is not perceived as credible, then any added interest or drama is all for naught. For that reason, avoid making a witness so interesting that they become a distraction rather than an asset to the team's overall effort. Accordingly, limit yourself to one or two ways of adding interest to a witness and focus your remaining energy on the advice in the rest of this chapter.

Our second caveat is that any "interest" added to a witness must not materially alter the import of the witness's written testimony. In other words, in making a witness more interesting, a team cannot make the substance of the witness's testimony more helpful to its case. As we discuss elsewhere, witnesses in mock trials are limited to testifying to the facts set forth in their witness statements and reasonable inferences drawn therefrom. If in making a witness more interesting a team essentially adds favorable facts to the case to increase the likelihood it will prevail, then the team is violating that procedural rule and may be penalized or even disqualified. (See Section III(I) below and Chapter Seven, Section IV(B) for fuller discussions of reasonable inferences.)

Consequently, examine whether your added "interest" is aimed at making the witness's testimony stronger for the case. If it is, then in adding that interest the team has likely overstepped at least the spirit of the competition rules, which is always wrong.

III. Techniques for Handling Direct and Cross-Examination

Testifying as a witness can be an intimidating experience. Being questioned by lawyers (or even people pretending to be lawyers) can be stressful. Lawyers are good with words and when it comes to testifying under oath, words matter. And while precision may not always be possible, trial lawyers will still strive to achieve it.

Some lawyers—even experienced trial lawyers who question witnesses in court for a living—are not good at asking clear questions. Other lawyers deliberately try to confuse witnesses into giving favorable answers.

Even though the process can be intimidating, it is imperative that witnesses listen critically to the questions asked of them.

A.   Listen Critically to Each Question and Pause Before Answering

Listen carefully to each question you are asked and pause briefly before answering. Ask yourself whether you understand exactly what information the question is intended to elicit. One way to get into this habit is to intentionally take a breath after each question that is posed on direct or cross-examination. That very brief pause will give you time to consider whether you understand what information the question is attempting to elicit. If you have any confusion whatsoever about the information a question seeks, ask the questioner for clarification before attempting to answer.

You must understand each question posed because if you do not understand the question, the chances are good that the factfinder (who is much less familiar with the facts of the case) does not understand the question either. And when confusing questions are answered by a witness who thinks they understand the question, but is not sure, the answer can compound the factfinder's confusion.

Think of it this way: as a witness your job is to tell your part of the trial story in the clearest way possible. A confusing question makes your job harder, so it is best if you do not answer confusing questions. Instead, take action to ensure that the questions you are asked are clear and straightforward, which sets the stage for the jurors to fully understand and digest your answers.

If you are not sure you understand a question you have been asked, say so. There are many ways to do that politely and respectfully and avoid being perceived as an evasive or difficult witness. Examples include:

- "I'm not sure I understand your question. Can you please repeat it?"
- "Is it possible for you to word that question differently for me?"
- "Can you please explain what you mean by [insert potentially confusing word]?"
- "Please help me understand what you are asking—I'm not sure I follow."
- "Would you mind rephrasing the question so I can be sure I understand it?"
- "I'm sorry but I don't follow. Is it possible for you to ask that question another way?"

B. On Cross-Examination, Listen for Clues Within Objections

Even if you are confident you understand a question posed to you on cross-examination, you should still pause briefly before answering. If you get into the habit of taking a breath after each question, this will come naturally and will seem natural to the casual observer as well. In addition to giving you time to formulate your answer, the resulting pause will give the lawyer who called you as a witness the opportunity raise an objection to the form of the question you have been asked or to the information that question seeks to elicit.

When it comes to raising objections, it is greatly preferred for the objection to be made *before* the witness begins to answer. This is because some bells cannot be "unrung." In other words, while counsel or the court can ask the jurors to disregard an answer, there is no guarantee they will. Accordingly, the best course of action is to avoid answering the objectionable question to begin with.

You might be wondering why a lawyer would ask an objectionable question or seek to elicit objectionable information. There are several possible answers. One is that the lawyer may not realize the question violates a procedural or evidentiary rule or seeks to elicit information that will have that effect. It is also sometimes the case that a lawyer will intentionally ask an improper question. (This is unethical and not a practice we endorse.)

A different situation arises when, unbeknownst to the individual objecting, there is an exception to the procedural or evidentiary rule that makes the question permissible. Or it may be that reasonable minds can disagree as to whether the question posed, or the information it seeks to elicit, is improper at all, in which case the adversarial process must play out so the presiding judge can decide.

When an attorney asks an objectionable question, opposing counsel is responsible for bringing the matter to the attention of the presiding judge. And it is best to do that before the witness has started giving an answer that may stick in the minds of the factfinders. For that reason, always pause briefly before answering any question, particularly on cross-examination, to allow time for objections.

We discuss objections in detail in Chapter Thirteen. That chapter is intended for those playing attorneys in a mock trial, however. Below we provide basic guidance to help you understand certain objections you may hear while testifying—objections that can help inform the answers you may give in response.

Lawyers raise objections to halt the trial proceedings and seek an immediate ruling from the presiding judge on the propriety of something happening in the courtroom. Most common objections are prompted by questions posed of witnesses, but they can also be based on the substance of a witness's answer or anything else happening in the courtroom that one side or the other thinks may be improper.

An objection made while you are testifying is not your fault. It is up to the lawyers to ask appropriate questions. And it is up to the presiding judge to decide what questions are appropriate and whether one side or the other is attempting to elicit testimony that is inappropriate under the rules of procedure or evidence. Witnesses have no responsibility for, and play no role in resolving, objections.

If an objection is raised while you are testifying, pause your answer and wait until you receive clear direction on whether and how to proceed.

If an objection is "sustained," it means the judge agrees that the question posed was improper in some way, whether in form or in the substance it sought to elicit. A sustained objection means that you need not (and should not) answer. (An easy way to remember this is: **Sustained = Stop** answering.) In response to a sustained

Chapter Five

objection, the attorney who posed the question will typically ask a different question or word the inquiry in a different, non-objectionable way.

If an objection is "overruled," it means the judge does not believe the objection was valid or well-founded. In essence, in overruling an objection the judge is saying they disagree with the attorney who lodged the objection. When an objection is overruled it means it is okay for the witness to answer the question as posed. (An easy way to remember this is: **Overruled = Okay** to answer.)

Have no fear if you forget the difference between "sustained" and "overruled" when testifying. If you are not sure whether you can answer a question already posed or should wait for a new question to be asked, simply wait. If a few seconds pass and no one directs you how to proceed, turn to the judge or to the lawyer questioning you and ask whether it is okay for you to answer.

Some objections made during cross-examination can provide helpful clues to witnesses. That is particularly true of the following objections, as we will explain in detail below.

1. Vague

When an attorney objects that a question is vague, they are signaling to those present that they do not understand the question or that the question can be interpreted in more than one way and therefore its answer could confuse the factfinder. If you are being cross-examined and the attorney who called you to the stand objects to a question you are asked as "vague," proceed with caution before answering. It is possible the attorney knows or realizes something about the question that you do not, so carefully consider whether you understand the question and know what information it is seeking to elicit.

In response to a vague objection, the presiding judge will sometimes ask you, the witness, whether you understand the question. In response, express any uncertainty you have about the question. Ways to do that politely include:

- "I'm sorry—no, I don't believe I understand the question."
- "To be honest I'm not sure I do (understand the question)"
- "I think I do (understand the question) but am not positive."
- "Can you please explain it for me?"

Of course, only claim uncertainty if you are in fact uncertain; claiming uncertainty solely because of an objection, especially if you understood the question before the objection was raised, would be disingenuous and untruthful. It could also give the appearance that the objecting attorney is coaching you to testify in a certain way. Witness coaching is strictly prohibited; any whiff of its occurrence can damage your credibility as a witness (as well as that of the coaching attorney).

Playing an Effective Witness

If you are confident you understand the question as posed, then say so to the judge if asked. Your assurance that you understand the question will likely prompt the presiding judge to overrule the objection, clearing the way for you to answer the question.

2. Compound

A question is compound if it actually asks more than one question. An example of a compound question is "Did you run the red light and then speed down Main Street on May 6th?" That is really three questions, not one. It asks: 1) whether, as the witness, you ran a red light; 2) whether you sped down Main Street after running the red light; and 3) whether those events occurred on May 6th. Unless the answer to all three of those questions is "yes," an affirmative answer to this compound question is likely to confuse the factfinder.

A question is most likely to draw a compound objection if the answers to the subparts of the question differ. Going back to our example, imagine for a moment that your witness ran a red light on May 6th but did not speed down Main Street afterwards. Recognizing that, the attorney who called you is likely to object on compound grounds to alert you that multiple pieces of information are being sought in the question and to proceed with caution.

If a compound objection is overruled, break down your answer so that it addresses each separate aspect of the question posed to avoid confusing the jurors. In our example, that would mean answering something like: "Yes, I did run a red light on May 6th but I did not speed down Main Street afterwards—I turned onto Veteran's Drive."

3. Calls for Speculation

When an attorney objects that a question calls for speculation, they are signaling to those present that the witness lacks personal knowledge of the information sought by the question. Personal knowledge means firsthand knowledge—i.e., knowledge that something occurred because the witness personally saw, heard, tasted, touched, or otherwise witnessed it firsthand.

When you hear the "calls for speculation" objection, consider whether your answer is speculative in any way—in other words, would you be guessing or assuming any part of the answer because you do not have personal knowledge of the information the question seeks to elicit? If the objection is overruled and you are directed to answer the question anyway, try to differentiate between information you know firsthand and any information that is speculative, including any part of the answer that you learned about from someone else. When any portion of an answer is based on speculation, a guess, an assumption, or someone else's words, make that clear in your answer to allow the attorney who called you to object again, if appropriate.

Chapter Five

Generally speaking, witnesses are not supposed to testify based upon speculation. If they do, it is incumbent upon the side damaged by the speculation to object, move to strike the speculative testimony, and to ask the presiding judge to instruct the factfinder to disregard the prior answer (if appropriate). (When a motion to strike is granted, it is appropriate for the presiding judge to also instruct the jury to disregard the speculative testimony, though some judges will not give that instruction automatically and will instead wait for a request to be made.)

4. Relevance

When an attorney objects to a question on relevance grounds, they are signaling to those present that the answer is not important in the context of the case. Evidence is relevant if it has any tendency to make a fact at issue in the case more or less likely to be true. Irrelevant testimony should be excluded from evidence, especially if it has any tendency to confuse or mislead the jurors.

When responding to an objection that a question or the information it elicits is not relevant, focus your answer on any aspect of the information sought that *is* relevant to the issues in the case. That may not stop the cross-examining attorney from again inquiring into the allegedly irrelevant information, but at least your prior answer will allow the objecting attorney to argue that the remaining information the question seeks to elicit is not relevant. Of course, if the judge overrules the objection and directs you to provide the allegedly irrelevant information in response, you are obligated to do so. As with everything else that happens in a trial, it is up to the presiding judge to rule on objections; if the judge says the information sought is relevant and admissible, then you must testify to the information regardless of your personal opinion on the matter.

5. (Calls for) Hearsay or Double Hearsay

Hearsay is an out-of-court statement offered to prove the truth of the matter asserted. Out-of-court merely means the statement was made before the trial started and not in the presence of the factfinder. A statement is offered for its truth when it is recounted to prove not just what words were spoken, but that the words spoken were true or accurate.

Let's say that a month before trial a witness is heard to complain that a pink elephant visits their bedside each night while they sleep. The side not calling the witness might want to elicit testimony about the out-of-court statement to prove that the witness is delusional and seeing things that are not actually there. They could elicit the witness's out-of-court statement from them or from any other witness with knowledge of the statement because they are not using it prove the truth of the matter asserted (that a pink elephant really does visit the witness's bedside each night). In other words, the statement, although made out-of-court, is not hearsay because it is not being offered for its truth.

Most statements made out-of-court that one side or the other wishes to elicit at trial are offered for their truth, however. And those statements are hearsay unless an exception to the hearsay rule applies. (We discuss hearsay in detail in Chapter Six, Section IV, Chapter Eight, Sections II(F) and IV(E), and Chapter 13, Section IV(B)(1).)

Double hearsay describes a statement that contains two layers of hearsay. For example: "Meredith told me she overheard Delia complaining about Kyle's insubordination." Delia's description of Kyle is one layer of hearsay and Meredith's recounting of that statement is a second layer. For the testimony to be deemed admissible, each layer must be deemed not to be hearsay or to have an applicable exception to the hearsay rule.

Fortunately, witnesses need not understand the ins and outs of the hearsay rule to testify effectively. All you need to do, in response to a hearsay objection during cross-examination, is make clear if any part of your testimony relies upon or recounts something that was said outside of court. So, building on our example above, imagine that the witness was asked "Isn't it true Delia said that Kyle was insubordinate?" The witness's answer could be: "Well, Meredith told me she heard Delia make that statement, but I don't have firsthand knowledge that it was said or whether Kyle was in fact insubordinate."

Here is an easy reference chart that summarizes the advice provided above:

OBJECTION	ADVICE
Vague	The witness should answer the question as phrased only if they are sure they understand it. If they are not sure, they should say so.
Compound	The witness should break down their answer so that it addresses each separate aspect of the question asked and avoids confusing the jury.
Calls for Speculation	If the witness's answer would be based on the possibility of something happening that the witness does not know to have happened, the witness should say so in answering.
Relevance	The witness should initially confine their answer to the relevant facts but if pressed by the cross-examiner or directed to do so by the presiding judge, provide a full and complete answer regardless of their own opinion of its relevance.
(Calls for) Hearsay (or Double Hearsay)	If the witness's answer to the question relies on or repeats something they or someone else said outside of court, the witness should explicitly say so when answering.

Chapter Five

C. Address Internal Assumptions, Premises, or Predicates Separately

This is more likely to be an issue on cross-examination than it is direct. Sometimes sneaky lawyers (or lawyers-in-training) bury an assumption, premise, or predicate within a question and hope that you will answer the question affirmatively without addressing the internal assumption, premise, or predicate so they can later argue to the jury that you agreed with that part of the question too. The way to handle this tactic is to address the internal assumption, premise, or predicate directly before answering the question.

Say for example that an expert in computer forensics is testifying about how they extracted data from the internet cache of a computer. This question is posed: "Given that digital evidence can be manipulated, are your findings from the internet cache reliable?" Answering "Yes, my findings are reliable" or, worse, just "Yes" risks the factfinder concluding that digital evidence, which presumably would include evidence from the internet cache, can be manipulated. In response, the safest course for the witness is to address the premise (that digital evidence can be manipulated) first and then answer the question. For example: "Regarding digital evidence being manipulated, there are only a few ways that can occur and my forensic examination ruled out each of them. There is no basis for believing the digital evidence was manipulated in this case. Given that, yes, my findings from the cache are indeed reliable."

D. Be Succinct If Possible but Explain If Needed

As a general rule, answer the precise question you are asked. A classic test used to train witnesses to do this is to ask them "Do you know the time?" If the witness's answer goes beyond "yes" or "no"—for example, if the witness glances at their watch or cell phone and offers up the current time in response—they are not limiting their answer to the precise question asked.

Typically witnesses do this because they are trying to be helpful. But even so, offering more information than was sought can make you appear more as an advocate and less as a neutral unbiased participant. It is also sometimes counterproductive to volunteer more information than you're asked because if the questioner wanted to elicit that additional information, they would. Sometimes the questioner has a very good reason for not seeking the additional detail, for example when that information is inadmissible or otherwise improper and the questioner is deliberately avoiding it.

Given this, the safest course is simply to answer only the question you are asked and to provide only the information needed for your testimony to be properly understood and not taken out of context. Beyond that, trust the lawyers to ask any necessary follow-up questions.

Oftentimes, cross-examiners will try to force witnesses to answer their questions with just a "yes" or "no." Some questions—many questions!—cannot be answered that succinctly. There is no rule of procedure or evidence requiring you to give one-word definitive answers such as "yes" or "no" when testifying. If it is not possible to answer definitively in a single word, or if a one-word answer must be explained so as not to be misleading, say so and insist on explaining. If the cross-examiner cuts you off and insists you answer "yes" or "no," respond: "I cannot answer that question 'yes' or 'no,' given how it was phrased," or even "Answering that question 'yes' or 'no' without explaining further would be misleading."

If, for whatever reason, you are not allowed to explain your answer during the cross-examination, have no fear; if you have made it clear that further explanation is necessary, the attorney who questioned you on direct should invite you to explain your answer on redirect examination.

E. Ask to See Any Document Referenced

If, on direct examination, you are questioned about a document and are asked if your memory about the content of the document "is exhausted," the appropriate answer to give is almost always "yes." There is a reason you are being asked that question and likely it's because you haven't given the precise answer the person questioning you was expecting. Trust your teammate enough to acknowledge that your memory does need to be refreshed and be open to them pointing your attention to whatever fact you may have forgotten. If the fact is important enough for them to seek to refresh your recollection, it is an exercise worth undertaking so your testimony is accurate and complete.

It is not uncommon for cross-examiners to ask witnesses questions from a document, whether it is the witness's own prior statement or testimony, or an exhibit about which the witness has knowledge. If seeing that document will help you give a more precise and accurate answer to a question posed, there is nothing wrong with asking to see the document counsel is referring to in order to refresh your own recollection about what it says. Here are some ways you can do that without seeming to be evasive or unsure:

- "That sounds right but can I review the transcript to be sure?"
- "I'd feel better about answering if I could review the document you're referring to first."
- "Mind if I review that in context, just to refresh my recollection?"
- "Can I take a look at my report/statement before answering? I haven't memorized the words I used there."

If you are not permitted to review a document about which you are being questioned, be careful about how you characterize that document or its contents. Do not guess. If you do not remember, "I don't know" is more trustworthy than an erroneous guess.

Chapter Five

F. *Do Not Fight Necessary Admissions*

Every mock trial case file, and every witness statement or transcript therein, has facts that help and hurt each side. It is rare for a mock trial witness to help only the side that called the witness and not offer any helpful facts to the cross-examining side. That is to say, most cases and most witnesses come with unhelpful facts—facts one side or the other wishes they did not have to contend with at trial.

When it comes to bad facts, the best course of action is simply to admit them. Fighting, resisting, or attempting to explain away bad facts only highlights them for the jurors. It also risks the witness being impeached and perceived as an advocate, which as we discuss above and further below can be highly problematic.

Instead, readily admit bad facts on cross (or, even better, testify about them on direct examination to "draw the sting" as we explain in Chapter Six, Section III(B)) as doing so can make even the most damaging of facts seem like no big deal.

G. *Do Not Take on the Role of Advocate*

Most civil and criminal cases that go to trial end up in that posture because they are close cases. If they weren't close cases—if it were obvious from the facts or the law that one side or the other should win—civil parties would probably settle out of court and criminal defendants would probably plead guilty, because early case resolutions usually benefit the would-be loser. It is when either side has a chance of winning at trial that both parties are more likely to take the risk of losing at trial.

Mock trial case files are written with that idea in mind. They are meant to be close cases in which either side has a chance of winning at trial. That helps to keep the playing field even between teams and incentivizes participants to perform at their best.

Witnesses are called to testify in real trials because they have personal knowledge of the relevant facts or specialized knowledge which one party in the case believes will help the judge or jurors resolve the factual or legal questions at issue. Witnesses are not meant to be advocates for a particular outcome. In fact, a witness taking on the characteristics of an advocate is counterproductive for the side that called the witness because it makes the witness seem biased and less credible.

The risk of witnesses turning into advocates may be greater in a mock trial than in an actual trial. There are a few reasons for this. One is that mock trial witnesses are often members of the team who called them to testify. If a witness views opposing counsel as their opponent too, a sense of competitiveness can result. This can be exacerbated by the fact that, in some mock trial competitions, the witnesses for the defense become the attorneys for the prosecution in alternating rounds. Once in an "advocate" role, it can be difficult for some participants to resist the temptation to stay in that role. And because mock trial participants do not have actual, personal knowledge of the relevant facts at issue in the case, they may feel less wedded to the prior statements of the witnesses they play. Finally, unlike real witnesses, mock trial witnesses do not face potential perjury charges if they lie under oath. For those and possibly other reasons as well, there is always a danger that witnesses in mock trials will be tempted to take on the role of advocates.

Resist that temptation. A witness who comes off as an advocate undermines their own credibility and does more harm than good for their team. Even though you can't be prosecuted for perjury if you alter or embellish your testimony, you can be impeached and your team can be penalized or even disqualified if your actions violate the competition rules. Moreover, it is wrong and dishonorable.

Advocate-witnesses tend to fall into a trap of trying to "read into" the questions they are asked on cross-examination in hopes of cutting the examiner off at the knees. That is not a worthwhile endeavor. The questions posed on cross-examination are (or at least should be) based on information contained in the witness's own sworn statement or a transcript of their prior testimony. In mock trials some of that information is helpful to each side of the case. As we have explained, witnesses cannot avoid making an admission just because it hurts their side of the case; they are obligated to testify consistently with their prior statement, regardless of which side it helps. For that reason, there is little to be gained by trying to figure out the larger point a cross-examiner is building up to and seeking to prevent the point from being made. That effort is destined to fail if the cross-examiner is well-prepared and adept at impeachment, and the last thing you want to do as a witness is make the cross-examiner look good while highlighting a fact unhelpful to your side of the case.

The better practice is to let the examiner make any uncontestable points without putting up any fight whatsoever. In fact, if you act as though the points being made on cross are no big deal at all, you put the onus on the examiner and their teammates to explain the significance of the admitted fact(s) in their closing argument(s).

H.   Be the Same Person on Cross as Direct

A witness who is forthcoming and helpful on direct but obstinate, argumentative, and difficult on cross comes across as "two-faced" and loses all credibility with the jury. Other than in cases of overt provocation by the cross-examining attorney, an uncooperative witness (especially one who was very cooperative on direct) tends to diminish their own credibility.

Do not say or do anything on cross-examination that you would not say or do when being questioned on direct examination. Instead of becoming impatient, exasperated, or annoyed with a stubborn cross-examiner, offer them the same steady explanation you would offer to a difficult younger student.

Chapter Five

In short, be the same person on cross-examination as you were on direct. To make sure you're achieving that, ask a relative, friend, or fellow student you like and trust to watch you testify during a practice and tell you if your demeanor or tone changed from direct to cross-examination.

I.   Make Only Reasonable Inferences from the Case File

Mock trial cases are written to include facts helpful to each side. They are meant to be close cases that either side could win if they more adeptly marshal the facts through better witnesses and better advocacy.

To keep the playing field even for both sides in a mock trial, some competition rules prohibit all inferences. Others allow limited inferences of information not explicitly written into the case file. If such inferences are allowed, they are typically confined to only reasonable inferences. It is essential to know your competition's rules for witnesses' inferences.

What is a reasonable inference from the material written in a mock trial case file?

A reasonable inference is a factual connection or conclusion that a reasonable person would draw from a particular fact or set of facts contained in a mock trial case file, so long as it does not affect the outcome or create an unfair advantage. An inference is probably reasonable if it is supported by the facts contained in the witness's statement and is logical and predictable. Of course, the more facts that support an inference, the more reasonable it is. Likewise, the reasonableness of an inference correlates with the logic it employs and its overall believability.

To test an inference for reasonableness, ask yourself these questions: Are there facts in the case file that support this inference? Does it make sense that this witness would know this information? If I were a juror, would I be inclined to assume this fact from the witness's testimony based on everything else they say? If the answer to all of those questions is yes, the proposed inference is probably reasonable.

Remember that to be reasonable, an inference cannot be material to the case at bar. Here, "material" means the inference is not likely to make a difference in the case's outcome. Judging what is likely to change the outcome of a case can be a tricky matter, however. A more conservative method of judging whether a fact is material is to consider whether it makes any fact at issue in the case more or less likely to be true. If it does, the inference is in danger of being material and therefore inherently unreasonable if injected into a mock trial.

In real trials, the witnesses have personal knowledge of the relevant events. Attorneys, therefore, are free to fill in any details missing from a witness's pretrial statements by asking the witness additional questions at trial (subject to impeachment during cross-examination). But in mock trials, the people we call witnesses are not actually witnesses at all. They are student-actors bringing to life a script that, by necessity, cannot include every fact that would or could be documented in a real case. Accordingly, mock trial case files abound with "missing" facts that would be established by one side or the other during an actual case. Does that mean a mock trial team can simply "fill in" the facts they deem to be missing to better support their theory of the case? Absolutely not. In order to keep the playing field even for both sides in a mock trial, where competition rules allow for inferences to be made, they usually specify that students may not infer facts that are material to the case. In other words, it is one thing to add in a detail that is missing despite appearing obvious based on the information provided, but it is something else altogether (indeed, it is unethical) to simply make up facts to improve your case. (See Chapter Seven, Section IV(B) for a further discussion of reasonable inferences.) If while preparing as a witness you believe you could infer something from the facts in the case file, raise the issue well in advance of competition with your coach or faculty advisor and your teammates. Making an inference is definitely not something you should do on a whim without a thorough discussion with every other person on the team who may be affected by the decision.

In some mock trial competitions, organizers have become so frustrated with students making unreasonable inferences that they have barred witnesses from making any inferences at all. In those competitions, witnesses are not permitted to testify to any fact not explicitly written into the case file; violations of the rule can result in the deduction of points or even disqualification from the competition. Obviously, if your competition has adopted that rule, no prior discussion about reasonable or material inferences is needed. If inferences are not allowed under the rules of your mock trial, do not make them. Period.

Chapter Six

Evidence Made Simple

All mock trial competitions adopt rules of evidence, usually a simplified form of the Federal Rules of Evidence, that determine which testimony and exhibits will be admitted at trial. The presiding judge rules on the admissibility of the evidence at trial; they hear objections from counsel and rule upon them. If an objection is sustained, the testimony or evidence is inadmissible under the rules of evidence. If the judge overrules an objection, they have determined that the testimony or evidence is admissible under the rules of evidence.

There are two main types of objections: substantive and nonsubstantive. Substantive objections question the admissibility of the content of the testimony or exhibit at issue. Nonsubstantive objections raise the appropriateness of the manner in which the information is being sought or delivered to the court.

Understanding and knowing the rules of evidence used in your mock trial is crucial. If a portion of a witness's testimony or an exhibit is clearly not allowed under the rules of evidence, do not incorporate it into your story, theory, or theme at trial. Likewise, if you believe one of your opponent's witnesses will offer testimony or an exhibit that is not allowed under the rules of evidence, be prepared to object if it is offered at trial.

We will return to the nonsubstantive evidentiary rules in Chapter Thirteen. For now we will focus on the substantive rules, since they play the largest role as you prepare your case. The following is a short explanation of the most common substantive rules of evidence your mock trial is likely to follow. Because the rules of evidence used in mock trials vary, the explanations below are based on the Federal Rules of Evidence.

I.   Relevance

Irrelevant evidence is not permitted at trial. Evidence is irrelevant if it does not make any fact of consequence to the case more or less likely to be true. For example, the astrological sign of the defendant in a criminal case would not make any fact of consequence more or less probable—the fact that the defendant is a Leo does not make it any more likely that he killed his wife in the heat of passion. Be aware, however, that the relevance of evidence depends on the parties' theories of the case. The prosecution could conceivably argue that the defendant was enraged

Chapter Six

by reading his daily horoscope and acted accordingly. The presiding judge makes the final determination of what evidence is relevant.

II. Unfair Prejudice

By definition, all relevant evidence is prejudicial to some party—that is why it is offered at trial in the first place. Consequently, evidence cannot be excluded merely because it is prejudicial. Even so, relevant evidence may be excluded if its probative value is substantially outweighed by the danger of unfair prejudice that will result from its admission. The probative value of evidence refers to its helpfulness to the trier of fact in deciding the case. When the helpfulness of evidence is outweighed by the possibility that it will have an unfair impact on the factfinder, it is considered unduly or unfairly prejudicial.

For example, consider a murder case involving a shooting where the defendant is a member of the National Rifle Association (NRA). The prosecution wants to use this evidence to show that the defendant knows about guns and is likely to be trained in the use of guns. Thus, the prosecution argues that the defendant's NRA membership is probative of the defendant's exposure to and skill in using guns—it shows that they had the ability to commit the crime.

The defense argues, however, that the defendant's membership in the NRA may also cause a juror who opposes that organization's political views to form a negative opinion of the defendant. The defense points out that the defendant has never taken any training courses from the NRA and that, at the time of the murder, the defendant had only been an NRA member for two months. Thus, the defense argues that the probative value of the defendant's NRA membership is substantially outweighed by its potentially unfair impact.

As always, the presiding judge makes the final determination.

III. Lack of Personal Knowledge and Speculation

Witnesses (other than experts) must testify from their own personal knowledge and may not speculate about things they do not know firsthand. This means that witnesses may only testify about their sensory perceptions: what they saw, heard, smelled, touched, or tasted (subject to other evidentiary limitations). Witnesses may not testify to what they think might have happened, no matter how firmly they believe it.

For instance, the neighbor of the defendant in a murder trial may testify to seeing the defendant enter their apartment two hours before the murder took place. The witness may also testify that they did not see the defendant leave the apartment again that night. However, the witness may not testify that the defendant was definitely in the apartment at the time of the murder, unless the witness saw the defendant there at the time the crime was committed.

There is an exception, however, under the "lay opinion" rule for certain commonsense observations that are "rationally based on the witness's sensory perceptions." A witness may testify that another person appeared drunk or angry, so long as the opinion is the kind of conclusion most people can reach based on firsthand observation. Thus, a long-time colleague of a criminal defendant would likely be allowed to testify that the defendant appeared drunk at an office party, even though the witness did not administer a breathalyzer test or taste the beverage the defendant was drinking.

IV. Hearsay

Hearsay describes any out-of-court statement (even one made by the testifying witness) that is used in court to prove the truth of the matter asserted in the statement itself. Within this definition, a statement is a verbal, nonverbal, or written assertion of fact. A statement is "offered for its truth" only when it is being used to show that its content is true.

For example, assume that witness Taran testifies that "Ellis told me they saw a camel walking down the streets of New York City." On the surface, it appears that Taran's testimony about Ellis's statement is being used to prove that a camel was seen walking down the street in New York. If so, Ellis's statement would be hearsay. But what if counsel is merely trying to use Ellis's statement to show that their health is failing? In that case, the testimony is not asserting the truth of the matter; it is being offered to show that Ellis is becoming disoriented or perhaps dementia is setting in. When used for that purpose, the testimony would not be hearsay.

In addition to statements that are not offered for their truth, two other types of statements are recognized as nonhearsay. The first type is a prior sworn statement by the witness that is inconsistent with their testimony at trial. The second type comprises statements made by a party (the defendant in a criminal case; either the plaintiff or defendant in a civil case), if used against that party at trial. This category also includes statements by an agent of a party (for example, an employee) or by a co-conspirator of the party. These statements are called "party admissions" or "admissions of a party-opponent." In a criminal trial, for example, the prosecution can use any statements made by the defendant or one of their co-conspirators, if a conspiracy is alleged and proven, as admissions of a party-opponent.

There are also many exceptions to the hearsay rule. A witness is allowed to repeat an out-of-court statement offered for its truth if it fits into any of the following categories:

- It describes an event or occurrence and was made while the speaker observed the event or occurrence or immediately afterward (called a "present sense impression");

Chapter Six

- It is a statement relating to a startling event made while the speaker was still under the stress of excitement caused by that event (called an "excited utterance");

- It illustrates the declarant's mental state, as in the camel example above, or it is being used to show the effect of the statement on the listener (called the "state of mind" exception);

- It is a record of a regularly conducted activity, usually that of a business (called a "business record"); or

- It is a statement by a dying person about the cause or circumstances of what the person believed to be impending death (called a "dying declaration").

Other exceptions exist, though these are the most common ones in mock trials.

Hearsay is discussed further in Chapter Thirteen.

This table illustrates how to recognize the most common forms of hearsay.

	Checklist	
	IS THIS ADMISSIBLE HEARSAY?	
☑	**Is it an out-of-court statement being offered to prove the truth of the matter asserted?**	Does it assert some fact? Are you using the statement to prove the truth of that fact? *If the answer to both of these questions is yes, go on to the section below.*
☑	**Is it an admission of a party-opponent?**	In criminal cases: did the defendant or a co-conspirator of the defendant make the statement, and is it being offered by the prosecution? In civil cases: did the plaintiff or defendant or any of their agents make the statement, and is it being offered against that party now? *If the answer to the applicable question is no, the statement is hearsay. Go on to the section below to determine whether an exception to the hearsay rule applies.*

Evidence Made Simple

Checklist	
IS THIS ADMISSIBLE HEARSAY?	
☑ **Is there an exception that applies?**	Is the statement a present sense impression? Is the statement an excited utterance? Is the statement being used to illustrate the declarant's state of mind or the effect of the statement on a person who heard it? Is the statement itself a business record? Is the statement a dying declaration? *If the answer to any of these questions is yes, the statement is admissible. If the answer to each question is no, check the less common hearsay exceptions to see if one applies. If none apply, the statement is inadmissible.*

Note that there is also such a thing as "double hearsay" or "hearsay within hearsay," which describes the possibility of hearsay statements being made within other hearsay statements. For example, see the statement by the testifying witness below.

In this example, the first level of potential hearsay is Julie's statement to Bob that "I am the one who got that brooch." The second layer of potential hearsay is Bob's statement to the testifying witness that "Julie told me that she took the brooch." To pass the test of admissibility, each layer of hearsay must be independently allowable under the rules of evidence. So, you must answer the question, "Is this inadmissible hearsay?" (as outlined in the table above) for each of these statements. The reason

Chapter Six

for this rule is obvious from the example: the more a statement is repeated, the more likely it is that its content will change. The rules of evidence are designed to make it difficult to admit unreliable testimony at trial.

V. Improper Character Evidence Generally

Character evidence is generally not admissible to prove that because a person did something in the past, that person is more likely to have done it (or "acted in conformity" with that character) again. For example, a driver's past involvement in a hit-and-run accident generally cannot be offered as proof that the driver was negligent in a later collision.

There are exceptions to this rule. First, when criminal defendants choose to offer proof of their good character, the prosecution may then (and only then) rebut that evidence with proof of their bad character. Also, past crimes and bad acts may be offered to prove a person's motive, opportunity, intent, preparation, plan, knowledge, identity, or absence of mistake, assuming one or more of those are relevant to the case.

A. *Conviction of Crime*

The commission, and even the conviction, of past crimes is not admissible to prove guilt in the current matter. This follows logically from the principle that all defendants, even those with criminal records, are presumed innocent until proven guilty at trial.

The credibility of a witness who takes the stand and testifies, however, may be impeached on the basis of a prior criminal conviction, but only if the crime was either a felony or one that involved dishonesty or false statement.

With felonies, the evidence is generally not admissible unless the conviction occurred within the last ten years (juvenile adjudications, regardless of how long ago they occurred, are almost never admissible). Some convictions that are more than ten years old may still be admissible if the court determines that their probative value, supported by specific facts and circumstances in the case, substantially outweighs their prejudicial effect.

If the crime was not a felony, the conviction may still be admissible if it involved dishonesty. For example, if a witness was found guilty of committing fraud (making false representations that were reasonably relied upon by others) two years before testifying, that conviction is admissible even if the crime was only a misdemeanor.

Note that conviction evidence is generally limited to the fact of conviction, the name of the crime, and the sentence received. The details and events that constituted the crime are generally inadmissible.

Evidence Made Simple

B. Character for Untruthfulness

The past acts of a person may not be offered as proof that they subsequently committed similar acts. These acts, called "specific instances of conduct," are only admissible for the limited purpose of attacking or supporting the witness's credibility. Thus, a witness may be cross-examined concerning past acts when they reflect upon the witness's truthfulness or untruthfulness.

Evidence of a witness's reputation is admissible only if it is probative of the witness's character for truthfulness or untruthfulness. Thus, a witness's reputation as a "dirty, rotten scoundrel" is only admissible if it shows they were well known as untruthful. A witness's reputation as "loud, obnoxious, and contemptuous" is inadmissible.

Below is a general checklist you can use when considering the admissibility of the facts set forth in a witness's statement.

	Checklist	
	IS THIS EVIDENCE ADMISSIBLE?	
☑	**Is this evidence irrelevant?**	Does this information fail to make at least one fact of consequence to the case more or less probable? *If so, it is irrelevant.*
☑	**Is this evidence more prejudicial than probative?**	Does the unfairly prejudicial nature of this evidence outweigh its probative value? *If so, it is unduly prejudicial.*
☑	**Is this an opinion only an expert could reach?**	Is this an opinion that requires special training, education, or knowledge? *If so, the witness is giving an improper lay opinion.*
☑	**Is this inadmissible hearsay?**	Is this an assertion that is being used to prove its truth? If so, does a hearsay exception apply? *If not, the statement is hearsay.*

Chapter Six

Checklist	
IS THIS EVIDENCE ADMISSIBLE?	
☑ **Is this improper character evidence?**	Can this prior act be used to prove motive, opportunity, intent, preparation, plan, knowledge, identity, or absence of mistake? Does this information go to the witness's truthfulness? Is this a felony that occurred within the past ten years? *Unless the answer to at least one of the above questions is yes, the information is improper character evidence.*

Chapter Seven

Direct Examination

I. The Role of Direct Examination

Direct examinations are the heart of your case. On direct examination, you present your witnesses' testimony through questions and answers; you develop your persuasive trial story and the evidence that supports that story.

The importance of conducting effective direct examinations therefore cannot be overstated. Every other aspect of the trial derives from direct examination. Opening statements and final arguments are the lawyers' opportunity to discuss what the witnesses have to say; cross-examination exists solely to challenge or controvert direct examination testimony.

Effective direct examinations accomplish many or all of the following basic goals.

A. Set Forth Your Theory of the Case

Conduct each direct examination to aid the jurors in better understanding your theory of the case.

As discussed in Chapter Two, Section II(B), some mock trial case files contain the statements of more witnesses than their rules permit each side to call. In those mock trials, the participants must decide which witnesses are essential to establishing their theory of the case. Participants must also adapt their theories in response to the witnesses chosen by the opposing side. Witness selection is crucial—in competitions allowing it—because it must coincide with the theory you argue and prove to the factfinder.

B. Introduce the Undisputed Facts

Every trial contains undisputed facts that establish one or more elements of each side's case. Although not controverted by the parties, these facts cannot be considered by the judge or jury until and unless they are placed in evidence through a witness's testimony.

Chapter Seven

Assume, for example, that you represent the prosecution in a murder case and that the defendant claims self-defense. Even if the question of who killed the victim is not in dispute, the death of the victim is still an element of your case and must be proved through testimony on direct examination.

C.   *Enhance the Likelihood of Disputed Facts*

The most important facts in a trial will normally be those in dispute. Direct examination is your opportunity to advance your side's version of the disputed facts and persuasively introduce evidence that supports that version. The true art of direct examination is establishing the certainty of facts that the other side claims are uncertain or untrue.

D.   *Lay Foundation for Introducing Exhibits*

Documents, photographs, writings, tangible objects, and other forms of evidence will often be central to your case. With some exceptions, the direct testimony of a witness is necessary to lay the foundation for the admission of these exhibits.

E.   *Reflect upon Witness Credibility*

A witness's credibility is always in issue. Every direct examination, whatever its ultimate purpose, must also attend to the credibility of the witness's own testimony. For this reason, direct examinations usually begin with background information about the witness. What do they do for a living? Where did they go to school? How long have they lived in the community? Even if their credibility will not be challenged, this sort of information helps to humanize the witness, adding weight to their testimony.

The credibility of some witnesses will be attacked on cross-examination. In these situations, you can blunt the assault by establishing the witness's believability during direct examination. Strengthen the witness by eliciting their basis of knowledge, ability to observe, or lack of bias or interest in the outcome of the case.

You may also use a witness's direct examination to reflect adversely on the credibility of another witness's testimony by introducing negative character or reputation evidence concerning that witness. Alternatively, you may use a witness's direct examination to provide evidence of another witness's bias or motive or simply to contradict the other's testimony.

F.   *Hold the Factfinder's Attention*

No matter which of the above purposes predominates, conduct the direct examination in a manner that holds the attention of the judge or jury. Though the heart of your case, direct examination also has the highest potential for dissolving into boredom, inattention, and routine. Since it has none of the inherent drama or tension of cross-examination, you must take extreme care to prepare your direct examination to maximize impact. Preparing an interesting and memorable direct examination is especially vital in mock trials, since the participants playing the roles of attorney and witness have weeks or even months to plan and practice their exchange.

II. The Rules of Direct Examination

Whenever you have a reasonable theory of admissibility for a particular piece of evidence that helps your case, offer that evidence on direct. As Chapter Two explained, each mock trial competition dictates the rules of evidence that govern your trial, and the testimony you elicit from your witnesses must be admissible under those rules. The admissibility of a particular piece of evidence is ultimately determined by the presiding judge, so craft your theories of admissibility as carefully as you plan your questions to the witness.

Remember to stand near the end of the jury box when conducting direct examinations so that your witnesses can easily be heard by, and make eye contact with, all of the jurors. If there is no jury present and you are not treating the mock trial as a jury trial (see Chapter Four, Section I(A)), where you stand is less important than being seen and heard, so stand wherever you are most comfortable. Remember that overreliance on notes during direct will prevent you from making eye contact with the witness and from watching and evaluating the jurors' and/or judges' reactions to the testimony. Direct examination should sound like a conversation between two friends, where the lawyer prompts the testimony and the witness explains their testimony; your position relative to the jurors and/or those judging your performance is crucial to achieving this effect.

Additionally, keep in mind that the use of visual aids can greatly improve a witness's testimony. Whether this means making a list of important points as a witness testifies to emphasize those points to the factfinder, or having a witness use a map, diagram, or picture to illustrate their testimony, the factfinder will retain the information better if it is laid out visually as well as orally. This also applies to physical and vocal demonstrations; if the factfinder sees and hears specific facts as they are explained, they are more likely to remember them. Consult the rules of your mock trial competition to determine whether demonstrative aids may be used and, if so, whether the competition limits how and when they can be used.

The following are specific rules regarding the manner in which you may present your witnesses' testimony on direct examination. Once you understand these rules, you can plan your direct examinations.

A. *Ask Only Nonleading Questions*

The principal rule of direct examination is that the attorney may not "lead" the witness. Leading questions contain or suggest their own answers. These questions

Chapter Seven

are prohibited during direct examination to ensure that the testimony is truly the witness's and not simply dictated by the lawyer.

Whether a particular question is leading is frequently an issue of tone or delivery as much as one of form. The distinction, moreover, is often finely drawn. For example, there is no doubt that this question is leading:

> QUESTION: Of course, you crossed the street, didn't you?

Not only does the question contain its own answer, its format also virtually guarantees that it will be answered in the affirmative.

On the other hand, this question is not leading:

> QUESTION: Did you cross the street?

Although this question is specific and calls for a yes or no answer, it does not suggest the witness's response.

Finally, this question falls in the middle:

> QUESTION: Didn't you cross the street?

If the examiner's tone of voice and inflection indicate that this is meant as a true query, the question probably will not be considered leading. If the question is stated more as an assertion, however, it violates the leading question rule.

There are some exceptions to the rule against leading questions on direct examination. A lawyer is generally permitted to lead a witness to lay foundation and make a transition in the testimony. An example of a leading question intended to lay foundation is: "You have done extensive research in psycho-cybernetics, isn't that right, doctor?" An example of a leading question intended to make a transition is: "Will you tell the jury about your extensive work in psycho-cybernetics, doctor?" Although generally permissible, these types of leading questions can still draw objections from opposing counsel; if they do, be prepared to explain that you are laying foundation or using the question to signal a transition in the testimony.

B.   Avoid Questions That Elicit "Narrative" Responses

Witnesses may not testify in narrative form. The term "narrative" has no precise definition, but it is usually taken to mean an answer that goes beyond responding to a single specific question. Questions that invite a lengthy or run-on reply are said to call for a narrative answer. An example of a non-narrative question is: "What did you do next?" The objectionable, narrative version would be, "Tell us everything that you did that day." In mock trials, there is added incentive to avoid questions that elicit narrative responses: they take up too much time and diminish the role of the student attorney conducting the examination.

Rather than narrative questions, keep witnesses on track with short, incremental questions. The line of questions that follows uses short, incremental questions to demonstrate the accuracy of an identification.

QUESTION:	Were you able to get a good look at the robber, Ms. Kearney?
ANSWER:	Yes, I was able to see him clearly.
QUESTION:	How tall was he?
ANSWER:	About six feet tall.
QUESTION:	How heavy was he?
ANSWER:	He was heavy like a football player; broad shoulders and a thick torso. He must have weighed over 200 pounds.
QUESTION:	What race was he?
ANSWER:	He was white.
QUESTION:	And his complexion?
ANSWER:	His complexion was fair.
QUESTION:	What color was his hair?
ANSWER:	He didn't have any hair—he was bald.
QUESTION:	Did he have any facial hair?
ANSWER:	Yes, he had a goatee.
QUESTION:	Could you see his eyes?
ANSWER:	Yes, he came right up to me.
QUESTION:	What color were they?
ANSWER:	Brown.

Depending upon the witness's knowledge, further questions could inquire into other facts. Could the witness see the robber's shirt? What color was it? His trousers? His shoes? Any jewelry? Glasses? Tattoos?

As you can see, this line of questioning drives home the accuracy of the witness's identification without allowing the witness to get lost in a narrative answer. It also allows the listener to compile a very detailed mental picture of the assailant one physical characteristic at a time. Using this technique would be especially useful if you wanted to draw attention to a particular aspect of the assailant's appearance, such as his bald head. If that is your aim, consider pausing after that portion of the witness's answer to allow the testimony to sink in, or writing it out on a demonstrative board to make clear to the factfinder that it is an important fact worth remembering.

C.   *Obey the Nonopinion Rule*

Witnesses are expected to testify to their sensory observations. What did the witness see, hear, smell, touch, taste, or do? If a witness's testimony goes beyond their own sensory observations, the testimony runs the risk of being speculative, lacking foundation, or venturing into the territory of an improper lay opinion.

Witnesses other than experts are generally limited to giving opinions that are rationally based upon their own perceptions; they may not characterize the events. Thus, witnesses will usually be permitted to draw conclusions on issues such as speed, distance, volume, time, weight, temperature, and weather conditions. However, in order for a lay witness to offer that sort of testimony, the attorney eliciting the testimony must lay a proper foundation demonstrating the witness's ability to observe and interpret the events.

Similarly, lay witnesses may characterize the behavior of other people as angry, drunken, affectionate, busy, or even insane. But once again in order to elicit that testimony, the attorney asking the questions must establish that the witness had ample opportunity to observe and interpret the other person's behavior.

D. Refresh the Witness's Recollection When Necessary

Most mock trials witnesses are played by students, who are often friends with or fellow team members of those playing the roles of the attorneys. As a result, the attorneys and the witnesses will likely have days, weeks, or even months to practice the direct examinations together. In these situations, the need to refresh a witness's recollection is not likely to arise.

There are some mock trial organizers, however, who strive to more closely simulate real trials. One of the ways they do this is by bringing in volunteers to play the witnesses. These volunteers have not had time to run through the direct examination with counsel in advance of the trial. This format prevents teams from presenting the kinds of "scripted" direct examinations that often result when both the questioner and witness have practiced a direct over and over. Instead, those playing the attorney and witness roles are given a very limited amount of time to meet in advance of trial. Because it is not possible to map out an entire examination in that timeframe, give your witnesses a broad overview of the subjects to be covered and ask the witnesses to answer only the questions asked and not to volunteer additional information. These are the situations in which refreshing a witness's recollection during direct examination is more likely to arise in a mock trial.

But even scripted directs can go off the rails due to imperfect witness memories. Competition is stressful and nervous witnesses sometimes forget material facts. Thus, regardless of the format of your mock trial, become adept at refreshing a witness's recollection in a non-leading manner.

In most cases, you will refresh a witness's memory using their own prior testimony. First confirm that the witness's memory is exhausted concerning the specific issue or event by asking, "Is your memory about this fact exhausted?" Then ask, "Is there anything that might refresh your recollection?"

When the witness identifies their statement, follow the same steps you would follow if you were offering the exhibit into evidence:

- show the document, and any specific portion to which you will refer the witness, to opposing counsel;
- ask for the judge's permission to approach the witness;
- hand the exhibit to the witness and describe your actions verbally for the record;
- ask the witness to identify the exhibit and authenticate it (usually by identifying their signature if present at the end of the statement); and
- ask the witness to review the document or a specific portion thereof, and to signal you when their memory is refreshed.

As mentioned, you can and should direct opposing counsel's and the witness's attention to the particular page or line number where the forgotten fact appears. Doing this saves time and keeps the testimony flowing more smoothly.

Once the witness has the information that will refresh their recollection, either step to the side of the jury box or return to your position at the end of the jury box or at counsel table; standing over the witness and pointing out their testimony will give the appearance that you are coaching the witness. When the witness has indicated that their memory is refreshed, retrieve the document from the witness or have the witness place it face-down on the witness stand and re-ask your initial question.

Here is an example that takes you through these steps:

QUESTION: Were you able to get a good look at the robber, Ms. Kearney?

ANSWER: Yes, I saw him clearly as he exited the building and climbed into a blue sedan.

QUESTION: How tall was he?

ANSWER: I really don't remember now.

QUESTION: Was there a time when you did remember this information?

ANSWER: Yes, I gave the police a complete description right after the robbery.

QUESTION: Is your memory as to the robber's height exhausted now?

ANSWER: Yes, I'm sorry, it is.

QUESTION: Would looking at the statement you gave to the police immediately after the robbery refresh your recollection?

Chapter Seven

> ANSWER: Yes, it would.
> TO
> COUNSEL: I'm showing the witness her statement, marked as Exhibit 3 for identification.

[Show opposing counsel the page and line number to which you intend to direct the witness.]

> TO JUDGE: Permission to approach the witness, Your Honor?
> JUDGE: Granted.
> QUESTION: Ms. Kearney, I'm handing you what has been marked as Exhibit 3 for identification. Do you recognize that?
> ANSWER: Yes, that is the statement I gave to the police right after the robbery.
> QUESTION: How do you know that is your statement?
> ANSWER: Because I signed the back page.
> QUESTION: Please take a moment to look over the second page of that statement beginning at line 12 and signal me when your memory about the robber's appearance is refreshed.
> ANSWER: (pause) Oh yes, now I remember.
> QUESTION: (retrieving document) Ms. Kearney, please tell the jury how tall the individual you saw was.
> ANSWER: He was about six feet tall.

The more fluently you perform this procedure, the more you will restore the witness's credibility, despite their memory lapse. If you act shocked and confused at the witness's failure to remember an important fact, you will only highlight their inadequacy for the trier of fact. Refresh the witness's recollection quickly and calmly, as though it is the most natural thing in the world. This skill is so important that witnesses in some trial competitions are told by organizers to "forget" an important fact during direct examination so the scoring judges can determine how successfully each student attorney refreshed the witness's recollection.

E. Have the Appropriate Witnesses Identify the Defendant (Prosecution Only)

In a criminal prosecution, the government must prove that the person sitting in the courtroom is, in fact, the same person named in the charging document, and, of course, the same person who committed the crime. Prosecutors therefore must obtain from at least one witness an in-court identification of the defendant in criminal cases. In-court identifications can also be quite powerful when done effectively.

To enable a witness to properly identify the defendant in court, first establish the witness's familiarity with the defendant. Are they a relative of the defendant? A good friend? The arresting officer? The victim of, or eyewitness to, the crime? Whatever the witness's relationship, show the factfinder that the witness is qualified to identify the defendant. Next, ask the witness to identify the defendant in the courtroom by pointing to the defendant and briefly describing the individual physically. Finally, note for the record that the witness has identified the defendant.

Below is an example of an effective in-court identification.

QUESTION: Did you get a good look at the robber, Ms. Kearney?
ANSWER: Yes. As I said, I saw him clearly as he left the building and climbed into a blue sedan.
QUESTION: Please take a minute to look around the courtroom. Do you see the robber here in the courtroom today?
ANSWER: Yes, I do.
QUESTION: Please point to him and identify an item of clothing he is wearing.
ANSWER: He's right there (pointing) and he's wearing a blue suit with pinstripes.
TO JUDGE: Your Honor, let the record reflect that the witness has pointed to and properly identified the defendant, Mr. Thomas Ratcliffe.

F. Use Stipulations When Helpful

Stipulations are evidentiary agreements between the parties. For example, in the firetruck case, the parties might stipulate that the plaintiff's medical treatments following the collision cost a total of $4,500. In the context of a real trial, the plaintiff might agree to that stipulation to save time during trial and to avoid testifying about complicated medical records that jurors are not likely to find interesting. The defendant, who has no reason to doubt the authenticity of the records, might agree to the stipulation to avoid drawing unnecessary attention to the various injuries the plaintiff suffered and the tests and procedures required to diagnose and treat those injuries.

Stipulations are often included in mock trial case files to limit the number of exhibits the case file drafter has to create or to cut down the length of a particular witness's statement. If an agreed fact is important to your case in a mock trial, incorporate the stipulation into your direct examination.

In Chapter Four, Section I(E), we recommended that you ask the presiding judge to read stipulations to the jury. If the presiding judge agrees to do that, all that is left for you to do is decide when the stipulation should be read and, at the appropriate time, turn to the court and say, "At this time we ask that the court read Stipulation 4 on page 12 of the case file to the members of the jury."

Chapter Seven

If the court declines to read the stipulations, read the stipulation to the jurors yourself. Taking our stipulated cost of $4,500 for the plaintiff's medical treatment in the firetruck case as an example, plaintiff's counsel might establish this fact during their client's direct examination as follows.

QUESTION:	How many medical visits did you have following your initial treatment after the collision?
ANSWER:	I went to see a doctor and physical therapist at least ten times following my initial treatment.
QUESTION:	Was this expensive?
ANSWER:	Yes, it most certainly was.
QUESTION:	Did you keep track of all of the expenses you incurred as a result of the medical treatments you required after the collision?
ANSWER:	Yes, I did.
TO JUDGE:	Your Honor, at this time I would like to read a stipulation between the parties aloud for the jury.
JUDGE:	Proceed.
COUNSEL:	(To defense counsel) I'm going to read Stipulation 4 on page 12. (To jury) Members of the jury: "The plaintiff and the defendant agree that the plaintiff's medical treatment following the collision cost a total of $4,500." (To defense counsel) So stipulated, counsel?
DEFENSE:	Yes, so stipulated.

Not only are the jurors now aware of the plaintiff's medical costs, but they also know that the parties agreed to the total amount. From this point on, there can be no disputing that the collision cost the plaintiff $4,500 in medical bills.

If the factfinder in your trial is a judge, you may want to simply direct the court's attention to the particular stipulation rather than reading it aloud. Judges, unlike juries, are aware of the stipulations made between counsel since they have access to the court documents filed by the parties. There is no need to read facts to a judge who is already familiar with them. Thus, counsel would instead state:

TO JUDGE:	Your Honor, at this time we would direct the court's attention to Stipulation 4 on page 12 of the case file, wherein the parties agreed that the total cost of the plaintiff's medical bills following the collision was $4,500.
JUDGE:	Yes, I have that . . . you may proceed.

Here is a checklist you can use to ensure you have followed the rules of direct examination.

Direct Examination

	Checklist	
	HAVE YOU FOLLOWED THE RULES OF DIRECT EXAMINATION?	
☑	**Are all of your questions non-leading?**	Do any of the questions you plan to ask suggest the answer desired?
		If so, they are leading; rephrase them.
☑	**Did you avoid asking questions that seek narrative responses?**	Do any of your questions ask the witness to provide a lengthy summary or to describe a chain of events in a single answer?
		If so, break up the witness's testimony by asking more questions.
☑	**Did you avoid speculative testimony and refrain from asking the witness to offer an opinion they are not qualified to give?**	Do any of your witness's answers include phrases such as, "I assumed" or "I'm not sure but . . ."?
		If so, the witness is speculating and you should avoid eliciting the response.
		Do any of your witness's answers give opinions that would normally come from an expert?
		If so, the witness is giving an improper lay opinion and you should avoid eliciting that information.
☑	**Are you prepared to refresh the witness's recollection if necessary?**	Have you practiced refreshing recollection? Are you able to do it without skipping a beat?
		If not, keep practicing until you are comfortable refreshing recollection.
☑	**(Prosecution only) Did you have the witness identify the defendant?**	If you represent the prosecution in a criminal case and your witness is able to identify the defendant, did you ask the witness to do so during the direct?
		If not, you should add an in-court identification to the direct examination.

Mock Trials: Preparing, Presenting, and *Winning* Your Case

Chapter Seven

Checklist	
HAVE YOU FOLLOWED THE RULES OF DIRECT EXAMINATION?	
☑ Did you incorporate stipulations when helpful?	Did you include every stipulation that is helpful to your witness's testimony in the direct examination? *If not, consider adding those stipulations to your direct examination.*

III. Planning Direct Examinations

Your principal tool in presenting a persuasive direct examination is, of course, the knowledge of the witness. If the underlying content of the examination is not accurate and believable, organizing it perfectly is unlikely to make any noticeable difference. Your first concern, then, must be content—the existence of the facts that you intend to prove.

A. Content

Recall that direct examination provides your best opportunity to prove your case. To do so effectively, the examination must either establish some aspect of your theory or contribute to the persuasiveness of your theme. Preferably, it will do both.

In considering the content of a direct examination, return to the summary you created in Chapter Two and pick up where you left off. Prioritize those facts that are most helpful to your case and eliminate those that are extraneous. This is a ruthless process. In direct examination, length is your enemy. Eliminate all nonessential facts that are questionable, subject to impeachment, cumulative, distasteful, implausible, distracting, or just plain boring.

1. What to Include

First, decide what to include. Review your summary of the helpful facts this witness adds to your case, and determine which facts are necessary to prove your theory. What is the single most important thing that the witness has to say? What are the witness's other facts that will make the central information more plausible? What is the next most important part of the potential testimony? What secondary facts make that testimony more believable? Continue this process for every element of your case.

For example, assume that in our fire engine case one of your witnesses saw the defendant driver at an automobile repair shop just a few days before the accident. The witness's statement indicates that the defendant was advised that their brakes were in poor repair, but that they left without having them fixed. This is a fact of central importance (since it shows recklessness), and you will no doubt present it in the direct examination of the witness. The facts that support this testimony include corroborative details such as the time of day, the witness's location during the crucial conversation about the brakes, and why the witness can identify the defendant. These details, while not strictly relevant to your theory, give weight and believability to the crucial testimony.

Remember to also include those thematic facts that give your case moral appeal. Returning to the firetruck case, remember that at the time of the collision the defendant was already late for an important meeting. How can your theme, "Too busy to be careful," be developed in the testimony of the auto shop witness described above? The answer is to look for supportive details in the witness's statement. Was the defendant curt or abrupt with the repairperson? Was the defendant constantly checking the time? Was the defendant trying to read important-looking papers while discussing the brakes? Did the defendant rush out of the shop? In other words, search for details that support your image of the defendant as busy, preoccupied, and unconcerned with safety. Those will underscore the key aspect of the witness's testimony: that the defendant needed to, but chose not to, have his brakes fixed prior to the accident.

In addition to central facts and supporting details, your "content checklist" should include reasons and explanations whenever possible. Remember, stories are more persuasive when they include reasons for the way people act. A direct examination usually should include the reasons for the witness's own actions and, with qualified witnesses, reasons for the actions of another. Likewise, when a witness's testimony is not self-explanatory or where it raises obvious questions, consider whether you can ask the witness to explain. In the above repair shop scenario, it may not be immediately apparent that a casual observer would recall the defendant's actions in such detail. Thus, ask the witness for an explanation:

> QUESTION: How is it that you can remember seeing and hearing what the defendant did that morning?
> ANSWER: I was at the shop to have my brakes fixed, and it really made an impression on me that the defendant was leaving without taking care of theirs.

This explanation is logical and believable and bolsters the witness's testimony against the defendant. (Of course, you cannot add such an explanation unless it is based upon facts included in, or can be reasonably inferred from, facts included in your mock trial case file.)

Additionally, as we explained above, devote some part of every direct examination to establishing the credibility of the witness. You can enhance credibility in numerous ways. Show that the witness is neutral and disinterested. Demonstrate that the witness had an adequate opportunity to observe. Allow the witness to address and deny any expected charges of bias or misconduct. Elicit personal background to demonstrate that the witness is a hardworking, honest person.

Chapter Seven

2. What to Exclude

Now begin the process of elimination. Unless you have an extraordinarily compelling reason to include them, discard all facts that fall into the categories discussed below.

Clutter may be the single greatest vice in direct examination. Details are essential to corroborating important evidence, but they are a distraction everywhere else. In the auto shop example, for instance, the witness's proximity to the service counter is an essential detail. The color of the paint in the waiting room is not.

Exclude facts that can be successfully disputed at trial. While perhaps not false, the vigorous and effective dispute likely renders them unusable. Is the witness the only person who claims to have observed a certain event, while many other credible witnesses present at the scene swear it did not occur? Is your witness less than certain? Is the testimony contradicted by credible documentary evidence?

It is usually better to pass up a line of inquiry than to pursue it and ultimately have it rejected by the factfinder. This is not, however, a hard and fast rule. Many true facts will be disputed by the other side, and your case will virtually always turn upon your ability to persuade the jurors that your version is correct. Sometimes your case depends entirely upon the testimony of a single witness who, though certain and truthful, will come under massive attack. Still, evaluate all of the potential testimony against the standards of provability and need. If you cannot prove it, do not use it—especially if you do not need it.

Next, exclude any implausible facts. An implausible fact does not need to be disputed in order to collapse under its own weight. It might be true, it might be useful, it might be free from possible contradiction, but it still may not fly. Return to the auto shop case and assume that the witness's statement said that they recognized the defendant because they had once ridden in the same elevator fifteen years previously. You may have no reason to disbelieve the witness, and it is certainly unlikely that anyone could contradict or disprove this testimony. The testimony might even add some support to your theme, say, if the defendant had rushed out of the elevator in an obvious hurry to get to work. Nonetheless, the testimony is pretty far-fetched. If offered, it gives the trier of fact something unnecessary to worry about; it injects a reason to doubt the other testimony of the witness.

Note, however, that implausibility must be weighed against importance. If the case involved a disputed identification of the defendant, then proof of an earlier encounter might be of sufficient value to risk its introduction.

Leave out direct testimony that opens the door for inquiries on cross-examination that otherwise would not be allowed. Door openers are dangerous because fairness requires that the cross-examiner be allowed to explore any topic that was deliberately introduced on direct. For example, in the intersection case, the defendant almost certainly would not be allowed to introduce the fact that the plaintiff had been under the care of a psychiatrist. On the other hand, assume that the plaintiff testified on direct that the accident had forced her to miss an important appointment with her doctor, the appointment could not be rescheduled for a week, and missing it caused mental distress to the plaintiff. In these circumstances, the door would be opened, at a minimum, to a cross-examination that covered the nature of the appointment; in other words, that the plaintiff was on her way to see her psychiatrist. If asking a question possibly opens the door to a worse fact coming to light through cross-examination, resist the temptation.

B.   Organization

Organization translates the facts included in a witness's statement into a coherent and persuasive story. A trial lawyer does not simply ask a witness to "tell us everything you know," but instead uses the placement and sequence of the information to heighten and clarify its value. In Chapter Three, Section III, we discussed a number of methods you can employ when organizing your direct examinations, including repetition and duration, reflective questioning, apposition, headlines, and enumeration. Be sure to refer back to that chapter often as you compose your direct examination.

Although there is no set pattern for the structure of a direct examination, we recommend you follow these loose guidelines.

1.   Start Strong and End Strong

In most cases, it will be necessary to use the opening part of a direct examination to introduce the witness and establish their basic background. Thus, when we refer to the "beginning" of the direct examination, we're referring to the beginning of the witness's substantive testimony.

a.   The Overall Examination

In every direct examination, no matter how else it is organized, begin and end on strong points. The definition of a strong point will differ from trial to trial. It may be the most gripping and dramatic aspect of the entire examination, the single matter on which the witness expresses the greatest certainty, the most hotly disputed issue of the case, or it may be a crucial predicate for other testimony. Whatever the specifics, the strong points of your overall examination should have some or all of these features:

Admissibility. There is little worse than having an objection sustained right at the beginning, or end, of a direct examination. Be absolutely certain of the admissibility of your opening and closing points.

Theory value. The very definition of a strong point is that it makes a significant contribution to your theory. What does the witness have to say that is most central to the proof of your case?

Chapter Seven

Thematic value. Ideally, your strongest points will reinforce the moral weight of your case. Try to phrase them in the same language you use to invoke your theme.

Dramatic impact. Dramatic impact at the beginning of an examination will keep the judge or jurors listening. Dramatic impact at the end of the examination will help fix the testimony in their memories.

Undeniability. Choose strong points in the hope that they will be vividly remembered. It will do you little good if they are remembered as being questionable or controverted.

b. The Sub-Examinations

Each full direct examination is actually a combination of many smaller sub-examinations. As you move from topic to topic, you constantly conclude and reinitiate the subparts of the direct testimony. Apply the "start strong and end strong" rule not only to the organization of the full direct, but also to the structure of its individual components.

In our intersection case, you might wish to begin and end the substantive part of the plaintiff's examination with evidence about the firetruck. In between, however, you will cover many other issues, including the plaintiff's relevant background, the scene of the collision, and the plaintiff's injuries and damages. Begin and end each of these component parts of the direct on a strong point, if possible.

In something as simple as setting the scene, consider what elements of the description are most important to your case. Then begin with one and end with another. In the intersection case you might lead off with the clarity of the weather conditions in order to establish visibility, then conclude the scene-setting portion of the examination with this description of the traffic:

QUESTION: Of all the cars that were present, how many stopped for the firetruck?
ANSWER: All of them, except the car driven by the defendant.

2. Use Topical Organization

Chronology is the easiest form of organization. What could be more obvious than beginning at the beginning and ending at the end? In trial advocacy, however, easiest is not always best. Instead, consider organizing topically or thematically. Can you arrange one component of the witness's testimony to reinforce another component? It might also allow you to isolate weak points and persuasively develop your theory. The order in which events occurred is usually fortuitous. Your duty as an advocate is to rearrange the telling, when necessary, to provide the story with maximum logical force.

Even in a matter as simple as our firetruck case, conducting a strictly chronological direct examination of the plaintiff could fail to be either dramatic or persuasive.

A chronological examination of the day of the accident would set forth these facts in this order: the time that the plaintiff left home that morning; her destination and her estimated travel time; the weather and traffic conditions; her route from street to street until she arrives at the fateful intersection; the appearance of the firetruck; the plaintiff's reaction; and, finally, the collision. After slogging through this series of details—some important and some not—the direct examination finally arrives at the most important event: the accident itself. But by that point, is the factfinder still interested in what the witness has to say?

It would be more dramatic to: 1) begin with the collision; 2) explain why the plaintiff stopped her car; 3) describe the firetruck; 4) describe the response of the surrounding traffic; and 5) contrast that with the actions of the defendant. This leads us directly to our next point.

3. Get to the Point

A direct examination is not a treasure hunt or murder mystery; do not keep the jurors in suspense. The best organization explains exactly where the testimony is headed and then goes directly there. For example:

QUESTION: Please introduce yourself to the members of the jury.
ANSWER: My name is Len Rubinowitz. I'm a law professor at Northwestern Law School here in Chicago.
QUESTION: Professor Rubinowitz, I want to ask you this right up front, so the jurors know—why is it that you are here today?
ANSWER: I'm here to testify about the bank robbery I witnessed last August 1.

4. Tell the Story

Once the trier of fact knows why the witness is testifying, they will be anxious to hear the witness's account of what happened. While you may need to revert back to the witness's background, as in the example above, keep that portion brief and then proceed directly to the witness's story using a headline to alert the factfinder to where you're going. For example:

QUESTION: Let's go directly to the robbery you witnessed on August first last year, Professor. Where were you when you witnessed the robbery?
ANSWER: I was inside the bank, standing at the adjacent teller window.
QUESTION: Tell the jurors what you saw.
ANSWER: I saw a person with a mask approach the next teller window. The masked person gave a slip of paper to

Chapter Seven

	the teller working at the window and as soon as the teller took it, the masked person pulled out a gun.
QUESTION:	Then what happened?

And so on until the story has been told.

5. Do Not Interrupt the Action

Every direct examination is likely to involve one, two, or more key events or occurrences. The witness may describe physical activity such as an automobile collision, an arrest, the failure of a piece of equipment, or a surgical procedure gone awry. Alternatively, the witness may testify about something less tangible, such as the formation of a contract, the effect of an insult, the making of a threat, the breach of a promise, or the existence of pain following an injury. Whatever the precise subject, divide the testimony into "action" on the one hand and supporting details and descriptions on the other.

As the witness describes an event such as the armed robbery of a bank described above, a cardinal rule for the organization of direct is to never interrupt the action. Do not disrupt the dramatic flow of the witness's description of crucial events in order to fill in minor details. For example, it would be unwise to stop in the middle of Professor Rubinowitz's testimony describing the bank robbery to ask how many other people were in the bank at the time or what the lighting conditions were like inside the bank. While these details may be important, they cannot possibly be important enough to justify fracturing the natural flow of the occurrence testimony.

Cover supporting information after you have elicited the occurrence testimony. Use that testimony as the framework on which to hang the details. For example:

QUESTION:	Now that we've covered what you saw and heard that day, I need to take you back through your description to fill in some details, Professor Rubinowitz.
ANSWER:	OK.
QUESTION:	How many other people were in the bank when you entered?
ANSWER:	Four or five. It was early in the morning—the bank had just opened.
QUESTION:	What were the lighting conditions like inside the bank when you saw the defendant approach the teller window?
ANSWER:	It was bright. There were windows on the east side and the morning sun was beaming in through blinds, which were open. Also, all of the lights inside the bank were on.

Direct Examination

This method has the added advantage of allowing you to repeat much of the witness's crucial testimony, since you are now seeking its clarification. Repeating or referring back to a witness's testimony, in turn, increases the likelihood that the factfinder will remember it.

6. Affirm Before Refuting

Witnesses are often called to testify to give both affirmative evidence and to refute the testimony of others. In such cases, it is usually best to offer the affirmative evidence before proceeding to refutation. In this manner, you will accentuate the positive aspects of your case and avoid making the witness appear biased. As a general organizing principle, think of this as building your own case before destroying your opposition's.

7. Draw the Sting

Witness statements in mock trials are like buffets: there's something for everyone. If each side's witnesses knew only facts that helped their side, there would be nothing worthwhile for the other team to draw out during cross-examination. That would make mock trials a lot less interesting to prepare for and to judge. To avoid that, drafters of mock trial case files are careful to include facts in each witness statement that help each side. In mock trials where some or all witnesses can be called by either side, this balanced approach makes determining which witnesses to call more complex and interesting.

One of the true arts of direct examination lies in deciding when to bring out potentially harmful or embarrassing facts. The goal is to blunt their impact during cross-examination. This is known as drawing the sting of the bad facts. The theory behind drawing the sting is that the bad information will be less damaging if the witness offers and explains it on direct, rather than giving opposing counsel the satisfaction of bringing it out for the first time on cross-examination. Be careful only to draw the sting when you are sure that the information will be admissible if offered by the other side—otherwise, asking about it on direct opens the door for the cross-examiner.

Assuming that you have decided to bring out damaging information on direct, be sure not to do it at the beginning or end of the examination. Remember the principles of primacy and recency: bad facts must never be the strongest points; always bury them in the middle of the direct examination.

Also, allow the factfinder to get to know your witness before you introduce harmful information. It is a normal human tendency to want to believe the best of people whom you like. Give the trier of fact every possible reason to like your witness before offering anything that might have a contrary effect.

8. End with a Clincher

End every examination with a clincher—a single fact that encapsulates your trial theory or theme. To qualify as a clincher, a fact must be: 1) absolutely admissible; 2) reasonably dramatic; 3) simple and memorable; and 4) stated with certainty. Depending upon the nature of the evidence and the theory on which you are proceeding, the final question to the plaintiff in our automobile case might be any of the following:

QUESTION: How long was the fire engine visible before the defendant's car struck yours?

ANSWER: It was visible for at least ten seconds because I had already seen it and stopped for a while when the defendant ran into me.

Or,

QUESTION: Did the defendant begin talking on the phone before or after checking on your injuries?

ANSWER: The defendant started the call without even looking at me.

Or,

QUESTION: Do you know whether you will ever be able to walk again without pain?

ANSWER: The doctors say that they can't do anything more for me, but I am still praying.

9. Ignore Any Rule When Necessary

By now, you may have noticed that the above principles may not be consistent with one another. In any given case, you may not be able to start strong, organize topically, affirm before refuting and yet still get to the point without interrupting the action and ending with a clincher. Which rules should you follow? The answer lies in your own good judgment and can only be arrived at in the context of each specific case. If you need another principle to help interpret the others, it is this: apply whichever rules best advance your theory and theme and skip the others—this time around.

Summary
DIRECT EXAMINATION ORGANIZATION
• Start strong and end strong in the overall and sub-examinations • Use topical organization • Get to the point • Tell the story • Do not interrupt the action

> **Summary**
> **DIRECT EXAMINATION ORGANIZATION**
> - Affirm before refuting
> - Draw the sting
> - End with a clincher
> - Ignore any rule when necessary

IV. The Ethics of Direct Examination

The two most common ethical issues counsel face when preparing for direct examination in a mock trial are discussed below.

A. Asking Objectionable Questions

As we discussed in Chapter Two, assessing the likely admissibility of evidence is an essential component of trial preparation. There is no question that attorneys may offer any evidence that they believe is either clearly or probably admissible. What about evidence that is probably inadmissible? Is it ethical to offer such testimony in the hope that opposing counsel will fail to object or that the judge will make an erroneous ruling?

It is ethical to offer any evidence for which you have a reasonable theory of admissibility. Our adversary system calls upon each attorney to present the best case possible, and relies upon the judge to rule on disputed issues of law. Valuable evidence should not be preemptively excluded on the basis of counsel's assessment, so long as there is a reasonable basis in the law for its admission.

When does counsel reasonably believe evidence is admissible? It is improper to offer evidence that cannot be supported by a theory of admissibility expressed in words. More specifically, counsel should be able to complete, with specific and recognizable legal arguments, a sentence that begins, "This evidence is admissible because . . . ."

If the only conclusion for the sentence counsel can think of is "it helps my case," then there is no reasonable basis for the offer.

And whenever in doubt, ask your mock trial coach or faculty advisor for guidance. No person is an island when it comes to the practice of law; even experienced trial attorneys consult their colleagues and supervisors before making difficult evidentiary decisions.

In summary, on direct examination, attempt to elicit any information that is certainly or probably admissible, but refrain from attempting to elicit information that has no reasonable basis of admissibility.

Chapter Seven

B. *Eliciting Unreasonable Inferences*

This rule is unique to mock trials.

In real trials, the witnesses actually observed the relevant events and therefore attorneys are free to fill in any details missing from a witness's pretrial statements by asking the witness additional questions at trial (subject to impeachment during cross-examination). But in mock trials, the people we call witnesses are actually not witnesses at all. They are actors bringing to life a script that, by necessity, cannot include every fact that would or could be documented in a real case. Accordingly, mock trial case files are bound to be missing facts that would likely be established by one side or the other during an actual case.

Does that mean a mock trial team can simply fill in the facts they deem to be missing to better support their theory of the case? Absolutely not. To keep the playing field even for both sides in a mock trial, many competitions do not allow the witnesses to make any inferences. Where competition rules allow inferences, they usually prohibit inferring facts that are material to the case. In other words, it is one thing to add in a detail that appears obvious based on the information provided, but it is something else altogether (indeed, unethical) to simply make up facts to improve your case. The rule adopted by most mock trial organizers is that witnesses are limited to their prior written statements and reasonable inferences drawn from those statements. We discussed this concept in Chapter Four, Section II(B), in addressing the use of demonstrative exhibits at trial, but will discuss it in greater depth below.

What is a reasonable inference? A reasonable inference is a factual connection or conclusion that a reasonable person would draw from a particular fact or set of facts contained in a mock trial case file, so long as it does not affect the outcome or create an unfair advantage. An inference is probably reasonable if it is supported by the facts that are contained in the witness's statement and it is natural, logical and believable. Of course, the more facts that support an inference, the more reasonable it is. Likewise, the reasonableness of an inference is also correlated with the logic it employs and its overall believability.

To test an inference for reasonableness, ask yourself these questions: Are there facts in the case file that support this inference? Does it make sense that this witness would know this information? If I were a juror, would I be inclined to assume this fact from the witness's testimony based on everything else the witness says? If the answer to all those questions is yes, the proposed inference is probably reasonable.

The example we gave previously is apt: if a criminal mock trial case file says the defendant was found in their bedroom lying down and a gun was found in the nightstand next to them, it would be reasonable to infer that the defendant was found on a bed. Why? Because bedrooms contain beds, nightstands sit next to beds, and a bed is a place where people commonly lie down in bedrooms. Is it possible the defendant happened to be found lying on the ground next to a nightstand? Yes, that is possible. But given the known facts, it seems more reasonable to infer that the defendant was found lying on a bed than it would be to infer that the defendant was lying on the floor.

But what if positioning the defendant on a bed as opposed to the floor made it a lot more likely that the defendant would be found guilty? For example, what if the applicable law stated that when a convicted felon is found within six inches of a firearm, the felon is presumed to have intentionally possessed that firearm? If that were the law, having a witness testify that the defendant was on a bed (instead of merely lying down, as written in the case file) when found could affect the outcome of the case. In our example, the fact we are considering inferring is now a material fact and that makes the inference impermissible, no matter how reasonable it might otherwise seem. Facts that are material to a case are expressly written into each mock trial case file and should *never* be inferred by the participants.

So, what is a material fact? In a criminal case, a fact is material if it directly supports or contradicts an element of the offense charged or a defense thereto (as in our felon in possession of a firearm example above). In a civil case, a fact is material if it directly supports or contradicts a claim or a counterclaim in the lawsuit. If a fact that you are tempted to infer from the information provided in a case file is clearly material, do *not* have a witness testify to the inference during a mock trial.

But just because a fact is not clearly material does not mean it is acceptable for a team to introduce during a mock trial. The rule to follow is the inverse of our advice concerning objectionable questions in the preceding section. If there is an articulable theory that a fact is material, you should avoid eliciting that fact during a mock trial. We reiterate our reasoning: mock trials are meant to test students' abilities to present the facts and evidence they have been given within the framework of the evidentiary and procedural rules that govern trials; they are not tests of creativity meant to reward the team who makes up the best facts to support their theory of the case.

Once again, when in doubt, consult your mock trial coach or faculty advisor for guidance. Eliciting unreasonable inferences on direct examination—and especially material facts not included in the case file—can cost you dearly. Judges penalize students for inventing facts, and tournament organizers can disqualify mock trial teams from entire competitions if observers or opposing teams feel the line between inference and invention was crossed. It is also just wrong. So, if in preparing for a mock trial, you find yourself or your team debating whether an inference is reasonable or a fact you are inferring is material, ask yourself this instead: Is it worth risking all of the hard work we have put in to preparing for this competition to elicit this testimony, given the possible consequences if others disagree with our analysis? If you get to the point where you are asking that question, the answer is surely no.

Chapter Seven

As we said, in some mock trial competitions, organizers have become so frustrated with and concerned about students making unreasonable inferences that they have barred any inferences at all from being made by witnesses. In those competitions, witnesses are not permitted to testify to any fact not explicitly written into the case file and violations of the rule can result in the deduction of points or even disqualification from the competition. Obviously, if your competition has adopted that rule, do not concern yourself with the prior discussion about whether a particular inference is reasonable or a fact being inferred is material. If inferences are not allowed under the rules of your mock trial, explicitly prohibit your witnesses from making them. Period.

Chapter Eight

Foundations and Exhibits

I. Evidentiary Foundations Generally

A. *The Requirement of Foundation*

Before substantive testimony and the content of tangible evidence can be considered at trial, the attorney offering the evidence must show that there is some basis for believing the evidence to be relevant, authentic, and admissible. This basis is called the foundation for the evidence, and the process of establishing foundation is referred to as laying foundation. The lawyer seeking the admission of evidence is referred to as the proponent of the evidence.

Say, for example, your mock trial case file includes a contract. A contract is a legal document. Before a witness can testify to the content of any document, the proponent of the evidence must first lay the foundation for the document. Laying the foundation for a contract consists of asking a witness whatever questions are necessary to establish that the contract is relevant to the case, that it is authentic, and that it is admissible. Until all three of those requirements have been met, no witness can testify to the content of the contract.

Depending upon the nature of the evidence, the necessary foundation may be painfully complex or strikingly simple. The rules of evidence used in your mock trial govern which facts form the basis for the admission of testimony and exhibits. The question of foundation is directed to the presiding judge, who decides whether the evidence will be received.

With many kinds of testimony, the necessary foundation is obvious. For example, the basic foundation for eyewitness testimony is that the witness observed the relevant events and is able to recall them. This foundation would typically be established shortly after introducing the witness. For example:

> QUESTION: Where were you on the afternoon of December 29?
> ANSWER: I was at the corner of Alta Vista and Craycroft.
> QUESTION: What did you see?
> ANSWER: I saw an automobile collision.

It has now been shown that the witness has personal knowledge of the collision in our firetruck case. On the basis of this foundation, and in the absence of some objection that is not apparent from the example, the witness should be allowed to describe the collision. Of course, not all foundations are so straightforward. Many require proof of other foundational facts, as discussed below.

The Basics	
THE COMPONENTS OF FOUNDATION	
Relevance:	All testimony and exhibits must be shown to make some fact at issue in the case more or less likely to be true.
Authenticity:	All testimony and exhibits must be shown to be what the proponent claims them to be.
Specific Admissibility:	All testimony and facts must be shown to be otherwise admissible under the mock trial rules of evidence.

B. Components of Foundation

As explained above, there are three universal aspects to virtually all evidentiary foundations. To be received, evidence must be shown to be relevant, authentic, and otherwise admissible under the rules of evidence in your mock trial.

1. Relevance

Relevance defines the relationship between the proffered evidence and some fact that is at issue in the case. Evidence will not be admitted simply because it is interesting or imaginative; it must make a disputed fact in the case either more or less likely to be true. The relevance of most evidence is generally apparent from the context of the case, but occasionally it must be demonstrated by the establishment of foundational facts.

In the example above, the relevance of the testimony is made clear by the recitation of the date and place of the witness's observation. The witness is about to testify concerning the collision in the firetruck case, not just any accident. Note, however, that this basic foundation might not always be adequate. Had there been more than one accident on December 29 at the corner of Craycroft and Alta Vista, the witness would have to provide additional identifying facts before testifying to the events. What time was the witness there? What colors were the automobiles involved?

2. Authenticity

The concept of authenticity refers to the requirement of proof that evidence actually is what the proponent claims it to be. In other words, evidence may not be admitted until there has been a showing that it is "the real thing."

We generally think of authentication as it applies to tangible evidence such as documents, physical objects, or photographs. Say, for instance, a case file includes a document containing the name of a business and an address, along with a date and time, followed by a list of items purchased, a total charge, the last four digits of a credit card number, and the name and signature of a person. Based on its content, the piece of evidence appears to be a receipt, right? In trial, a document that appears to be a receipt cannot be admitted in evidence unless a witness with personal knowledge about the document authenticates it. The foundation establishing the authenticity of a receipt might be as simple as this:

QUESTION: I'm handing you what has been marked as Government Exhibit 5. Do you recognize it?
ANSWER: Yes, I do.
QUESTION: Please tell us what it is.
ANSWER: This is a receipt for the food I purchased at Dominick's grocery store on the morning of April 2.

The above foundation adequately supports the proponent's claim of authenticity—i.e., that the document is what it appears to be (a grocery receipt).

The requirement of authenticity is not, however, limited to tangible objects. It also applies to certain testimonial evidence. For example, a witness generally may not testify to a telephone conversation without first establishing a basis for recognizing the voice of the person on the other end of the line. That is, the identity of the other speaker must be authenticated.

The judge decides whether evidence has been sufficiently authenticated, and the criteria vary according to the nature of the evidence involved.

It is common for mock trial case files to contain stipulations to the authenticity of the documentary or physical evidence included in the materials. In fact, in many mock trials, the authenticity of all the exhibits included in the case file is stipulated in the competition rules. If there is no such broad stipulation in the case file—and likewise no stipulations establishing the authenticity of a particular exhibit or testimony—you must lay the necessary foundation to establish the authenticity of the evidence.

Even if your case file includes a blanket stipulation that every witness statement and piece of documentary evidence provided is authentic, we nonetheless recommend that you establish the authenticity of at least the key pieces of the evidence you present during a mock trial. Our rationale for recommending this seemingly unnecessary step is simple: the people judging you will expect you to lay this foundation. They

Chapter Eight

have been "programmed" to ask these questions, whether by their law school professors, their partners, or perhaps the judges before whom they appear. Consequently, if you skip that step during your direct examination due to the stipulation in your case file, your examination may seem incomplete to those judging your performance.

It also bears mentioning here that authenticity stipulations are included in mock trial case files not to save evidentiary proponents time and energy. Instead, they are included to prevent opposing teams from successfully excluding evidence included in the case file on authenticity grounds. Mock trial case files are, after all, fictional and thus none of the documents included are actually authentic. To avoid authenticity challenges, case file drafters include a blanket stipulation that all documents in the case file are deemed authentic.

3. Specific Admissibility

While evidence will generally be received if it is relevant and authentic, the rules of evidence in your mock trial govern its further admissibility. In many cases, evidence can be admitted only once you establish foundational facts that illustrate to the presiding judge that the evidence is admissible. Be aware of the rules of evidence governing each fact you intend to offer at trial. As discussed in detail below, the foundation you lay can then be tailored to meet the evidentiary rule's requirements.

C. *Establishing Foundations*

There are multiple combinations of ways to establish the foundation for testimony or exhibits. A lawyer may establish foundation using one witness or several witnesses, including even witnesses called by opposing counsel.

1. Using a Single Witness

The most common approach to establishing a foundation is to ask questions of a witness who can provide the necessary facts, and then to offer the evidence after eliciting that testimony. Consider this example from the direct examination of the plaintiff in our firetruck case:

QUESTION: Do you recognize the object that I am showing you, which has been marked as Plaintiff's Exhibit 12?
ANSWER: Yes, it is the neck brace that I got from my doctor.
QUESTION: When did you get it from your doctor?
ANSWER: When I was discharged from the hospital following the accident.
QUESTION: What is it made of?
ANSWER: Stiff plastic.
QUESTION: Do you still wear it?
ANSWER: Yes, I have to wear it at least eight hours a day.

Counsel may now offer the neck brace into evidence. Its relevance to the issue of damages is apparent from the context of the case, its authenticity as the actual neck brace worn by the plaintiff has been established by that witness, and there are no special evidentiary considerations that govern the admission of this piece of tangible evidence.

2. Using Multiple Witnesses

Some foundations cannot be laid by a single witness. In such cases, counsel must establish separate parts of the foundation from each of several witnesses before offering the evidence. In a bag-snatching case, for example, it may be necessary to question two witnesses in order to lay the foundation for the admission of the stolen bag. First, the arresting officer:

QUESTION: Officer, do you recognize Prosecution Exhibit 1?
ANSWER: Yes. It is a messenger bag that was in the possession of the defendant at the time of arrest.

The officer has laid some of the foundation, but not all of it. The defendant's possession of a bag is not relevant until it is shown to have been stolen. It is therefore necessary to then ask the victim:

QUESTION: Do you recognize Prosecution Exhibit 1?
ANSWER: Yes. It is my bag.
QUESTION: Before today, when was the last time that you saw it?
ANSWER: The last time I saw it was when it was ripped off my shoulder by a bag snatcher.

Now the bag is admissible. The victim provided the missing aspect of relevance, and also authenticated the bag as the object that was stolen.

You can use both direct and cross-examination to lay a single foundation. Thus, defense counsel can begin to lay a foundation during the cross-examination of a plaintiff's witness and can conclude the foundation during the defendant's case-in-chief. Assume, for example, that the defendant wants to introduce a letter from the plaintiff. To be admissible, it must be shown both that the plaintiff wrote the letter and that the defendant received it. Defense counsel can begin the foundation during the plaintiff's case by having the plaintiff authenticate their own signature on cross-examination. The foundation can later be completed by asking the defendant on direct whether the letter was actually received.

3. Cross-Examination

Foundation requirements apply equally during cross- and direct examinations. Testimonial foundations must be laid on cross-examination for personal knowledge, voice identification, hearsay exceptions, and in every other circumstance

Chapter Eight

where a foundation would be necessary on direct examination. In addition, there are special foundations for impeachment by omission or prior inconsistent statement. We discuss impeachment in depth in Chapter Ten. It is also often necessary to use cross-examination to lay the foundation for admitting exhibits.

4. Conditional Admissibility

As illustrated above, it is not always possible to complete a foundation during the testimony of a single witness. However, a witness who is responsible for part of the foundation will sometimes have other important information to offer concerning the exhibit. In the absence of a special rule, this witness could not testify about the exhibit until the foundation was complete. Fortunately, the doctrine of conditional admissibility allows the temporary or conditional admission of the evidence based upon counsel's representation that the foundation will be completed through the testimony of a subsequent witness.

In the above bag-snatching case, the prosecution might want to elicit further testimony about the bag from the arresting officer:

PROSECUTOR:	Officer, do you recognize Prosecution Exhibit 1?
ANSWER:	Yes. It is the messenger bag that the defendant was concealing under their jacket when I arrested them.
PROSECUTOR:	Officer, please show us how the defendant was concealing the bag when you made the arrest.
DEFENSE:	Objection. The foundation for this exhibit is incomplete.
PROSECUTOR:	Your Honor, we will complete the foundation when we call the victim, who will testify that Exhibit 1 is the same bag that was stolen. In the meantime, we ask that the bag be conditionally admitted so we may ask this witness additional questions about it.
COURT:	On the basis of counsel's representation, the objection is overruled.

The further testimony of the officer has been conditionally allowed, subject to the perfection of the foundation for the bag. Of course, in the event that the victim does not identify the bag, all of the conditionally accepted testimony may be stricken from the record at the request of opposing counsel.

Accordingly, when your opponent seeks to have a piece of evidence conditionally admitted, make a note to yourself to ensure that your opponent later succeeds in perfecting the foundation. If they do not, bring the matter to the attention of the presiding judge as soon as practicable. For example, address the court as follows: "Your

Honor, during the testimony of the arresting officer in this case, the prosecution asked the court to conditionally admit Prosecution Exhibit 1, subject to the perfection of the foundation through the victim. However, no such foundation was laid during the victim's testimony. Consequently, the defense now moves to strike arresting officer's testimony about the bag, which was conditioned upon further foundation being laid. We also ask that you instruct the jurors to disregard that testimony."

II. Foundations for Testimonial Evidence

A. *Personal Knowledge*

Witnesses are expected to testify from personal knowledge. The most common personal knowledge is direct sensory perception: information gained through sight, hearing, touch, taste, and smell. Witnesses may also have personal knowledge of more subjective information such as their own intentions or emotions or the reputation of another person.

Whatever the content of the witness's testimony, it is necessary to lay a foundation showing that the witness is testifying either from personal knowledge or on the basis of an acceptable substitute, as in the case of expert testimony, which will be discussed in Chapter Twelve.

In the case of a witness testifying based upon sensory perception, the basic foundation is simply that the witness was in a position to observe or otherwise experience the relevant facts, as explained above in the example of eyewitness testimony in the firetruck case. Witnesses are assumed to have all of their senses in order, so, for example, counsel is not required to show that the witness's eyesight is unimpaired.

In some situations, however, additional foundation may be called for to fully establish the basis of the witness's testimony:

> QUESTION: What happened when you were standing in the workshop?
> ANSWER: I heard a high-pitched, mechanical, whining sound in the next room.
> QUESTION: Could you tell what it was?
> ANSWER: Yes.
> QUESTION: How could you tell?
> ANSWER: I have worked in the workshop before, and I heard that sound when I saw the machines operating.
> QUESTION: What was the sound?

B. *Conversations*

In addition to establishing the personal knowledge of the witness, conversations between two or more parties require further foundation, depending on whether the

Chapter Eight

conversation is taking place in person or over the telephone. Below we explain the foundation you must lay for each.

1. Conversations That Occur in Person

Before a witness can testify to an in-person conversation with another person, foundation must be given to establish the date, time, and place of the conversation, as well as the persons present at the time. For example:

QUESTION: Did you complain to anyone about the quality of the printing job?

ANSWER: Yes, I spoke to the store manager, Pete Surdo.

QUESTION: When did you speak to the manager?

ANSWER: On April 18, the same day that I refused to accept the product.

QUESTION: About what time was that?

ANSWER: I believe that it was just before noon, but it may have been somewhat later.

QUESTION: Where were you when you spoke?

ANSWER: We were at the service counter.

QUESTION: Was anybody else present?

ANSWER: There was a clerk nearby, but not involved in the conversation.

QUESTION: Please tell us what was said during that conversation.

The witness's ability to relate the time, date, place, and participants provides sufficient evidence that the conversation happened as the witness says it did. It is not necessary to lay the foundation with minute precision. In the above scenario, the witness would not be required to provide the clerk's name or the exact time of the conversation. The foundation is sufficient so long as it fulfills its purpose of providing opposing counsel with reasonably sufficient information with which to challenge or contest the witness's testimony.

Note, however, that the foundation for the conversation does not resolve any hearsay or other evidentiary problems that may be raised by its content. Those issues must be addressed separately, often necessitating the development of additional foundation, as we discuss below.

2. Conversations That Occur Over the Telephone

The foundation for a telephone conversation includes the additional element of voice identification or of a reasonable circumstantial substitute. For instance, a witness can testify to recognizing the voice of the person to whom the witness spoke because they had spoken to each other before or since the incident (either in person or on the phone).

QUESTION: Did you complain to anyone about the quality of the printing job?
ANSWER: Yes, I telephoned the store manager, Pete Surdo, as soon as I opened the first package.
QUESTION: How do you know that you were speaking to Surdo?
ANSWER: I recognized his voice. I have been going to that print shop for years, and I have spoken to Pete many times in person.

In the absence of a basis for voice identification, circumstantial evidence can be used as the foundation for a telephone conversation.

QUESTION: Did you complain to anyone about the quality of the printing job?
ANSWER: Yes, I telephoned the store as soon as I opened the first package.
QUESTION: How did you obtain the number?
ANSWER: I looked it up online.
QUESTION: Did you dial the number that was listed online?
ANSWER: Yes.
QUESTION: What did you say when the telephone was answered?
ANSWER: I said that I wanted to complain about the quality of the printing job that I had just picked up.

C. Prior Identification

A witness may testify to their previous out-of-court identification of an individual. While such evidence is most commonly offered in criminal cases to support the in-court identification of the defendant made at trial, it also has its uses in civil matters. The foundation for this testimony is that the out-of-court identification was made by the witness after perceiving the person identified.

QUESTION: Were you able to see the person who stole your car?
ANSWER: Yes. He was driving away in it just as I got home from work. I saw him from the shoulders up.
QUESTION: How far away were you when you first saw him?
ANSWER: I was about thirty feet away.
QUESTION: Did you ever see him again?
ANSWER: Yes, I picked him out of a lineup.
QUESTION: When was that?
ANSWER: About four days later at the police station.
QUESTION: Please describe the circumstances of the lineup.
ANSWER: There were five men standing in a row. They were all about the same height and they were all wearing blue

Chapter Eight

QUESTION:	jeans and flannel shirts. I identified the man who was second from the left. Was that the same man whom you identified here in court today?
ANSWER:	Yes.

D. Habit and Routine

Testimonial evidence of habit or routine practice may be admitted as circumstantial evidence that a person or organization acted in a similar fashion on a particular occasion. The subject matter of such testimony can range from an individual's clothing preferences to a business's routine for mailing letters. In each case, the evidence of a regular custom or practice is offered to prove that the individual or business acted in the same way at a time relevant to the issues at trial.

To lay the foundation for evidence of habit or routine practice, it is necessary to call a witness with personal knowledge of the regular conduct of the person or organization involved. Furthermore, you must establish that the asserted conduct was, in fact, of a consistently repeated nature. This can be accomplished through proof of either extended observation or of the existence of a formal policy or procedure.

In order to lay this sort of foundation in the context of a mock trial, a witness statement must make clear that the witness has had sufficient opportunity to observe the habits of the person, or the routines of the business, about whom or which they are being questioned. Referring back to our discussion in Chapter Seven, Section IV(B), it would be an unreasonable inference for a witness to testify to another person's habit or to a business's routine practice if the witness's statement did not include details directly supporting such an inference.

In the following example, assume that the defendant is charged with stabbing a person to death. Pleading self-defense, the defendant claims that it was the victim who attacked the defendant with a knife, which the defendant took away and used for defense. The ownership of the knife—was it the victim's or the defendant's?—will be a contested issue at trial. Habit evidence could be offered by the prosecution to show that the defendant always carried a knife.

QUESTION:	How long have you known the defendant?
ANSWER:	About five years.
QUESTION:	In what context do you know the defendant?
ANSWER:	We are neighbors. The defendant lives next door to me.
QUESTION:	During the last five years, how often have you seen the defendant?
ANSWER:	On average, I would say that I have seen the defendant at least twice a week.

QUESTION:	On those occasions, did you ever see the defendant carry a knife?
ANSWER:	Yes. The defendant always carried a hunting knife strapped to their belt.
QUESTION:	How often did you see the defendant with a hunting knife?
ANSWER:	Whenever the defendant went out of the house, they always had that knife on their belt.
QUESTION:	Did you ever see the defendant go out of the house without a knife on their belt?
ANSWER:	Only once.
QUESTION:	What was that occasion?
ANSWER:	The defendant was going to a wedding and wearing formal clothes.

The evidence of the defendant's constant habit over an extended period of time is admissible to prove that the defendant was carrying a knife on the date in question. Likewise, a routine practice of a business or organization may be established either through direct observation or through evidence of an existing policy or practice. Once the routine business practice is established, it may be used to show that the company adhered to that custom during the time period in question.

E. Character and Reputation

Evidence of a person's character generally is not admissible to prove that the person acted in conformity with their character on a particular occasion. For example, counsel may not offer proof of a person's dislike of children as evidence that they physically abused a child. There are, however, a few exceptions that allow the admission of character evidence for various purposes. Each exception requires the establishment of its own foundation.

1. Other Crimes or Past Misconduct

Other than in cases involving the sexual abuse or exploitation of a minor, evidence of past crimes or other wrongful conduct is not admissible to prove the occurrence of a specific subsequent event.

For example, the mere fact that a defendant committed three previous burglaries cannot be offered to show that the defendant is a burglar and therefore committed the burglary in a current case. Past misconduct, including uncharged crimes, may, however, be admitted for other purposes such as proof of motive, opportunity, intent, preparation, plan, knowledge, identity, or absence of mistake or accident. Let's return to our burglary example. Recall that counsel would not be permitted to use the defendant's prior burglary convictions merely to prove

Chapter Eight

that the defendant is a burglar, for example, by arguing, "Once a burglar, always a burglar!"

The defendant's prior burglary convictions may be admitted, however, if they are deemed relevant to proving the defendant's motive, opportunity, or intent to commit the crime charged, or the defendant's preparation, plan, knowledge, identity, or absence of mistake or accident in committing the crime. Imagine, for example, that the defendant had previously robbed three jewelry stores in the middle of the night by using a glass cutter to gain entry to the stores. You could seek to admit evidence of those prior crimes in a criminal case where the evidence showed that the culprit committed the offense in the middle of the night by using a glass cutter to gain entry to the store. In so doing, you would argue to the presiding judge that the prior convictions should be admissible because they are directly relevant to the defendant's intent, knowledge, preparation, and plan.

Evidence proving up one or more prior "bad acts" of a defendant has the potential to be incredibly prejudicial. If the probative value of that evidence is substantially outweighed by its prejudicial effect, it will not be admitted by the presiding judge. We talked about this rule in Chapter Six, Section II. Because of its high potential for causing prejudice, seek a ruling in advance on the admissibility of this type of evidence before presenting it during a mock trial.

If your competition rules allow pretrial evidentiary motions, we recommend moving in limine to admit evidence of a defendant's prior bad acts. We discuss motions in limine in Chapter Four, Section II.

If pretrial motions are not allowed, raise the matter after the witness is called but before you begin eliciting testimony regarding the prior bad acts. You can do this by asking the court if you may be heard at sidebar (or may assume you are being heard at sidebar, as explained in Chapter Four, Section I(B)). If the judge agrees, explain that you are about to elicit testimony about the defendant's prior bad acts and that you want to provide opposing counsel with an opportunity to object outside the hearing of the jury. This is exactly what a savvy trial lawyer would do in a real trial. If evidence of a defendant's prior bad acts were put before a jury and later deemed inadmissible for any reason, the chances are great that the presiding judge would declare a mistrial. Although mock trials are not real trials, they are designed to train people to become trial lawyers and all lawyers must learn to avoid eliciting testimony or evidence that could result in a mistrial.

Assuming you have sought a ruling in advance and the presiding judge in your mock trial has deemed the evidence of the defendant's prior crimes, wrongs, or other acts admissible, your next task is to lay the proper foundation for this evidence so the factfinder can consider it within the proper context.

The foundation for such evidence must include the specifics of the past act as well as the circumstances that make it usable for a permissible purpose in the case at trial. Assume that the defendant in the following example is an employer who is being prosecuted for intentionally failing to pay last year's employee withholding taxes to the government. The defendant admits the conduct but claims that it was an unintentional oversight—the defendant meant to pay withholding taxes to the government but simply forgot to do so in the charged instance. The prosecution has called a tax examiner to the stand.

> QUESTION: What is your occupation?
> ANSWER: I am an auditor for the Internal Revenue Service.
> QUESTION: Have you audited the records of the defendant's business?
> ANSWER: Yes, I audited the records for the last seven years.
> QUESTION: Exactly what records did you review?
> ANSWER: I looked at all of the payroll records, including the time sheets and check stubs for every employee.
> QUESTION: Were you able to determine anything with regard to withholding taxes?
> ANSWER: Yes. In each of the last seven years, the amount of money withheld from employees' paychecks was more than the amount paid over to the government.
> QUESTION: What was the difference last year?
> ANSWER: Last year, the defendant withheld $55,000 more from employees than was paid to the government for their withholding taxes.
> QUESTION: And in the preceding six years?
> ANSWER: The amounts for the previous six years were $40,000; $32,000; $51,000; $39,000; $46,000; and $42,000.
> QUESTION: Did the defendant submit withholding tax returns in each of the last seven years?
> ANSWER: Yes. They were submitted and signed by the defendant in each of the last seven years, but they never accurately reflected the amount of money deducted from employees' paychecks.

The defendant has not been charged with failing to pay withholding taxes other than in the most recent tax year. The government may not offer the evidence regarding the previous years' tax records to show that the defendant was a habitual tax cheat, as doing so would violate the rule against admitting improper character evidence. Nonetheless, evidence of the defendant's past misconduct should be admissible to show intent and the absence of any mistake or accident on the defendant's part when filing last year's return. The fact that the defendant made the same "oversight" in each of the last seven years tends to show that it was not an oversight at all, but rather was knowing and intentional.

Chapter Eight

Note that the foundation included the basis of the witness's knowledge, the precise records that were reviewed, the relationship of the records to the withholding return, the years in which underpayments were made, and the defendant's personal involvement in signing the returns.

Evidence of prior crimes—even when properly admitted—must be handled carefully during final argument. See Chapter Fifteen, Section II(C)(2), for a detailed discussion of this issue.

2. Reputation for Untruthfulness

Evidence of a person's reputation for untruthfulness is admissible if it reflects on the credibility of another person's testimony as a witness in the trial—i.e., it gives the jurors a reason to doubt that the witness's testimony is truthful. Such evidence must be offered by someone who has knowledge of the other witness's reputation in the community.

The foundation for such reputation evidence includes identification of the relevant community, the basis of the witness's knowledge, and the nature of the other witness's reputation during a relevant time period. Note that the "community" involved may be residential, professional, social, or the like. Returning to our firetruck case, a witness for the defendant may testify as follows:

> QUESTION: Do you know the plaintiff?
> ANSWER: Yes, I have known her for four years.
> QUESTION: In what context do you know her?
> ANSWER: We belong to the same hiking club. It's called the Campside Walkers.
> QUESTION: Are you familiar with the plaintiff's reputation for truth and veracity among the Campside Walkers?
> ANSWER: Yes, I am. Her reputation is very bad. She is regarded within the club as an untruthful person.

A witness may also testify about their opinion of another witness's untruthfulness. The foundation is similar to that for reputation testimony.

> QUESTION: Do you know the plaintiff?
> ANSWER: Yes, I have known her for four years.
> QUESTION: In what context do you know her?
> ANSWER: We belong to the same hiking club, the Campside Walkers.
> QUESTION: How often have you spoken to the plaintiff during those four years?
> ANSWER: Well, the club meets once a month and both of us usually attend the meetings. In addition, we have gone on many long hikes together, and on at least three occasions we went on weekend camping trips.

QUESTION: Based on your contacts with the plaintiff, do you have an opinion concerning her truthfulness?
ANSWER: Yes, I do. My opinion is that she is not a truthful person.

Once a witness has given reputation or opinion evidence concerning another's untruthfulness, the cross-examiner may inquire about relevant specific instances of conduct.

F. Foundations for Hearsay Statements

The rule against hearsay excludes evidence of out-of-court statements if offered to prove the truth of the matter asserted. Numerous exceptions to the hearsay rule allow for the admissibility of out-of-court statements, provided that the necessary foundation is established. The foundations for exceptions that apply primarily to testimonial evidence are discussed below. Those that typically apply to documentary evidence are discussed in Section IV of this chapter, further below.

1. Party Admissions

Out-of-court statements made by an opposing party (meaning the plaintiff or the defendant in a civil case or the defendant in a criminal case) are admissible to prove the truth of the matter asserted. The proponent of such evidence must lay foundation to show that the witness heard the statement and can identify it as having been made by the party against whom it is being offered. The content of the statement itself can demonstrate its adverse nature. The party admission doctrine applies only to statements offered against the party-declarant. A defendant cannot elicit their own favorable statements made to a third party unless allowed by another hearsay exception, such as the state of mind or excited utterance exceptions.

The party admission exception also applies to statements made by an agent or employee of a party. In these situations, there are two additional elements to the foundation: 1) the declarant was an agent or employee of the opposing party at the time the statement was made, and 2) the statement concerned a matter that was within the scope of the agency or employment. In the following example, assume that the plaintiff is the Quickset Printing Company, which has sued the defendant for nonpayment on a large duplicating order. The defendant is testifying on direct examination.

QUESTION: Did you speak to anyone at Quickset after you received the order?
ANSWER: Yes. I went back to the shop and I spoke to the manager, Mr. Pete Surdo.
QUESTION: How do you know that you were speaking to Surdo?
ANSWER: I have been doing business with Quickset for years, and I have spoken to Pete many times.

Chapter Eight

QUESTION:	What did you say to Mr. Surdo?
ANSWER:	I said that the order was defective and that I would not pay for it.
QUESTION:	Did the manager respond?
ANSWER:	Yes. He said that no one should have to pay for defective work and that he would speak to the owner of the company.

Since agency and scope have been established, the manager's out-of-court statement is admissible. Note that the testimony also contained a reference to the defendant's own out-of-court statement concerning the defective nature of the order. The defendant cannot offer their own statement as a party admission. In this case, however, it is not being offered for the truth of the matter asserted, but rather to provide the context for the manager's response. Therefore, it is not hearsay and is admissible.

2. Present Sense Impression

The present sense impression exception to the hearsay rule allows the admission of out-of-court statements describing or explaining an event or condition made while the declarant was perceiving the event or condition, or immediately thereafter. A witness may testify to their own previous expression of a present sense impression, as in this example from the firetruck case:

QUESTION:	Where were you at about 8:20 a.m. last December 29?
ANSWER:	I was at the corner of Craycroft and Alta Vista, walking west on Alta Vista.
QUESTION:	Were you with anyone?
ANSWER:	Yes, I was with my two children, who are four and six years old. My neighbor was also with us.
QUESTION:	Was your attention drawn to a vehicle at that time?
ANSWER:	I saw a fire engine headed west on Alta Vista.
QUESTION:	Was the fire engine using its warning signals?
ANSWER:	It was flashing its lights.
QUESTION:	Did you say anything about the fire engine to anyone?
ANSWER:	Yes. I told my children to look at the firetruck. I think that my exact words were something like, "Look kids, a firetruck with its lights on. There must be a fire somewhere near here."
QUESTION:	When did you say that to your children?
ANSWER:	Right as the firetruck was passing.

A witness may also testify to another person's present sense impression statement. In these instances, it is generally necessary for the statement to have been made in the witness's presence in order to satisfy the foundational requirement of personal knowledge.

3. Excited Utterance

The excited utterance exception is similar to the present sense impression rule, allowing for the admission of a hearsay statement that relates to a startling event or condition and is made while the declarant was under the stress of excitement caused by the event or condition.

To lay foundation for an excited utterance, you must show that the declarant perceived a startling event or experienced a stressful condition and that the declarant's statement was made while they were under the stress of the event or condition.

As with present sense impressions, a witness may testify to their own excited utterance or to that of another so long as the proper foundation precedes the testimony.

QUESTION: Directing your attention to last December 29 at approximately 8:20 a.m. Do you remember where you were at that time?

ANSWER: I was on my morning walk, and I was just approaching Alta Vista walking south down Craycroft with the traffic.

QUESTION: Were you with anyone?

ANSWER: No, I was alone.

QUESTION: Was your attention drawn to a vehicle at that time?

ANSWER: Yes, it was. I heard brakes and looked up. In the car next to me, I heard a man yell at the driver of the car in front of him.

QUESTION: Were you able to hear what he said?

ANSWER: Yes, I heard it clearly.

QUESTION: Would you say the man was under the stress of excitement caused by an event or condition?

ANSWER: Absolutely. He was angry because the driver in front of him wasn't paying attention and rammed right into the car ahead. The driver of this car was able to avoid a collision but just barely.

QUESTION: What did you hear this other driver say?

ANSWER: He said, "If you weren't texting and driving, you would have noticed the firetruck sooner!"

QUESTION: What did you do after that?

ANSWER: I stayed to talk to the police officer. I'm retired, so I had nothing better to do, and I noticed that the driver who yelled about texting did not stay to talk to the police about what he saw.

Chapter Eight

4. State of Mind

The state of mind exception is one of the broadest exceptions to the hearsay rule. It allows the admission of statements concerning the declarant's then-existing state of mind, emotion, sensation, or physical condition (such as intent, plan, motive, design, mental feeling, pain, and bodily health). Examples include statements such as, "I feel sick," "I hate Ralph," or "Let's play a trick on the professor."

The foundation for this exception is that the statement must actually tend to prove the declarant's mental, emotional, or physical condition, which must be relevant to the case. This can best be demonstrated by the content and context of the statement itself. Apart from the content of the statement, there is no special foundation for the state of mind exception. However, the witness must still be able to describe when, where, and in front of whom the statement was made.

Let's say you represent the defendant in a criminal case who is charged with aggravated identity theft—that is, using the identity of another person to obtain something of value, knowing that the stolen identity belonged to a living person (as opposed to a deceased individual). Due to the nature of the charge, the state of mind of the defendant is inherently relevant to the case. Your client admits to using a stolen identity to purchase food for his family, but he swears he did not know the identity was stolen from a living person. You call as a witness a friend of the defendant who saw him in the store where the stolen identity was used to purchase groceries. Normally, statements by your client would not be admissible except when offered by the prosecution. However, in this instance, you will seek to admit your client's own statements as proof of his state of mind at the time of the offense.

QUESTION: Directing your attention to the early morning hours of August 7 last year, did you run into someone you know at that time?

ANSWER: Yes, I did. I ran into Jared Harris, a friend from high school.

QUESTION: Where did you see him?

ANSWER: In an aisle at Dominick's grocery store. He was filling a grocery cart with canned vegetables.

QUESTION: Did you speak to him?

ANSWER: I did. I said, "Hey man, I thought you just lost your job. How are you going to pay for all that?"

QUESTION: Did he say anything in response?

ANSWER: He did. He told me he found a credit card in the street after a horrible traffic accident and was using it to buy food to feed his family. I specifically remember him saying, "The poor driver who died can't buy groceries, so I figured I would!"

5. Dying Declaration

The hearsay exception for dying declarations requires two elements: 1) that the declarant made a statement while believing that their death was imminent; and 2) that the statement concerned what they believed to be the cause of their death. The declarant's belief that death was imminent can be established by surrounding circumstances, such as the nature of an illness or injury, or by the declarant's own words. The content of the statement will generally be sufficient to show that it related to the declarant's belief of the cause of death.

Let's say a murder victim is brought in to an emergency room and makes a dying declaration to one of the nurses treating him. The foundation for seeking to admit the statement at the trial of the person charged with the murder might go as follows:

QUESTION: Were you working the midnight shift at the hospital on the night of February 14 last year?

ANSWER: I was. That was a Friday night, and I always work Friday nights.

QUESTION: Do you recall a particular patient who came into the emergency room that night?

ANSWER: I do. I remember a man by the name of Mr. Love came in. I realized after the fact that it was ironic that a man with that last name was shot and killed on Valentine's Day.

QUESTION: What were Mr. Love's injuries upon his arrival at the ER?

ANSWER: He had suffered a gunshot wound to the back—the bullet just missed his heart.

QUESTION: Was he still breathing?

ANSWER: He was, but just barely.

QUESTION: Did you talk to him?

ANSWER: I did. As we were wheeling him into the operating room I put my head close to his and asked, "Mr. Love, who did this to you?" He told me it was his "woman" who shot him. His final words were, "I guess I should have treated her better." He died a few hours later in surgery. The blood loss was just too much for his heart to take.

The Basics
FOUNDATIONS FOR TESTIMONIAL EVIDENCE

Personal Knowledge:	Testimony by all witnesses (except expert witnesses) must be shown to be based on personal knowledge.

Chapter Eight

The Basics	
FOUNDATIONS FOR TESTIMONIAL EVIDENCE	
Conversations:	Testimony about conversations must include when and where the conversation took place, a listing of the parties present, and (in the case of telephone conversations) how the other person's voice was authenticated.
Prior Identification:	Testimony about a prior identification must include the circumstances under which that identification was originally made.
Habit and Routine:	Testimony about another's habit or routine practice must be shown to be based on personal knowledge of a consistently repeated activity.
Character and Reputation:	Testimony about another's character or reputation must be shown to be used for an admissible purpose and must include the specifics of how that information was learned and why it is reliable.
Hearsay:	Testimony of an out-of-court statement that is used to prove the truth of the matter asserted must be shown to be nonhearsay or to fit into an exception to the hearsay rule.

III. Exhibits Generally

A. The Role of Exhibits

Exhibits are the tangible objects, documents, photographs, and other items that are offered for the factfinder's consideration. Spoken testimony typically presents the trier of fact with a recitation of the witness's memories and perceptions. As effective as testimony might be, it remains a secondhand account that is, at best, once removed from the factfinder's own experiences. Exhibits, on the other hand, allow the jurors to use their own senses and perceptions. It is one thing to hear somebody describe, for example, the texture of a piece of cloth; it is far more striking to actually run your hand over the material. Direct experiences are infinitely more informative than listening to another person's description. Having touched the cloth, you will remember it better, you will appreciate more of its nuances and details, and you will be much less likely to change your mind about it in the future.

At trial, exhibits enhance or supplement the testimony of the witnesses. Exhibits can make information clearer, more concrete, more understandable, and more reliable. The sections immediately following will discuss the general procedures for the introduction of exhibits.

B.   Types of Exhibits

While the categories tend to overlap and the lines cannot be drawn with precision, exhibits generally fall into these three categories: 1) real or tangible evidence; 2) demonstrative evidence; and 3) documentary evidence.

1.   Real or Tangible Evidence

Real evidence generally refers to tangible objects that played an actual role in the events at issue in the trial. The murder weapon, for example, is often introduced in homicide trials. Real evidence is also used in all categories of civil cases. In personal injury cases, it is common for plaintiff's counsel to introduce objects that allegedly caused or contributed to the injury. Photographs, while obviously different from tangible objects, are so close to reality that they are also often treated as real evidence.

2.   Demonstrative Evidence

Demonstrative evidence consists of exhibits that did not play an actual role in the events underlying the case but instead illustrate or clarify a witness's testimony. As we explained in Chapter Four, Section II(B), demonstrative evidence can take the form of models, graphs, diagrams, charts, drawings, or any other objects that can explain or illustrate issues in the case.

A familiar form of demonstrative evidence is the simple intersection diagram on which a witness can indicate the locations of the automobiles involved in an accident. The intersection itself, not the diagram, would constitute real evidence of the configuration of the streets. The diagram, however, demonstrates the relative positions of the cars, traffic signals, and witnesses. It is easy to see why demonstrative evidence can be superior to real evidence—the intersection cannot be transported into the courtroom.

In mock trials, the author of the case sometimes develops demonstrative evidence and includes it along with the real and documentary evidence provided in the case file. Unless prohibited by your mock trial rules, feel free to create demonstrative evidence.

3.   Documentary Evidence

Documentary evidence refers to virtually all writings, including letters, statements, contracts, leases, memoranda, reports, ledgers, printouts, and business records. Written documents, almost by definition, contain out-of-court statements,

Chapter Eight

and they are typically offered because their contents are relevant to the case. Thus, most documents face hearsay hurdles that real and demonstrative exhibits do not; tangible objects are admitted into evidence because of what they *are,* whereas documentary exhibits are admitted because of what they *say*.

The value of documentary evidence cannot be overstated. It has the power to document past events, which is often the best proof possible. Imagine a criminal case in which the defendant has raised an alibi defense, claiming that on the day of the crime they were visiting relatives in a distant city. The testimony of the defendant and their family is relevant and admissible to establish the alibi, but it will be subject to vigorous attack on cross-examination. A signed hotel receipt for the date in question stands to be far more persuasive than any witness in proving the defendant's whereabouts.

C.   *Offering Exhibits at Trial*

Whether they consist of real, demonstrative, or documentary evidence, there is one basic protocol for offering exhibits at trial. Although the details vary somewhat depending on the mock trial competition in which you are participating, the following steps form a nearly universal procedure.

1.   Mark the Exhibit for Identification

Mark every exhibit for identification before offering it into evidence or even referring to it in the course of a trial. Marking the exhibit identifies it for the record so that it will be uniquely and immediately recognizable to everyone at trial.

In some mock trial competitions, all the exhibits are premarked in the case file itself without regard to which party will use them or in what order. In other competitions, the exhibits are not premarked and you will be responsible for their identification. In these competitions, exhibits are typically marked sequentially as they are introduced into evidence and further identified according to the designation of the party who has first offered them. Thus, the exhibits in a two-party trial will be called Plaintiff's Exhibit 1, Plaintiff's Exhibit 2, Defendant's Exhibit A, Defendant's Exhibit B, and so forth. It is often helpful for one side to use numbers for their exhibits, while the other side uses letters. Hence, Plaintiff's Exhibit 1 and Defendant's Exhibit A. What marking system you use is unimportant so long as it produces a clear and understandable indication of which exhibit is which.

To mark your exhibits for identification, write the number or letter on one corner of the exhibit. It does not matter which corner you choose, so long as you are consistent with all of your exhibits. The term "marked for identification" means that the exhibit has been marked and can be referred to in court but has not yet been admitted into evidence. Exhibits that have been marked for identification may be shown to witnesses and may be the subject of limited examinations for the purpose of establishing a foundation, but they usually may not be shown to the factfinder.

2. Identify the Exhibit for Opposing Counsel

Identify exhibits for opposing counsel before showing them to a witness or the trier of fact at trial. This may be done by handing or displaying the exhibit to opposing counsel and announcing the exhibit number as follows:

> COUNSEL: I'm going to show the witness what has been marked as Plaintiff's Exhibit 11 for identification.

This common courtesy allows opposing counsel to confirm that the exhibit has not been altered in any way. Opposing counsel is also afforded an opportunity to make an early objection to the use of the exhibit.

Having identified the exhibit, you may now proceed to lay the foundation for its admission.

3. Show the Exhibit to the Witness

Request permission to approach the witness before handing the witness an exhibit. Once you obtain the judge's permission, approach the witness and announce for the record what you are doing, using a shorthand description of the exhibit as well as its identification number. The process should proceed as follows:

> COUNSEL: Your Honor, may I approach the witness?
> JUDGE: Yes, you may.
> COUNSEL: Ms. Strawn, I am handing you Plaintiff's Exhibit 11, a one-page, one-sided document.

If yours is a jury trial, also give a copy of the exhibit to the presiding judge.

4. Have the Witness Identify the Exhibit

The next step is to have the witness identify the exhibit. The witness should state the basis for their familiarity with the exhibit and then describe it in some detail. For example:

> QUESTION: Have you ever seen Plaintiff's Exhibit 11 before, Ms. Wuletich?
> ANSWER: Yes, I have seen it many times.
> QUESTION: What is Plaintiff's Exhibit 11?
> ANSWER: It is a piece of the stationery I received when my order was delivered from Quickset Printing.
> QUESTION: How is it that you recognize it?
> ANSWER: I remember how it looked when I took it out of the box.

Numerous variations are possible once the witness has examined the exhibit: "Are you familiar with the exhibit?" "Do you recognize the exhibit?" "Are you

Chapter Eight

able to identify the exhibit?" While it is technically necessary to initially establish that the witness has a basis for giving a description, it is often possible to elicit the description first by asking, "What is it?" followed by, "How do you know?"

5. Complete the Foundation for the Exhibit

In some situations, particularly those involving real evidence, the identification of the exhibit will provide a sufficient foundation for admission. In other circumstances, the foundation will be much more elaborate, perhaps calling for the establishment of a chain of custody or an applicable hearsay exception. These and other foundations for the introduction of real, demonstrative, and documentary evidence are discussed at length later in this chapter.

6. Offer the Exhibit into Evidence

Once you complete the foundation, offer the exhibit into evidence. There are several ways in which this may be done, some more formal than others. In the simplest version:

> COUNSEL: Your Honor, we offer Exhibit 11 into evidence.

Or, for a more formal presentation:

> COUNSEL: Your Honor, we move that the identifying mark be stricken and that Plaintiff's Exhibit 11 be received in evidence.

In any case, the judge will then ask opposing counsel if there are any objections to its admission. The process for arguing objections will be discussed in Chapter Thirteen. At this point it is sufficient to note that objecting counsel is entitled to request a limited cross-examination of the witness (called "voir dire"), which will be restricted to the subject of the admissibility of the exhibit. Following any objections or voir dire by opposing counsel, the judge will rule on the admissibility of the exhibit.

7. Publish and Use the Exhibit

Once the court receives an exhibit, it can be published to the factfinder and used as a basis for further testimony.

a. *Publishing an Exhibit*

To "publish" an exhibit is to communicate its contents to the factfinder. Exhibits may be published in a variety of ways. Diagrams or models are usually displayed in front of the trier of fact. Smaller objects typically are handed to the jurors and passed among them. Documents can be enlarged and displayed, passed among the jurors, or read aloud. The choice of publication method is customarily left to counsel, although the court may deny leave to use overly dramatic, prejudicial, or dangerous means. Persuasive uses of exhibits will be discussed in greater detail later, as will effective methods of publication.

If yours is a bench trial, simply hand a copy of the exhibit to the judge once it has been admitted. In jury trials, however, it is necessary to obtain the judge's permission to publish an exhibit to the jury.

> COUNSEL: Your Honor, permission to publish Defendant's Exhibit F to the jury?

Or,

> COUNSEL: May I have leave to publish Plaintiff's Exhibit 3 by passing it among the jurors, Judge?

Or,

> COUNSEL: Your Honor, may the witness read Prosecution Exhibit 9 to the jurors?

b. Using an Exhibit

Once your exhibit has been admitted in evidence, use it to illustrate or amplify a witness's testimony.

Use tangible objects in demonstrations. Have your witness show how a gun was aimed or how a tool was used. Use maps, diagrams, and photographs to illustrate the movement of persons and vehicles, the locations of incidents, or the relationship and distances between stationary objects. Your witness can mark directly on an exhibit if doing so will help explain their testimony and not impermissibly deface or change the exhibit. (If marking on an exhibit will change it but would still be helpful to your case, make a copy of the exhibit, marking it as a variation of the original [e.g., "Exhibit 10B" where the original was "Exhibit 10"], have the witness mark on it, and then move that exhibit into evidence as well.)

In a real trial, a court reporter writes down everything that is said in court. Although mock trials are not transcribed by court reporters, a mock trial is intended to allow participants to demonstrate that they are capable of trying a real case. So, demonstrate that you understand that the written record (regardless of whether one is actually being made) must accurately reflect what took place during trial. For example, if you have an exhibit that is a diagram of a parking lot and your witness uses a finger on the diagram to point out the direction of travel of a vehicle during their testimony, say something like, "Let the record show that the witness just used their index finger to trace the direction of travel of the defendant's vehicle from the top of the diagram outside the grocery store to the southeast exit on the bottom right-hand corner of the exhibit." The court will usually respond to your request by saying something like "The record will so reflect."

Chapter Eight

In addition to publishing the exhibit to the finder of fact and engaging in demonstrations, a witness's testimony can interpret or otherwise explain the significance of any exhibit that has been admitted in evidence.

> QUESTION: Why was the color of the stationery, Plaintiff's Exhibit 1, so important to you?

Or,

> QUESTION: What did you do once you received Plaintiff's Exhibit 12?

Or,

> QUESTION: What was your reaction when you saw Ms. Collins holding Defendant's Exhibit D?

Also be aware that once an exhibit has been admitted it may be used, subject to the rules of evidence, in the examination of any witness—not just the witness who introduced it.

The Basics
OFFERING AN EXHIBIT AT TRIAL

STEP	EXAMPLE
Mark the exhibit for identification:	• Prosecution Exhibit 10.
Identify the exhibit for opposing counsel:	• (To counsel) I'm going to show the witness what has been marked Prosecution Exhibit 10.
Show the exhibit to the witness:	• (To judge) Your Honor, may I approach the witness? • (To witness) Detective Duncan, I'm handing you what has been marked as Prosecution Exhibit 10.
Ask the witness to identify the exhibit:	• (To witness) Please tell the jury what that is. • How do you know that is the knife found at the defendant's home? • Why do you put your initials on items recovered from crime scenes? • On what day was this knife found?

The Basics	
OFFERING AN EXHIBIT AT TRIAL	
STEP	**EXAMPLE**
Complete the foundation:	• Please tell the jury exactly what you did with the knife after you found it. • Did anyone else have access to the evidence locker at the police station? • Who brought the knife to court today?
Offer the exhibit into evidence:	• (To judge) The People move the admission of Exhibit 10 into evidence.
Publish the exhibit and use it in the witness's testimony:	• (To witness) Detective, please describe how this knife looked on the day you found it. • Where was the knife within the defendant's home? • Did you ask the defendant about the knife? • What was his response? • (To judge) Your Honor, may we have permission to publish the knife by displaying it to the jurors?

IV. Specific Foundations for Exhibits

The remaining portion of this chapter will discuss the specific foundations required for various types of real, demonstrative, and documentary evidence. For the sake of brevity, these examples are limited to the necessary evidentiary foundations and do not include all of the steps described in the previous section for offering exhibits. You should assume that, in each example, the sponsoring attorney will follow the general procedure outlined above for offering exhibits.

A. Real Evidence/Tangible Objects

Real evidence must be shown to be relevant and authentic. Did the object actually play a role in the facts of the case? Does it tend to prove (or disprove) some issue in contention? Is the object in court really the one that we are talking about? If these conditions are met, the evidence will usually be admitted unless it is unduly prejudicial.

Chapter Eight

The relevance of real evidence is typically established by the context of the case and often requires no additional attention when it comes to laying foundation. Authenticity, on the other hand, must always be carefully established, as it is the fact of authenticity that qualifies the exhibit as real evidence. In Section I(B)(2), above, we discussed the fact that most mock trial case files include a stipulation that all of the documentary evidence included therein is authentic. Nonetheless, for the reasons we explained, we recommend that whenever possible, you establish the authenticity of evidence used during a mock trial.

1. Establishing Authenticity

You can establish the authenticity of real evidence through the testimony of a witness who is able to recognize the item in question. Many objects can be identified by virtue of their unique features. Others may have been given some identifying mark in anticipation of litigation. In either case, the witness must testify that they were familiar with the object at the time of the underlying events, and that the witness is able to recognize the exhibit in court as that very same object.

In the following example, the plaintiff in a property damage case will be asked to lay the foundation for an item of personal property:

QUESTION: Do you recognize Plaintiff's Exhibit 1?
ANSWER: Yes, it is an oil painting that was left to me by my grandmother.
QUESTION: How is it that you can recognize it?
ANSWER: Until the fire, it hung over our mantel and I used to look at it almost every day.
QUESTION: Was it in your house at the time of the fire?
ANSWER: Yes, it was. It was one of the first things that I tried to salvage after we were allowed back into the house.
QUESTION: Is Plaintiff's Exhibit 1 in substantially the same condition as it was when you removed it from your house after the fire?
ANSWER: Yes, it is.

This testimony is sufficient to establish the authenticity of the oil painting. The final question regarding the condition of the exhibit is necessary because the damaged painting is being offered to show the destruction caused by the fire. While an oil painting is likely to be unique and easily recognizable, other exhibits are harder to identify specifically. Police officers and others who are familiar with litigation often solve this problem by placing identifying marks on tangible objects. In the following example, a police officer will lay the foundation for a child's safety seat that was found at the scene of an automobile collision:

QUESTION:	Officer, I'm handing you what has been marked as Defendant's Exhibit F. What is that?
ANSWER:	It is the child safety seat I removed from the plaintiff's automobile on the day of the accident.
QUESTION:	How do you know that Defendant's Exhibit F is the same seat?
ANSWER:	Because when I removed it from the plaintiff's car, I wrote my initials and the date on the back of the seat.
QUESTION:	Do you recognize your initials on that seat now?
ANSWER:	Yes, they are right here (pointing).
QUESTION:	(To judge) Let the record show that the witness is pointing to the back of Defendant's Exhibit F.

The above foundation is sufficient to admit the car seat, so long as the exhibit is being offered only to prove the presence of the child seat in the plaintiff's automobile. If the condition of the car seat were in issue (as with the damaged oil painting above), it would also be necessary to ask whether the seat is in "the same or substantially the same condition" as when it was retrieved.

In both the oil painting and the car seat examples, it was unnecessary for the witness to account for the whereabouts of the exhibit between the incident and the trial. This is because the witnesses were able to supply all of the information necessary to authenticate the exhibits. In other circumstances, however, the foundation will need to include a "chain of custody" for a particular exhibit.

2. Showing the Chain of Custody

A chain of custody establishes the location, handling, and care of an object between the time of its recovery and the time of trial. A chain of custody must be shown whenever an exhibit is not uniquely recognizable and was not specially marked as in the example above, or when an exhibit's physical properties are in issue.

Establishing an object's chain of custody can be necessary when a witness is not likely to recognize the relevant object with any certainty, when the exhibit has been subjected to testing or analysis, when aspects of its condition or composition are at issue in the case, and/or when there is a plausible claim of tampering. In each of these instances, the chain of custody negates the possibility that the object was mishandled, tampered with, or altered.

A chain of custody must, at a minimum, be sufficient to show that the object in the courtroom is the same one that was involved in the events being considered at trial. This can usually be accomplished by tracing the possession of the item as it passed from hand to hand. In some situations, it is also necessary to show that the object was stored during the intervening period (between the event at issue and the trial)

Chapter Eight

in a manner that was secure from tampering. In either case, it may be necessary to call more than one witness in order to complete the chain.

In the following example, an automobile mechanic was injured when a tire exploded as it was being mounted. The tire manufacturer has been sued, and the defective tire will be offered solely to show that it was manufactured by the defendant. The first witness is the garage manager.

QUESTION: Where were you when the plaintiff was injured?
ANSWER: I was standing about thirty feet away when I heard the noise of a loud explosion.
QUESTION: What did you do?
ANSWER: I ran over to where the plaintiff was lying on the ground. The plaintiff was covered with blood, and there was a ragged tire lying right next to them.
QUESTION: Were there any other tires nearby?
ANSWER: No, that was the only one.
QUESTION: Did you do anything with the tire?
ANSWER: Yes. I picked it up and put it in my office.
QUESTION: Were there any other tires in your office at the time?
ANSWER: No.
QUESTION: Did you ever do anything else with the tire that you found next to the plaintiff?
ANSWER: Yes. About a week later, a company superintendent came to investigate the injury. She asked to take the tire, and I gave it to her.
QUESTION: Had the tire been in your office the entire time between the injury to the plaintiff and the time that you gave it to the company superintendent?
ANSWER: Yes.

The garage manager has completed the first part of the chain. Note that the tire has not yet been produced in court. The next witness is the company superintendent.

QUESTION: Did you obtain a tire in the course of your investigation of this injury?
ANSWER: Yes. I went to speak to the garage manager about two weeks after the incident, and he gave me a tire that he had kept in his office.
QUESTION: What did you do with that tire?
ANSWER: I brought it back to company headquarters and placed it in my office.
QUESTION: Did the tire that you got from the garage manager ever leave your office?

ANSWER: Yes, I brought it with me to court today.
QUESTION: Showing you Plaintiff's Exhibit 1, is this the same tire that you obtained from the garage manager and that you brought with you to court today?
ANSWER: Yes, it is.

The chain of custody is now sufficient to establish the identity of the tire. Even though the company superintendent did not witness the accident or initially recover the tire, there is enough evidence to show the continuity of possession. Since in this example the tire is being offered only to prove who manufactured it, physical properties are not in issue. It is therefore unnecessary to show that the tire was kept under lock and key during the intervening period.

B. Photographs

Photographs bridge the gap between real and demonstrative evidence. While a visual recording of any sort is, strictly speaking, an illustration of a past event, its capacity to portray a scene with accuracy is so great that many courts treat photographs as real evidence.

The basic foundation for the admission of a still photograph is that it "fairly and accurately" portrays the scene shown. It is generally possible to introduce a photograph through the testimony of any witness who is familiar with the scene as it appeared at a relevant time. In the following example, the witness is the owner of a home that was destroyed by fire. A photograph of the house will be offered as evidence of damages.

QUESTION: Are you the owner of the house located at 4604 Desert Drive?
ANSWER: Yes.
QUESTION: How long did you live there?
ANSWER: About eight years, until the fire.
QUESTION: So, of course, you are familiar with the appearance of your home before the fire.
ANSWER: Yes, certainly.
QUESTION: Does Plaintiff's Exhibit 11 fairly and accurately show your home at 4604 Desert Drive as it appeared on the day before the fire?
ANSWER: Yes, it does.

C. Demonstrative Evidence

As we have discussed previously, demonstrative evidence illustrates, clarifies, or explains other testimony or real evidence.

Chapter Eight

1. Maps, Charts, and Diagrams

The foundation for a map, chart, blueprint, or other diagram is essentially the same as that for a photograph. The witness must be familiar with the scene, location, or structure as it appeared at a relevant time and must testify that the exhibit constitutes a fair representation of that scene, location, or structure. Additional foundation is necessary if the exhibit is drawn to scale. If the witness prepared the exhibit, they should also testify to the manner in which they prepared it and the steps they took to ensure its accuracy.

> QUESTION: What is Government Exhibit 4, Special Agent Chicantek?
>
> ANSWER: It is a diagram of the defendant's residence.
>
> QUESTION: Who created it?
>
> ANSWER: I did, based on my observations the day the search warrant was executed.
>
> QUESTION: Is it to scale?
>
> ANSWER: It is, roughly. I took some measurements that day and used them to create the diagram. The rooms are to scale. I did not measure the yard sizes, so those areas may not be to scale.
>
> QUESTION: Does this diagram fairly and accurately represent the layout of the rooms in the defendant's residence on the day you searched his house for firearms?
>
> ANSWER: It does.

2. Illustrative Aids

Exhibits that are insufficiently accurate to be allowed into evidence may often still be used for illustrative purposes. The foundation includes a witness's testimony that the exhibit will assist in explaining their testimony, as well as a general explanation or description of the inaccuracy of the exhibit. In the following example, the witness has produced a freehand drawing of an intersection:

> QUESTION: What is Plaintiff's Exhibit 5?
>
> ANSWER: It is a drawing of the intersection of Craycroft and Alta Vista.
>
> QUESTION: Did you make that drawing yourself?
>
> ANSWER: Yes, I did.
>
> QUESTION: Does Plaintiff's Exhibit 5 generally show the configuration of the streets at Craycroft and Alta Vista as they appeared on the date of the accident?
>
> ANSWER: Yes, it shows the location of the streets and traffic signs.
>
> QUESTION: Is Plaintiff's Exhibit 5 drawn to scale?

ANSWER:	It is the best I could do, but it is not drawn to scale.
QUESTION:	Would Plaintiff's Exhibit 5 still help you to explain your testimony about the accident?
ANSWER:	Yes, it would.

The above foundation is sufficient to allow the witness to use the diagram in the course of their testimony.

D. Documentary Evidence

In addition to the usual issue of relevance, the foundation for a document typically includes two other elements.

1. Authentication

Authenticating documents typically requires proof of authorship or origin and may also call for proof of transmission or receipt. The existence of a lease, for example, may not be probative unless it can be shown to bear the signatures of the contending parties. Thus, unlike tangible objects, the foundation for documentary evidence may include more than simple recognition.

On the other hand, it is unusual for the physical condition or safekeeping of a document to be in issue. Chain of custody, therefore, is seldom a component of the foundation for documentary evidence, although it may be required if the paper has been subjected to testing or if the writing appears to have been altered or amended.

a. *Handwriting and Signature*

You can authenticate the signature or other handwriting on a document through a variety of means. A witness may recognize a signature based on past observation or may authenticate it on the basis of circumstantial evidence. Other possibilities include expert testimony and in-court comparison by the trier of fact.

A witness may always authenticate their own handwriting or signature. A witness may also authenticate the handwriting of another if sufficient familiarity can be shown.

QUESTION:	Please examine Defendant's Exhibit 2 and tell me if you recognize the signature at the bottom of the page.
ANSWER:	Yes, I do recognize the signature.
QUESTION:	Whose signature is it?
ANSWER:	It is Meredith Edwards's signature.
QUESTION:	How are you able to recognize it?
ANSWER:	I have seen Meredith sign her name many times, and I recognize the handwriting as hers.

Chapter Eight

It is not necessary, however, for the witness actually to have seen the person sign their name before. Circumstantial evidence can also support the required degree of familiarity.

> QUESTION: How is it that you are able to recognize Meredith Edwards's signature?
>
> ANSWER: We have corresponded over the years, and it is the same signature that I have seen on her letters.
>
> QUESTION: How do you know that those letters came from Ms. Edwards?
>
> ANSWER: Because her name and address were on the envelope as the sender and she would usually answer questions in her letters that I had written to her in my letters.

Note that extended correspondence is not required. A nonexpert witness can identify a signature on the basis of a single past event or sample so long as familiarity was not acquired for the purpose of testifying at trial.

b. *Circumstantial Evidence of Authorship or Origin*

Many documents are printed or typewritten and do not contain signatures or other handwriting. Unless such a document is somehow uniquely marked, it will need to be authenticated via circumstantial evidence. Such evidence can be in the form of a letterhead, seal, or stamp, or it can be provided by the context of the case.

> QUESTION: Do you recognize Defendant's Exhibit 6?
>
> ANSWER: Yes, it is a price list that I received from Quickset Printing.
>
> QUESTION: How do you know that Defendant's Exhibit 6 came from Quickset Printing?
>
> ANSWER: Well, it is on stationery that says Quickset Printing at the top of the page.
>
> QUESTION: Is there any other reason that you know that Defendant's Exhibit 6 came from Quickset Printing?
>
> ANSWER: Yes. I called the telephone number listed for Quickset online, and I asked the person who answered the phone to send me a price list. This price list arrived in the mail two days later.

The above foundation is more than sufficient to authenticate the document. Note that, even if the document is shown to be authentic, the opposing party may still contest its admissibility. Authentication is a threshold question, and it is not dispositive of admissibility.

c. Mailing or Transmission

The admissibility of a document will often depend upon its receipt by, or at least transmission to, another party. This is an authenticity issue since the document is made admissible only by its status as one that was actually or constructively received. In other words, proof of mailing authenticates the document as truly having been sent to the other party.

Mailing can be proven either directly or through evidence of a routine business practice. Direct proof of mailing can be given in a single sentence: "I placed the document in an envelope with the correct address, and I deposited it in the United States mail with sufficient postage."

The basic foundation for proof of transmission is the same no matter what mode of communication is utilized. A witness may provide direct proof of transmission ("I put it in Google Docs, and I had the program send a notification," or "I hit 'send' in my email program.") or may testify as to the organization's practice for handling outgoing documents.

E. Hearsay Exceptions

The offer of a document inevitably sets the hearsay bell ringing in opposing counsel's mind. While writings may be admissible for nonhearsay purposes, such as proof of notice or acceptance, they are frequently submitted into evidence precisely to prove that their contents are true. Various exceptions are available to allow for the use of such documents, each requiring its own foundation. The more common exceptions are discussed in the following sections.

1. Business Records

Business records can include ledgers, accounts, calendar entries, memoranda, notices, reports, statements, computer printouts, summaries of records or events, and similar writings of a company. All of these documents constitute hearsay if they are offered to prove that their contents are true. Thus, the entries in a loan company's account book would be hearsay if submitted as proof that a certain loan was not repaid in time.

The business records exception to the hearsay rule allows for the admission of most such records, so long as they can be shown to meet certain requirements. Under most mock trial competition rules, the records of any regularly conducted activity are admissible if they were made by a person with knowledge as part of a regular business practice and they were kept in the course of that regularly conducted business activity.

It is not uncommon to use the approximate words of the evidentiary rule in order to lay a foundation for the exception. Judges are accustomed to hearing the foundation's magic words, and objections are less likely to be made or sustained when you use them too.

> QUESTION: Ms. Strawn, are you employed by the Quickset Printing Company?
> ANSWER: Yes, I am the accountant and bookkeeper.
> QUESTION: Do you recognize Plaintiff's Exhibit 3?
> ANSWER: Yes I do. It is our ledger book.
> QUESTION: What is the function of your ledger book?
> ANSWER: We use it to record all of our credit sales and all of the payments that we receive.
> QUESTION: Are the entries in Plaintiff's Exhibit 3 made at or near the time of the sales or payments?
> ANSWER: Yes.
> QUESTION: Are the entries made by or transmitted from a person with knowledge of the sales and payments?
> ANSWER: Yes.
> QUESTION: Are those entries made as a part of the regular business practice of Quickset Printing?
> ANSWER: Yes.
> QUESTION: Is the ledger book, Plaintiff's Exhibit 3, kept in the regular course of business?
> ANSWER: Yes, it is.

The foundation for the exception is now complete.

The basic foundation for the business records exception can be expanded upon as circumstances dictate. In dealing with records that are more complex, intricate, questionable, or exotic than ledger books, it is often desirable to have the witness spend more time explaining their use and reliability.

2. Public Records

There is also a hearsay exception for public records, statistics, and reports. Such records are generally admissible if they were made by a public office or agency and they set forth the activities of the office or agency; or matters observed pursuant to a duty imposed by law; or in limited circumstances, certain investigative findings; or officially required records of vital statistics.

Because most government records are "self-authenticating," it is not usually necessary to call a witness to testify to their authenticity.

Two limits may be placed on the use of this hearsay exception in criminal cases. First, matters observed by police officers and other law enforcement personnel do not qualify for the exception, even if contained in a report made pursuant to a duty imposed by law. Second, investigative findings are admissible in criminal cases only if offered against the government. Read your mock trial rules carefully to see if either of these exceptions apply to your case.

3. **Party Admissions**

The party admission exception applies to documents as well as to oral statements. A party admission can be contained in a letter, report, memorandum, journal, progress chart, or virtually any other form of writing. Once the exhibit has been authenticated, the only remaining foundation is that it was made or adopted by a party against whom it is being offered or by an agent, servant, or employee of such a party.

An example of an exhibit that contains a party admission that would be admissible at trial is a letter written by a defendant in a criminal case from jail apologizing to the victim of their crime; such a letter would be admissible if offered by the prosecution, but would not be admissible if offered by the defense.

The Basics	
SPECIFIC FOUNDATIONS FOR REAL, DEMONSTRATIVE, AND DOCUMENTARY EVIDENCE	
Tangible Objects:	Tangible objects must be shown to be what the proponent claims them to be.
Chain of Custody:	Chain of custody must be established when 1) the exhibit is not readily identifiable, 2) the specific condition of the object is at issue, or 3) there has been a possibility of tampering.
Photographs:	Photographs must be shown to fairly and accurately represent their subject matter.
Demonstrative Evidence:	Demonstrative evidence must be shown to be helpful in the illustration, clarification, or explanation of the testimony or real evidence offered at trial.
Documentary Evidence:	Documentary evidence must be shown to be what the proponent claims it to be and admissible under the hearsay rule and its exceptions.

Chapter Nine

Cross-Examination

I. The Purpose of Cross-Examination

Cross-examination is the ultimate challenge for a trial lawyer. It is frequently dramatic, often exciting, and in many ways it defines our adversarial system of justice. Although a poor direct examination can be aimless and boring, the worst thing you can do is leave something out and at least you know that the witness will try to be helpful. A poor cross-examination, on the other hand, can be truly disastrous; the witnesses can range from uncooperative to hostile, and you constantly run the risk of adding weight or sympathy to the other side's case. Moreover, most cross-examinations will inevitably be perceived as a contest between the lawyer and witness. You can seldom afford to appear to lose, especially in mock trial competitions.

In other words, cross-examination is inherently risky. The witness may argue with you. The witness may fill in gaps that were left in the direct testimony. The witness may make you look bad. You may make yourself look bad. And whatever good you accomplish may be subject to immediate cure on redirect examination. None of these problems can be avoided entirely, but they can be minimized by conducting careful cross-examinations and setting realistic goals.

To begin, cross-examination should be undertaken only to serve some greater purpose within your theory of the case. Thus, it must tell your client's story even though it is being elicited from opposing witnesses. A useful cross-examination should fulfill at least one of the following objectives.

A. Repair or Minimize Damage Done on Direct

If a witness's direct examination hurts your case, look to cross-examination as your opportunity to rectify or minimize that damage whenever possible. Ask yourself whether the witness can be made to retract or back away from their testimony or whether additional facts can be elicited that will minimize its impact. If so, demonstrate the witness's lack of certainty, confidence, or opportunity to observe, or highlight the internal inconsistencies or inherent implausibility of their testimony, or show that this testimony conflicts with the testimony of other, more credible witnesses.

Chapter Nine

B. Enhance Your Case

Opposing witnesses may also be able to provide positive facts that support or contribute to your version of the events. This is especially true in mock trials, where facts helpful to each side are typically included in every witness's statement or affidavit. This helpful information can and should be brought out during your cross-examination. Your challenge is figuring out the most effective way to elicit the information.

C. Detract from Your Opponent's Case

There are also times when an opposing witness can establish facts that are detrimental to your opponent's case. Mock trial case file drafters often include several such "nuggets" of information to keep things challenging and interesting. This information, which is likely to be left out of the direct examination, should be elicited during cross-examination to create inconsistency among the other side's witnesses.

D. Lay the Foundation for Introducing Exhibits

This objective is particularly important in mock trials, which prohibit recalling adverse witnesses and, as a result, typically allow exhibits to be offered during cross-examination. (Real trials may prohibit this practice since each side may call or recall any witness.) Only introduce evidence during cross-examination, however, when an opposing witness is the only one able to lay the proper foundation for an exhibit. Admitting exhibits during cross-examination is difficult and should be avoided if possible.

E. Discredit the Witness or Another Witness

You can also use cross-examination to discredit the witness testifying by revealing their bias or interest in the outcome of the case; motivations to stretch, misrepresent, or fabricate testimony; and past instances of untruthfulness. You might also be able to use the witness to elicit discrediting information about other witnesses in the case.

F. Stay in Control

The essential technique of cross-examination is witness control. Since the object of cross-examination is to tell your client's story, make certain that you set the agenda for the examination, you determine the flow of information, and you require the witness to answer your questions. In short, always control the witness and the testimony. This does not mean, by the way, that you must be domineering, rude, or overbearing toward the witness. In this context, control means only that the examination follows the course you have selected and that the information elicited is only that which you have determined helpful.

With a cooperative witness, this may mean nothing more than asking the right questions and getting the right answers. Hostile, evasive, or argumentative witnesses require more assertive means. Because mock trials are competitions and in most cases the opposing team provides the witnesses you cross-examine, be prepared to employ assertive questioning to effectively cross-examine witnesses. (Note: Never prepare your own witnesses to be unreasonable or uncooperative during cross-examination. As we explain in Chapter Five, Section III(H), witnesses who appear reasonable and cooperative on direct but become unreasonable and uncooperative during cross are perceived as far less credible than their consistent counterparts. It is also just plain wrong.)

Following the basic rules of cross-examination is a good start toward achieving witness control.

II. The Rules of Cross-Examination

As with direct examinations, the rules of evidence used in your mock trial govern the content of your cross-examinations; in order to elicit testimony from an opposing witness, you must have a reasonable theory of admissibility for that evidence. Beyond admissibility, adhere to the rules below to stay in control during your cross-examination.

One rule that applies to cross-examinations in actual trials is not discussed at length here: the rule that every cross-examination must stay "within the scope" of the direct examination preceding it. Within the scope means that questions asked on cross must be about the same topics covered during the direct examination. There is an exception to this rule: questions that address the witness's bias or character are always allowed.

Understandably, the scope rule is largely abandoned in mock trials because there are strict time limits and witnesses cannot be recalled by either side. If you do face a "beyond the scope" objection in a mock trial, it is usually adequate to respond by saying, "Your Honor, due to the format of today's trial, I will not have the opportunity to recall this witness for questions on this subject. Therefore, I respectfully request the court's permission to ask these questions now." When a cross-examination is allowed to exceed the scope of direct, the court may require counsel to refrain from asking leading questions. For that reason, if you think it likely you will question a witness beyond the scope of their direct, be prepared to ask your questions in a nonleading manner.

Remember to stand in the center of the courtroom while cross-examining, if allowed, so that you can command the attention of everyone in the courtroom

Chapter Nine

and better control the opposing witness. Also, remember that relying on notes will harm your ability to make eye contact and to use movement for emphasis.

A. Ask Only Leading Questions

The cardinal rule of cross-examination is to ask only leading questions. As discussed in Chapter Seven, Section II(A), leading questions contain or suggest their own answers. Although generally prohibited during direct examination, leading questions are allowed during cross-examination because it is assumed that your adversary's witnesses will not cooperate with you. The right to ask leading questions is also usually understood to include the right to insist on receiving a responsive answer from the witness.

Cross-examination is no time to seek the witness's interpretation of the facts; rather, it is the time for you to tell a story by obtaining the witness's assent. A non-leading question invites the witness to wander away from your story, taking your control away as well. For example, you can control a witness this way:

> QUESTION: You were thirty feet away from plaintiff's car when you first applied your brakes, correct?

But you lose control when you ask:

> QUESTION: How far were you from the plaintiff's car when you applied your brakes?

How can you be sure to ask only leading questions? The answer is preparation. Read through your case file thoroughly until you are confident of what testimony the witness must provide. If you are unsure of where the witness applied their brakes, of course you will not tell them that it was thirty feet. So be sure. Read the witness's affidavit, scour the police report, and read the other witnesses' affidavits. Then, once you are certain that there is no plausible denial, tell the witness exactly what they did. Because your leading question is based upon a verifiable fact, the witness will have no choice but to agree with you.

B. Get In and Get Out

Brevity is an excellent discipline. Many trial lawyers suggest limiting cross-examinations to a maximum of three points. While circumstances may require departing from such a hard and fast rule, shorter cross-examinations have much to commend themselves. In terms of your own preparation, a mental limit for the length of the cross will concentrate and organize your thinking. Conducting a short examination will minimize risk, add panache, and usually make the result more memorable.

The length of your cross-examination will generally depend upon how many of the above goals you expect to be able to fulfill. It is not necessary, and it may not be possible, to achieve them all. You will often stand to lose more than you can gain by overreaching. Therefore, be selective.

C. Ask Only Questions to Which You Already Know the Answers

This rule seems simple enough. If you do not know how a witness will answer a question, do not ask it. Do not go on a "fishing expedition" during cross-examination. While practicing lawyers may have no choice but to violate this rule every now and then when their gut suggests they can or their professional obligations tell them they must, this is one principle that a mock trial participant must scrupulously follow. Resist every temptation to ask a witness any variation of a "how" or "why" question on cross. If you already know the explanation, you should use leading questions to tell it to the witness. If you do not already know the explanation, then asking for it on cross-examination is like sending an invitation to the witness to invent facts that will not help your case. Never give a witness the opportunity to explain during cross-examination.

Suppose you do refrain from asking the witness to explain and instead the witness asks you if they may explain. Again, resist the temptation; if a witness is volunteering an explanation, there is no chance the answer will help your case. The best way to handle this awkward situation is to politely decline to respond to the witness's question. For example:

QUESTION: So it takes you at least ten minutes to get from your garage to your office, right?

ANSWER: No, that is not right. I usually make it in three to five minutes. Would you like me to explain how?

QUESTION: Your lawyer can ask you to explain that. I have other questions I'd like to ask you instead.

Asking or allowing a witness to explain is the equivalent of saying, "I've grown tired of controlling this cross-examination. Why don't you take over for a while?"

D. Do Not Invite Objections or Argue with Witnesses

Objections can be distracting and unsettling. Young attorneys often lose their stride when interrupted by an objection during cross-examination. And objections are more common during cross-examination than any other phase of the trial. This is a logical phenomenon; of course the other side will want to prevent you from making strides at the expense of their witnesses. While they may not always be successful in stopping the attack, they are bound to try. Thus, although you cannot prevent opposing counsel from objecting during your cross, you can make doing so more challenging.

The easiest objections to raise during cross are to the form of the questions asked. For instance, assume that you represent the defendant in the firetruck case and the plaintiff's attorney asks the defendant on cross-examination, "You had an important meeting that morning that you didn't want to be late for, didn't you?" The easiest way for you to prevent this question from being answered is to object that it is compound. The question *is* compound and counsel should be forced to rephrase it. Now, put yourself in the plaintiff's attorney's shoes. If the question can be rephrased (by breaking it into two separate questions), what was gained by asking it the wrong way to begin with? Nothing.

By asking questions in proper form, you force opposing counsel to object to the substance of your questions, which is a much more challenging task.

1. Ask Short Questions

Cross-examination questions must be short in both execution and concept. If a question is more than fifteen words long, it is not short in execution. Shorten it. If a question contains more than one fact or assertion, it is not short in concept. Divide it.

Short, single-fact, propositional questions enable you to control witnesses during cross-examination. Long questions contain an almost limitless capacity to deprive a cross-examiner of witness control and to be easily forgotten or misunderstood. The more words you use, the greater chance a witness will become confused by them or refuse to adopt them all.

Divide areas of questioning into their smallest component parts. For example, assume that you are cross-examining the defendant in the firetruck case. You want to establish the distance from his parking garage to his office in order to show that he was in a hurry to get to his meeting that morning. You could ask one question: "Your parking garage is located three blocks from your office, isn't it?" If the witness says yes you will have achieved your purpose, but what will you do if the witness says no? You see, the defendant may decide that the distance is somewhere between two and three blocks, since his office building is not exactly on the corner, or he may quibble with you over whether you can call the parking lot "his" garage. You can head off such potential problems by asking incremental questions, such as these:

QUESTION: You have a monthly parking contract at the Garrick garage?

QUESTION: The Garrick garage is located at the northwest corner of Randolph and Dearborn?

QUESTION: Your office is located at 48 South Dearborn?

QUESTION: The shortest distance from the Garrick to your office is to go south on Dearborn, right?

QUESTION: First, you must cross Randolph?

QUESTION: Then you must cross Washington?

QUESTION: Then you must cross Madison?

QUESTION: And your office is farther south on that block, isn't it?

This technique allows you to do two things. First, it cuts off the escape route for a witness who is inclined to argue or prevaricate. The incremental questions provide small targets for a witness's inventiveness. More importantly, it lets you know early in the sequence whether the witness is likely to disagree with you.

2. Ask Fair Questions

Your right to lead the witness during cross-examination does not include a right to mislead the witness. It is objectionable to mischaracterize a witness's testimony. If a witness has testified that it was dark outside, it would mischaracterize the testimony to ask, "So you admit that it was too dark to see anything?"

Furthermore, you don't have to mischaracterize a witness's testimony in order to lose control during cross-examination; adding any sort of characterization to the witness's prior testimony may lead to the same dismal result. Assume that you are cross-examining the complaining witness in a robbery case. The witness testified on direct that the crime occurred at night on a seldom-traveled country road. Your defense is misidentification. Wishing to take advantage of the time and place of the events, you ask, "It was too dark to see very well, wasn't it?" You have just asked the witness to agree with your characterization of the lighting conditions. The witness, being nobody's fool, answers, "I could see just fine."

Instead, ask the witness about the facts that led you to the characterization: the sun had gone down, the moon was not out that night, there were no street lamps, there were no house lights, and there were no illuminated signs. Save the characterization that it was too dark to see well for final argument—when the witness may no longer refute it.

In addition to avoiding questions that mischaracterize answers, you also risk objections if you ask cumulative, vague, and argumentative questions during your cross-examination. Cumulative, or "asked and answered," questions are objectionable because they cover the same ground twice (or more). Vague questions are objectionable because answers to them are also vague. Questions are argumentative when they insist the witness agree with a conclusion or characterization, rather than a statement of fact.

E. Do Not Ask the Ultimate Question

You will be tempted to confront an adverse witness with one last conclusory question: "So, you just ignored the firetruck, didn't you?" Resist this temptation. If you have already established all of the incremental facts that lead to your conclusion, then you have little to gain by making the question explicit. At best, you repeat what has become obvious, and at worst, you give the witness an opportunity to recant or amend the foundational testimony.

Even worse, you may not have established the incremental facts as fully as you thought. Under these circumstances, the witness will not only disagree with your ultimate proposition, but will explain exactly why you are wrong.

Chapter Nine

Elicit all the facts that lead to the ultimate conclusion. Then stop. Save the final proposition for final argument. When you save the ultimate point for final argument, the witness cannot change or add to the testimony. To a certain extent, you also avoid informing opposing counsel of your argument, thereby diminishing the likelihood of having your position refuted either on redirect or through another witness.

There is one exception to this rule, and it applies only to the prosecution in a criminal case where the defendant testifies in their own defense. The ultimate question in that scenario is asserting that the defendant is guilty—an assertion the defendant will flatly deny. Nonetheless, even if it is only symbolic, many believe it is important to confront and directly accuse the defendant of committing the crime or crimes with which they have been charged. Because you can count on the defendant denying the charges, craft an entire accusatory line of questions in advance so that the defendant's denials do not unnerve you in front of the jurors. After each denial, simply go to the next question in your arsenal and fire another shot. Be sure, of course, that you have a good-faith basis for every factual assertion you make. As we have discussed, counsel is never free to assert facts on cross unless there is a good-faith basis for believing the facts to be true. In the context of a mock trial, your good faith can be based on information in the case file or proper reasonable inferences drawn from it. Remember to end your cross of the defendant on a strong, preferably irrefutable point.

This kind of questioning might go as follows in the prosecution of the jilted lover for her Valentine's Day murder of Mr. Love:

QUESTION: You and Mr. Love had been dating for ten years, hadn't you?

QUESTION: February 14 was your anniversary, correct?

QUESTION: You were expecting a proposal that night, weren't you?

QUESTION: You wanted to have a family together, didn't you?

QUESTION: But he just mocked you, right?

QUESTION: You claim that he threatened you?

QUESTION: You claim that he raised his fist?

QUESTION: You claim that he had hit you before, right?

QUESTION: And that made you angry, didn't it? Especially that night?

QUESTION: So you followed Mr. Love to his car with your .9 mm and shot him, didn't you?

QUESTION: His fist was not raised when he was sitting in the car, was it?

QUESTION: And afterwards, you made up that story about the two of you being mugged on your way home from dinner, didn't you?

The defendant's denials in response to these questions quickly become irrelevant; what matters is that the jurors see that you believe your theory of the case and aren't afraid to confront the defendant with the facts. While this is a fine tactic to use, it can be overused. If the trier of fact hears a witness deny every question you ask (or even the majority of questions), the factfinder may believe that none of your factual assertions were true. Thus, the start of your cross-examination should include questions with which the witness is likely to agree. Save your arsenal of accusations toward the criminal defendant for your cross-examination finale—after they have agreed with most everything else you have said.

F. Insist on a Responsive Answer

There is more to controlling a witness on cross-examination than asking the right questions. You must also make sure that you have gotten the correct answers. This requires that you listen to the witness. Of course, when a defendant accused of committing a serious crime chooses to take the case to trial, as in our example above, you know the defendant will deny the accusation. In every other instance, however, you must listen carefully to make sure the witness gives the answer that was derived from the witness's own prior statements in the mock trial case file.

Even the most painstakingly prepared question can elicit the wrong answer. The witness may not have understood you, they may have detected an ambiguity in your inquiry, or they may simply argue with you for the sake of argument. In any event, you must always listen carefully to ensure that the testimony is what you expected.

Below are some methods you can use to insist on a responsive answer.

1. Correct the Problem Yourself

You can often correct an unresponsive answer by simply re-asking your question.

Consider the following scenario from the firetruck case:

QUESTION:	Isn't it true that all of the other traffic stopped for the firetruck?
ANSWER:	How would they know to stop? There was no horn or bell.
QUESTION:	You didn't answer my question. All of the other cars stopped?
ANSWER:	Yes.

In the above example, the defendant decided that they did not want to respond to the cross-examiner's question, so they deflected it by answering a different question. An inattentive lawyer might have interpreted that answer as a denial or otherwise let it go by. The advocate above listened more carefully, however, and was able to obtain the precise information sought.

Chapter Nine

There are other ways of accomplishing the same outcome. You can repeat your question but this time ask it more slowly or use simpler language to make sure you are being clear. You can stop, look at the jury, and say, "I don't think you gave the jurors an answer to that question," which is a bit more bold and direct. You can be polite and say, "I'm sorry, perhaps my question wasn't clear" and then restate the question. The possibilities are endless.

Choose a particular method with which you are comfortable and be consistent so that you can effectively "train" the witness to answer your questions. Say, for example you adopted the method of stopping, looking at the jury, and saying "I don't think you gave the jurors an answer to that question." After doing that a time or two, the witness is likely to realize that each time you turn and face the jury, you are about to accuse them of not giving the jurors an answer to your question. If done effectively, eventually the witness will answer as soon as they see you turn toward the jury box—you may not even have to speak.

Your effectiveness in reining the witness back in depends in large part upon the level of control that you establish at the outset of your examination of the witness. A witness accustomed to answering short, leading, propositional questions will be more likely to stop offering explanations. In contrast, a witness repeatedly given latitude to explain will be inclined to keep it up. Additionally, your own level of confidence, not to mention the witness's natural degree of argumentativeness, play a large part in your ability to reassert control through these and other means.

2. Enlist the Judge's Help, If Necessary

Not all witnesses are inclined to play fairly. Some witnesses are overtly partisan, some are subtly uncooperative, and some are just plain ornery. While nothing requires a witness to facilitate or enhance the goals of your cross-examination, witnesses are required to provide fair answers to fair questions. When it is clear that a witness is utterly incapable of fulfilling this responsibility, you have earned the right to bring in the big gun: the judge, who is obliged to ensure not only that the witness responds to your questions, but also to "strike" any answers that are unresponsive once you request that action. Thus, the ultimate solution to the problem of the impermissibly uncooperative witness is to seek the judge's intervention.

> QUESTION: Your Honor, could you please instruct the witness to answer my question?
>
> Or,
>
> QUESTION: Your Honor, could you please direct the witness to answer the question yes or no?
>
> Or,
>
> QUESTION: I move to strike that answer as nonresponsive to my question and request that the court instruct the jury to disregard it.

Checklist		
HAVE YOU FOLLOWED THE RULES OF CROSS-EXAMINATION?		
☑	Are all of your questions leading?	Does each question you ask suggest the answer desired? *If not, rephrase your questions so they do.*
☑	Did you get in and get out?	Are you asking about more than three or four topics? *If so, consider cutting down your cross to make it as short as possible.*
☑	Are you asking only questions to which you already know the answers?	Is there any answer that the witness might give that will surprise you? *If so, rephrase the question to eliminate this possibility or strike the question altogether.*
☑	Are your questions short, fair, and in proper form?	Can opposing counsel object to any of your questions as compound, cumulative, vague, argumentative, or otherwise improper? *If so, rephrase those questions now to avoid unnecessary interruptions at trial.*
☑	Did you avoid asking that ultimate question?	Did you ask any questions that summarize an argument you will make during your closing and that the witness is unlikely to agree to on cross? *If so (unless you are cross-examining the defendant in a criminal case), omit the question and save the point for closing argument.*
☑	Are you comfortable insisting that the witness answer your questions?	Have you practiced methods you can use to rein a witness back in if she fails to answer your questions? *If not, be sure you take time to practice techniques for witness control.*

III. Planning Cross-Examination

Like direct examinations, the two fundamental aspects to planning your cross-examination are content and organization.

A. Content

Your work outlining the case according to the method we suggested in Chapter Two will come in very handy when considering what to include in your cross-examinations. Look over your final summary of the facts for the witnesses you will

Chapter Nine

cross-examine. Focus on those facts that are helpful to your case or that diminish opposing witnesses' credibility. This, along with any information that may be conspicuously missing from each witness's affidavit, is likely the universe of information you will use to construct your cross-examinations.

1. Determining the Usable Universe

Boil the universe of facts you may use in each cross-examination down to what we like to call the "usable universe." Consider the following factors as you decide which facts to include in your cross-examination.

Can one of your own witnesses testify to the same fact?

Why wrestle answers from an unwilling source if a friendly witness can provide you with the same information? Cross-examination always runs the risk that the witness will argue or hedge or that the information will not be developed as clearly as you would like. Unless you stand to benefit specifically from repetition of the testimony, consider bypassing cross-examination questions that merely repeat evidence.

Of course, you must cross-examine on important facts that are solely within the knowledge or control of the adverse witness. Such information will range from the foundation for the admission of a document to evidence of the witness's own prior actions.

Some information, though available from a variety of sources, will be particularly valuable when elicited on cross-examination. In the firetruck case, for example, the defendant's own testimony that he loved driving fast cars would be preferable to accusations about his driving from other witnesses. It is generally desirable to obtain negative or contested evidence from the mouths of the opposition witnesses, when possible.

Will the witness agree with your assertion of each fact?

The best cross-examination questions come directly from a witness's prior statement because the witness must concede those answers. There will also be times, however, when you cross-examine a witness about facts documented in exhibits or other witnesses' testimony. As we explained above, in some instances you will want to confront a witness (especially the defendant) with information they are likely to deny.

The construction of your usable universe depends almost entirely on your mastery of the case as a whole. To prepare for cross-examination, you must know everything that the particular witness is liable to say as well as what facts might be obtained from any other witness, document, or exhibit. Choosing effective cross-examination topics depends on your ability to choose those areas that will do you the most good while risking the least harm.

The chart that follows will help you determine which facts should be included in your cross-examinations.

Cross-Examination

Checklist		
SHOULD YOU INCLUDE THIS FACT IN YOUR CROSS-EXAMINATION?		
☑	**Is a friendly witness available to testify to the same fact?**	Can one of your own witnesses testify to this fact? *If so, eliminate the question unless you stand to benefit from having this witness repeat it.*
☑	**Do you benefit from having this witness testify to the fact?**	Is this witness the only person who can testify to this fact or is this something the factfinder should learn directly from this witness? *If so, keep it in your cross regardless of whether it will be repeated by another witness.*
☑	**How certain is it that the witness will agree with your assertion of the fact?**	Can the witness plausibly deny this fact? *If so, take it out of your cross-examination unless the denial itself is useful to your case.*

2. **Preparing Your Questions**

Once you have selected the topics for each cross-examination, write out short, single-thought, strictly factual sentences that develop each topic. For example, assume that the defendant's affidavit in the firetruck case includes the following statements:

> I awoke on the morning of the accident at 7:00 a.m. (page 3, line 5)

> I had to be downtown later that morning to meet an important new client. (page 3, lines 5–6)

> Yes, I wanted to get that client's business. (page 3, line 7) And yes, I stood to make a lot of money. (page 3, lines 7–8) The meeting was scheduled for 8:30 a.m. (page 3, line 12) I live about sixteen miles from my office. (page 2, line 15)

> I also rent a monthly parking spot in a garage two blocks from my office. (page 2, line 17)

> I left my home at 7:55 a.m. that morning. (page 1, line 20) There was a lot of traffic that morning. (page 2, line 2)

> The accident occurred at an intersection seven miles from downtown. (page 2, line 11)

> The accident happened at 8:20 a.m. (page 2, lines 11–12)

Chapter Nine

This lays out the facts in the defendant's affidavit that underlie the theory that he was rushed that morning. Now convert this list into cross-examination questions by taking each first-person sentence and rephrasing it into a second-person question. Leave the sentence in the form of a declaration and make it a question through voice inflection or by adding an interrogative phrase at the end. The above list then becomes the following cross-examination of the defendant:

> QUESTION: You awoke at 7:00 a.m. on the morning of the accident, isn't that right? (page 3, line 5)
>
> QUESTION: You had to be downtown later that morning, correct? (page 3, lines 5–6)
>
> QUESTION: You were meeting an important new client? (page 3, lines 5–6)
>
> QUESTION: You wanted to get that client's business? (page 3, line 7)
>
> QUESTION: You stood to make a lot of money? (page 3, lines 7–8)
>
> QUESTION: The meeting was scheduled for 8:30 a.m., correct? (page 3, line 12)
>
> QUESTION: You lived sixteen miles from your office? (page 2, line 15)
>
> QUESTION: You rented a monthly parking spot? (page 2, line 17)
>
> QUESTION: That spot was in a garage located two blocks from your office? (page 2, line 17)
>
> QUESTION: You left your home at 7:55 a.m., right? (page 1, line 20)
>
> QUESTION: There was a lot of traffic that morning? (page 2, line 2)
>
> QUESTION: The accident occurred at an intersection seven miles from downtown? (page 2, line 11)
>
> QUESTION: It happened at 8:20 a.m., isn't that right? (page 2, lines 11–12)

These questions fit neatly into the usable universe. Many of these facts are unlikely to be available from friendly witnesses. Most others are of the sort that will be most valuable if conceded by the defendant himself. Finally, and best of all, all the facts are documented in the witness's own prior sworn testimony.

This technique is useful for developing the content of your cross-examination. Organizing the examination and structuring your individual questions will depend upon additional analysis.

B. Organization

As with direct examination, you can organize a cross-examination based on the principles of primacy and recency, apposition, repetition, and duration. Unlike direct examination, however, on cross-examination the witness is often reluctant to help your case. Temper your plan in recognition of this reality, occasionally sacrificing maximum clarity and persuasion to avoid "telegraphing" your strategy to the uncooperative witness. Use these additional organizing principles of indirection and misdirection when planning cross-examinations.

1. General Tips for Organizing Cross-Examinations

Recall that cross-examination lets you tell part of your client's story in the middle of the other side's case. Your goal is to focus attention away from the witness's direct testimony and onto matters that are helpful to your case. On cross-examination, *you* want to tell the story. To do so, control the testimony and the witness.

Remember, too, that effective cross-examination often succeeds through implication and innuendo. Do not ask a witness the ultimate question. Final argument is your opportunity to point out the relationship between facts, make characterizations, and draw conclusions based upon the accumulation of details. Do not expect an opposing witness to do this for you.

a. *Do Not Worry About Starting Strong*

In an ideal world, you could begin every cross-examination with a strong, memorable point that absolutely drives home your theory and theme. Unfortunately, this will not always be possible. Many cross-examinations must begin with a preliminary period during which you acclimate yourself to the tenor of the witness's responses and attempt to put the witness in a cooperative frame of mind. Unless you can start with a true bombshell, take time to establish predicate facts through indirection.

b. *Use Topical Organization*

Topical organization is essential in cross-examination. Your goal on cross-examination is not to retell the witness's story, but rather to establish a small number of additional or discrediting points. A topical format allows you to move from area to area. Cluster facts in the same manner that you would on direct examination; or separate facts to hide your strategy from the witness.

Assume you are cross-examining the defendant in the firetruck case to show how busy he was on the day of the collision. You know that he had an important meeting to attend that morning, but he will be unlikely to admit that he risked losing the client (and a lot of money) if he arrived late. Solve this problem by organizing your cross-examination into two distinct topics: one dealing with the nature of the defendant's business and the other covering his appointment on the fateful morning.

First, show that the defendant is an independent management consultant employed in a very competitive business in which client relations are extremely important. Part of his work involves seeking out potential new clients, whom he is always anxious to please. Since he is a sole proprietor, every client means more money. As a consultant, he must pride himself on professionalism, timeliness, and efficiency. He bills his clients by the hour. Time is money. In short, examine the witness on his business background without ever bringing up the subject of the accident.

Later in the examination, after covering several other areas, shift topics to the defendant's agenda on the day of the accident. Establish the details of his planned meeting and the fact that he was still miles from downtown minutes before it was scheduled to begin.

You do not need to obtain an admission that the defendant was running late or was preoccupied. Through topical organization, you developed the predicate facts for that argument before the witness was aware of their implications.

There is another advantage to topical organization on cross-examination. Assume, in the example above, that the witness was well prepared and that he immediately recognized your reasons for inquiring into his business practices. Because your examination was segmented, however, he could scarcely deny the facts that you suggested. In the portion of the examination limited to the operation of his business, it would be implausible for him to deny that his clients value "professionalism, efficiency, and timeliness." Denying your perfectly reasonable propositions would make him look either untrustworthy or defensive.

You would not obtain the same result without topical organization. In the middle of discussing the morning of the accident, it would be quite plausible for the defendant to testify that this particular new client was not dominating their thoughts or that they did not actually need the new client's business.

Be sure that, as you organize your cross-examination questions, you continue to reference the page and line number where that fact appears in the witness's affidavit or deposition transcript. Referencing allows you to seamlessly impeach or contradict witnesses who give you evasive, unexpected, or false answers during cross.

If you followed the steps in Chapter Two, you will have already referenced every fact in each witness's affidavit. Remember that in addition to affidavits and deposition transcripts, reference sources can come from letters, reports, memoranda, notes, and even photographs. The best sources, of course, are the witness's own prior words. Adequate secondary sources may include documents that the witness reviewed, acted upon, or affirmed by silence.

Avoid referring to the testimony of a different person to impeach the current witness. That testimony, though perhaps useful, will not be a reliable source for supporting a cross-examination question, given that different witnesses perceive events differently. Only risk such reliance if there is no other source, and if the disparity between the current testimony and a provable fact is so blatant that you are confident the jurors can only accept your (and the other witness's) version of events. It is better to move on from a point you cannot win than to give the witness "wiggle room."

c. Give the Details First

Details are, if anything, more important on cross-examination than they are on direct. On direct examination, a witness tells the gist of the story, unimpeded by the examining attorney; details add strength and veracity to the basic testimony. On cross-examination, however, you are the one telling a story, and the witness will frequently disagree with the gist of the story that you want to tell. Details therefore become the primary method of making your points. You may elicit details to lay the groundwork for future argument, to draw out internal inconsistencies in the witness's testimony, to point out inconsistencies between witnesses, to lead the witness into implausible assertions, or to create implications that the witness will be unable to deny later.

Within each segment of your cross-examination, give the details first. No matter what your goal, the witness will be far more likely to agree with a series of small, incremental facts before the thrust of the examination becomes apparent. Once you have challenged, confronted, or closely questioned a witness, they will fight your attempt to go back and fill in the details necessary to make the challenge stick.

d. Scatter the Circumstantial Evidence

Inferential or circumstantial evidence is most persuasive when you combine a series of facts or events to create a logical path to the desired conclusion. Unfortunately, facts arranged in this manner on cross-examination will also be highly transparent to the witness. As you stack inference upon inference, your direction will become increasingly clear. A hostile or unfriendly witness will then become increasingly uncooperative, perhaps to the point of thwarting your examination. Instead, scatter the circumstantial evidence throughout the examination, drawing it together only during final argument to avoid telegraphing points to the witness, thereby inviting the witness to refute them.

e. Save a Zinger for the End

The final moment of cross-examination may well be the most important. No matter how low-key or friendly your style, almost every cross-examination will in some sense be viewed as a contest between you and the witness. Were you able to shake the adverse testimony? Did you do what you set out to do? In this regard, the final impression that you leave is likely to be the most lasting. Did you finish on a high note, or simply give up?

Carefully plan the very last point that you intend to make on cross-examination. It must be a guaranteed winner. Then, if your entire examination seems to fail, the witness denies every proposition, and the judge sustains every objection, you can always skip to your last question and finish with a flourish. Satisfied that you have made this single, telling, case-sealing point, you may proudly announce, "No further questions," and sit down.

How do you identify your fail-safe zinger? The following guidelines should help.

It must be absolutely admissible

Nothing smacks more of defeat than ending a cross-examination on a sustained objection. If you suspect even for a moment that your zinger might not be allowed, abandon it and choose another. In fact, make an entry in the margin of your notes that reminds you of your theory of admissibility. Why is the point relevant? Why isn't it hearsay? How has the foundation been established? Why isn't it speculation?

It must be undeniable

The end of your cross is not the time to argue or quibble with the witness. There are two good ways to ensure undeniability. First, choose a documented fact—the best "gift" given to you in the witness's statement. Second, phrase your question using the exact language the witness used, making it impossible for the witness to deny you the simple answer you seek.

It must be stated with conviction

No matter what your closing question, you must be able to deliver it with an attitude of satisfied completion. If the subject makes you nervous, worried, or embarrassed, then you must choose another. It is neither necessary nor desirable to smirk, but you must exhibit confidence that your parting inquiry has done its work.

Summary
CROSS-EXAMINATION ORGANIZATION
• Do not worry about starting strong • Use topical organization • Give the details first • Scatter the circumstantial evidence • Follow the classic format to maximize witness cooperation • Save a zinger for the end

2. A Classic Format for Cross-Examination

Because almost all cross-examinations will be topical, there can be no standard or prescribed form of organization. The following "classic format" maximizes witness cooperation. Of course, you may have a goal in mind for your cross-examination other than witness cooperation; in that case, feel free to ignore or alter this approach. As a rule of thumb, however, you can best control witnesses on cross-examination by following this questioning order.

a. Friendly Information

Be friendly first, asking all questions that the witness will regard as nonthreatening. These will often be background questions. For example, medical malpractice cases are often based upon errors of omission, and you may intend to argue in closing that the defendant physician, by virtue of their extraordinary training, should have known about certain available tests. Start your cross-examination, then, by asking friendly questions about the defendant's medical education, residency, fellowships, and awards. Most people, even defendants on trial, like to talk about their achievements. There is little doubt that a witness will be the most forthcoming when asked about flattering information at the very outset of the cross-examination.

b. Affirmative Information

After exhausting the friendly information, ask questions that build up the value of your case rather than tear down the opposition's. Much of this information will fill in gaps in the direct testimony. In fact, a good way to plan this portion of the cross is to list the information that you reasonably hope will be included in the direct. Build your affirmative information section from whatever opposing counsel omitted from the witness's direct testimony. Although adverse witnesses may not be enthusiastic about supplying you with helpful information, they will be unlikely to fight you over answers that might logically have been included in their own direct. Be careful, though, not to simply repeat the testimony given during direct in your cross-examination; doing so only reinforces it and bores everyone in the room.

c. Uncontrovertible Information

Now inquire about facts that damage the opposition's case or detract from the witness's testimony, so long as they are documented in the case file. With these questions, the witness may be inclined to hedge or quibble, but you can minimize this possibility by sticking to the information that ultimately must be conceded.

d. Challenging Information

Few witnesses will cooperate once you challenge their memory, perception, accuracy, conduct, or other aspects of their testimony. At some point, however, you must

Chapter Nine

ask most witnesses questions that they will recognize as challenges: "The fact is that the first thing you did after the collision was to telephone your office?" Such questions are necessary and, when used in their proper place, will not prevent you from first exploiting the other, more cooperative testimony from the witness.

e. Hostile Information

Hostile information involves confronting the witness directly. You may extract the necessary answers to hostile questions, but often at the cost of eliminating all hope of cooperation both then and thereafter. Hostile questions involve assaults on the witness's honesty, probity, peacefulness, character, or background. "Didn't you spend time in prison?" "You never intended to live up to the contract?" "That was a lie, wasn't it?"

f. Zinger

Always end with a zinger. You know why.

IV. The Ethics of Cross-Examination

While lawyers generally consider cross-examination to be an engine of truth-seeking, we are often criticized for using cross as a device for distortion and confusion. And in truth, as with all powerful rhetorical tools, cross-examination can be used to mislead and deceive. Accordingly, certain ethical principles have developed that circumscribe a lawyer's use of cross-examination.

Many cross-examinations contain inherent assertions of fact. Indeed, many of the best cross-examination questions are strictly propositional. Consider this example from the fire engine case:

> QUESTION: You were on your way to an important business meeting, right?

This question contains a single fact that counsel is urging to be true. The danger arises when counsel proposes baseless or knowingly false points. The witness, of course, can deny any untrue assertions, but the denials are likely to ring hollow in the face of an attorney's presumably superior persuasive skills. False or groundless accusations can inflict enormous damage. Imagine the impact of this examination in our firetruck case:

> QUESTION: Isn't it true that you had been drinking on the morning of the accident?
> ANSWER: No, not at all.
> QUESTION: Didn't you arrive at the Kingfisher Bar at 7:00 a.m.?
> ANSWER: Certainly not.

QUESTION:	Well, the truth is that you ran up a $24 tab that morning, didn't you?
ANSWER:	No.
QUESTION:	$24 would cover at least four drinks, right?
ANSWER:	I'm telling you that I wasn't drinking.

The precision of the details in the questions, such as the exact amount of the supposed bar tab, appears to add weight to the cross-examination, while the denials can be made to appear superficial. The cross-examiner's ability to control the interchange puts the witness at an extreme disadvantage. This cross-examination raises no problems if you have a good faith basis to believe that the witness was indeed drinking at the Kingfisher Bar and ran up a $24 tab, but it is absolutely unethical if those claims are baseless.

To protect against the unscrupulous use of cross-examination, every question is required to have a good-faith basis in fact. You are not free to make up assertions.

As a predicate to any propositional question, you must be aware of specific facts that support the allegation.

In addition, the good-faith basis for a cross-examination question cannot be composed solely of inadmissible evidence. Counsel cannot allude to any matter that will not be supported by admissible evidence. Thus, a good-faith basis cannot be provided by rumors, uncorroborated hearsay, or pure speculation.

Allegations lacking a basis in admissible evidence may lead to a sustained objection and even a strong admonition from the court.

Chapter Ten

Impeachment

I. The Role of Impeachment

Impeachment is the act of discrediting a witness as a reliable source of information on cross-examination. Successful impeachment renders the witness less worthy of belief, as opposed to merely unobservant, mistaken, or otherwise subject to contradiction.

Contrary to popular belief, the clouds will not part and lightning will not strike when you impeach a witness, nor is the witness likely to give up and admit that you were right all along. If you play your cards right, though, the effect of your impeachment will be felt during your closing argument. Closing argument is your opportunity to argue that the factfinder should disregard the impeached witness's testimony because they are not credible.

We will focus on impeachment by prior inconsistent statement, impeachment by omission, and impeachment through the use of character and case-specific motive evidence in this chapter.

Impeachment by prior inconsistent statement is conducted when a witness's testimony at trial is different from, and conflicts with, the information included in their prior statement. For example, say that a defendant in a hit-and-run case takes the stand and testifies during their direct examination that the traffic light was green at the time of the accident. Upon hearing this, opposing counsel remembers that in their earlier statement or testimony the defendant said the traffic light was red when the accident occurred. This situation calls for impeachment by prior inconsistent statement.

Impeachment by omission is conducted when a witness adds important facts at trial that were not included in their prior statement. To illustrate, imagine that the witness in the example above did not include the color of the traffic light in their prior sworn testimony but then added it during direct examination. The cross-examiner will want to point out that omission through impeachment.

In both cases, the inconsistency demonstrates that the witness's current testimony is at odds with their previous testimony. In essence, these forms of impeachment assert, "Do not believe this witness because they changed their story."

Chapter Ten

Mock trial witnesses, just like real witnesses, sometimes add details or change details from their written statements when testifying. This sometimes happens intentionally, when the opposing side tries to make their case stronger. We counsel strongly against that sort of conduct, but you do need to be prepared in case it happens. (See Chapter Seven, Section IV(B) for a discussion of the ethics of doing so intentionally.) More often, witnesses simply forget or become confused, or there is a good-faith disagreement about the inferences that can be drawn from the case file. Either way, if the change is significant enough, impeach the witness on cross-examination.

The third and fourth methods are called character impeachment. This form of impeachment is aimed at demonstrating that the witness possesses some trait or characteristic that renders their testimony less credible. Perhaps the witness is a convicted felon or suffers a memory defect. This examination says, "This witness is not trustworthy on any matter, because of who they are." Likewise, case-specific motive evidence can establish that the witness is not reliable in the context of the case at trial. For example, a witness might have a financial interest in the outcome of the case or might be prejudiced against one of the parties.

The Basics	
THE FORMS OF IMPEACHMENT	
TYPE	**USED WHEN**
Prior Inconsistent Statement:	A witness's trial testimony conflicts with their prior sworn statement
Omission:	A witness adds facts to their testimony at trial that were not included in their prior sworn statement
Character and Case-Specific Motive:	An aspect of the witness's character renders their testimony less credible

II. The Rules of Impeachment

Impeachment is a powerful tool. Unlike standard cross-examination, which may rely on unspoken premises and subtle misdirection, there should be no mistaking or hiding the intended impact of impeachment. Impeachment is inherently confrontational; it challenges the witness's believability, perhaps even their veracity. Below are rules to consider when deciding whether to impeach a witness.

A. *Impeach Only on Significant Matters*

Avoid impeaching witnesses on irrelevant, trivial, or petty inconsistencies. If the "punch line" fails to justify the buildup, the result can be embarrassing or damaging to your case. Imagine this scenario where the plaintiff in our firetruck case is being cross-examined:

QUESTION: You testified on direct examination that you saw the flashing lights and then realized that there was a firetruck behind you and so you slowed down, correct?
ANSWER: Correct.
QUESTION: You have given an earlier statement?
ANSWER: Why, yes, I did.
QUESTION: You spoke to the investigating police officer?
ANSWER: That is right.
QUESTION: You knew that you had to be truthful with the police officer?
ANSWER: Of course.
QUESTION: Didn't your earlier statement say, "I realized that there was a firetruck behind me when I saw its flashing lights, which caused me to slow down at once"?
ANSWER: Yes, I believe that is what I said.

Although the plaintiff has, in some technical sense, been impeached, the inconsistency involved is inconsequential. What difference does it make what triggered the witness to first realize there was a firetruck behind her? The essential point—that the firetruck was using its warning signals and that traffic slowed down—remains completely intact. The cross-examiner, however, has squandered valuable capital by confronting the witness, wasting time, and emerging with nothing to show for those efforts. A jury's response would be, "Is that all you can do?" A judge's response would be even less charitable.

This principle of significance also applies to impeachment by omission. The test of whether a "surprise" fact is important enough to point out through impeachment is whether the fact arguably makes it more or less likely that one side will prevail.

B. *Impeach Only on Actual Inconsistencies*

Impeach through prior inconsistency to show that the witness has made contradictory statements. The technique only works, however, when the two statements cannot both be true. If the two statements can be harmonized, explained, or rationalized, the impeachment will fail. For example:

QUESTION: You testified on direct that the bank robbers drove away in a blue sedan, correct?
ANSWER: Yes.
QUESTION: You gave a statement to the police right after the robbery, didn't you?

Chapter Ten

>ANSWER: Yes, I did.
>QUESTION: You told the police that the robbers drove off in a turquoise sedan, didn't you?

Although different words were used, the two statements are not inconsistent. It does not detract from the witness's credibility that they once referred to the car as turquoise and later called it blue.

C. Be Sure of Success Before Beginning

Failed impeachment can be disastrous. A lawyer who begins an assault they cannot complete looks ineffective at best and foolishly overbearing at worst. Because of this, be absolutely sure you can prove up an impeachment before you begin it.

If you are impeaching a witness by prior inconsistent statement, each question you ask will tell you whether you can prove up an impeachment. Take the questions you ask directly from the witness's statement, referencing the page and line numbers. Begin your impeachment only when you have the statement in hand and have located the page and line that contradicts the current testimony.

A smart precautionary measure (and also a good way to demonstrate teamwork in competition) is to involve your co-counsel in this process. Before beginning your cross-examination, give a copy of your indexed questions to your co-counsel. Then, when the witness refuses to agree to a question taken directly from their statement, turn toward your co-counsel and await the signal of whether it is safe to proceed. Your co-counsel, who was diligently following along, should nod to you if the question you asked is supported by a reference to the exact page and line number where the information appears in the witness's statement. Having received the go-ahead, walk to your counsel table, retrieve the witness's statement, and confidently proceed with the impeachment.

D. Do Not Impeach Favorable Information

You gain nothing by casting doubt on testimony that helps your case. So, even if an opposing witness has given a prior inconsistent statement, do not use it to impeach favorable trial testimony.

Assume that the defendant in the firetruck case testified at trial that immediately after the accident he used his cell phone to call his office. In contrast, in his affidavit he testified that his first action was to check the damage to his BMW and that he called his office only after making sure that the plaintiff was not seriously injured. The two statements are clearly inconsistent, and the witness is technically open to impeachment. The trial testimony, however, is actually more helpful to the cross-examiner's case. Recall the possible plaintiff's themes that the defendant was "too busy to be careful" or "too late to be safe." The defendant's admission that his first thought was to telephone his office fits beautifully into either theme. While his hard-heartedness in checking on his BMW before looking into the plaintiff's injuries might also be useful to the cross-examiner's case, this information does not go directly to any theory of liability or damages. The cross-examiner therefore will not want to undercut the trial testimony (about the immediate phone call) by impeaching it with the affidavit (about first checking on his BMW and the plaintiff).

E. *Consider the Impact of Multiple Impeachment*

In some cases, a witness may make multiple potentially impeaching statements. Though no single statement may be of great significance, the sheer volume of self-contradiction may be sufficient to take on a life of its own. Thus, it may be worthwhile to impeach the witness on a series of relatively minor inconsistent statements. Consider this impeachment of a bystander witness in the firetruck case:

QUESTION: You testified today that you were standing on the northeast corner of Craycroft and Alta Vista, correct?

QUESTION: But you told the police officer that you were standing on the southeast corner, didn't you?

QUESTION: You told the jury that you saw the accident while you were waiting for a bus?

QUESTION: But your affidavit said that you were out for a walk.

QUESTION: Today you said that you were on your way to work that day.

QUESTION: In your affidavit, though, you said you were going to the beach.

QUESTION: Today's testimony was that you were the only person on the corner.

QUESTION: You told the police, however, that there was a jogger standing right next to you, didn't you?

In isolation, none of the above details impacts the witness's credibility. In aggregation, however, they paint a picture of a confused person who is very likely uncertain about what they saw.

Multiple impeachment is a refined tool. It can be overdone, and the point lost. On the other hand, when deftly executed and well conceived, the whole impeachment can be much greater than the sum of its parts.

F. *Consider the Timing of Impeachment*

Effective impeachment may fit into the overall strategy of your cross-examination. If you intend to impeach a statement the witness made during direct examination, you are free to place it wherever you see fit in your cross-examination.

Chapter Ten

The basic organizing principles of cross-examination also apply to impeachment: maximize cooperation by beginning with inquiries that do not challenge or threaten the witness; employ initial questions that build up your own case, as opposed to controverting the opposition's; impeach only when you have exhausted the favorable information that you intend to obtain from the witness. These are not absolute rules, but they do form a sound framework within which to begin thinking about organization.

On the other hand, you might want to "discipline" the witness by conducting a good, strong impeachment at the very beginning of the cross-examination. Use this technique when you anticipate great difficulty in controlling the witness. By teaching the witness right from the start of the examination that you have the tools to compel the answers that you are entitled to, you may minimize the witness's tendency to wander or argue. This approach sacrifices cooperation, but this is a witness from whom you had not expected cooperation in the first place.

But what if you do not have the luxury of deciding when to impeach, as is the case when the witness changes their story while you are cross examining them? At that point there is no reason to wait or experiment with the niceties of fine organization. If you have the ammunition, impeach the witness on the spot.

Checklist		
IS THIS IMPEACHMENT PROPER?		
☑	**Is this worth impeaching?**	Does this testimony make it any more or less likely that your client will prevail at trial?
		If not, skip the impeachment unless you can impeach on multiple grounds at once and you believe doing so would advance your theory of the case.
☑	**Is this an actual inconsistency?**	Does this testimony truly conflict with the witness's prior testimony?
		If not, there is no point in impeaching.
☑	**Are you sure to succeed?**	Is the inconsistent testimony written in the witness's own statement or in some other usable document?
		If not, consider skipping the impeachment to save yourself from the possibility of a failed attempt.

Checklist		
IS THIS IMPEACHMENT PROPER?		
☑	**Is this information actually *favorable* to your case?**	Do the additional or changed facts actually support your theory or theme of the case?
		If so, skip the impeachment and argue the facts in your closing argument.
☑	**Can you perform a multiple impeachment?**	Are the points you plan to make through the impeachment small enough that they will be stronger if grouped together?
		If so, impeach the witness in a series of questions.
☑	**Is this the right time to impeach on this fact?**	Are you impeaching based on the witness's direct examination testimony?
		If so, add the impeachment to the confrontational section of your cross.
		Are you impeaching based on the witness's response to a question during cross-examination?
		If so, launch into the impeachment right away.

III. The Types of Impeachment

A. *Prior Inconsistent Statements*

One of the most dramatic aspects of any trial is the confrontation of a witness with their own prior inconsistent statement. This is the moment that trial attorneys live for—the opportunity to show that the witness's current testimony is contradicted by their own earlier words. Properly conducted, this form of impeachment is not only effective on cross-examination; it also can provide an extremely fruitful final argument.

> Members of the jury, Ms. Starnella is simply unworthy of belief. They couldn't even keep the story straight. Right after the accident, they told Officer Hernandez that the light was red. By the time of trial, it had mysteriously changed to green. The best you can say is that Ms. Starnella doesn't know what color the light was.

Chapter Ten

Prior inconsistent statements damage a witness's credibility because they demonstrate that the witness has changed their story. Depending upon the nature and seriousness of the change, the witness may be shown to be evasive, opportunistic, error-prone, or even lying.

There are three steps necessary to impeach a witness with a prior inconsistent statement: 1) recommit, 2) validate, and 3) confront. Recommit the witness to the current testimony by restating it and asking the witness to verify that they made the statement under oath. Then, validate the prior testimony by getting the witness to agree that it too was under oath and that the witness had a chance to correct it for errors. Finally, confront the witness with their prior testimony by reading it aloud for the court.

1. Recommit the Witness

Recommit the witness to their current testimony by asking, for example:

> QUESTION: You testified on direct examination that the light was green for the southbound traffic, correct?

Or,

> QUESTION: Are you telling this jury today that the light was green for southbound traffic?

2. Accredit the Witness's Prior Opportunity to Tell the Full Story

If your mock trial case file includes witness statements or affidavits, it is reasonable to conclude that each of the witnesses was given a previous opportunity to tell their story accurately. After all, witness statements and affidavits are summaries of the witness's testimony and the important facts. Likewise, if your case file includes copies of witness depositions, it is reasonable to conclude that the witnesses were given the opportunity to read over their depositions and correct any inaccuracies. (We are speaking here in generalities; confirm whether the rules and materials in your specific competition permit these assumptions.)

If the prior testimony was in the form of an affidavit, the accreditation might proceed as follows:

> QUESTION: You recall giving a statement in this case, right?
> QUESTION: When you gave that statement, you were under oath?
> QUESTION: You swore to tell the truth, the whole truth, and nothing but the truth?
> QUESTION: That was the same oath that you took here in court today?
> QUESTION: When you were asked to give that statement, you were told to include all relevant information, right?

Impeachment

QUESTION:	Then, when you were done writing it, you were asked to read it over?
QUESTION:	To make sure it was accurate?
QUESTION:	And you did that, didn't you?
QUESTION:	You were able to make any corrections that you wanted?
QUESTION:	When you were done, you signed the statement affirming that it was accurate, right?

In the context of a deposition, the accreditation might go as follows:

QUESTION:	You gave a deposition in this case, right?
QUESTION:	That was where you came to my office?
QUESTION:	I asked you questions.
QUESTION:	You gave me answers.
QUESTION:	You were under oath when you answered those questions, right?
QUESTION:	You swore to tell the truth, the whole truth, and nothing but the truth?
QUESTION:	That was the same oath that you took here in court today?
QUESTION:	You later had an opportunity to go over your deposition, correct?
QUESTION:	To make sure everything you said was accurate, right?
QUESTION:	And you did that, didn't you?
QUESTION:	You were able to make any corrections that you wanted?
QUESTION:	When you were done, you signed your deposition affirming that it was accurate, right?

If your mock trial case file includes unsworn statements by witnesses that were made orally—for example, statements made to a law enforcement officer during an investigation—you can still set up the impeachment by prior inconsistent statement by asking the witness questions such as these during cross-examination:

QUESTION:	You talked with Officer Hernandez after the collision, correct?
QUESTION:	She asked you questions about what you saw?
QUESTION:	You answered her questions to the best of your ability, right?
QUESTION:	And when you talked with her, the events you witnessed were fresh in your mind, were they not?

In addition to validating the witness's prior statement or testimony, it is often a good idea to accredit it—that is, to state reasons why the factfinder might find it more accurate than the witness's current testimony. Since the two statements are by

Chapter Ten

definition mutually exclusive, there is a natural syllogism: if the earlier statement is true, then the current testimony must be wrong. Accrediting the prior inconsistent statement can further detract from the witness's credibility.

Accredit a witness's prior testimony by showing that the witness had a strong motive for recalling all the important facts accurately when it was given, as in a physical description given when the perpetrator of a crime was still at large. As illustrated above, you can also accredit a prior statement by showing that it was given closely in time to the events in the case or that the witness was under a legal duty to be accurate at the time.

3. Confront the Witness with the Prior Statement

The final stage of impeachment is to confront the witness with the prior statement to get the witness to admit that the earlier statement was indeed made. This confrontation need not always be confrontational. It is sufficient merely to require the witness to admit making the impeaching statement, particularly when the impeachment is based upon the witness's forgetfulness, confusion, or embellishment. Reserve hostility or accusation for those situations when you can show that the witness is lying or acting out of some ill motive.

To be effective, confront the witness in a clear and concise manner that leaves no room for evasion or argument by the witness or their attorney. The classic approach is to alert the court to the page and line number of the witness's statement to which you will be referring and then to read the witness's own words.

> TO COURT: I'm referring to the first page, line 10, of the witness's statement.
> QUESTION: Isn't it true that in your statement you said, "At the time of the accident, the traffic light was red for the southbound traffic."
> ANSWER: Yes.

Or, in the case of a deposition:

> TO COURT: I'm referring to the first page, lines 10 through 15 of the witness's deposition transcript.
> QUESTION: Isn't it true that during your deposition I asked you this question and you gave this answer: "Question: What color was the traffic light for southbound traffic when the accident occurred? Answer: It was red."
> ANSWER: Yes.

Consider giving the witness a copy of the impeaching statement or deposition transcript and direct the witness to read along with you:

Impeachment

QUESTION:	Please take a look at Exhibit 14. Isn't that the affidavit you signed?
ANSWER:	Yes, it is.
QUESTION:	Now please look at line 10 of the first page and read silently along with me. Doesn't your affidavit say, "At the time of the accident, the traffic light was red for the southbound traffic"?

Do not ask the witness to read the testimony aloud and do not ask the witness to explain the inconsistency between their current and prior testimony. Doing either of these surrenders your control over the examination. If the witness reads the statement, you cannot control how clearly, loudly, or accurately it is read and whether voice inflection will be used to emphasize the inconsistency. It is even riskier to ask the witness to explain the inconsistency; at best, the witness will take the opportunity to muddle the clarity of the impeachment and at worst the witness will launch into an explanation that undercuts the entire line of examination.

In the same vein, do not ask a witness to agree that the two statements are inconsistent or different. And never ask a witness to concede that they have changed their story. These are the "one too many" questions you want to avoid. The witness is not going to admit to them on the stand; instead they will only take issue with your assumption that they are lying or that the statements are contradictory. Such questions only produce argument, and argument is likely to engender explanation.

What do you do if the witness's prior statement was oral rather than written? Assume Ms. Starnella spoke to Officer Hernandez but did not sign a written statement. Even if Officer Hernandez included verbatim notes in the police report, that document cannot be used for impeachment because it was not the witness's own prior statement. You could ask if Ms. Starnella made the statement to Officer Hernandez, but they may deny it. In this case, the only sure-fire way to complete the impeachment would be to question Officer Hernandez about the description given orally during the investigation.

QUESTION:	Did you interview Ms. Starnella immediately after the accident?
ANSWER:	Yes, I did.
QUESTION:	Do you remember what they told you regarding what color the light was for southbound traffic at the time of the accident?
ANSWER:	Yes, that it definitely was red.

This testimony is admissible as nonhearsay because it impeaches the prior witness.

Chapter Ten

\multicolumn{2}{c}{**The Basics**}
\multicolumn{2}{c}{**IMPEACHMENT BY PRIOR INCONSISTENT STATEMENT**}
STEP	**ANOTHER EXAMPLE**
Recommit the witness:	• Mr. Kaeser, you testified during direct examination that you left your apartment at 10:15 p.m. on the night of September 10, correct?
Validate the prior statement:	• You remember speaking to Detective Judson Brown the following day, don't you?
	• Detective Brown came to your apartment?
	• It was at noon?
	• You were wide awake?
	• You didn't have any trouble remembering what you had done the night before, did you?
	• In fact, you voluntarily gave a statement to the detective, didn't you?
	• Because, as you put it, you had "nothing to hide," right?
	• Detective Brown asked you when you left your apartment the night before, correct?
	• And you told him you were certain of the time because you had just finished watching a rerun of *Seinfeld* before you left, correct?
	• A few days later, Detective Brown returned to your apartment with a summary of the statement you had given?
	• Detective Brown gave you a chance to review that statement and correct any information that was incorrect?
	• After reviewing the statement, you swore under oath that it was accurate, didn't you?
Confront the witness with his prior statement:	• Isn't it true, Mr. Kaeser, that your sworn statement says that you left your apartment at 9:30 p.m. on September 10?

B. *Impeachment by Omission*

In addition to prior inconsistent statements, a witness may also be impeached by pointing out that their current testimony includes facts that were not included in their prior statements or testimony. This type of impeachment follows the same theory as impeachment by a prior inconsistent statement: the current testimony is rendered less credible because when the witness told the same story earlier it did not contain facts that the witness now claims are true. In essence, the impeachment is saying, "Do not believe this witness because they are adding facts to their story." Or, in other words, "If those things are true, why didn't you say them before?"

In mock trials, it is easy to see what is really taking place when facts are included at trial that are not found in the case file: they are either reasonable inferences from the case materials that explain the information and events described in the case file, or they are unreasonable inferences that bolster the witness's testimony or opposing counsel's case. As discussed in previous chapters, witnesses in most mock trial competitions are allowed to make reasonable inferences from the case materials. Witnesses are not, however, allowed to go beyond reasonable inferences by making up material facts in order to strengthen their side of the case. We discussed this already in Chapter Seven, Section IV(B), among other places, but it is an important aspect of mock trials, so further discussion is warranted.

If mock trial participants are not supposed to make up facts, why do some people do it? Unfortunately, teams make up facts because they forget that competitions are not about getting a verdict in their favor; they are really about demonstrating sound trial advocacy skills. Making up facts is unethical. Accordingly, it is not unheard of for judges to penalize teams who make unreasonable inferences from the case file. Some judges even believe it should be cause for automatic loss of the competition round. Given the seriousness of the possible consequences and the pointlessness of the prohibited conduct, we do not understand why some participants continue to engage in this behavior.

If you encounter participants who make up material facts during your trials, resist the temptation to object and say, "Your Honor, the witness is making up that fact—it isn't in the case file." Stay in character and deal with surprises the same way trial lawyers do: by impeaching the witness by omission. Learning the steps of an effective impeachment by omission equips you with a tool just as—if not more—important for mock trial participants as learning to impeach by prior inconsistent statement.

When impeaching by omission, follow these three general steps: 1) recommit, 2) accredit, and 3) confront. Recommit the witness to the new testimony given during the trial. Next, accredit the previous testimony, emphasizing that the witness swore to tell the whole truth and also had an opportunity to read the statement to make sure they included all relevant facts or reported all of the information they believed to be relevant. Finally, confront the witness with the fact that these new facts were not in their original testimony or statement.

Let's return to our example of testimony about the color of the traffic light. This time, we'll assume that Ms. Starnella's prior statement did not include any information about the color of the light at the time of the collision. Despite that, Ms. Starnella testified on direct that the light was green for southbound traffic.

Chapter Ten

1. Recommit the Witness

Recommit the witness to having testified to a certain fact during direct or cross-examination.

> QUESTION: You testified on direct examination that the light was green for the southbound traffic, correct?

Or,

> QUESTION: Are you telling this jury today that the light was green for southbound traffic?

2. Accredit the Witness's Prior Opportunity to Tell the Full Story

If your case file includes witness statements or affidavits, it is reasonable to conclude that each of the witnesses was given the opportunity to tell their story in full therein. After all, both witness statements and affidavits are summaries of the witness's testimony and would include all the important facts. Likewise, if your case file includes copies of witness depositions, it is reasonable to conclude that each witness was given the opportunity to read over their deposition and add any information relevant to the case. (Again, we are speaking in generalities. Check that the rules of your competition, or the materials provided to you, allow or support these assumptions.)

If the prior testimony was in the form of an affidavit, the accreditation might proceed as follows:

> QUESTION: You recall giving a statement in this case, right?
> QUESTION: When you gave that statement you were under oath?
> QUESTION: You swore to tell the truth, the whole truth, and nothing but the truth?
> QUESTION: That was the same oath that you took here in court today?
> QUESTION: When you were asked to give that statement, you were told to include all relevant information, right?
> QUESTION: Then, when you were done writing it, you were asked to read it over?
> QUESTION: To make sure it was complete?
> QUESTION: And you did that, didn't you?
> QUESTION: You were able to make additions that you wanted?
> QUESTION: When you were done, you signed the statement affirming that it was complete, right?

In the context of a deposition, the accreditation might go as follows:

> QUESTION: You gave a deposition in this case, right?
> QUESTION: That was where you came to my office?
> QUESTION: I asked you questions.

QUESTION:	You gave me answers.
QUESTION:	You were under oath when you answered those questions, right?
QUESTION:	You swore to tell the truth, the whole truth, and nothing but the truth?
QUESTION:	That was the same oath that you took here in court today?
QUESTION:	You later had an opportunity to go over your deposition, correct?
QUESTION:	To make sure you included all of the relevant information, right?
QUESTION:	To make sure it was complete?
QUESTION:	And you did that, didn't you?
QUESTION:	You were able to make any additions that you wanted?
QUESTION:	When you were done, you signed your deposition affirming that it was complete, right?

If your mock trial case file includes unsworn statements by witnesses that were made orally—for example, statements made to a law enforcement officer during an investigation—you can still set up the impeachment by omission by asking the witness questions such as these during cross-examination:

QUESTION:	You talked with Officer Hernandez after the collision, correct?
QUESTION:	Officer Hernandez asked you questions about what you saw?
QUESTION:	You answered the questions to the best of your ability, right?
QUESTION:	You told Officer Hernandez everything you could remember, did you not?
QUESTION:	Officer Hernandez didn't prevent you from including anything you thought was important, did she?
QUESTION:	And when you talked with Officer Hernandez, the events you witnessed were fresh in your mind, were they not?

3. Confront the Witness

Here is where you point out that the witness testified to facts that were not included in their affidavit or deposition:

QUESTION:	Isn't it true that nowhere in your affidavit did you mention the light being green for southbound traffic at the time of the collision?

Chapter Ten

Or, in the case of a deposition:

QUESTION: During your deposition you did not tell me that the light was green for southbound traffic, did you?

QUESTION: Even after your deposition, you did not add that information to your deposition transcript when given the opportunity, did you?

You can also give the witness a copy of the affidavit or deposition transcript and ask the witness to indicate where it includes the pertinent fact. This allows the factfinder to hear the witness's admission, in their own words, that the fact was not included. The downfall of using this method in mock trial competitions is that it takes more time to execute than the method outlined above. Given the time limits typically set in mock trials, it is not wise to waste even one minute on having an opposing witness authenticate their own affidavit and then read through it to look for a pertinent fact. After all, there is always the risk that the witness will take the time to read their entire affidavit before answering—in which case one minute can easily become five. If you can spare the time and choose to take this route, the confrontation might go as follows:

QUESTION: This is your affidavit, isn't it?

QUESTION: Directing your attention to the last page. That is your signature, is it not?

QUESTION: Please take a minute to find the place in your affidavit where you said the light was green for southbound traffic at the time of the collision.

QUESTION: Isn't it true that nowhere in your statement did you say that?

As we explained previously, when the witness's prior statement was oral rather than written, you will need to call the person to whom the statement was made to perfect the impeachment. So, going back to our example, you would want to call Officer Hernandez to confirm that the witness never said the light was green when they spoke.

QUESTION: Did you interview the witness immediately after the accident?

ANSWER: Yes, I did.

QUESTION: Did they tell you the color of the light for the southbound traffic?

ANSWER: They did not. I would have included it in my report if they had told me.

Because this testimony is impeaching, it is admissible.

The Basics
IMPEACHMENT BY OMISSION

STEP	ANOTHER EXAMPLE
Recommit the witness:	• Ms. Combe, you told the jury during your direct examination that immediately upon riding the bicycle manufactured by my client, you noticed that it was unstable, correct?
Validate the prior statement:	• You were deposed in this case, were you not? • You came to my office. • I asked you questions, and you did your best to answer my questions, correct? • That was after you purchased the same make and model of bicycle that the plaintiff purchased, right? • And you were under oath when you answered my questions, right?
Confront the witness with the prior statement:	• (Directing counsel to the deposition transcript generally.) Ms. Combe, isn't it true that at no time during your deposition did you complain about the bicycle being unstable? • In fact, didn't you say that you have enjoyed having the bike and were grateful to your husband for buying it for you?

C. Character and Case-Specific Motive Impeachment

1. Impeachment Based on the Witness's Character or Characteristics

Character impeachment uses some inherent trait or particular characteristic of the witness, essentially unrelated to the case at hand, to render the witness's testimony less credible. The thrust of the impeachment is to show that the witness, for some demonstrable reason, is simply not trustworthy.

The most common forms of characteristic impeachment include conviction of a crime, defect in memory or perception, and past untruthfulness.

Chapter Ten

a. Conviction of a Crime

A witness may be impeached on the basis of their past conviction of certain crimes. To determine which crimes are admissible, consult the rules of evidence followed in your competition.

Once you have determined that you can use a conviction for impeachment, relatively little technique is involved in the cross-examination.

> QUESTION: Isn't it true, Mr. Halawith, that you were once convicted of the crime of aggravated battery?
> ANSWER: Yes.
> QUESTION: You were convicted on October 12, 2013, correct?
> ANSWER: Yes.
> QUESTION: That was a felony?
> ANSWER: It was.
> QUESTION: And you were sentenced to two years of probation?
> ANSWER: I was.

As a rule, you are allowed to impeach the witness by showing that the witness was convicted of a certain type of crime. However, the facts and details of the crime (e.g., who the witness injured, why, when, etc.) are generally not allowed. Because of this, it is effective to draw out the impeaching information, as in the above example, in a series of short questions, each of which deals with a single fact. Repetition of terms such as "crime," "conviction," and even "convicted felon" will add weight to the impeachment.

b. Past Untruthfulness and Other Bad Acts

We have discussed the rules governing impeachment on the basis of a criminal conviction. What about a witness's bad acts that were not the subject of a conviction? A witness who has lied in the past, regardless of whether prosecuted and under oath, may well be likely to lie during current testimony. On the other hand, past misconduct of some sort is a near-universal human condition, and trials would become bogged down if lawyers were allowed free rein to cross-examine witnesses on any and all of their past misdeeds.

Again, determine whether your rules of evidence allow you to go into instances of a witness's untruthfulness and other bad acts. The procedure for examining the witness once you have a good faith basis to believe the evidence will be deemed admissible is the same as above.

c. Impaired Perception or Recollection

A witness can also be impeached on the basis of inability to perceive or recall events. Perception can be adversely affected by a wide variety of circumstances. The witness may have been distracted at the time of the events, or their vision may have been obscured. The witness may have been sleepy, frightened, or intoxicated. The witness may have poor eyesight or may suffer from some other sensory deficit. Any of these or other similar facts can be used to impeach the credibility of a witness's testimony.

Of course, you must have a good-faith basis for asserting on cross-examination that a witness had impaired perception or recollection. In a mock trial, look for that good-faith basis in the information provided in your case file and, if allowed, any reasonable inferences that can be drawn from that information.

For example, if the witness's own statement included the line, "Ever since I turned 70 my eyesight has been going downhill quickly and I can't seem to keep up with my glasses prescriptions," you can elicit that information on cross to establish the witness's impaired perception. Rather than attempt to argue with the witness about whether they actually saw what they testified on direct examination to seeing, wait for closing and argue that the witness's impaired perception draws their testimony into serious question.

2. Case-Specific Motive Impeachment

Some facts are impeaching only within the circumstances of a particular case. They would be innocuous, or perhaps even helpful, in any other context. The most common forms of case-specific motive impeachment are based on the witness's personal interest, bias, or prejudice.

A witness who is personally interested in the outcome of a case may be inclined to testify with less than absolute candor. Whether consciously or subconsciously, humans possess a well-recognized tendency to shape their recollection in the direction of the desired outcome. Impeachment on the basis of personal interest takes advantage of this phenomenon by pointing out just how the witness stands to gain or lose as a consequence of the resolution of the case. The technique is common in both civil and criminal cases, and it may be applied to both party and nonparty witnesses. Perhaps the clearest example of impeachment on the basis of personal interest arises when the witness has a financial stake in the factfinder's verdict.

A witness's testimony may be affected by a case-specific motive other than personal interest; the witness may have a professional stake in the issues being litigated or may have some other reason to prefer one outcome to another. For example, where a witness's prior judgment is being questioned, that witness has a motive to testify in such a way as to vindicate their earlier judgment. Likewise, an expert who adheres to a particular school of thought in their profession has a motive to defend it at trial when it is challenged by other experts in the field.

Bias and prejudice generally refer to a witness's relationship to one of the parties. A witness may be well disposed, or ill inclined, toward either party. Sadly, some

Chapter Ten

witnesses harbor prejudices against entire groups of people. Bias in favor of a party is often the consequence of friendship or affinity.

> QUESTION: You are the defendant's younger brother?
> QUESTION: You grew up together?
> QUESTION: You have helped each other out throughout your lives?
> QUESTION: Now your brother is charged with a crime?
> QUESTION: He is in trouble?
> QUESTION: He needs help?
> QUESTION: And you are here to testify?

Nothing is more case-specific than this sort of impeachment. It has forensic value if and only if the witness's brother is the defendant in the case and the two had a strong relationship. Of course, if they didn't, the other side might be able to use the same facts to its advantage.

> QUESTION: You are the defendant's younger brother?
> QUESTION: You grew up together?
> QUESTION: He was always beating you up?
> QUESTION: He seemed to have all of life's advantages?
> QUESTION: It was hard to follow in his successful footsteps?
> QUESTION: Everyone was always comparing you to him?
> QUESTION: He teased you and called you names?
> QUESTION: You were always resentful of him?
> QUESTION: You swore that you would get even?
> QUESTION: Now your older brother is charged with a crime?
> QUESTION: After all these years, his success seems to have run out?
> QUESTION: And you have come to court today to testify against him?

As with all case-specific motive impeachment, the establishment of bias or prejudice requires careful development through the use of small, individual facts.

As always, you must have a good-faith basis for suggesting during cross-examination that a witness has a case-specific motive. That good-faith basis should come from the information provided in your case file and, if allowed, any reasonable inferences that can be drawn from that information.

Chapter Eleven

Redirect and Recross-Examinations

I. Redirect Examination

A. *The Purpose of Redirect Examination*

Redirect examination, which allows counsel an opportunity to respond to the cross-examination, may be used for a number of purposes. The witness may be asked to explain points that were explored during the cross, to untangle seeming inconsistencies, to correct errors or misstatements, or to rebut new charges or inferences. In other words, use redirect to minimize or undo the damage, if any, that was done during cross-examination.

B. *The Rules of Redirect*

1. Follow the Same Rules as Direct Examination

All of the rules of direct examination apply equally to redirect examination. Leading questions are prohibited, witnesses may not testify in narrative form, testimony must come from personal knowledge, lay opinions are limited to sensory perceptions, and the proper foundation must be laid to refresh recollection.

Many judges, however, allow a certain amount of latitude during redirect, especially with leading questions. Even without indulgence, leading questions are always permissible to direct the witness's attention or to introduce an area of questioning. A certain amount of leading may be necessary on redirect to focus the examination on the segment of the cross-examination that you wish to explain or rebut. Of course, you should also be able to accomplish this by using headlines or transitional questions (discussed in Chapter Three, Section III(I)), followed by non-leading questions.

2. Stay Within the Scope of the Cross-Examination

Although most mock trial competitions do not apply the scope rule to cross-examinations as we discussed in Section II of Chapter Nine, it is typically applied to redirect examinations. Accordingly, limit the subject matter of the material covered on redirect to topics brought up on cross. You cannot introduce on redirect a general subject that was not covered during cross-examination.

Redirect examination is therefore not an opportunity to ask questions that were overlooked during the witness's direct examination, unless opposing counsel touched upon the subject matter during cross. For example, if the defendant in the firetruck case was not cross-examined regarding his vision and his ability to see the approaching vehicle, redirect questions on that subject will draw an objection that they are "beyond the scope of cross-examination." This is true even if the witness's statement contained helpful information on that subject, such as an assertion that "I have 20/20 vision and have never needed corrective lenses."

Because of this rule, prepare for and ask your witnesses about all topics and evidence during direct examination; do not save evidence for after the cross. Likewise, if you forget to ask your witness a question or a series of questions during your direct examination and that subject is not explored on cross-examination, do not expect to ask the questions on redirect unless you can tie the evidence to a subject that was raised during the cross-examination.

C. Planning Redirect Examination

Each redirect must respond to the preceding cross-examination; it is seldom possible to plan out every question you will ask to rehabilitate a witness. Even so, you can anticipate that certain subjects will be addressed and prepare at least part of your redirect.

Although we have stated that you should never reserve important evidence for redirect, it may be wise to withhold certain explanatory information until after the cross. Where your witness has an effective response to a potential line of cross-examination questions and where there is no guarantee that opposing counsel will bring up that subject on cross, it is a good idea to save the explanation for redirect.

Say, for example, that the defendant in a murder case was asked by a police officer whether he hit the victim with a shovel on the night of the alleged murder and the police officer says the defendant responded, "Hmm . . . maybe." While there may be a number of perfectly reasonable responses to the apparent inconsistency (e.g., the police officer is mistaken about what the defendant said or the police officer misunderstood what the defendant's statement meant), there is no point in eliciting the explanation during direct examination if the issue may not be raised during the cross-examination.

D. Waiving Redirect Examination

Redirect examination is not necessary. Only pursue redirect if it will contribute to your theory of the case, either by eliciting new evidence within the scope of the cross-examination or by rehabilitating, and thus strengthening, the evidence the witness testified to previously.

There is no need to redirect a witness who was not appreciably hurt by the cross-examination. And some damage cannot be repaired; it is a mistake to engage in redirect examination if you cannot improve the situation. The worst miscalculation of all is to surprise a witness by asking for an explanation the witness is not prepared to give.

As a further hazard, redirect examination may expose the witness to recross-examination in mock trial competitions where it is allowed. If redirect is waived, there can be no additional cross. Even a single question on redirect, however, can subject the witness to significant further recross, so long as it stays within the applicable scope.

Finally, an unnecessary redirect risks repeating, and therefore reemphasizing, the cross-examination. It can also trivialize the effect of the direct by rehashing minor points.

The point of all these warnings is that you should redirect your witness only when it is necessary, possible, and anticipated by the witness—that is, when success is very likely. Otherwise, you are essentially reopening the closet door and inviting opposing counsel in to play with the witness's skeletons.

E. Conducting Redirect Examination

Content is the most important aspect of redirect examination. Concentrate the redirect on a few significant points that can definitely be developed. Inexperienced students often make the mistake of attempting to repeat many of the same questions that were asked during direct examination. This is not allowed due to the "asked and answered" objection, which bars the same lawyer from asking the same witness a question more than one time. You can instead ask very similar questions by rephrasing those asked on direct to elicit the same or similar information, though you should do so with caution.

A good rule to follow in a mock trial is to never ask more than five questions during a redirect examination. Asking more will broadcast to everyone in the courtroom that cross did significant damage. Ideally, limit your redirect to the one or two questions that will best rehabilitate your witness so that the last words they speak on the stand help your case.

Clearly express to the witness the information you seek. First, focus the witness's attention on the pertinent area of the cross-examination. Then, simply ask the witness to explain, clarify, or respond as necessary.

> QUESTION: Defense counsel pointed out that you did not visit your doctor immediately following your camping trip at Eagle River Falls. Why didn't you go to the doctor right away?

Chapter Eleven

Or,

> QUESTION: You were asked about why you didn't mention in your affidavit the pain you experienced while camping. Is there a reason you left it out?

This latter question is a good example of rehabilitating an impeached witness (in this case by omission) by allowing the witness to explain away the impeachment, if possible. Assuming that the witness's answer is something to the effect of, "I thought it was clear when I said I have been in pain every day since the accident that the days I spent camping were no exception," your question accomplishes that task.

You can also use redirect examination to bring out clarifying facts that were made relevant by the cross-examination. For example, you might simply ask the plaintiff:

> QUESTION: How soon after the camping trip did you visit the doctor?

Yet another use for redirect is to point out when the level of control exerted by the cross-examiner on the witness seemed unfair or unjustified. This method is especially useful where your witness became even slightly caustic during the cross, since your subtle attack on opposing counsel may justify the witness's response. Consider:

> QUESTION: Defense counsel seemed very concerned that you did not go to the doctor immediately after your camping trip, but didn't ask you for an explanation. Would you like to explain?

Or,

> QUESTION: I noticed that defense counsel cut you off when you tried to continue your answer about the camping trip. What was it that you wanted to say?

While the introductions in the above examples are arguably leading, they are probably permissible efforts to lay foundation or direct the witness's attention.

Nonetheless, do not overuse preambles of this sort. They are likely to be effective only where the cross-examination truly was overbearing or oppressive.

II. Recross-Examination

The purpose of recross-examination is to discredit the explanation, clarification, or response a witness offers during redirect. So long as subsequent questions stay within the scope of earlier examinations, redirect and recross can theoretically go on and on to the extent permitted by the competition rules or the presiding judge (or the timekeeper, if the duration of your witness examinations is limited).

Redirect and recross are more and more focused than direct and cross-examinations. The rules of many competitions, however, limit each side to one redirect or recross per witness.

Recross-examination follows the same rules as cross-examination with the added requirement that it remain within the scope of the redirect examination: only ask leading questions to which you already know the answers; maintain control of the witness at all times; and get in and get out even faster than you did before.

In order to conduct a successful recross, listen carefully to the witness's explanations during the redirect examination. Recross-examinations are spontaneous and cannot be planned. If you trust your instincts and think a few more questions are needed, go for it. When in doubt, skip it. More times than not, the best recross-examinations begin and end with the words, "Nothing further."

	The Basics	
	REDIRECT EXAMINATION	**RECROSS-EXAMINATION**
Purpose:	Offering explanations for, clarifications of, or responses to, evidence brought out on cross-examination.	Discrediting the explanation, clarification, or response a witness offered on redirect examination.
Rules:	Follow the same rules that apply to direct.	Follow the same rules that apply to cross.
	All redirect questions must be within the scope of the cross.	All recross questions must be within the scope of the redirect.
Length:	Ideally, one to five questions.	The shorter the better.

Chapter Twelve

Expert Testimony

I. The Purpose of Expert Testimony

Most witnesses are called to the stand because they have seen, heard, or done something relevant to the issues in the case. Such persons are often referred to as "ordinary" or "lay" witnesses. The testimony of these witnesses is generally limited to things they have directly observed or experienced, as well as reasonable conclusions they can draw from those sensory perceptions. In short, lay witnesses must testify from personal knowledge, and they may not offer opinions unless the proper foundation can be laid.

Expert witnesses constitute an entirely different category. Expert witnesses are not limited to personal knowledge and may base their testimony on information that was gathered solely for the purpose of testifying at trial. Moreover, an expert witness may offer opinions that go well beyond their direct sensory impressions. Experts may opine on the cause or consequences of occurrences, interpret the actions of other persons, draw conclusions on the basis of circumstances, comment on the likelihood of events, and even state their beliefs regarding such issues as fault, damage, negligence, avoidability, and the like.

Experts can be used in commercial cases to interpret complex financial data, in personal injury cases to explain the nature of injuries, and in criminal cases to translate underworld slang into everyday language, among many possible other scenarios. Properly qualified, an expert can be asked to peer into the past, as when a forensic anthropologist determines the cause of death or a computer forensic examiner tracks the usage of a computer or other electronic device. Other experts may predict the future, as when an economist projects the expected life earnings of the deceased in a wrongful death case.

II. The Standards for Expert Testimony

Expert testimony must conform to the following standards:

Chapter Twelve

A. Areas of Expertise

Expert opinions are admissible where the expert's scientific, technical, or other specialized knowledge will assist the trier of fact in understanding the evidence or a fact at issue in the case. There are two threshold questions: Does the witness possess sufficient scientific, technical, or other specialized knowledge to testify as an expert? And if so, will that knowledge be helpful to the trier of fact?

In real trials, these questions can sometimes be the subject of extensive argument prior to trial. In mock trials, however, the experts are usually identified in the case files, and every expert is typically qualified to provide at least one admissible opinion.

B. Scope of Opinion

Generally, experts can testify on any subject within their area of expertise. Expert testimony may even be about an ultimate issue to be decided by the trier of fact. The only exception is that an expert in a criminal case may not opine about guilt or innocence, or whether the defendant possessed the mental state or condition constituting an element of the crime charged or a defense thereto. For example, in a murder case where temporary insanity is raised as a defense, an expert may not testify that the defendant was temporarily insane at the time of the crime.

C. Bases for Opinion

An expert may testify to their opinion with or without explaining the facts or data on which the opinion is based. This allows the witness to state their opinion at the beginning of the examination, followed by explanation, rather than having to set forth all of the data at the outset before giving her opinion.

Additionally, an expert may testify on the basis of facts made known to them at or before the trial. Moreover, those facts or data need not be admissible in evidence so long as they are of a type "reasonably relied upon" by experts in the particular field.

The Basics	
THE STANDARDS OF EXPERT TESTIMONY	
Areas of Expertise:	An expert's opinion is only admissible if their scientific, technical, or other specialized knowledge will assist the factfinder in understanding the evidence.
Scope of Opinion:	An expert's opinion may embrace an ultimate issue to be decided by the factfinder (except in criminal cases where an expert may not testify about the defendant's state of mind when it is an element of the crime).

> **The Basics**
>
> **THE STANDARDS OF EXPERT TESTIMONY**
>
> **Bases for Opinion:** An expert's opinion need not be preceded by an explanation of the underlying data. Also, the underlying data need not be admissible so long as it is the type reasonably relied upon by experts in the same field.

III. Direct Examination of Experts

A. Planning Expert Testimony

In addition to following the techniques discussed in Chapter Three and Chapter Seven, the rules below will help you achieve a successful direct examination of an expert witness.

1. Determine the Expert's Theory

Just as a lawyer cannot succeed without developing a comprehensive theory of the case, neither will an expert's testimony be effective without a viable, articulated theory. An expert's theory is an overview or summary of their entire opinion. The theory must not only state a conclusion, but must also explain, in commonsense terms, why the expert is correct. Why did the expert settle upon a certain methodology? Why did they review particular data? Why is this approach reliable? Why is the opposing expert wrong? In other words, the expert witness must present a coherent narrative that provides the trier of fact with reasons for accepting the expert's point of view.

The need for a theory is especially true in mock trial cases involving "dueling experts," where each side has its own expert witness and the experts' opinions vary. In these cases, the trier of fact is faced with the task of sorting through the opinion testimony and choosing which witness to believe. It is likely that both experts will be amply qualified, and it is unlikely that either will make a glaring error in their analysis or testimony. The trier of fact will therefore be inclined to credit the expert whose theory is most believable.

Consider the following case. The plaintiff operated a statewide chain of drive-in restaurants but was put out of business by the defendant's allegedly unfair competition. Assume that in the first trial the judge found that the defendant did participate in unfair competition and your mock trial is to be held to determine the amount of damages the defendant must pay to the plaintiff to compensate for the illegal commercial practice. Each side retained an expert witness who generated a damage model.

Chapter Twelve

Not surprisingly, the plaintiff's expert, Dr. Abha Gupta, found that the restaurants would have earned millions of dollars over the following five years had they not been driven out of business. Conversely, the defendant's expert, Dr. Thomas Harris, held the view that the stores would have been marginally profitable, with total profits amounting to no more than a few hundred thousand dollars. Each witness backed up their opinions with computer printouts, charts, and graphs. Both used reliable data, and all of their figures were rigorously accurate.

The rival experts reached different conclusions because they followed different routes. Dr. Gupta calculated lost profits as a function of population growth and driving habits, concluding that the revenues at drive-in restaurants would rise in proportion to expected increases in population and miles driven. Dr. Harris, on the other hand, estimated damages on a "profit-per-store" basis, taking the plaintiff's average profit for the existing restaurants and multiplying them by the number of outlets that the plaintiff planned to build.

Faced with this discrepancy, your task is to present the expert testimony in its most persuasive form. Whichever side you represent, a simple recitation of your expert's methods will not carry the day. After all, both experts were meticulously careful within the confines of their respective approaches. For the same reason, the trier of fact will probably be unimpressed by an expert who reviews in detail all of their calculations. Numbers are boring in any event, and both experts are sure to have been accurate in their arithmetic.

Instead, the key to this case is to persuade the trier of fact that your expert chose the correct approach. Dr. Gupta must be asked to explain why lost profits can be determined on the basis of population growth; Dr. Harris has to support relying on profits per store. The prevailing expert will not be the one with the greatest mastery of the details, but rather the one who most successfully conveys the superiority of their theory. The most painstakingly prepared projection of population growth cannot succeed in persuading a judge or jury if they ultimately decide that only an analysis of profits per store accurately assesses the damages.

The importance of theory extends to all types of expert testimony. It is necessary, but not sufficient, for your expert to be thorough, exacting, highly regarded, incisive, honorable, and well prepared. Despite all this, an expert's testimony will suffer if the witness cannot support their opinion with commonsense reasons.

2. Encourage Using Plain Language

Virtually every field of expertise creates its own technical and shorthand terms. The affidavits of any expert witnesses in your case file may be rife with arcane and jargon-laden speech. If your expert repeats these terms while testifying, have them define and explain what each term means in plain language. For example:

QUESTION:	Dr. Gettleman, do you have an opinion as to why the pressure plate failed?
ANSWER:	Yes. My tests indicate that the fastening bolts were over-torqued.
QUESTION:	What do you mean when you say over-torqued?
ANSWER:	I mean that the bolts were turned too far when they were tightened.

Finally, do not adopt the expert's terminology. Many students, perhaps out of a desire to appear knowledgeable, examine expert witnesses using the expert's own jargon. Such examinations become a private—and completely inaccessible—conversation between the lawyer and the witness. Consider the following:

QUESTION:	Dr. Winters, what injuries did you observe?
ANSWER:	I observed multiple contusions on the anterior upper extremities.
QUESTION:	Was there anything remarkable about the contusions?
ANSWER:	Yes. They varied in color, which indicated that they had been inflicted at different times.
QUESTION:	Did the anterior location of the contusions indicate anything further to you?
ANSWER:	Yes. Their anterior location suggested that they had been inflicted from a superior position.

The lawyer and doctor are talking about bruises. The witness used the term "contusions" because it is medically precise, and the lawyer adopted the term, encouraging the doctor to continue using it. The lawyer demonstrated medical sophistication, but at the cost of the factfinder's comprehension. Juries are made up of regular people from all walks of life; when you break down complicated terms and concepts simply at trial, you demonstrate your ability to inform and therefore persuade a jury.

3. Help to Avoid Narratives

Long narratives are hard to follow and hard to digest. Anyone who ever sat through a long lecture or speech should understand how difficult it is to pay attention to a speaker for an extended period of time. This is particularly true of expert testimony, which often concentrates on complex or intricate details. Allowing an expert to testify in a long, unbroken stretch invites inattention.

Avoid narrative answers and reinitiate primacy by punctuating the expert's testimony at logical breaking points, for example:

QUESTION:	Dr. Harris, what is the significance of location in projecting profits for a chain of drive-in restaurants?

Chapter Twelve

> ANSWER: Location is probably the single most important factor when it comes to profitability in any retail business. Even if the overall trend in an industry is upward, a poorly located business is unlikely to benefit. This is especially true of the restaurant business.
>
> QUESTION: Please explain.
>
> ANSWER: The restaurant business is intensely local in nature. There are very few restaurants that attract people from great distances. Most people eat near their homes, their places of work, or their shopping destinations. So a restaurant in an undesirable neighborhood or in a declining business district simply will not draw customers.
>
> QUESTION: Why is that?
>
> ANSWER: Many restaurants depend heavily on luncheon trade. People on their lunch break usually do not have more than an hour, so a restaurant will not draw this business unless it is located near a fairly large number of employers. No matter how well the economy is doing, a restaurant will not do well at lunchtime if it is located in an area that has experienced a downturn.

The lawyer in this example did not cut off the witness and did not limit the expert to unnaturally short answers. The lawyer did, however, use strategically interjected questions to break up the narrative, thereby continually reemphasizing the expert's testimony.

a. *Prompt the Witness to Give Internal Summaries*

Think of the expert's testimony as a series of steps or elements. At the conclusion of each step, the expert should explain how they got there, why it is important, and where they are going next, as in the following example from the testimony of the defendant's expert in the drive-in case:

> QUESTION: Dr. Harris, please summarize your objections to Dr. Gupta's methodology.
>
> ANSWER: The problem with Dr. Gupta's approach is that she failed to consider several of the most important factors in determining profitability. Reliance on population and vehicle miles led Dr. Gupta to dramatically overestimate the restaurant chain's likely profitability. Dr. Gupta's study was especially deficient because it did not account for either location or potential competition.

QUESTION:	Were you able to conduct a more comprehensive study?
ANSWER:	Yes. I conducted a study that included the six most important factors, all of which were omitted by Dr. Gupta.

b. Use Visual Aids

Visual displays enhance the direct examination of almost every expert. Since expert testimony may be hard to follow, use charts, graphs, drawings, or models to portray or simplify the expert's concepts.

The possibilities for visual aids are practically infinite. Bring to life a physician's testimony, for example, with an anatomical model or a series of colored overlays. Illustrate financial expert testimony with graphs or tables. Use diagrams or scale models for architectural or engineering experts.

Check the rules of procedure in your mock trial competition to see if demonstrative exhibits are allowed. If so, use the exhibits provided to you or, if competition rules permit, create your own to help explain the expert testimony. Do not look only at your own expert's exhibits; if you have the opposing expert's documents, can you make a demonstrative that your expert can use to refute the opposing testimony?

	Checklist	
	ARE YOU GETTING THE MOST FROM YOUR EXPERT?	
☑	**Does your expert's testimony have a clear theory?**	Does your expert's testimony state a clear theory as to why the factfinder should believe their findings? *If not, rework your direct examination to include an overriding theory of the expert's testimony.*
☑	**Are you encouraging your expert to use plain language?**	Do you prompt your expert to explain complicated concepts using plain language? Do you refrain from using the expert's jargon yourself? *If not, the content and purpose of your expert's testimony may not be understood by the factfinder.*
☑	**Are you helping the expert to avoid giving narrative answers?**	Do any of your expert's answers span longer than a few sentences? *If so, divide the answers with more questions to ensure that the factfinder will remain interested throughout the testimony.*

Chapter Twelve

Checklist		
ARE YOU GETTING THE MOST FROM YOUR EXPERT?		
☑	**Are you prompting your expert to give internal summaries?**	Is there an internal summary at the end of each major section of your expert's testimony? *If not, add them to clarify and emphasize the witness's testimony.*
☑	**Did you make use of visual aids?**	Does your expert use maps, charts, diagrams, or the like to explain the testimony? *If not, use demonstrative exhibits that enable your expert to better explain the testimony.*

B. *Organizing Expert Testimony*

There is a certain logic to the direct examination of most experts. While the particulars and details vary, a limited number of possible patterns exist for organizing the testimony. The following is a broad outline that can accommodate the specifics of most expert testimony.

1. Introduce the Witness and Foreshadow the Testimony

The first step is to introduce the expert and explain their involvement in the case. Since expert testimony differs from lay testimony, clarify its purposes for the factfinder so that the information that follows will be understood. Ask how the witness became involved in the case and why they are present in court. Then ask the expert to explain how their opinion fits into the case. Do these things at the very outset of the examination so the factfinder will understand the purpose and import of the witness's testimony from the start.

The plaintiff's damages expert in the example from the preceding section might be introduced as follows:

QUESTION: Please state your name.
ANSWER: Dr. Abha Gupta.
QUESTION: Dr. Gupta, have you been retained to reach an expert opinion in this case?
ANSWER: Yes.
QUESTION: Did you reach an opinion concerning the plaintiff's lost profits?
ANSWER: Yes, I have calculated the amount of money that the plaintiff would have earned if they had remained in business.

Expert Testimony

QUESTION: We'll talk about your opinion in detail in a few minutes, but right now I'd like to ask you about what qualifies you to testify as an expert in this case.

2. Elicit the Expert's Qualifications

To testify as an expert, a witness must be qualified by reason of knowledge, skill, experience, training, or education. This is a threshold question for the judge, who must determine whether the witness is qualified before permitting opinion testimony. Qualifying the witness, then, is a necessary predicate for all of the testimony to follow. Take care to qualify the expert in a manner that is both technically adequate and persuasive.

Although it is generally understood in mock trials that an expert witness whose affidavit is included in the case file is qualified to give opinions, demonstrate your understanding of the qualification process prior to eliciting the expert's opinions.

a. *Fulfill the Technical Requirements*

The technical requirements for qualifying an expert witness are straightforward. It is usually adequate to show that the witness possesses some specialized skill or knowledge, acquired through appropriate experience or education, and that the witness is able to apply that skill or knowledge in a manner relevant to the issues in the case. Thus, the minimal qualifications for the financial expert in the restaurant case could be established as follows:

QUESTION: Dr. Gupta, could you please tell the jury about your education?

ANSWER: Certainly. I have an undergraduate degree in business from the University of Michigan and a PhD in economics from Northwestern University.

QUESTION: What work have you done since earning your doctorate?

ANSWER: I was a professor in the economics department at Washington University for six years. Then I left to start my own consulting firm, which is called Gupta & Associates.

QUESTION: Do you have a specialty within the field of economics?
ANSWER: Yes, my specialty is business valuation.
QUESTION: Has business valuation been your specialty both at Washington University and at Gupta & Associates?
ANSWER: Yes.
QUESTION: What is the field of business valuation?

ANSWER: It is the study of all of the components that contribute to the fair value of a business, including anticipated future profits, assets, receivables, good will, and investment potential.

The above examination confirms the expert's qualifications by reason of both education and experience. Dr. Gupta should now be able to give an opinion as to the projected profits for the restaurant chain.

Establishing basic qualifications is not your entire objective. It is equally important, if not more so, to qualify the witness as persuasively as possible.

b. Be Persuasive When Qualifying

The technical qualification of an expert merely allows the witness to testify in the form of an opinion. Your ultimate goal is to ensure that the factfinder accepts that opinion. Persuasive qualification is particularly important in cases involving competing experts, since their relative qualifications may be one basis on which the factfinder will decide which expert to believe.

It is a mistake, however, to think that more qualifications are necessarily more persuasive. An endless repetition of degrees, publications, awards, and appointments may easily overload any judge or juror's ability, not to mention desire, to pay careful attention to the witness.

Concentrate on a witness's specific expertise, as opposed to more generic or remote qualifications. Every economist, for example, likely holds a doctorate; in cases with dueling economists, there is likely no need to waste valuable time expounding your expert's academic degrees. Similarly, ignore matters such as the subject of the witness's doctoral thesis, unless it bears directly on some issue in the case.

On the other hand, you can greatly enhance an expert's credibility by singling out qualifications that relate specifically to the particular case. Point out, for example, that the witness has published several articles directly relevant to the issues in the case. Avoid, on the other hand, taking the witness through a long list of extraneous articles, even if they appeared in prestigious journals. Look for other case-specific qualifications to highlight, such as consulting work or teaching experience that is connected to an issue in the case.

Experience is often more impressive than academic background. A medical expert may be more impressive if they have actually practiced in the applicable specialty, as opposed to possessing knowledge that is strictly theoretical. When presenting such a witness, then, dwell on the expert's experience, pointing out details such as the number of procedures performed, the hospitals where they are on staff, and the numbers of other physicians who have consulted the expert.

Finally, it is frequently effective to emphasize areas of qualification where you know the opposing expert to be lacking. If your expert has a superior academic background, use the direct examination to point out why academic training is important. If your expert holds a certification that the opposing expert lacks, have the expert explain how difficult it is to become certified.

c. Tender the Witness (If Allowed)

Depending on your mock trial rules, the next step will be to tender the witness to the court as an expert in the specified field. Tendering the witness informs the court that qualification has been completed and gives opposing counsel an opportunity either to conduct a voir dire examination of the witness (which we will discuss later in this chapter) or to object to the tender. In the restaurant example above, the financial expert would be tendered as follows:

COUNSEL: Your Honor, we tender Dr. Abha Gupta as an expert witness in the field of business valuation and the projection of profits.

Summary

AN EXPERT'S QUALIFICATION MAY INCLUDE

- Education
- Teaching and lecturing positions
- Work experience
- Licenses and certifications
- Specialized training
- Publications
- Continuing education courses
- Consulting experience
- Professional memberships
- Professional awards or honors

---

3. Elicit the Expert's Opinion and Theory

Following qualification, the next step in the direct examination of an expert witness is to elicit firm statements of opinion and theory.

a. Have the Expert State Opinions Up Front

Once qualified (and accepted as an expert through a formal tender and ruling, if allowed), the witness may express opinions without additional foundation. In other words, the witness may state conclusions without first detailing the nature or extent of their background work or investigation.

Take advantage of this opportunity. Expert testimony can be boring. The factfinder will not be interested in the intricate details of an expert's preparation—chances are they won't even understand them. Details, if they are offered in a void, will be even less captivating. On the other hand, a clear statement of the expert's conclusion can provide the context for the balance of the explanatory testimony. For example:

QUESTION: Dr. Gupta, do you have an opinion as to the profits that the plaintiff's restaurant chain would have made, if they hadn't been forced out of business?

ANSWER: Yes, I do.

QUESTION: What is your opinion?

ANSWER: I believe that the restaurant chain would have earned at least $3.2 million in profits over the next five years if they had been able to stay in business.

QUESTION: How did you reach that opinion?

ANSWER: I based my calculations on the state's projected population growth, combined with the probable demand for fast-food, drive-in restaurants.

By providing this opinion at the outset, the expert allows the trier of fact to comprehend the significance of the following details, which counsel is then free to inquire about further.

b. Elicit the Expert's Theory

Once the expert's opinion has been stated, immediately provide the underlying theory. The theory should furnish the nexus between the expert's conclusion and the data supporting the conclusion. In other words, the examination should follow this pattern: 1) here is my opinion; 2) here are the principles supporting my opinion; 3) here is what I did to reach my final conclusion.

In the fast-food example, craft questions that will draw out the expert's theory that population growth and vehicle miles are reliable indicators of projected profits.

QUESTION: Dr. Gupta, why did you base your calculations on the state's projected population growth?

ANSWER: The demand for fast food will rise as population grows. This is particularly true because teenagers and parents of young children are the largest purchasers of fast food, and they are also two of the groups that increase most rapidly as population goes up.

QUESTION:	Why did you also consider growth in vehicle miles?
ANSWER:	Drive-in restaurants are especially sensitive to vehicle miles. As people drive more, they are exposed to more drive-in restaurants, and they therefore buy more meals.
QUESTION:	What did you conclude from these relationships?
ANSWER:	I concluded that the profitability of a drive-in restaurant chain will rise in proportion to a combination of general population growth and increases in miles driven.
QUESTION:	Did you consider only population growth and vehicle miles?
ANSWER:	Of course not. I began by determining the chain's profits under current conditions, and I used those figures as a base. Then I projected them forward for five years, using the government's statistics for population and driving.
QUESTION:	Please tell us now exactly how you did that.

This examination both states the theory and provides the context for the explanation to follow.

4. Elicit the Explanation and Support for the Expert's Opinion

Having stated and supported their theory choice, the expert can now go on to detail the nature of their investigation and calculations. The trier of fact cannot be expected to take the expert at their word, so establish the validity and accuracy of their data and assumptions.

a. Have the Expert Explain the Data

Ask how the expert chose and obtained data. Ask the expert to explain why this information is reliable. In the scenario above, for example, the expert could point out that government statistics on population and vehicle miles are used to make many crucial decisions such as the configuration of traffic lights, the expansion of highways, and even the construction of schools.

Ask the expert to describe any tests or computations that they performed. It is not sufficient for the expert simply to relate the nature of the data. Rather, have the expert explain how and why the data support these conclusions.

Handling underlying data is one of the trickiest aspects of expert testimony. Elicit a sufficiently detailed treatment of the data to persuade the factfinder of its reliability but stop well short of the point where their attention span is exhausted. Whenever possible, provide the factfinder with a way to visualize the data upon which the expert relied. Showing the jurors the evidence so they can draw their

Chapter Twelve

own conclusion is always more persuasive than telling them what conclusion to draw. Moreover, once a juror reaches their own conclusion, it is harder for opposing counsel to persuade them otherwise.

b. Be Clear About What Assumptions Were Made

Many experts rely upon assumptions. The financial expert in the fast-food case, for example, would no doubt assume that the relationship between sales and population growth would continue at historical rates. The expert would also probably assume a certain financial "discount rate" for reducing the dollars in their projection to present value. There is obviously nothing wrong with using appropriate presumptions, but their validity should be explained.

> QUESTION: Dr. Gupta, did you make any assumptions in reaching your opinion that the plaintiff's restaurant chain would have earned $3.2 million in profits?
>
> ANSWER: Yes, I assumed that fast-food sales would continue to increase in proportion to population at the same rate as they had in the past.
>
> QUESTION: Why did you make that assumption?
>
> ANSWER: The restaurant chain was put out of business, so there were no actual sales to examine. I therefore had to project their most likely sales, and for that I had to assume a base figure to project forward.
>
> QUESTION: What did you use as your base figure?
>
> ANSWER: I used the average growth for the entire industry.
>
> QUESTION: Why did you use the industry average?
>
> ANSWER: I used the industry average precisely because it is an average of all of the companies in that particular business. That way I could be sure that I wasn't using a figure that was abnormally high or abnormally low.

It is not necessary to explain or outline every hypothesis used by your expert, but note and support the most important assumptions.

5. Use Theory Differentiation If Your Case Involves Dueling Experts

Cases involving dueling experts also involve competing theories. Properly prepared and presented, each expert will attempt to explain why the trier of fact should accept their theory. It can be particularly effective, therefore, to ask your expert to comment on the opposing expert's work. This technique, called "theory differentiation," is most convincing when your expert discusses the shortcomings of the opposition theory.

In previous sections, we have seen illustrations taken from the testimony of the plaintiff's financial expert in a case involving lost profits. Now consider this example of theory differentiation, offered by the expert witness for the defendant in the same case, who has already been identified and qualified:

QUESTION: Dr. Harris, have you had an opportunity to review the work done in this case by Dr. Gupta?
ANSWER: Yes, I have.
QUESTION: Do you agree with Dr. Gupta's damage projections?
ANSWER: No, I do not.
QUESTION: Why not?
ANSWER: Dr. Gupta based the estimate on a combination of population growth and mileage assumptions, and this approach cannot yield a reliable result.
QUESTION: Why is that?
ANSWER: Because it assumes too much. Dr. Gupta's theory is that restaurant revenues will inevitably rise with population and automobile miles. While this might be true for the entire restaurant industry, there is no reason to think that it would be true for any particular chain of restaurants. To reach a dependable result for an individual chain, you would have to consider many other factors.
QUESTION: What factors are those?
ANSWER: At a minimum, you would have to consider location, market niche, product recognition, potential competition, specific demographics, and general economic climate.
QUESTION: Did Dr. Gupta consider any of those factors?
ANSWER: No, Dr. Gupta did not.
QUESTION: Please give us an example of how location could affect the profit projections.
ANSWER: Certainly. Population always grows unevenly. Even if the overall population rises in a state or a city, it might stay constant or fall in certain areas. Therefore, a restaurant chain cannot take advantage of population increases if its restaurants are in stagnant or declining locations.

The defense expert has deftly exposed the flaws in the plaintiff's theory. There are two advantages to this use of theory differentiation. First, it enables the expert to concentrate on major issues, as opposed to picking out petty mistakes. Second, it allows the expert to avoid personal attacks. In essence, the above example has Dr. Harris saying: "I have no personal quarrel with Dr. Gupta; they simply chose an inadequate theory." This "high road" approach contributes to the dignity and persuasiveness of the witness.

Chapter Twelve

The timing of theory differentiation is important. Generally, it is best to build up your expert's credibility through explanation of their opinion before attempting to tear down opposing counsel's expert and their opinion. Because the order of trials dictates that the defendant presents its case after the plaintiff, however, defense counsel may prefer to cover this ground early in the examination to rebut the plaintiff's expert immediately and forcefully.

6. Send the Expert Out with a Bang

Complete your expert's direct examination with a powerful restatement of the witness's most important conclusions.

Summary

ORGANIZING AN EXPERT'S DIRECT

- Introduce the expert and foreshadow the testimony
- Elicit the expert's qualifications
- Have the expert provide an opinion and theory
- Elicit the expert's explanation and support for the opinion
- Utilize theory differentiation in cases with competing experts
- Have the expert restate the most important conclusions

IV. Cross-Examining Experts

Apply the same rules and guidelines for content and organization discussed in Chapter Nine to the cross-examination of experts. Below is a list of additional techniques you can use with expert witnesses. Each mock trial case file is different, and only some of the following techniques will be useful in any particular case. So, consider all of the following, but use only those that clearly apply to your facts.

A. Challenge the Witness's Credentials

You can challenge an expert witness's credentials either on voir dire (a concept we explain below) or during cross-examination. Use voir dire to object to the legal sufficiency of the expert's qualifications; use cross-examination to attack the weight the factfinder should give to expert's conclusions.

1. Voir Dire on Credentials

Many courts, and therefore many mock trial competitions, require that experts be "tendered" to the court prior to eliciting any opinion(s). The tender is a request that the court recognize the witness as an expert in a particular field. After the tender, opposing counsel is entitled to request an opportunity to conduct a mini-cross-examination, limited to challenging the witness's qualifications to testify as an expert. This mini-cross-examination, which is conducted toward the beginning of the proponent's direct examination, is called voir dire. Most courts allow or even encourage voir dire of experts, but many mock trial competitions do not permit it.

Here is an example of how this exchange might transpire:

PROPONENT: Your Honor, we tender Dr. Thomas Harris as an expert on the subject of lost profits.
COURT: Any objection, counsel?
OPPONENT: Your Honor, we would like the opportunity to conduct a voir dire examination.
COURT: You may examine the witness on the subject of his qualifications to testify.

If the rules of procedure in your mock trial do not provide for the tendering of experts, then listen carefully and object at the point of the direct examination where the witness begins to offer an opinion. It is not necessary to wait for an invitation from the court.

PROPONENT: Dr. Harris, do you have an opinion about the profits that the plaintiff would have earned if the restaurant chain had not been driven out of business?
OPPONENT: Objection. Your Honor, we would like an opportunity to voir dire this witness before he is allowed to give opinion testimony.
COURT: You may examine the witness on the subject of their qualifications to testify.

Voir dire addresses the admissibility of evidence; it is not the time to launch into a wide-ranging attack on the expert's integrity, methods, data, or bias. Thus, when conducting voir dire of an expert's credentials, restrict questions to the witness's qualifications to give an expert opinion: Is the witness qualified to testify as an expert by way of their knowledge, skill, experience, training, or education? The witness may testify so long as they meet this minimum requirement.

It is frequently an uphill battle to persuade a judge that a proffered witness should not be allowed to testify as an expert, especially in mock trials where judges want to give all of the students the chance to participate in the trial. Even so, your ability to voir dire an expert and challenge their qualifications will be noted and, if done well, considered in the score you receive on cross-examination.

Chapter Twelve

2. Cross-Examine on Credentials

A court's ruling that a witness may testify as an expert means only that the witness possesses sufficient credentials to pass the evidentiary threshold. It still may be possible to diminish the weight of the witness's qualifications during cross-examination. There are three basic methods for discrediting the value of an expert's credentials.

a. *Limit the Scope of the Witness's Expertise*

Although an expert may be well-qualified in a certain area or subspecialty, consider whether you can recast the issues of the case to place them beyond the witness's competence. Assume, for example, that the plaintiff's expert in the restaurant scenario was tendered and accepted as an expert on lost profits.

> QUESTION: Dr. Gupta, your primary consulting work involves business valuation, correct?
>
> ANSWER: That is my profession.
>
> QUESTION: Issues of valuation usually involve an existing business, right?
>
> ANSWER: That is the usual case.
>
> QUESTION: People come to you when they want to buy or sell a business, value it for estate tax purposes, or perhaps when there is a divorce?
>
> ANSWER: Yes, those are all typical situations for business valuation.
>
> QUESTION: You wouldn't call yourself a management consultant, would you?
>
> ANSWER: No, I do not get involved in operations.
>
> QUESTION: Because your work is basically evaluative?
>
> ANSWER: Exactly.
>
> QUESTION: So someone who wanted assistance in expanding a business would need to go to a different consultant, wouldn't they?
>
> ANSWER: Correct.
>
> QUESTION: For example, there are consultants who specialize in site evaluation, correct?
>
> ANSWER: Yes, there are.
>
> QUESTION: But you do not do that yourself?
>
> ANSWER: No, I do not.
>
> QUESTION: So if I wanted to evaluate the best possible locations for my business outlets, you would recommend that I consult someone else, isn't that right?
>
> ANSWER: Yes, I suppose that I would refer you.

Expert Testimony

By limiting the scope of the witness's expertise, counsel can now claim during closing argument that the crucial issue of location is beyond Dr. Gupta's expertise and therefore their opinion regarding lost profits should be discounted.

b. Stress Missing Credentials

An expert witness may be qualified to testify but lack important certifications, degrees, or licenses. Assume for example that the plaintiff in a personal injury case has called their psychotherapist to testify on the issue of damages. The witness was tendered and accepted as an expert and has completed direct testimony. This cross-examination followed:

QUESTION: Mr. Zanzi, your degree is in social work, correct?
ANSWER: Yes, I have an MSW, and I am a licensed psychotherapist.
QUESTION: You do not have a doctorate in clinical psychology, do you?
ANSWER: No, I do not.
QUESTION: And of course you are not a psychiatrist?
ANSWER: That is correct.
QUESTION: I notice that your stationery lists your name as Abizer Zanzi, MSW.
ANSWER: Yes, that is right.
QUESTION: I have seen other social workers with the letters ACSW after their names. What does ACSW stand for?
ANSWER: It stands for Accredited Clinical Social Worker.
QUESTION: That is an additional certification that some social workers earn, correct?
ANSWER: Yes, that is correct.
QUESTION: But you have not achieved that certification, have you?

c. Contrast Your Expert's Credentials

When possible, point out an adverse witness's missing credentials and contrast them with your own expert's superior qualifications. In the following example, assume that the plaintiff called a practicing attorney as an expert witness in a legal malpractice case. This scenario is taken from the defendant's cross-examination:

QUESTION: Ms. Chang-Adiga, I understand that you are a member of the American Bar Association Section of Litigation, correct?

ANSWER: Yes, I am.
QUESTION: The American Bar Association Section of Litigation is open to any lawyer who is willing to pay the dues, correct?
ANSWER: That is right.
QUESTION: So you were not elected or chosen by your peers for membership in that section, were you?
ANSWER: Nobody is.
QUESTION: I assume that you are familiar with the American College of Trial Lawyers?
ANSWER: I am.
QUESTION: That organization consists of lawyers who specialize in litigation and the trial of cases, correct?
ANSWER: I believe so.
QUESTION: Membership in the American College of Trial Lawyers is limited to two percent of the lawyers in any given state, isn't that right?
ANSWER: I think that is right.
QUESTION: And individuals have to be proposed and elected to membership in the American College of Trial Lawyers?
ANSWER: I understand that to be the process.
QUESTION: You are not a member of the American College of Trial Lawyers, are you?
ANSWER: No, I am not.
QUESTION: Are you aware that Karla Chrobak, the defendant's expert witness, is a member of the American College of Trial Lawyers?
ANSWER: I am aware, yes.

You can contrast experts' credentials on bases other than certification. It is fair game to point out your own witness's greater or more specific experience, your witness's teaching or publication record, or any other disparity that will enhance your expert and diminish the opposition.

Note, however, that all the rules of basic cross-examination apply here as well. You must be satisfied to elicit the fact of the contrasting qualifications. It will do you little good to argue with the opposing expert witness or to try to extract a concession that their credentials are inadequate. If given the opportunity, the other side's expert will adeptly explain why those credentials, whatever they may be, are superior to your expert's. Stop short of offering up such an opportunity.

B. Obtain Favorable Information

It will often be possible to obtain favorable concessions from the opposing party's expert witness. As with all cross-examination, extract this information near the beginning of the examination. Needless to say, you must be positive of the answers before launching into this sort of cross-examination.

In general, the helpful material available from opposing experts will fall into the following categories.

1. Affirm Your Own Expert

Even experts who ultimately disagree may have many shared understandings. You may, therefore, accredit your own expert by asking the opposing expert to acknowledge the reliability of your expert's data, the validity of your expert's assumptions, or the caliber or your expert's credentials.

If this sort of helpful information is either obvious, given in the expert's affidavit, or implicit in the expert's conclusions, it is fair game for your cross-examination. Do not, however, attempt to elicit such affirmation out of thin air in a mock trial, as witnesses are not prone to provide helpful information unless they will look plain silly disagreeing, they can be impeached for disagreeing, or their own conclusions will be questioned if they disagree.

2. Elicit Areas of Agreement

In addition, it may be possible to elicit concessions from the opposing expert that go to the merits of the case. The adverse expert may, for example, be willing to agree with several of your major premises, even while disagreeing with your ultimate conclusion. Consider this cross-examination of the defense expert in the drive-in restaurant case:

> QUESTION: Dr. Harris, you are dissatisfied with the nature of Dr. Gupta's study of lost profits, correct?
> ANSWER: Yes, I have trouble with Dr. Gupta's methodology.
> QUESTION: But you do agree, don't you, that the chain had made a profit every year it was in business?
> ANSWER: I believe that is correct.
> QUESTION: And every one of its outlets was profitable, correct?
> ANSWER: I think that is right.
> QUESTION: So someone must have been able to select profitable locations, right?
> ANSWER: I suppose so.
> QUESTION: Dr. Gupta assumed that the chain would continue to choose good locations, isn't that right?

ANSWER: That is implicit in Dr. Gupta's model.
QUESTION: And you did not conduct an independent study of favorable or unfavorable restaurant locations, did you?
ANSWER: No, I did not.
QUESTION: So you have no data that you can point to that would contradict Dr. Gupta's assumption?
ANSWER: I do not.

3. Criticize the Opposing Party's Conduct

Finally, if the expert's affidavit or deposition transcript includes criticisms of the opposing party's conduct, bring out those criticisms on cross. For example:

QUESTION: Dr. Gupta, in order for you to reach your opinion on damages, you reviewed all of the plaintiff's financial records, correct?
ANSWER: Yes, that is correct.
QUESTION: Isn't it true that the plaintiff's company did not keep accurate store-by-store records?
ANSWER: Yes, they aggregated their financial information, rather than breaking it down store by store.
QUESTION: The absence of store-by-store information must have made your job more difficult.
ANSWER: I found that I was able to achieve accurate results on the basis of statewide projections.
QUESTION: Still, you could have projected profits for each individual restaurant if the available financial data had been more precise, isn't that true?
ANSWER: Yes, that is true.
QUESTION: But because of the plaintiff's aggregate record keeping, you were not able to do that?
ANSWER: No, I was not.

C. *Challenge the Witness's Impartiality*

Expert witnesses are supposed to be independent analysts, not advocates. The worst accusation you can make against an expert witness is that they altered their opinion to fit a party's needs—and, sadly, expert witnesses are sometimes guilty of this. Accordingly, cross-examine an expert on the issue of bias if the material is there to be exploited. Cross-examination on bias falls into three basic categories.

Expert Testimony

1. Question Fees

Cross-examine an expert concerning fees only in fairly limited circumstances. For example, an especially large fee, compared to another expert in the case, may demonstrate bias, especially if the other expert is a public employee who is not being additionally compensated. Similarly, a large unpaid fee outstanding at the time of testimony may be evidence of something less than objectivity.

2. Question the Expert's Relationship with the Participants

An expert's relationship with a party or with counsel may also indicate a lack of impartiality. If your case file indicates that the witness has worked with the opposing party's lawyers repeatedly or has testified to similar conclusions in case after case, establish those facts during cross-examination.

Some cases may involve testimony by in-house experts, perhaps a company's own accountant or engineer. Such experts are susceptible to the same suggestion of bias as any other employee of a party to litigation. It is safe to assume that all employees want to see their employer succeed and prosper. It is equally safe to assume that all employees would prefer not to be responsible for harm done to their employer or for excessive costs incurred. In these circumstances, use cross-examination to bring out the witness's personal stake in the outcome of the litigation.

3. Question the Expert's Positional Bias

With or without regard to past retention, some experts seem wedded to certain professional, scientific, or intellectual positions. Experts frequently come to testify only for plaintiffs or only for defendants. Others reach only one of a range of conclusions. For example, some psychiatrists seem to conclude that every criminal defendant is insane or incompetent to stand trial. Where they are supported by facts in your case file, such rigidly held positional biases can be exploited effectively on cross-examination.

D. Point Out Omissions

Experts may be vulnerable on cross-examination if they failed to conduct essential tests or procedures, or neglected to consider all significant factors. As with questioning an expert's fees, relationship to the participants, and personal biases, only question neglected tests or experiments if there is evidence of such omissions in your case file.

Other sorts of omissions are more commonplace. Witnesses are frequently asked to evaluate the validity or accuracy of other experts' work. A consulting pathologist, for example, might be asked to reevaluate the protocol of an autopsy conducted by the local medical examiner. No matter how prominent, a "second-opinion" witness can almost always be undermined by the fact that they did not conduct the primary investigation.

QUESTION: Dr. Combe, you reach a conclusion quite different from the conclusions reached by Dr. Goretskaya, correct?

ANSWER: Yes.

QUESTION: Of course, you did not perform an autopsy yourself, did you?

ANSWER: No, I did not.

QUESTION: In fact, your information comes exclusively from Dr. Goretskaya's autopsy protocol?

ANSWER: That is right.

QUESTION: So you have relied on Dr. Goretskaya for all of your factual information, isn't that right?

ANSWER: Yes, I have.

QUESTION: You know nothing of the actual circumstances of the autopsy, other than what you have learned from Dr. Goretskaya's report?

ANSWER: Correct.

QUESTION: So at least with regard to gathering information, you have trusted Dr. Goretskaya's work.

This technique is not limited to "reevaluating" experts. It can be employed, in different form, with regard to any witness who relies exclusively on information provided by others.

QUESTION: Dr. Rozenblat, you base your opinion solely on an examination of hospital records, correct?

ANSWER: Correct.

QUESTION: You did not examine the decedent yourself, did you?

ANSWER: No, I did not.

QUESTION: So your opinion can only be as good as the information you received, right?

ANSWER: I suppose so.

QUESTION: If any of that information were faulty, that could affect the basis for your opinion, correct?

ANSWER: Yes, depending upon the circumstances.

QUESTION: The same would be true of missing information, right?

ANSWER: Right.

QUESTION: You'll agree with me, won't you, that firsthand observation is preferred for the purpose of diagnosis?

ANSWER: Yes, it is preferred.

Finally, many experts testify based on statistics or studies compiled from other sources. Frequently, such experts do not investigate the reliability of the underlying data, and this can leave them vulnerable to cross-examination.

E. Substitute Information

1. Change Assumptions

Almost all experts use assumptions of one sort or another in the course of formulating their opinions. An expert's assumptions, however, might be unrealistic, unreliable, or unreasonably favorable to the party for whom the expert is testifying. It can be extremely effective, therefore, to ask the witness to alter an assumption, substituting one that you believe to be more in keeping with the evidence in the case. Consider this scenario from the drive-in restaurant case:

QUESTION: Dr. Gupta, your lost-profits calculation includes an assumption that vehicle miles will continue to grow at the rate of four percent, correct?

ANSWER: Yes, that is the figure I used.

QUESTION: Will you agree that numerous factors can influence the growth of vehicle miles?

ANSWER: Yes, I think that is obvious.

QUESTION: For example, vehicle miles actually fell during the pandemic?

ANSWER: I believe that is true.

QUESTION: And if vehicle miles were to rise at a rate of less than four percent, your estimate of lost profits would have to be reduced, correct?

ANSWER: Yes, that is right.

QUESTION: In fact, if we used an assumption of two percent, your estimate of lost profits would have to be reduced by over $600,000?

ANSWER: I haven't done the calculation, but it should be something in that range.

When the substituted assumption calls for recalculation, do the math in advance, rather than asking the witness to do it on the spot.

2. Maximize Any Uncertainty

Challenge an expert's degree of certainty by suggesting alternative scenarios or explanations that are included in your case file.

Chapter Twelve

> QUESTION: Dr. Harris, you believe that the plaintiff's history of profitability is largely attributable to location, correct?
>
> ANSWER: Yes, I think that location is, and has been, the most important factor.
>
> QUESTION: But there are other factors that contribute to profitability, correct?
>
> ANSWER: Certainly.
>
> QUESTION: Some of those factors would be product quality, value, or market demand, correct?
>
> ANSWER: Yes.
>
> QUESTION: You are familiar with the term "destination shopping," aren't you?
>
> ANSWER: Of course.
>
> QUESTION: That means that people will travel to seek out value or quality or amenities, regardless of the location, correct?
>
> ANSWER: That does happen.
>
> QUESTION: Well, you didn't interview the plaintiff's customers, did you?
>
> ANSWER: Of course not.
>
> QUESTION: So you cannot be sure that location was of primary importance to them, can you?
>
> ANSWER: I can't look into their minds.
>
> QUESTION: Isn't it possible that the plaintiff's customers sought out their restaurants because of value or quality?
>
> ANSWER: It is possible.
>
> QUESTION: So it is also possible that location was not the primary factor in plaintiff's profitability?

F. Challenge Technique or Theory

The most difficult, though frequently the most tempting, form of expert cross-examination is to challenge the witness's method, theory, or logic. It is possible, but extremely unlikely, that an expert will agree that they made a mistake or that their reasoning is faulty. In most cases, you gain little by confronting an expert with any but the most glaring flaws, since that will only afford the expert an opportunity to explain. Instead, point out the opposition's errors (using your expert, if possible) and draw your own conclusions during final argument.

Checklist
HOW CAN YOU OPPOSE THIS EXPERT'S TESTIMONY?

☑	**Can you challenge the witness's credentials?**	Are the witness's credentials arguably inadequate for an expert in the field?
		If so, point out that insufficiency by conducting voir dire during the direct examination.
		Are the expert's credentials weak in some area?
		If so, point out that weakness during cross-examination.
☑	**Can you obtain favorable information from the witness?**	Can you get the expert to affirm your expert, agree with your expert in certain areas, or criticize their own party's conduct?
		If so, elicit this helpful information early in your cross-examination.
☑	**Can you challenge the witness's impartiality?**	Are the expert's fees unusually high? Does the expert have an ongoing relationship with the party or counsel calling them? Does the witness seem wedded to certain positions?
		If so, exploit this information during cross-examination.
☑	**Can you point out omissions by the witness?**	Did someone besides the expert conduct the tests or compile the information upon which the expert relied?
		If so, point out the expert's reliance on others during cross-examination.
☑	**Can you challenge the witness's technique or theory?**	Are there *glaring* flaws in the witness's technique or theory that can be exposed?
		If so, point them out during cross-examination only if you cannot elicit the information from another witness.

Chapter Thirteen

Objections

I. The Purpose of Objections

Objections raise and resolve evidentiary disputes. You may object to the questions posed by attorneys, the testimony given by witnesses, the introduction or use of exhibits, or to the demeanor or behavior of any of the participants of a trial.

Although most people associate the process of objecting with contentiousness and even hostility, that need not be the case. Our adversary system relies upon opposing attorneys to present evidence and the judge to decide upon its admissibility. An objection, then, is nothing more than a signal to the judge that there is a disagreement between counsel concerning the rules of evidence or procedure.

When there are no objections, which is the overwhelming majority of the time, the judge can allow evidence to come into the record without a specific ruling. If we had no process of objecting, the trial judge would have to rule upon every separate answer and item of evidence. Thus, unless the process is abused or misused, trials are actually expedited by the judge's ability to rely upon counsel to object to questionable evidence.

Recall from Chapter Two and from Chapter Six that you determine the admissibility of information or conduct using the rules of evidence adopted by your mock trial organizer. If the rules allow a piece of evidence, it is admissible; evidence that is not allowed is inadmissible. The presiding judge determines the admissibility of the evidence at trial; the judge hears objections from counsel and rules upon them.

Objections that the judge sustains were appropriately raised and deemed applicable to the given situation; overruled objections were either inappropriately raised or deemed not applicable under the rules.

The lawyer objecting is called the opponent of the evidence, whereas the lawyer attempting to present the evidence is the proponent.

There are two main types of objections: substantive and nonsubstantive. Substantive objections bring into question the admissibility of the content of the testimony or exhibit at issue. Nonsubstantive objections raise the appropriateness of the manner in which the information is being sought or delivered to the court.

Chapter Thirteen

A. Nonsubstantive Objections

The most common nonsubstantive objections are challenges to the form of a question asked. For example, a leading question on direct examination is improper because it tells the witness what answer is expected. Even if the answer itself would be admissible, the question is not allowed because of its suggestiveness. Likewise, compound questions, vague questions, and argumentative questions, to name a few, are also objectionable because of their form.

Nonsubstantive objections may also be made to anything else that might have an impermissible impact on the trier of fact. For instance, a lawyer can object if opposing counsel raises their voice to a witness or approaches the witness in an intimidating manner. Likewise, counsel may object to the manner in which exhibits are displayed or to the position of chairs and tables in the courtroom.

B. Substantive Objections

Even if a question is phrased in the proper form, it may nonetheless call for inadmissible evidence. The information sought may be irrelevant, unduly prejudicial, or hearsay. For instance, the question, "What is your religious affiliation?" is in proper form but any answer would be inadmissible under most rules of evidence since it is almost certainly irrelevant.

In addition, even if a question is not objectionable, a witness may respond with an inadmissible answer. The answer might volunteer irrelevant information, it might contain unanticipated hearsay, or it might consist entirely of speculation. For example, a direct examiner could ask the perfectly allowable question, "How do you know that the traffic light was red?" only to receive the hearsay reply, "Because Karen Trumbull told me just last week." Hearing this response, opposing counsel would no doubt object to the answer and move that it be stricken from the record.

II. The Rules of Objecting

This portion of the chapter is aimed at giving you guidance to follow in determining whether, when, and how to object, as well as how to respond to and recover from objections.

A. Consider Objections Carefully

In Chapter Two, we explained in detail how to outline your case for trial. By following this method, you have already compiled a list of all the facts to which each witness may testify and every possible substantive objection (and response) that may be raised. You have also taken this process one step further by determining which substantive objections are worth making. Knowing this information will make your job at trial much easier since it will enable you to anticipate many substantive objections with the comfort of a planned response.

Despite this, there will always be instances in a mock trial when you will want to object to the manner in which information is sought or delivered to the court. These nonsubstantive objections are impossible to anticipate. Instead, in the heat of trial, you must consider whether to object on a split-second basis.

When deciding whether to object, ask yourself if the objection is truly necessary. Not every valid objection needs to be made. Objections can be tiresome: they interrupt the flow of the evidence, they distract attention from the real issues at hand, and they have an awful tendency to degenerate into whining. You may even lose points with the judge by incessantly interrupting your opposition only to point out your incredible grasp of the rules of evidence.

For instance, there is little point to objecting if opposing counsel will be able to rectify the problem simply by rephrasing the question, as is the case with most nonsubstantive objections that address the improper form of a question. This is particularly true of leading questions on direct examination.

PROPONENT: Isn't it true that you had the green light as you approached the intersection?
OPPONENT: Objection, counsel is leading their own witness.
THE COURT: The objection is sustained.
PROPONENT: What color was the traffic light as you approached the intersection?
ANSWER: It was green.

In this example, the objection to the leading question excluded no evidence and may actually have emphasized the witness's testimony that the light was green. Although it was technically proper, counsel would have been just as well off not making the objection.

Of course, the persistent use of leading questions to feed answers to a witness is quite another matter. In those circumstances, an objection should almost always be made.

B. Direct All Arguments to the Judge

Objections at trial are conducted as a conversation between counsel and the court. Ideally, the opponent of the evidence argues first, followed by the proponent of the evidence and concluding with a reply from the opponent. In practice, however, the format is often much less formal, with the judge asking questions and counsel responding.

No matter what, do not argue with, or even address, opposing counsel. It is the judge who will make the ruling and the judge who must be convinced. It is

Chapter Thirteen

ineffective, distracting, and even insulting to the court when counsel turn to each other to argue their objections.

> OPPONENT: Objection, Your Honor, lack of foundation.
> PROPONENT: What more foundation could you want, counselor?
> OPPONENT: Well, you could start with a basis for personal knowledge.
> PROPONENT: He already testified that he is the comptroller. Isn't that enough for you?

No matter how foolish, trite, or easily disposed of the other side's position seems, always avoid speaking directly to opposing counsel. Make all of your arguments to the court.

C. In Jury Trials, Request Sidebars

Occasionally, during a jury trial, the jury should not hear the content of counsels' arguments following objections. This is true when counsel must recite the expected testimony so the judge can rule on the objection, or refer to other evidence that has not yet been admitted. The most common way of insulating the jury from the attorneys' argument is for counsel to approach the bench and hold, in whispered tones, a sidebar conference with the presiding judge. A sidebar can be called by the court or requested by either the party simply by asking, "Sidebar, Your Honor?"

Some mock trial rules of procedure do not allow for sidebar conferences, both to save time and to ensure that everyone in the courtroom can listen to and learn from exchanges between counsel and the court. If sidebar conferences are not allowed, you can still demonstrate your recognition that one is called for by making your objection and, before proceeding to argument, asking, "May we assume we are out of the presence of the jury, Your Honor?" (as we recommended in Chapter Four, Section I(B)).

If, prior to trial, you asked the judge whether you should assume objections are being argued at sidebar and the judge responded affirmatively, you do not need to take the extra step of asking this question before launching into a sensitive argument. But if there is no standing assumption in effect, this is a good opportunity for you to demonstrate that you know the proper way to handle sensitive factual or legal issues.

D. Raise Objections Appropriately

The accepted format for making and meeting objections may differ from court to court. The majority approach is as follows.

1. Stand Up

Stand whenever you speak to the presiding judge, including when you raise objections. Sitting while objecting can be seen as a sign of disrespect to the judge.

Some judges refuse to entertain objections from seated counsel. Even if a judge allows you to object while sitting, most will not be pleased by the practice. Stand when you object unless the presiding judge requires that you remain seated instead, which is the rule in a few jurisdictions.

Aside from showing respect to the court, there is another benefit to standing while objecting. Since the purpose of objecting is to keep inadmissible information from being introduced at trial, standing to make your objection draws the physical attention of everyone in the courtroom away from the current action and onto you.

2. Object and State Your Grounds

The best way to state your objection is clearly and concisely. For instance: "Objection, Your Honor, relevance." "Objection, counsel is leading the witness." "Your Honor, we object—hearsay." "Objection, lack of foundation."

You may also refer directly to the precise rule of evidence on which your objection relies. Many competitions use the Federal Rules of Evidence, in which case references could include: "Objection, Your Honor, this information is irrelevant under Rule 401." "Objection, Your Honor, this is improper character evidence under Rule 404(b)." "Your Honor, we object to hearsay under Rule 801."

This method demonstrates your knowledge of the rules and impeccable trial preparation, in addition to signaling to the judge the specific nature of your objection.

Use objections to educate the jurors about the kinds of evidence that the law recognizes as inherently unreliable. The following are good examples: "Objection, hearsay, Your Honor. Under Rule 801 this witness cannot testify to what somebody else said." "Objection, Your Honor, leading; counsel is testifying instead of the witness."

While it is reasonable to explain the nature of your objection to be sure the judge and jury understand, there is no need to comment further on the inadequacy of the evidence. Lawyers who make objections such as, "Your Honor, I fail to see the relevance of counsel's last question" are often met with rebukes from the judge: "It doesn't matter whether or not you see it. Just make an objection if you have one, counsel." It is improper to use a lengthy objection—sometimes called a "speaking objection"—as a disguised argument to the jury.

3. Pause for the Judge to Consider the Objection

Some attorneys feel the need to launch into an extended discourse on the bases for their objections before allowing the judge to rule or opposing counsel to speak. Such a "speaking objection" might sound like this:

> Objection, Your Honor, that question calls for hearsay. The witness's personal notes constitute an out-of-court statement, even though the witness is present on the stand. They do not qualify either as business

Chapter Thirteen

records or as past recollection recorded, and in any event there has been no foundation.

While there is no absolute rule against speaking objections, most judges do not like them because they take up time when the judge might be willing to rule immediately. Judges also recognize that lawyers sometimes use speaking objections to argue their case to the jury, which is the purpose of closing arguments and not objections.

Rather than launching into a narrative, simply state the basis for your objection and remain standing until the judge responds. The judge may respond in one of five ways: 1) overrule your objection; 2) sustain your objection; 3) ask opposing counsel to respond; 4) ask you to further explain your grounds; or 5) simply pause for a moment to collect their thoughts on the matter.

4.   If Appropriate, Respond to the Court

If the judge sustains your objection immediately, your job is done. If the judge overrules it, you may wish to politely ask the judge if you may be heard on the matter further by stating, "Your Honor, may I be heard?" Use this technique prudently, however. If the judge allows you to be heard after ruling against you once and your additional statements do not change their mind, the judge is unlikely to allow you the luxury again.

If the judge seeks a response from opposing counsel, the court will usually return to you so you may have the last say. If the judge does not invite your reply, let your instincts tell you whether it is appropriate for you to ask to be heard on the matter again. You might say, "May I respond, Your Honor?" This technique is also useful for those times when the judge appears to be wavering on the ruling or pausing in thought. It is usually safe to take these cues as invitations to further explain your argument. Always ask permission to argue before you do so.

Any additional assertions you make beyond your initial objection and statement of grounds must be different from those you have already expressed. Repeating or simply restating the same grounds will only wear on the judge's patience and lessen your credibility. If you have nothing more to say, be honest about it with the judge and say, "I have nothing further, Your Honor," or "I stand on my objection, Your Honor."

5.   Special Considerations

There are a couple types of objections that merit special handling.

a.   *Repeated Objections*

It is sometimes necessary to raise the same objection to a number of questions in a row. Perhaps your initial objection was sustained, but your opponent is persistent in attempting to introduce the inadmissible evidence through other means. Perhaps your initial objection was overruled, and you feel bound to continue objecting as opposing counsel asks a series of questions in elaboration. In any event, an awkward situation inevitably arises when you must object repeatedly, on the same ground, to question after question.

The least obtrusive way to raise a repeated objection is to say "same objection" at the end of each of opposing counsel's questions. The judge can then repeat the ruling and the trial can proceed in a relatively uninterrupted fashion. If your objections are being sustained, the judge will no doubt tire of reiterating the ruling and will eventually instruct opposing counsel to move on to another line of questioning.

If your "same objections" are being consistently overruled, the judge is likely to tire of them even sooner. Under the Federal Rules of Evidence, it is not necessary to renew objections once the court "has ruled definitively." In many state jurisdictions, however, counsel may need to handle this situation by requesting a "standing objection." When a standing objection is granted, a single objection will be considered to "stand" or apply to an entire line of questioning, without the need for repeated interruptions. In most instances, the judge will grant your request for a standing objection, saying, for example:

THE COURT: Counsel, you may have a standing objection to that line of questioning.

OPPONENT: Thank you, Your Honor. For the record, we object to all further testimony concerning any conversations between the defendant and Ms. Wallace, including Ms. Wallace's alleged references to the investigative report. Ms. Wallace's statements are hearsay and the comments on the content of the report are double hearsay.

THE COURT: Very well. (To proponent) Ask your next question.

In the example above, the opponent makes what lawyers refer to as an "offer of proof" once their request for a standing objection has been granted. An offer of proof is a statement made for the record that enunciates the proponent's or opponent's basis for believing that certain evidence is admissible (in the case of the proponent) or inadmissible (opponent). If yours is a jury trial, be cognizant of whether you want the jurors to hear your offer of proof; if you do not, ask to be heard at sidebar (if allowed) or ask if you may assume you are being heard outside the presence of the jury.

In actual trials, lawyers make offers of proof to preserve their objections for appeal in case the outcome of the trial is not favorable to their client. Then, on appeal, lawyers cite to the appropriate page in the trial record to show that they attempted to offer or opposed the particular evidence in question and stated their grounds. The point of all this is to argue that the judge's decision in the matter was incorrect and that the trial outcome should not stand.

Advanced mock trial participants may want to make an offer of proof when they believe the presiding judge in a trial has ruled incorrectly. To make an offer of proof, simply ask the presiding judge, "May I make an offer of proof?" once the adverse ruling has been made. Judges know, of course, what an offer of proof is, and most are not likely to appreciate your assertion that they are wrong. Because of this, be absolutely sure that you are right and be polite when making an offer of proof in a mock trial. Most importantly, do so sparingly.

Think of it this way: in mock trials, your goal is to impress the presiding judge who scores your performance. There is no appeal process for mock trials. Any offer of proof you make will be useless once the trial is over. Thus, while you may want to show that you know how to make an offer of proof by doing so politely once or (at most) twice during a mock trial, nothing good will come to you if you become indignant or appear to relish pointing out the judge's error.

One final word of caution about offers of proof: by definition, they are opportunities to offer proof that is not already in the record. Thus, they are appropriate only when counsel has not otherwise had the opportunity to argue the basis for offering or opposing the admission of the evidence. Using an offer of proof to restate an argument you have already made will not only upset the presiding judge, it likely will cost you valuable points in your score since it demonstrates your lack of understanding of this trial advocacy procedure.

b. Requests for Voir Dire of the Witness

The basis for an objection may not always be apparent from the question or even the answer. Counsel may have access to information that is not yet in the record but which negates the admissibility of some part of a witness's testimony or some exhibit being offered into evidence. This information can be brought to the judge's attention through witness voir dire, a concept we introduced in Chapter Eight, Section II(C)(6) and explained in detail in Chapter Twelve, Section IV(A), in discussing expert witnesses. The term voir dire is derived from "law French" which was once in use in English courts; it means "speak the truth."

In the context of a lay witness examination, voir dire refers to a limited cross-examination for the purpose of determining the admissibility of evidence. The voir dire examination interrupts the direct and gives the opposing lawyer a chance to bring out additional facts that bear directly on the admissibility of some part of the balance of the testimony. Some mock trial competitions permit voir dire of witnesses; others do not. Even when permitted, an attorney who wishes to conduct voir dire must ask permission of the judge.

PROPONENT:	Whose signature is on that document?
ANSWER:	It appears to be the defendant's.
OPPONENT:	Your Honor, we object to that testimony and ask leave to conduct a limited voir dire of the witness.
THE COURT:	You may proceed with voir dire of the witness.
OPPONENT:	You did not see the document being signed, did you?
ANSWER:	No.
OPPONENT:	You have never seen the defendant sign their name, have you?
ANSWER:	No.
OPPONENT:	You have never received any signed correspondence from the defendant, have you?
ANSWER:	No.
OPPONENT:	Your Honor, the witness cannot identify the signature from personal knowledge. We renew our objection to the testimony and move to strike the previous answer.

Voir dire examination is most commonly utilized with regard to the qualifications of an expert witness (as discussed in the previous chapter) or the foundation for a document or exhibit, but it can be used in other situations as well. Note that at the conclusion of voir dire the offering attorney is entitled to ask additional questions—a mini redirect examination, if you will—aimed at reestablishing the admissibility of the evidence.

E. *Time Objections Appropriately*

Having determined what to say in raising an objection, consider when to say it. The general rule is that an objection must be made as soon as it is apparent that it is called for. On the other hand, an objection may be premature if it interrupts an incomplete question or if it anticipates testimony that may or may not be given.

Most objections to questions should be held until the examiner has had the opportunity to complete the question. Not only is it rude to interrupt, but the final version may turn out not to be objectionable. For this reason, many judges will refuse to rule on an objection until the question has been completed.

There are times, however, when it is necessary to interrupt the questioner. Some questions are objectionable not because of what they will elicit, but because of what they assert. A question may contain a damaging suggestion or proposition that, once heard by the factfinder, cannot be wholly remedied by objection. Such questions must be interrupted in order to cut off the interrogator's inadmissible statement. For example, a cross-examiner may be about to question a witness about an inadmissible criminal conviction. Imagine this scenario:

Chapter Thirteen

> PROPONENT: Isn't it true that you were convicted—
> OPPONENT: Objection, Your Honor. Counsel is seeking information prohibited by Rule 609(d).
> THE COURT: Sustained.

This is an example of a situation where the opponent of evidence is wise to refer only to the rule number calling for its exclusion rather than making clear to the jury that counsel is seeking to exclude evidence of a prior conviction.

Timing objections to questions is relatively easy. Often, however, a witness will respond to a seemingly proper question with a wholly inadmissible answer. The timing in these situations is trickier since, by definition, the answer was not foreshadowed by the question. The general rule is that an objection must be made as soon as the inadmissible nature of the testimony becomes apparent. This necessarily means interrupting the witness. For example:

> PROPONENT: When did you begin your investigation of the defendant's financial situation?
> ANSWER: I began the investigation as soon as I received an anonymous letter charging that—
> OPPONENT: We object on the grounds of hearsay and foundation.
> THE COURT: Sustained.

It will not do to allow the witness to finish the answer because by then the factfinder would have heard the inadmissible testimony and the harm would be done. Remember, you cannot un-ring a bell.

Unfortunately, it is not always possible to recognize and respond to inadmissible testimony before it happens. Counsel may be momentarily distracted or may suffer from rusty reflexes. And some witnesses, either innocently or by design, have a way of slipping improper testimony into the record. When this happens, your only recourse is to make a motion to strike.

A motion to strike, when granted, notes for the record that the improper testimony is not to be considered as part of the evidence for appeal purposes. Although there is no appeals process following a mock trial, you should still demonstrate your knowledge of trial skills by making motions to strike. Here is an example of the effective use of a motion to strike:

> PROPONENT: Are you the comptroller of the defendant corporation?
> ANSWER: The only thing I knew about skimming funds came through the rumor mill.
> OPPONENT: Objection, hearsay. We move to strike that answer.
> THE COURT: Sustained. The answer will be stricken from the record.

If your mock trial is being conducted as a jury trial, you should also ask the judge to instruct the jurors to disregard the inadmissible answer.

> OPPONENT: Will Your Honor please instruct the jury to disregard that last answer?
>
> THE COURT: Yes, certainly. Members of the jury, you are to disregard the answer that the witness just gave. (To counsel) Proceed.

While this sort of curative instruction is hardly a satisfying remedy, it is the best that can be done under the circumstances.

F. Respond to Objections Appropriately

The etiquette for the attorney responding to an objection is much the same as for the objecting attorney. Recall that the judge may react to an objection in one of five ways: 1) sustain it; 2) overrule it; 3) ask you to respond to it; 4) ask the attorney objecting to explain the grounds further; or 5) pause to collect their thoughts.

1. Wait for the Judge's Cue to Respond

Many judges like to rule on objections immediately after they are made. Therefore, keep quiet until you are invited to respond, either verbally or nonverbally, by the judge. If the judge overrules the objection immediately, your job is done.

Other judges prefer to hear argument from counsel before ruling on objections. In this case, the judge might turn to you and say, "Response, counsel?" or nod in your direction, signaling that it is safe to respond.

2. If Appropriate, Request to Be Heard

Many objections cannot be quickly decided because they raise subtle or complex legal issues. Aspects of an objection may escape the judge or may require consideration of additional information that is not already apparent to the judge. In these circumstances, you cannot rely on an invitation to argue from the judge and will need to inform the court, as politely as possible, that argument is necessary.

It is preferable to do this before the judge has ruled, if that can be accomplished without interrupting. An effective signal is to stand while the objection is being made or, if you are already standing, to take a step toward the bench, in order to alert the judge that argument is desired.

If the judge sustains opposing counsel's objection without asking for your input, do not be shy about letting the judge know that there is another side to the objection.

> PROPONENT: What did the police officer say to you?
> OPPONENT: Objection, hearsay.

THE COURT: Sustained.
PROPONENT: Your Honor, may I be heard on that?
THE COURT: Very well, what do you have to say?
PROPONENT: The statement falls under the "present sense impression" exception.
THE COURT: I see. Overruled. The witness may answer.

3. **Respond Specifically**

The key to responding to any objection is specificity. A judge who has agreed to listen to argument on an objection has indicated that they are persuadable. A good argument will result in the admission of the evidence only if it provides the judge with a good reason to overrule the objection. Tell the judge exactly why the proffered evidence is admissible. Some lawyers, for reasons known only to themselves, respond to objections by repeating the evidence and exhorting the judge to admit it. The following scenario is not at all unusual:

PROPONENT: What did the defendant do immediately after the accident?
ANSWER: He began yelling at his eight-year-old son.
OPPONENT: Objection. The defendant's relationship with his son is irrelevant.
THE COURT: It does seem irrelevant. What do you have to say, counsel?
PROPONENT: It is very relevant, Your Honor. It shows that he was yelling at his child.

This response communicates very little to the judge. What is the probative value of the defendant's conduct? Note how much more effective it is when counsel explains why the evidence is being offered to the court.

PROPONENT: What did the defendant do immediately after the accident?
ANSWER: He began yelling at his eight-year-old son.
OPPONENT: Objection. The defendant's relationship with his son is irrelevant.
THE COURT: It does seem irrelevant. What do you have to say, counsel?
PROPONENT: The defendant's anger at his son tends to show that he was distracted by the child just before the accident. It goes directly to negligence, Your Honor.

The judge may or may not agree with the proponent's assessment of the evidence, but at least they will have the benefit of counsel's analysis.

a. Inform the Court of Limited Admissibility

Evidence may be inadmissible for some purposes yet admissible for others. When responding to objections, it is extremely important to advise the judge of the admissible purpose for which the evidence is offered.

For example, evidence that a dangerous condition has been repaired is generally inadmissible to prove negligence. Counsel cannot argue to the trier of fact, "Of course the owner of the car took inadequate care of the automobile; he had his brakes repaired just two days after the accident." On the other hand, evidence of the repair is admissible to prove ownership of the automobile if that is at issue in the case. Counsel can argue, "The defendant denies that he was responsible for the upkeep of the car, but he was the one who ordered and paid for the repair of the brakes just two days after the accident."

With this dichotomy in mind, consider these possible objections and responses in the cross-examination of the defendant in our traffic collision case.

PROPONENT: Didn't you have your brakes repaired just two days after the accident?

OPPONENT: Objection, Your Honor, subsequent remedial measures are inadmissible.

THE COURT: What do you have to say, counsel?

PROPONENT: We are offering it only to prove ownership and control, Your Honor.

THE COURT: The evidence will be received, but only for that limited purpose. Members of the jury, you are to consider this evidence only for the purpose of showing ownership and control of the automobile. You must not consider it as proof of any negligence on the part of the defendant.

If the court does not immediately give a limiting instruction, one should be requested by the attorney whose objection was overruled.

b. Inform the Court of a Conditional Offer

The admissibility of certain testimony, particularly with regard to relevance, may not always be immediately clear as it may depend upon other testimony to be developed through later witnesses. In these circumstances, counsel may respond to an objection by making a "conditional offer." This is done either by promising to "tie it up later" or, preferably, by explaining to the court the nature of the evidence that is expected to follow. For example:

PROPONENT: Isn't it true that you had an important meeting scheduled for the morning of the accident?

OPPONENT: Objection. The witness's business schedule is not relevant.
THE COURT: What is the relevance of that inquiry, counsel?
PROPONENT: We intend to introduce evidence that the defendant had a meeting scheduled with a prospective client, that he was already late for the meeting at the time of the accident, and that he stood to lose a great deal of money if he didn't arrive on time. The question is therefore directly relevant to show that he was speeding and inattentive.
THE COURT: Based on that representation, I will allow the testimony, subject to a motion to strike if you don't tie it up.

A conditional offer is always subject to the actual later production of evidence. Keep track of conditional offers made by the other side. If opposing counsel fails to elicit the promised testimony, raise an objection and move to strike the earlier evidence at the end of opposing counsel's case-in-chief. If testimony or evidence heard by the jury is later stricken from the record, ask the court to instruct the jurors to disregard the information in its entirety. Testimony that has been stricken cannot be mentioned in final argument; if opposing counsel mentions it anyway, object again and ask to be heard at sidebar (or a constructive sidebar) so you can remind the court that the evidence was stricken and ask again that the jurors be instructed to disregard it.

4. Cure the Objection Whenever Possible

It is not necessary to fight to the death over every objection. Counsel can frequently avoid or overcome an objection by rephrasing the offending question, either before or after the judge rules.

Since the precise language of a question is seldom of vital importance, it should be possible to circumnavigate virtually any "form" objection. Leading questions, compound questions, and vague questions can all be cured. Even if your original question was perfectly fine, you may be able to move the trial along, and earn the gratitude of judge and jury, by posing the same inquiry in different words.

Other objections that can be undercut through rephrasing include personal knowledge, foundation, and even relevance. For example:

PROPONENT: Did the plaintiff follow his doctor's advice?
OPPONENT: Objection. Lack of personal knowledge.
PROPONENT: Let me put it this way. Did the plaintiff say anything to you about his doctor's advice?
ANSWER: Yes.

PROPONENT:	What did he say?
ANSWER:	He said that he would rather risk the consequences than stay in bed all day.

In this scenario, the examination was made stronger by rephrasing the question in response to the objection.

Making and meeting objections involves a certain amount of gamesmanship. No lawyer likes to be seen as an evidentiary pushover. From time to time, it may be tactically important to stand behind a question, if only to establish your mastery of the rules. Another alternative is to rephrase a question without saying so. In the above example, the attorney neither withdrew the question nor overtly rephrased it, but rather said, "Let me put it this way." Problem solved.

G. Follow Up on the Judge's Ruling

The judge's ruling on an objection is not necessarily the end of the matter. Counsel must remain alert to ensure that the ruling is carried out and that the grounds for the ruling are followed. Both the proponent of the evidence and the opponent may have more yet to do.

1. Objection Overruled

a. Proponent's Job

The proponent's job when an objection is overruled is to ensure that the evidence actually makes its way into the record. In other words, the proponent must make sure that the witness answers the question or provides whatever testimony the judge has just ruled to be permissible. The following is an all-too-frequent scenario:

PROPONENT:	After the accident, what did the crossing guard say to you?
OPPONENT:	Objection, Your Honor, the question calls for hearsay.
PROPONENT:	May I respond, Your Honor?
THE COURT:	Yes.
PROPONENT:	Your Honor, it has already been established that the crossing guard observed the accident immediately before making the declaration, so it qualifies as either an excited utterance or a present sense impression.
THE COURT:	Yes, I think there is a hearsay exception there. Overruled.
PROPONENT:	What is the next thing that you did?
ANSWER:	I took out my cell phone and dialed 911.

Chapter Thirteen

Despite the court's ruling, the witness was never directed to answer the original question. The proponent, apparently flushed with victory, just went on to another subject.

Lawyers make similar mistakes when a witness's answer has been interrupted or when the arguments on the objection overlap the testimony. Sometimes, even when the witness was able to get an answer out, the import of the testimony may have been drowned out by the subsequent wrangling over the objection.

In all of these instances, the proponent's safest course is to repeat the question that triggered the objection and to be sure to get a clear answer from the witness. Experienced attorneys will take this job one step further by emphasizing the allowed testimony. For instance:

> PROPONENT: After the accident, what did the crossing guard say to you?
>
> OPPONENT: Objection, Your Honor, the question calls for hearsay.
>
> PROPONENT: Response, Your Honor?
>
> THE COURT: Yes, certainly.
>
> PROPONENT: Since the crossing guard observed the accident just before making the declaration, it is an excited utterance or a present sense impression.
>
> THE COURT: The objection is overruled.
>
> PROPONENT: You were about to tell us what the crossing guard said immediately after witnessing the accident.
>
> ANSWER: Oh yes, he said that the yellow car ran the red light and smashed right into the blue car.

This technique allows counsel to repeat the question and also to emphasize the favorable circumstances under which it was made.

b. Opponent's Job

The opponent's job following an overruled objection is to stay alert to the possibility of excluding all or some of the remaining offending evidence. Perhaps the witness will not testify in the manner that was promised by the proponent of the evidence in argument to the court. For example:

> PROPONENT: After the accident, what did the crossing guard say to you?
>
> OPPONENT: Objection, Your Honor, the question calls for hearsay.
>
> PROPONENT: Your Honor, if I may be heard?
>
> THE COURT: Yes.

PROPONENT:	The statement of the crossing guard qualifies as a present sense impression.
THE COURT:	Yes, I think so. Overruled.
ANSWER:	He said that he didn't really see what happened, but that it looked as though . . .
OPPONENT:	Your Honor, I renew my objection. If the witness didn't really see the accident then this cannot be a present sense impression.
THE COURT:	Yes. The objection will be sustained on those grounds.

Alternatively, other grounds for objection may become clear in the course of the testimony, or perhaps the witness will begin volunteering evidence that is inadmissible for some additional reason. In the above scenario counsel could also have objected on the ground that the crossing guard's statement ("it looked as though . . .") was speculative.

2. Objection Sustained

a. *Proponent's Job*

A sustained objection means that the proponent of the evidence has been denied the opportunity to introduce the testimony or exhibit at trial. Following this ruling, the proponent's job is to keep trying to have the evidence admitted, if possible. When a judge sustains an objection, the ruling usually applies only to the specific question (or answer) and grounds that were then before the court. Unless the judge says so explicitly, the ruling does not extend to the ultimate admissibility of the underlying evidence. In other words, a sustained objection says only that "the evidence cannot be admitted based on the testimony and arguments heard so far." It does not say that "the evidence cannot ever be admitted no matter what you do." Counsel generally has the option to offer the evidence through other means.

These "other means" may consist of nothing more than rephrasing a question. Any objection as to form—leading, compound, vague, argumentative—can be cured by altering the language of the inquiry. Leading questions on direct examination can easily be restated.

PROPONENT:	You had the green light when the defendant's car hit yours, didn't you?
OPPONENT:	Objection, leading.
THE COURT:	Sustained.
PROPONENT:	What color was your light when the defendant's car hit yours?
ANSWER:	It was green.

Chapter Thirteen

Objections are frequently sustained not because of the form of the question but because of some missing predicate in the testimony. Objections to foundation can be cured by eliciting additional foundation. Objections to a witness's lack of personal knowledge can be remedied with further questions showing the basis of the witness's information. Relevance objections can be overcome through continued questioning aimed at demonstrating the probative value of the original question. Note the following cross-examination of the defendant in our firetruck case:

PROPONENT:	Immediately after the accident you started yelling at your eight-year-old son, didn't you?
OPPONENT:	Objection, relevance.
THE COURT:	Sustained.
PROPONENT:	Well, your eight-year-old son was in the car at the time of the accident, wasn't he?
ANSWER:	Yes.
PROPONENT:	He was sitting in the front seat with a portable stereo, right?
ANSWER:	Yes, he was.
PROPONENT:	And he was playing a loud rap song on the stereo?
ANSWER:	Yes.
PROPONENT:	And to be clear, he wasn't using headphones was he?
ANSWER:	He was not.
PROPONENT:	Many adults find loud rap music annoying, don't they?
ANSWER:	I couldn't really say.
PROPONENT:	And immediately after the accident you yelled at your son, didn't you?
OPPONENT:	Same objection.
PROPONENT:	Your Honor, I believe we have established the likelihood that the defendant was distracted by his son's music. Yelling at the child is probative on that issue.
THE COURT:	Yes, I see your point. Overruled.

The same approach can work for hearsay objections. Additional facts can often be established that will qualify a statement for an exception to the hearsay rule. Moreover, out-of-court statements may sometimes be recast in the form of conduct or observations. In the following example, a police officer has just testified on direct examination that they received a radio dispatch that a crime had been committed.

PROPONENT:	What was the content of the radio bulletin from the dispatcher?
OPPONENT:	Objection, hearsay.
THE COURT:	Sustained.

PROPONENT:	What did you do immediately after receiving the alert?
ANSWER:	I drove to the corner of Grand Avenue and State Street.
PROPONENT:	What did you do there?
ANSWER:	I began looking for a suspect wearing glasses and a white lab jacket.

The effect of the sustained hearsay objection was avoided by continuing the examination on the admissible subject of the witness's actions, as opposed to the inadmissible content of the dispatcher's out-of-court statement.

It is not always possible to overcome a sustained objection. Some testimony will be flatly inadmissible no matter how many approaches you attempt. On the other hand, there are often numerous routes to admissibility, and a sustained objection usually closes off only one. Keep trying.

b. Opponent's Job

When an objection is sustained, the opponent of the evidence has been successful. This should bring satisfaction to the objector, and in some cases even rejoicing, but it is never a reason to rest on your laurels. The very next question may ask for the identical evidence, in which case an additional objection must be made. A sustained objection will be a temporary victory indeed if the proponent of the evidence succeeds in having it admitted later in the witness's testimony. This is not uncommon. Successful objections can come undone as soon as the objector relaxes vigilance.

PROPONENT:	Who told you to begin your financial investigation?
ANSWER:	I received an anonymous note charging that—
OPPONENT:	Objection, hearsay.
THE COURT:	Sustained.
PROPONENT:	What caused you to begin investigating?
ANSWER:	There was a charge that money had been skimmed from one of the trust accounts.
PROPONENT:	How did you learn of the charge?
ANSWER:	I received a note.

The opponent of the evidence in this case let down their guard. When the first hearsay objection was successful, the opponent's attention lapsed. They therefore failed to notice that the identical testimony was being introduced as the "cause" of the investigation. The information, of course, is no less hearsay (and no less anonymous) the second time around. A second objection should have been made.

The cardinal rule when your objection is sustained is to remain just as vigilant as you were before.

Chapter Thirteen

H. Reevaluate Your Theory

Rulings on objections govern the flow of evidence at trial. The availability of evidence forms the underpinning of every attorney's theory of the case. Theory planning, in turn, involves calculated predictions as to the admissibility of evidence. In some cases, the court's ruling on a particularly important objection will require you to reevaluate your theory of the case.

Evidentiary rulings must be understood in the context of the entire case. They are not merely passing successes or failures; they can be crucial turning points in the progress of the trial. If an essential item of evidence is excluded, or if some controversial proof is admitted, you may have to switch to a new theory or alter your current one, even if this occurs in midtrial.

In some instances, the effect of an evidentiary ruling may be only to strengthen or weaken your case. If the court excludes some testimony of one of your witnesses, you might be able to proceed as planned but with a lesser volume of evidence. Recall the firetruck case that we have been using as an example. The plaintiff's theory was that the defendant caused the accident because he was hurrying to a business meeting for which he was already late. Assume that the court, for whatever reason, sustained an objection to testimony that the defendant was seen rushing from his home that morning with his tie undone and a coffee cup in his hand. This ruling diminishes the proof available to the plaintiff, but so long as other evidence is available, the "hurrying to work" theory can remain intact.

Summary
OBJECTION RULES
Consider objections carefully
Direct all arguments to the judge
Request sidebars (if allowed)
Raise objections appropriately
• Stand up
• Object and state your grounds
• Pause for the judge to consider the objection
• If appropriate, respond to the court
• Make repeated objections by saying "same objection"
• Request voir dire of the witness when necessary
• Time objections appropriately

Summary
OBJECTION RULES

Respond to objections appropriately
• Wait for the judge's cue to respond
• If appropriate, request to be heard
• Respond specifically and inform the court of limited admissibility or a conditional offer
• Cure the objection whenever possible
• Follow up the judge's ruling:
 	
    <u>Objection Overruled</u>
        Proponent's job: Ensure that the evidence is heard
        Opponent's job: Stay alert and try to exclude some or all remaining evidence
 	
    <u>Objection Sustained</u>
        Proponent's job: Keep trying to have the evidence admitted
        Opponent's job: Stay alert for different attempts to admit the same evidence. Reevaluate your case theory in light of rulings (if necessary)

III. Ethics and Objections

Ethical issues frequently arise in the context of making and meeting objections. Because the process of objecting is one of the most confrontational aspects of trials, it often tests counsel's reserves of good will, civility, restraint, and sense of fair play. The three most common problems are discussed below.

A. Asking Objectionable Questions

A corollary to counsel's right to offer evidence for which there is a reasonable basis is the obligation to refrain from offering evidence for which there is no reasonable basis. In other words, it is unethical to offer evidence knowing that there is no reasonable basis for its admission. Even though opposing counsel might neglect to object, and even though the court might err in its ruling, the adversary system does not extend so far as to allow the intentional use of improper evidence. Indeed, one of the justifications for the adversary system is precisely that counsel can be relied upon to perform this minimum level of self-policing.

Do not use the information contained in questions as a substitute for testimony that cannot be obtained. Some lawyers apparently believe that the idea of zealous advocacy allows them to slip information before a finder of fact by asserting it in a question, knowing full well that the witness will not be allowed to answer. An example might be:

> PROPONENT: Isn't it true that you were once fired from a job for being drunk?
>
> OPPONENT: Objection, relevance.
>
> PROPONENT: I withdraw the question. (Proponent's thought process: "Who cares about the ruling? I never expected to get it in, but now the jury knows that the witness is a drunk.")

This conduct, even if the information is true, is absolutely unethical. Testimony is to come from witnesses, with admissibility ruled upon by the court. It subverts the very purpose of an adversary trial when lawyers abuse their right to question witnesses in order to slip inadmissible evidence before the factfinder. Withdrawing an improper question does not in any way negate the unethical act of asking it.

B.   Making Improper Objections

The same general analysis applies to objecting as it does to offering evidence. You need not be positive that your objection will be sustained, but you must believe that there is a reasonable basis for making it. Again, under the adversary system, it is up to the judge to decide whether to admit the evidence.

The license to object is available only if counsel is truly interested in excluding the subject evidence. That is, an attorney may make reasonable or plausible objections, but only so long as the purpose of the objection is to obtain a ruling on the evidence. As we will see in the following section, objections may also be employed for a variety of ulterior purposes, most of which are unethical.

C.   Making "Tactical" Objections

Many lawyers, and at least a few trial advocacy texts, have touted the use of so-called "tactical" objections. Since an objection is the only means by which one lawyer can interrupt the examination of another, it has been suggested that objections should occasionally be made to "break up" the flow of a successful examination. An objection can throw the opposing lawyer off stride, give the witness a rest, or distract the finder of fact from the content of the testimony. This advice is usually tempered with the admonition that there must always be some evidentiary basis for the objection, but the real message is that an objection may be used for any purpose whatsoever so long as you can make it with a straight face.

This view is unfortunate, amounting to nothing more than the unprincipled use of objections for a wholly improper purpose. No judge would allow a lawyer to object on the ground that the opposition's examination is going too well. The fact that disruption can be accomplished without actually saying this does not justify the attempt. Do not make objections solely for the purpose of disrupting your adversary's case.

IV. A Short List of Common Objections

A complete discussion of evidentiary objections is beyond the scope of this book. The following list of some frequently made objections and responses is based on the Federal Rules of Evidence and is intended only as a reference or guide. Most mock trial organizers adopt the Federal Rules of Evidence or modify them slightly to fit the circumstances. Nonetheless, the following is not a substitute for your knowledge of the rules of evidence and procedure governing your mock trial.

This list provides an example of an improper question or of potentially inadmissible testimony, followed by the appropriate objection. We also list possible responses the proponent of the evidence may give to overcome the objection. In some cases, the best response is to reword the question or to ask a different question altogether.

A. Nonsubstantive Objections

1. Leading Question (On Direct Examination Only)

A leading question suggests or contains its own answer. Leading questions are objectionable on direct examination unless they are meant to signal a transition or lay foundation.

> PROPONENT: You saw the defendant flee the scene of the crime, right?
> OPPONENT: Objection, Your Honor, counsel is leading the witness.

Possible Responses: Explain that the question is transitional or foundational and therefore not impermissibly leading. If neither of those exceptions applies, rephrase the question so it is not leading. For example, "Did you see the defendant flee the scene of the crime?"

2. Compound Question

A compound question contains two separate inquiries that are not necessarily susceptible of a single answer.

> PROPONENT: Did you determine the point of impact from conversations with witnesses and from physical marks, such as debris in the road?
> OPPONENT: Objection, Your Honor, that question is compound.

Chapter Thirteen

Possible Responses: Dual inquiries are permissible if the question seeks to establish a relationship between two facts or events. For example, "Didn't he move forward and then reach into his pocket?" If your question does not seek to establish a relationship between two facts or events, break it up and ask each part separately. For example, "Did you determine the point of impact of the collision?" followed by, "Please explain what information or evidence you used to determine the point of impact."

3. **Vague Question**

A question is vague if it is incomprehensible, incomplete, or if any answer will necessarily be ambiguous.

PROPONENT: When do you leave your house in the morning?
OPPONENT: Objection, Your Honor, the question is vague since it does not specify a day of the week.

Possible Responses: If you believe the question is not vague, you can simply wait for the judge's decision. If the judge thought the question was vague, they will sustain the objection. A judge who understands the question, however, is likely to turn to the witness and confirm that the witness does as well. If both the judge and the witness understand the question, the objection is likely to be overruled. Unless the precise wording of your question is important, it may be easiest to simply rephrase a question that has drawn a "vague" objection.

4. **Argumentative Question**

An argumentative question asks the witness to accept the examiner's summary, inference, or conclusion rather than to agree with the existence (or nonexistence) of a fact. Questions can be made more or less argumentative depending upon the tone of voice of the examiner.

PROPONENT: Do you really expect this jury to believe that you are telling the truth?
OPPONENT: Objection, Your Honor, that question is argumentative.

Possible Responses: While it will not be persuasive to say, "Your Honor, I am not arguing," it might be persuasive to explain the nonargumentative point you are trying to make. Alternatively, make no response and let the judge decide. Or simply offer to rephrase the question.

5. **Narratives**

Witnesses are required to testify in the form of question and answer. This requirement ensures that opposing counsel will have the opportunity to frame objections to questions before answers are given. You can object to questions that call for a narrative answer, as well as to an answer that has become narrative. A narrative answer is one that proceeds at some length in the absence of questions. An answer that is more than a few sentences long can usually be classified as a narrative.

    PROPONENT: Tell us everything you did on July 14.
    OPPONENT: Objection, Your Honor, that question calls for a narrative answer.

Possible Responses: The best response is usually to ask another question that will simply break up the potential narrative answer. Note that expert witnesses are often allowed to testify in narrative fashion since technical explanations cannot be given easily in question-and-answer format. Even then, however, it is usually more persuasive to interject questions to break up long answers.

6. Asked and Answered

A question is "asked and answered" if it calls for the repetition of testimony from a witness who has previously given the same testimony in response to a question asked by the same counsel. Once an inquiry has been "asked and answered" by one side in a trial, further repetition by that side is objectionable. Variations on a theme, however, are permissible, so long as the identical information is not repeated. The asked and answered rule does not preclude inquiry on cross-examination into subjects covered fully on direct. Nor does it prevent asking identical questions of different witnesses.

    PROPONENT: Mr. Burns, you killed Homer, right?
    ANSWER: No, I did not.
    PROPONENT: Yes, you did kill him, didn't you?
    OPPONENT: Objection, Your Honor, asked and answered.

Possible Responses: If the question has not been asked and answered, point out to the judge the manner in which it differs from the earlier testimony. Otherwise, rephrase the question to vary the exact information sought.

7. Assumes Facts Not in Evidence

A question, usually on cross-examination, is objectionable if it includes as a predicate a statement of fact that has not been proven. The reason for this objection is that the question is unfair; it cannot be answered without conceding the unproven assumption.

    PROPONENT: You left your home so late that you only had fifteen minutes to get to your office, correct? (Where the witness's departure time was not previously established.)
    OPPONENT: Objection, that question assumes facts not in evidence, Your Honor.

Chapter Thirteen

Possible Responses: A question assumes facts not in evidence only when it utilizes an introductory predicate ("You left your home so late . . . ") as the basis for another inquiry ("that you only had fifteen minutes to get to your office"). Simple, one-part cross-examination questions do not need to be based upon facts that are already in evidence. For example, it would be proper to ask a witness, "Didn't you leave home late that morning?" regardless of whether there had already been evidence as to the time of the witness's departure. As a consequence of misunderstanding this distinction, "facts not in evidence" objections are often erroneously made to perfectly good cross-examination questions. If the objection is sustained by the judge, most questions can easily be divided in two.

8. Nonresponsive Answers (On Cross-Examination Only)

Testimony is "nonresponsive" if it does not answer the specific question asked. Counsel may ask to have the nonresponsive answer stricken from the record and/or to have the judge instruct the witness to answer the question.

PROPONENT:	You don't like Ms. Smith, do you?
ANSWER:	I would certainly prefer not to spend my time around her.
PROPONENT:	Like I said, you don't like her, do you?
ANSWER:	Sometimes she can be a real jerk.
PROPONENT:	Your Honor, I ask that the witness's answer be stricken as non-responsive.
THE COURT:	It will be stricken. Please answer the question "yes" or "no" if you are able to do so.

Possible Responses: If you believe the witness is answering the question to the best of their ability, stand up and inform the court.

B. Substantive Objections

1. Hearsay

Hearsay statements are verbal or written assertions previously made out of court that are being offered at trial to prove the truth of the matter asserted. Hearsay includes prior statements made by the witness testifying or statements made by others that are subsequently repeated by the testifying witness, as well as any information contained in documents, regardless of the author. Whenever a witness testifies, or is asked to testify, about what she or someone else said or wrote in the past, the statement should be subjected to hearsay analysis.

PROPONENT:	You told your mother that her heirloom bracelet had been stolen, isn't that right?
OPPONENT:	Your Honor, that question calls for hearsay.

Possible Responses: Out-of-court statements are admissible if they are not hearsay or if they fall within one of the exceptions to the hearsay rule. Remember that statements are not hearsay if they are offered for a purpose other than to "prove the truth of the matter asserted." Thus, in the above example, if the cross-examiner is using the statement for something other than to prove that the bracelet was indeed stolen—for example, to establish the mother's reaction to the statement—it is not being offered for its truth. Note that if a statement is not being offered for its truth, you may be called upon to explain why it is relevant.

    a.   **Statements That Are Not Hearsay**

In addition to statements that are not offered for their truth, two other types of statements are nonhearsay. A witness's own previous statement is not hearsay if it was given under oath and it is inconsistent with the witness's current testimony. Such statements are admissible at trial to impeach the witness by prior inconsistent statement.

Out-of-court statements by a party to the case may also be admitted into evidence, but only if they are offered against the party who made the statement. Such statements are called "admissions of a party-opponent." A party-opponent can be either the plaintiff or the defendant in a civil case or the defendant in a criminal case (or, generally, that person's agent—i.e., someone authorized to speak on his behalf, such as a high-level employee in the defendant's company). This rule allows prosecutors in criminal cases to bring into evidence prior incriminating statements of the defendant, such as text messages they sent, recorded conversations they participated in, and confessions they gave to law enforcement. A party cannot seek to admit their own self-serving prior statements, however; admissions of a party-opponent can only be offered by the other party to the case.

    b.   **Exceptions to the Hearsay Rule**

Some of the more frequently encountered exceptions to the hearsay rule follow.

Present Sense Impression. A statement describing an event made while the declarant is observing it (or immediately thereafter). For example, "Look, there goes the president" or "Did you see the president just walk by?"

Excited Utterance. A statement relating to a startling event made while the declarant was under the stress of excitement caused by the event. For example, "A piece of plaster just fell from the roof and nearly hit me!"

State of Mind. A statement of the declarant's mental state or condition. For example, "He said that he was so mad he couldn't see straight." Note that the state of mind of the declarant must be relevant.

Past Recollection Recorded. A memorandum or record of a matter about which the witness once had knowledge but which they have since forgotten. The record must have been made by the witness when the events were fresh in the witness's mind and must be shown to have been accurate when made.

Business Records. The business records exception applies to the records of any regularly conducted activity. Thus, school, hospital, or social club records, among others, can be considered business records. To qualify as an exception to the hearsay rule, the record must have been made at or near the time of the transaction by a person with knowledge or transmitted from a person with knowledge. It must also have been made and kept in the ordinary course of business. The foundation for a business record must be laid by the keeper of the record or by some other qualified witness.

Reputation as to Character. Evidence of a person's reputation for truth and veracity is an exception to the hearsay rule. Note that there are restrictions other than hearsay on the admissibility of character evidence.

Prior Testimony. Testimony given at a different proceeding, or in deposition, qualifies for this exception if: 1) the testimony was given under oath; 2) the opposing party had an opportunity to cross-examine the declarant; and 3) the declarant is not an available witness in the trial.

Dying Declaration. A statement by a dying person that relates to the cause or circumstances of what the declarant believed to be impending death. For example, "Kim just shot me." Dying declarations are admissible only in homicide prosecutions or civil cases.

Statement Against Interest. A statement so contrary to the declarant's pecuniary, proprietary, or penal interest that no reasonable person would have made it unless it was true. For example, "I can't believe I got away with robbing that store." The declarant must not be a possible witness in the trial, and other limitations may apply in criminal cases.

Catch-All Exception. Other hearsay statements may be admitted if their probative value outweighs the prejudice they may cause to the opposing party and/or if they contain other sufficient circumstantial guarantees of trustworthiness. The declarant must not be an available witness in the trial.

2. Irrelevant

Evidence is irrelevant if it does not make any fact of consequence to the case more or less probable. Evidence can be irrelevant if it proves nothing or if it tends to prove something that does not matter.

> PROPONENT: Please describe George's personal hygiene.
> OPPONENT: Objection, Your Honor, that information is irrelevant.

Possible Responses: Explain the relevance of the testimony. If it is not relevant, ask a different question.

3. Unfair Prejudice

Relevant evidence may be excluded if its probative value is substantially outweighed by the danger of unfair prejudice. Evidence cannot be excluded merely because it is prejudicial; by definition, all relevant evidence is prejudicial to one party or the other. Rather, the objection only applies if the testimony has little probative value and it is *unfairly* prejudicial. The classic example is a graphic and upsetting photograph of an injured crime victim offered to prove some fact of slight relevance, such as the clothing that the victim was wearing. The availability of other means to establish the same facts is usually also considered by the court. Thus, if the prosecution can establish the type of clothing that was worn by the victim through the testimony of a neighbor (who saw the victim leave their apartment just prior to the murder), the court is less likely to allow the photograph.

> PROPONENT: You're a card-carrying member of the NRA, aren't you, Mr. Gappa?
>
> OPPONENT: [Outside the presence of the jury] Objection, Your Honor, the probative value of Mr. Gappa's membership in the NRA is outweighed by the prejudicial nature of that information.

Possible Responses: Most judges are hesitant to exclude evidence on this basis. A measured explanation of the probative value of the testimony is the best response.

4. Improper Character Evidence Generally

Character evidence is generally not admissible to prove that a person acted in conformity with their character. For example, a driver's past accidents cannot be offered as proof of current negligence.

> PROPONENT: This isn't the first time you've been involved in a traffic accident, is it, Mr. Yoon?
>
> OPPONENT: Objection, Your Honor, that is improper character evidence.

Possible Responses: A criminal defendant may offer proof of good character, which the prosecution may then rebut. Also, past crimes and bad acts may be offered to prove motive, opportunity, intent, preparation, plan, knowledge, identity, or absence of mistake.

a. Conviction of Crime

The commission, and even the conviction, of past crimes is not admissible to prove current guilt.

The credibility of a witness who takes the stand and testifies, however, may be impeached on the basis of a prior criminal conviction, but only if the following

Chapter Thirteen

requirements are satisfied: the crime must have been either a felony or one that involved dishonesty or false statement, regardless of punishment. With certain exceptions, the evidence is not admissible unless it occurred within the last ten years. Juvenile adjudications are generally not admissible.

The impeachment is generally limited to the fact of conviction, the name of the crime, and the sentence received. The details and events of the crime are generally inadmissible.

> PROPONENT: Thirteen years ago you committed another robbery, didn't you?
>
> OPPONENT: (Outside the presence of the jury) Objection, Your Honor, that is improper character evidence because it occurred over ten years ago.

Possible Responses: If the crime was not a felony, the conviction may still be admissible if it involved dishonesty. If the conviction is more than ten years old, it may still be admissible if the court determines that its probative value, supported by specific facts and circumstances, substantially outweighs its prejudicial effect.

b. Untruthfulness

The past acts of a person may not be offered as proof that they committed similar acts. Specific instances of conduct are admissible for the limited purpose of attacking or supporting credibility. A witness may therefore be cross-examined concerning past bad acts only if they reflect upon the witness's truthfulness or untruthfulness.

> PROPONENT: You were audited by the IRS two years ago, weren't you?
>
> OPPONENT: Objection, that is improper character evidence.
>
> PROPONENT: Your Honor, if I may, Ms. Justus's audit by the IRS is probative of her truthfulness since she was forced to pay $10,000 in back taxes for unreported income following that audit.

Possible Responses: Explain the manner in which the witness's past bad acts are probative of untruthfulness, as illustrated above.

c. Reputation

Reputation evidence is admissible only with regard to an individual's character for truthfulness or untruthfulness. Moreover, evidence of a truthful character is admissible only after the character of the witness has been attacked.

> ANSWER: Bonnie is known as a real trickster among her friends—someone no one should trust.

OPPONENT:	Objection, Your Honor. This is improper character evidence.
PROPONENT:	May I respond?
THE COURT:	Go ahead.
PROPONENT:	Your Honor, this testimony, that Ms. Kane is known amongst her friends as an untrustworthy trickster, illustrates the defendant's reputation for truthfulness. As such, it is proper character evidence.

Possible Responses: Explain why the reputation evidence is probative of truthfulness or untruthfulness.

5. Speculation or Lack of Personal Knowledge

Witnesses (other than experts) must testify from personal knowledge, which is generally defined as their sensory perceptions—what they saw, heard, felt, smelled, or tasted. A witness's lack of personal knowledge may be obvious from the questioning, may be inherent in the testimony, or may be developed by questioning on voir dire.

PROPONENT:	Where was the defendant at the time of the crime?
ANSWER:	The defendant must have been back at the bar by that time.
OPPONENT:	Objection, Your Honor, the witness is speculating (or the witness lacks personal knowledge of the defendant's whereabouts at that time).

Possible Responses: Ask further questions that establish the witness's personal knowledge. Witnesses are permitted to make reasonable estimates rationally based upon perception.

6. Improper Lay Opinion

Lay witnesses (nonexperts) are generally precluded from testifying as to opinions, conclusions, or inferences.

PROPONENT:	How did the defendant look to you that night?
ANSWER:	He looked like he was high on cocaine to me.
OPPONENT:	Objection, Your Honor, improper lay opinion.

Possible Responses: Lay witnesses may testify to opinions or inferences if they are rationally based upon the perception of the witness. Common lay opinions include estimates of speed, distance, value, height, time, duration, and temperature. Lay witnesses are also commonly allowed to testify as to the mood, sanity, demeanor, sobriety, or tone of voice of another person.

7. Authenticity

Exhibits must be authenticated before they may be admitted. Authenticity refers to adequate proof that the exhibit actually is what it seems or purports to be. Virtually all documents and tangible objects must be authenticated.

Recall that in mock trials, the authenticity of exhibits is often the subject of stipulations listed in the case file. If the documents provided in your case file have been stipulated to be authentic, do not object to the admission of an exhibit found therein on authenticity grounds.

Since exhibits are authenticated by laying a foundation, objections may be raised on the ground of either authenticity or foundation. This subject is discussed in greater detail in Chapter Eight.

> PROPONENT: (To the court) At this time, the plaintiff moves Exhibit 2 into evidence.
>
> OPPONENT: Objection, Your Honor. The authenticity of the exhibit has not been established. Counsel has not shown that this document was in fact written by the witness.

Possible Responses: Ask additional questions that establish authenticity.

8. Lack of Foundation

Nearly all evidence, other than a witness's direct observation of events, requires some sort of predicate foundation for admissibility. An objection to lack of foundation requires the judge to make a preliminary ruling as to the admissibility of the evidence.

As discussed in greater detail in Chapter Eight, evidentiary foundations vary widely. For example, the foundation for the business record exception to the hearsay rule includes evidence that the records were made and kept in the ordinary course of business. The foundation for the introduction of certain scientific evidence requires the establishment of a chain of custody. The following list includes some, though by no means all, of the sorts of evidence that require special foundations for admissibility: voice identifications, telephone conversations, writings, business records, dying declarations, photographs, scientific tests, expert opinions, and many more.

> PROPONENT: (To the court) At this time, the plaintiff moves Exhibit 2 into evidence.
>
> THE COURT: Any objections?
>
> OPPONENT: Yes, Your Honor, we object to authenticity. Counsel has not shown that the knife is in substantially the same condition as when the witness first examined it.
>
> PROPONENT: I'll lay that foundation, Your Honor.
>
> THE COURT: Very well.

PROPONENT: Is this knife in the same condition as when you first examined it?
ANSWER: Other than the fact that the victim's blood has been cleaned off, yes.

Possible Responses: Ask additional questions that lay the necessary foundation, as illustrated above.

The Basics	
COMMON OBJECTIONS	
NONSUBSTANTIVE OBJECTIONS	
Leading (direct only):	A question that suggests its own answer
Compound:	A question with two inquiries, where a single answer may be misleading
Vague:	A question that is incomprehensible or incomplete
Argumentative:	A question that insists that the witness accept the examiner's summary, inference, or conclusion
(Calls for) Narrative:	(A question that attempts to elicit) an answer that is longer than a few sentences
Asked and Answered:	A question that is duplicative of one already asked of the witness by the same counsel
Assumes Facts Not in Evidence:	A question that includes a statement of fact not yet proven; used as a predicate for the inquiry
Nonresponsive (cross only):	Testimony that does not answer the specific question asked
SUBSTANTIVE OBJECTIONS	
(Calls for) Hearsay:	(A question that attempts to elicit) testimony that includes an out-of-court statement that is being used to prove the truth of the matter asserted
Irrelevant:	Testimony that does not make any fact of consequence to the case more or less probable
Unfair Prejudice:	Testimony whose probative value is substantially outweighed by the danger of unfair prejudice
Improper Character Evidence:	Testimony that attempts to show a person's action in conformity with past conduct or a character trait
Speculation/Lack of Personal Knowledge:	Testimony that goes beyond a lay witness's sensory perception
Improper Lay Opinion:	Testimony that gives a lay witness's opinion, conclusion, or inference on a matter

Chapter Fourteen

Opening Statement

I. The Purpose of the Opening Statement

Opening statement is your first opportunity to speak directly to the factfinder about the merits of your case. A good opening statement is a map and diary rolled into one; it anticipates where the trial path will go and highlights the testimony and evidence that witnesses will present.

The three general purposes of opening statements are to grab the factfinder's attention, to assist the factfinder in understanding the anticipated events of the trial, and to advocate your client's position.

A. *Grab the Opening Moment*

The competition for the factfinder's imagination begins the first time you and your opposing counsel speak. This moment is crucial. If you can place a mental image in the mind of the factfinder, you can directly influence the way they interpret the evidence at trial.

Consider, for example, the different mental images evoked by the terms "billiard parlor" and "pool hall." For most people, a billiard parlor is thought of as a formal, reserved, well-lit, and fairly respectable establishment. A pool hall, however, is more likely to be pictured as smoky, dark, perhaps slightly threatening, and probably a little seedy. Along with the contrasting images, the factfinder will make different inferences about events occurring in these two places. In general, things seem to happen differently in pool halls than they do in billiard parlors. Visibility is better in a billiard parlor, whereas things happen more furtively in a pool hall. A stranger might be questioned in a billiard parlor, but a confrontation is more likely in a pool hall. In other words, the initial mental image dictates, or at least suggests, a variety of assumptions about the nature, context, and likelihood of events.

Your task in an opening statement is to engage the factfinder's imagination—to help them begin to imagine the case your way. This task is complicated by the legal function that the opening statement plays in the conduct of the trial.

Chapter Fourteen

B. Explain the Anticipated Evidence

The legal function of an opening statement is to assist the trier of fact in understanding the evidence to be presented at trial. While we hope the evidence will be self-explanatory, even in the best-organized trials evidence is often developed in a disjointed manner.

To reduce this confusion, the courts developed the concept of the opening statement. The opening statement gives the parties the opportunity to present an overview of the case at the beginning of the trial so as to better equip the factfinder to make sense of the evidence as it is presented. This chance to give an overview of the expected testimony, however, is not an invitation to argue about it.

The "nonargument rule" states that opening statements may only be used to inform the trier of fact of "what the evidence will show." Thus, lawyers are restricted to offering a preview of the anticipated testimony, exhibits, and other evidence. This limitation results in a highly stylized set of rules for the presentation of opening statements, as lawyers strive to influence the factfinder without crossing the line into prohibited argument.

C. Advocate for Your Client

Use your opening statement as an opportunity to advance your theory of the case. This is not as easy or as obvious as it may sound.

The trick is to consider the relationship between the expected evidence and the conclusions that you want the judge or jury to reach. In the firetruck case, the expected evidence is that a firetruck approached the intersection and that the defendant did not stop his car. But that doesn't advocate anything. It is only when the expected evidence is combined with a case theory that the opening statement becomes persuasive. Build a persuasive opening statement from the plaintiff's theory: the evidence will show that the defendant had ample opportunity to observe the firetruck, which was flashing its lights and sounding its siren, but that he was so rushed and distracted he did not notice it.

So long as you avoid lapsing into argumentative form, you may develop your theory of the case. While you may not urge the trier of fact to reach certain conclusions, you may arrange your discussion of the facts so that the conclusions are inevitable. Many tools are available to accomplish this goal. A well-developed opening statement will take advantage of some or all of the following concepts:

Choice of facts. In every opening statement, decide which facts to include and which to leave out. While you will obviously want to emphasize the facts that you find helpful, there is considerable risk to telling an incomplete or illogical story.

Sequencing. The order of the facts may be as important as the nature of the facts.

Clarity of description. It is one thing to mention a fact, but it is better to describe it with so much detail and clarity that the factfinder creates their own mental portrait.

Common sense. An opening statement cannot be successful if its story does not resonate with everyday experience. Use a factfinder's reflexive resort to common sense to lead them to a desired conclusion. Consider an opening statement that begins this way: "The defendant woke up late, he had an important meeting to go to, the meeting was to be held far from his home, he skipped breakfast, went directly to his car and drove to the meeting." Without saying more, common sense suggests that the defendant was in a hurry when he was driving.

Moral attraction. Make your opening statement more attractive by telling a story that people want to accept. Describe the evidence in a context of shared values or civic virtues that adds moral force to your client's position. In the firetruck case, for example, the plaintiff's evidence will show that the plaintiff knew that it was important not to get in the way of a fire engine, so she stopped to let it pass.

In the final analysis, the most successful opening statements explain exactly how you intend to win your case.

II. The Rules of Opening Statement

The rules of evidence used in your mock trial govern what evidence is admitted at trial. Since the admission of a piece of evidence is left to the discretion of the presiding judge, you may not know exactly what facts will come out at trial when you are preparing your opening statement. To complicate matters, opening statements are limited to admissible evidence. The best method, then, is to use only those facts for which you have a solid theory of admissibility.

In addition to limiting your opening to only the facts that you believe will be admissible at trial, there are other specific rules that govern how you may present your opening statement. Once you understand these rules, you can plan exactly what you will say. Before we address those rules, however, we will briefly summarize successful techniques for delivering your opening statement.

First, if you have weeks or even months to prepare for your mock trial, memorize your opening statement. Where you have had less time, write out your opening statement and divide it into sections. At trial, use an outline that lists the sections or headings. By triggering your memory section by section, you can avoid reading your opening statement. Reading is your enemy during openings since it introduces you as stilted, labored, or unprepared. It also prevents you from making eye contact, picking up on the factfinder's reactions, moving about the courtroom, and quickly responding to objections and rulings by the court. If you represent the defense, reading your opening further prevents you from replying to challenges, weaknesses, and omissions in the plaintiff's or prosecution's opening statement.

Chapter Fourteen

Movement about the courtroom can also add considerable force to your opening statement; use it to transition from one topic to another or to emphasize a particular point. Begin your opening statement standing directly in front of the factfinder. Then, to signal transitions, take a step or two to one side or the other whenever you change topics. By using your body in this manner, you signal that one subject has ended and another is about to begin. This motion, in turn, will reinitiate primacy. The factfinder's attention will refocus, giving you a new "opening moment" in which to take advantage of their heightened concentration and retention.

Most judges will allow you to move freely about the courtroom during opening statements. Even so, you might encounter a judge who prefers that you argue your case from the lectern or behind counsel table. As explained in Chapter Four, Section I(C), we recommend asking the judge's preference before the trial begins.

Even if you are limited to the lectern, use movement as a signal. Stand very still while making one point, then shift your weight by taking half a step before tackling your next topic. If you avoid fidgeting and swaying, small movements can refocus the factfinder almost as well as free movement.

A.   Do Not Argue

As we noted above, argument is improper during opening statements.

1.   Defining Argument

Most judges recognize that "argument" is a relative concept and allow lawyers reasonable latitude. As with many other rules we have discussed, application of this rule will vary by competition and by presiding judge.

To help you through the uncertainty involved in determining whether a statement is an argument, ask yourself the following questions:

- Am I interpreting the evidence?

- Am I urging the factfinder to draw inferences from the facts?

- Am I explaining the importance of a certain piece of evidence or suggesting the weight it should be given in the factfinder's deliberations?

- Am I appealing overtly to the factfinder's sense of mercy or justice?

If the answer to any of these questions could be yes, you are probably arguing.

To illustrate to the application of our test, consider the following portions of opening statements that are based on a personal injury case:

> Just before the accident, the plaintiff was sitting in a bar. In less than an hour and a half, he consumed at least four shots of vodka. He

bought a round for the house, and then he left. He left in his car. The collision occurred within the next twenty minutes.

As compared to:

The plaintiff was obviously drunk. No person could drink four shots of vodka in that amount of time without feeling it. Only an alcoholic or a liar would claim to have been sober under those circumstances.

The first example passes our test, since the bartender will testify to the facts contained in the first three sentences and the police will verify the remainder of the information. The second example is more problematic. To begin, the drunkenness of the plaintiff is an inference based on the lawyer's conclusion "no person could drink four shots of vodka" without feeling it. Calling the plaintiff "an alcoholic or a liar" is pure argument; it characterizes the plaintiff's behavior. The second example fails our test and is therefore improper.

2. Other Considerations

In addition to the words you speak, a variety of other considerations may lead a judge to conclude that your opening statement has crossed the line into argument. A statement can be transformed into an argument simply by the way in which it is spoken, including the use sarcasm, volume, or vocal caricature.

In addition, the use of rhetorical questions is inherently argumentative, for example, a suggestion of disbelief as in, "What could he possibly have been thinking?" or a suggestion of incontrovertible certainty, "What other answer could there be?" Questions like these strongly signal argument when used in an opening statement.

Likewise, although an excellent persuasive device when used elsewhere in a trial, repetition can lead an opening statement into the forbidden territory of argument. Even the most innocent of facts can become provocative when repeated three times, each with greater emphasis.

B. Do Not Comment on the Law

Closely related to the rule against argument is the general proscription against discussing the law at length during opening statements. The rationale is the same: opening statements organize and preview the evidence for the finder of fact; they are not for arguing one's case based on the law.

Since it is virtually impossible to avoid some discussion of the law during any but the simplest opening statement, do so quickly and only to the extent necessary. For instance, at some point in the firetruck opening the plaintiff's attorney will have to raise the legal concept of "due care," if only to explain exactly how the defendant was negligent.

Remember when you do this, however, that it is never acceptable to advocate that the factfinder follow a particular interpretation or construction of the law.

C. Weave Your Theory and Theme into Your Trial Story

Your most important task when giving an opening statement is to tell the factfinder your theory and theme of the case. Start each trial by saying, in effect, "This is a case about. . . ."

Then tell the factfinder, in a single phrase or sentence, precisely why your client should win. See Chapter Two for a detailed explanation of theme and theory.

1. State Your Theory Clearly

You developed a coherent theory of the case in your pretrial preparation. The challenge now is to communicate it clearly, succinctly, and persuasively.

Recall that a trial theory adapts a factual story to the legal issues in the case. Your theory must contain a simple, logical, provable account of facts that, when viewed in light of the controlling law, will lead to the conclusion that your client should win. Use your opening statement to explain that theory to the trier of fact and show why the verdict should be in your favor.

A successful theory will be built around a persuasive story. Ideally, such a story will be told about people who have reasons for the way they act; it will explain all the known or undeniable facts; it will be told by credible witnesses; it will be supported by details; and it will accord with common sense. Tie this all together in your opening statement by, at some point and in some manner, addressing each of these elements.

What happened? Describe the crucial events in your story. The crucial events are those that speak to the legal elements of your claim or defense. For instance, if your client is charged with murder and is claiming self-defense, describe those events that led your client to believe their life was threatened by the deceased.

Why did it happen? It is not sufficient to list the facts. Persuade the factfinder by describing why events occurred as they did. Explain why individuals acted as they did, since a compelling reason for an action will tend to rule out alternatives. In a collision case, for example, state that the defendant was driving slowly and carefully just before the accident. Make your explanation more persuasive by supporting it with the fact that the defendant was returning from an antique auction, carrying an expensive and fragile chandelier in the back seat of the car. This reason for driving slowly not only supports the defendant's version of events, but it makes less likely a claim by the plaintiff that the defendant careened around a corner at high speed.

Which witnesses should be believed? Although it is improper to argue the credibility of witnesses in your opening statement, you may, and should, provide the trier of fact with facts that bolster your own witnesses and detract from the opposition's. Bias, motive, prejudice, and interest in the outcome of the case are always relevant to a witness's believability. Explain the facts that demonstrate your own witnesses' lack of bias; also include the facts that demonstrate the motive or interest of the opposition. For example:

> Two experts will testify about the cause of the fire. The plaintiff will call Fire Chief Miguel Morales, who will testify that he investigated the fire as part of his normal professional duties. Chief Morales concluded that the fire was accidental. He was not paid by either of the parties. He was simply doing his job. The defendant's expert is Ann Chihak. She does not work for the city or the state; she is a private investigator. All of her income is derived from private clients. She was hired by the defendant to reach an opinion about the cause of the fire in this case, and she was paid $500 an hour to do so. Ms. Chihak will testify that the fire was caused by arson.

How can we be sure? As should be apparent from the examples above, the persuasiveness of an opening statement, indeed the persuasiveness of virtually any aspect of a trial, is often established through the use of details. Broad assertions can stake out territory and raise issues, but the truth will be determined by the details. An essential element of an opening statement, then, is the judicious use of details in support of the accuracy, dependability, or believability of your facts.

Does it all make sense? Finally, the theory you present in opening, or at any other point in the trial, must make sense when measured against the everyday experiences of the factfinder. The provision of reasons, bases, or details, no matter how compelling they are to your way of thinking, will accomplish nothing if the judge or jurors cannot place them into a context that they understand and accept.

2. Introduce Your Theme

Your trial theme, as distinct from your theory, is a single sentence that captures the moral force of your case. A theme communicates to the finder of fact the reason that your side deserves to win. Introducing a theme in opening is particularly persuasive since it focuses the factfinder's attention on a cognitive image that you will return to throughout the trial.

Nonetheless, using a theme in your opening statement presents some difficulty. Unlike a trial theory, a theme reflects upon or interprets the evidence rather than simply describing or outlining it. Overuse or constant repetition of your theme may bring you perilously close to argument. Most judges, however, will allow the statement of a theme at both the beginning and end of an opening statement, especially when it is phrased in terms of fact, as opposed to opinion or characterization.

Chapter Fourteen

One of our previous themes for the plaintiff in the firetruck case is that the defendant was "too busy to be careful." This theme can be used at the beginning of the opening as a reference point for the information about the defendant's course of conduct on the morning of the accident.

> Members of the jury, this is a case about a driver who was too busy to be careful. On the morning of the accident, he woke up late. He had to be at an important meeting downtown and he had less than an hour left in which to get there.

Although there is a sense in which "too busy to be careful" is a conclusion, it is used here solely to introduce the facts that follow. Busyness and carefulness are ordinary incidents of life that are easily recognized without questionable inferences. Therefore, the theme "too busy to be careful" can almost certainly be invoked at the outset of the plaintiff's opening statement.

D. Order and Contrast the Facts Persuasively

While argument is prohibited during opening statements, persuasion is not. Indeed, persuasion is unavoidable. Few of the facts outlined in an opening statement will be neutral; most facts will be favorable to one side or the other. So long as you refrain from suggesting conclusions to be drawn from the facts, feel free to arrange them in an order that maximizes their favorable impact. Persuasive ordering of the facts assists the factfinder in understanding the case by making it easy to see just how the parties' stories diverge.

Persuasively order the facts either through incremental development or through contrast. Incremental development successively orders a series of discrete facts, each building upon the last, until the desired conclusion becomes obvious. Although the facts will be related, they need not be presented in chronological order. The following example demonstrates how the plaintiff might use incremental development in our firetruck case:

> The defendant awoke at 7:00 a.m. He had an important meeting scheduled with a potential new client for 8:30 that morning. The client had not yet decided whether to hire the defendant, and the account was worth a lot of money. The meeting was downtown, sixteen miles from the defendant's home. The defendant showered, shaved, and dressed, but he skipped breakfast. He hurried to his car, parked about a block away. All of this took approximately fifty minutes. By the time the defendant got to his car, it was 8:00 a.m. He had thirty minutes left before the new client was scheduled to arrive at his office.

The example begins when the defendant woke up, skips ahead to the information about the scheduled meeting, and then goes back to describe the rest of the defendant's morning routine. Other facts, of course, could be added to show how seriously late the defendant was, and therefore how likely he was to drive carelessly or too fast. The point is that the individual events build upon each other to explain, without saying so, why the defendant would have been driving negligently.

Another tool in opening statement contrasts or juxtaposes contradictory facts to demonstrate the implausibility of some aspect of the opposing case theory. The defendant in the fire engine case might use contrast this way:

> The plaintiff in this case is seeking damages for pain and suffering and lost income. She claims a permanent disability. You will see medical bills offered into evidence that start with the date of the accident and which continue right through to last December 10. But you will also see a receipt for a new backpack and camp stove, purchased by the plaintiff last August 17. She went to the doctor on August 15, bought her backpack on August 17, and went camping at Eagle River Falls on August 31. She returned to town on September 3. Her next visit to the doctor was not until October 19.

Without resort to argument, the simple contrast between the medical bills and the camping trip casts doubt on the plaintiff's allegation of permanent injury.

Checklist	
HAVE YOU FOLLOWED THE RULES FOR OPENING STATEMENTS?	
☑ **Did you refrain from arguing?**	Are you interpreting the evidence or urging the factfinder to draw inferences? Are you explaining the importance of evidence or suggesting the amount of weight it should be given? Are you appealing overtly to the factfinder's sense of mercy or justice? *If so, you are arguing and you should refrain from doing so.*
☑ **Did you refrain from commenting on the law?**	Are you going beyond giving explanations of the allegations of wrongdoing in the case? *If so, save the further discussion for closing argument.*
☑ **Did you weave your theory and theme into your trial story?**	Are you beginning with a clear statement of your theory and theme and then giving the supporting facts in narrative form? *If not, rework your opening statement to make it more persuasive.*

Chapter Fourteen

Checklist	
HAVE YOU FOLLOWED THE RULES FOR OPENING STATEMENTS?	
☑ Did you order and contrast the facts of your case persuasively?	Did you use incremental development of the facts to support your theory and theme? Did you use contrast to point out the opposing party's factual weaknesses? *If not, rework your opening statement to make it more persuasive.*

III. Planning Your Opening Statement

A great deal of thought is required to plan an effective opening statement. In addition to following the rules outlined above, use these guidelines when determining the content and organization of your opening statement.

A. Content

Every good opening statement, no matter what the case, contains enough information to help you win the trial but not so much that you distract the factfinder or risk exploitation by the other side. So, how do you know what to include? Although the content of openings will vary depending on the type of case, consider the following.

1. Include Only Provable Facts

Every fact that you include in your opening statement must be provable at trial. The law limits opening statements to a preview of the evidence that will be presented once the trial begins. Evidence that no witness can verify or that is inadmissible under the rules of competition is not provable.

Think of your opening as a promise to the factfinder. By making a definitive statement about the future evidence, you commit yourself to producing that evidence. If you do not deliver, at best you appear to have overstated your case and at worst factfinders may feel deliberately misled. Even if the trier of fact does not realize that there has been a gap between your opening and your proof, opposing counsel will certainly point it out during final argument.

2. Include the Necessary Facts

The most important part of any opening statement is its treatment of the operative facts. Although there is no recipe for determining which facts are necessary in a given case, you will no doubt want to include some or all of the following.

a. The Physical Scene

The meaning and legal significance of events is often dependent upon their location. Use your opening statement, therefore, to set the scene for the major events in your case.

Setting a scene involves describing a potentially unlimited number of details. Craft your opening statement to dwell only on those details significant to your case; avoid those that are merely clutter. In the firetruck case, for example, it is important for the plaintiff to note that the pavement was dry, since that would affect the defendant's stopping distance. The height of the curb, however, would be extraneous under virtually any theory of the case.

b. Action and Key Events

Most cases revolve around one or more actions or key events. In depicting actions and events, nouns and verbs are much more useful than adjectives and adverbs. This may seem strange since modifiers are commonly thought to add descriptive depth. Consider, however, which of the following accounts is more evocative of the crime. First, a short paragraph that makes maximum use of adverbs and adjectives.

> It was a heinous, horrible crime. The defendant's actions were inhuman and awful. He brutally grabbed at the victim's gold chain, fiercely yanking it away. He left an ugly, ugly bruise on the victim's neck.

Now consider a paragraph with virtually no modifiers at all.

> The defendant placed his knife against the victim's body. Without waiting, he grabbed the gold chain from the victim's neck and wrenched it until it snapped, leaving bruises on the victim's neck that did not heal for over a week.

The second paragraph is more vivid because it describes the deeds as they occurred whereas the first paragraph actually short-circuits the action by substituting value-laden modifiers for an account of the events themselves. The nouns and verbs in the second paragraph make it easier to picture the crime because the precise meaning of each word is clear.

The message here is to use nouns and verbs in your opening statement and limit modifiers, which are frequently judgments rather than descriptions (and as such are argumentative). Words like heinous, brutal, and awful may convey the lawyer's opinion about the nature of the crime, but they do not depict a vision of the event itself. Moreover, it is always better for lawyers to let jurors come to their own conclusions rather than trying to force-feed them theirs.

c. Transactions and Agreements

Civil cases are likely to involve written and oral communications far more than physical occurrences. In many ways, these nonphysical events may be more difficult

Chapter Fourteen

to describe during an opening statement since there is little or no activity to depict. Nonetheless, when a case turns on the interpretation of a document or the meaning of a series of telephone calls, counsel must search for a way to bring the transaction to life.

Transactions and agreements are brought to life by interpreting, in simple terms, what happened or was agreed upon and then filling in the necessary details. There is no need, for example, to recount every telephone conversation that went into the negotiation of a purchase order. It will usually be sufficient to delineate the terms of the order itself, supported by an account of one or two crucial conversations.

3. Include a Brief Reference to the Other Side's Case

It is always difficult to decide how much attention to give to the opposition's case. Plaintiff/prosecution counsel must determine whether to anticipate and respond to the expected defenses. Defendant's counsel has to consider whether and how much to react to the plaintiff/prosecution opening.

a. *Plaintiff/Prosecution Opening*

Unlike final arguments, there is no rebuttal in opening statements. You only get to address the factfinder once and without the advantage of knowing what the defendant's theory and theme will be. No matter what your opposing counsel says, you will not be able to respond directly until the end of the trial. This can be especially troublesome in cases where the defendant presents an affirmative defense. Since an affirmative defense, by definition, raises issues that go beyond the plaintiff's own case, the plaintiff faces a delicate problem in dealing with them during the opening statement. Should the plaintiff ignore the affirmative defense, thereby foregoing the opportunity to reply to it at the outset of the trial? Or should the plaintiff respond to the defense in advance, in essence forecasting the defendant's case? Here are some guidelines to responding to the other side's case.

First, give primary attention to the strongest aspects of your own case. The opening statement is your opportunity to capture the factfinder's imagination. Do not get them started imagining the things that might be wrong with your case. Accentuate the positive.

Acknowledge that you have the burden of proof in the case. State what the burden is (preponderance of the evidence if it is a civil case or proof beyond a reasonable doubt in criminal matters) and confidently predict that the evidence presented will meet that burden. Failure to mention and embrace the burden in your opening is likely to be noted by the defense during its opening; do not to provide this opportunity if you can avoid it.

Since you will know with some certainty which defenses will be raised, there is no reason to address all of the holes that the defendant might try to punch in your case. Concentrate on the most likely defenses. To the extent possible, treat the defenses raised by the other side as technicalities or annoyances. If you seem overly concerned or worried about a defense, it suggests that there are indeed problems with your case.

Finally, the Fifth Amendment prohibits prosecutors from suggesting that the defendant will testify (even if you know for a fact that the defendant will be called to testify per your case file materials). The Fifth Amendment does not, however, prevent the prosecutor from reading from a confession or prior statement of the defendant so long as they intend to seek admission of the statement at trial and are confident it will be admitted.

b. Defendant's Opening

Defense lawyers plan and outline opening statements just like their opposing counsel. But when the time comes to present their opening, good defense attorneys are flexible in determining the final content. Delivering the second opening statement is a tremendous advantage; capitalize on this opportunity by preparing to respond to at least some aspects of the plaintiff's opening.

Responding to opposing counsel's opening is not easy; you must listen carefully and pick your battles. If you are new to trial advocacy, it might be best for you to stick to a prepared outline. For the more confident and experienced students, there are a few techniques you can use when responding.

First, state your denial right up front. The civil plaintiff's opening statement, and even more so the criminal prosecutor's, is essentially an accusation. It accuses the defendant of negligence, breach of contract, criminal acts, or some other negative conduct. After hearing such an extended charge against the defendant, the trier of fact's first inclination will be to ask the question, "Well, is it true?" The defendant, then, absolutely must respond with a denial. Anything short of a denial is likely to be regarded as evasion, equivocation, or worse, an admission of fault.

Respond directly to the plaintiff's version of significant controverted evidence. Simply telling your own independent story is not sufficient; explain why the facts in support of your version are superior. Do not expect the trier of fact to keep the plaintiff's opening in mind and then to appreciate the implications of the contrary facts as you reveal them. Instead, make it apparent that you are contradicting the plaintiff's factual claims.

Finally, point out significant omissions in your opposing counsel's opening statement. As all trial lawyers learn, the absence of evidence can be as telling as the evidence itself. Be ready to respond not only to what was said in plaintiff's opening but also to what was not said. While it would be argumentative to accuse opposing counsel of concealing information, it is perfectly proper to point out evidentiary gaps in the plaintiff's opening statement by stating, for example, "What Plaintiff's counsel didn't tell you is . . . ."

Chapter Fourteen

	Checklist	
	IS THE CONTENT OF YOUR OPENING STATEMENT APPROPRIATE?	
☑	**Did you include only provable facts?**	Is each fact you mention in your opening statement likely to be brought out during trial?
		If not, take out the unprovables.
☑	**Did you include all the necessary facts?**	Does your story describe the physical scene, actions and key events, and any transactions and agreements?
		If not, add these operative facts to your trial story.
☑	**Did you include a reference to the other side's case (or are you prepared to do so at trial)?**	If you represent the plaintiff/prosecution, did you embrace your burden of proof and address the defense theory (if known) in your opening statement?
		If not, consider whether you can do so. (Remember the limitations imposed by the Fifth Amendment in criminal cases.)
		If you represent the defense, are you prepared to deny the opposition's accusations and address the controverted evidence in, or omissions from, their opening?
		If not, practice your opening until you are comfortable enough to do so.

B. Organization

1. Begin with Your Theme and Theory

Embrace the principle of primacy and get right to the point: state your theme; explain the most important part of your theory; lay the groundwork for a crucial direct or cross-examination; foreshadow your closing argument.

In the firetruck case, this is a good start to the plaintiff's opening:

> This is a case about a defendant who was too busy to be careful. Because he failed to stop for a firetruck, he smashed his car right into the back of the plaintiff's automobile. The firetruck was flashing its lights and sounding its siren. All of the other drivers noticed the

> firetruck and stopped—except the defendant. He had his mind on an important meeting and was distracted. He kept on driving until it was too late. The plaintiff will never take another step without feeling pain caused by the collision that resulted.

This opening is direct and to the point. It states plaintiff's theory and theme right at the outset and launches immediately into the facts that support their case. The three central points that the plaintiff will make are all mentioned: 1) the firetruck was clearly visible, 2) all of the other traffic stopped, and 3) the defendant was preoccupied and caused the accident.

In considering what to include in your opening paragraph, choose the information you want the factfinder to remember when the trial concludes. Ask yourself: "What facts most support a verdict in my favor?" "What issues will be most hotly contested?" "Which witness will be most relied upon?"

2. Introduce Yourself and Your Client

While there is a natural inclination to begin your opening statement by introducing yourself, your co-counsel. and your client, that wastes your opening moment. After providing the factfinder a summary of your theory and theme, you may then pause to introduce yourself and your co-counsel.

If you represent a specific person, now is the time to introduce them to the factfinder as well. This is your chance to humanize your client, to give the factfinder a chance to come to like them. Do not point and announce that your client is a great person. Stand next to them, place your hand on their shoulder, and introduce your client like you would your own grandparent. Explain your client's many fine qualities. Remember that likable people are more apt to be perceived as credible. Although there is no formula for how much information you give during your introduction, it is generally a good idea to share your client's age, marital status, educational background, occupation, and anything else relevant to your case.

If you represent the prosecution in a criminal case, it is a good idea to introduce the victim of the crime after introducing yourself. You might continue as follows:

> Members of the jury, you will hear Danielle Weeks referred to as the victim in this case, the deceased, and even, the body. But remember when you hear those terms we are talking about a real person—a person who used to be a bright, young, talented twenty-six-year-old actor. Danielle Weeks grew up here in Tucson as part of a family: she had a mother, a father, and two siblings. Danielle was heavily involved in acting, dance, and musical theatre classes throughout junior high and high school. The teachers all considered Danielle to be exceptionally talented.

Introducing the victim at the outset of your case humanizes them so that the judge and jurors will remember *who* the victim is or was and the gravity of the crime committed.

3. Tell the Full Story

Now that you have introduced the key participants, tell the factfinder the story of your case.

a. Avoid the Witness-by-Witness Approach

Recall that the very purpose of the opening statement, indeed its underlying justification, is to overcome the disjointed fashion in which the witnesses will produce evidence at trial. A witness-by-witness rendition of the facts rarely produces a coherent story when the witnesses take the stand and testify for themselves. This method of organization is not helpful because it simply substitutes a summary of the coming testimony for the actual direct and cross-examinations.

Imagine that plaintiff's counsel in the firetruck case opted for the witness-by-witness approach in her opening statement.

> Members of the jury, you will hear a number of witnesses testify in this case. Let me tell you about some of them.
>
> Lisa Gee will testify that on the morning of the accident she was driving south on Craycroft. As she approached the intersection of Craycroft and Alta Vista, she saw a firetruck approaching from the west. It was flashing its lights and sounding its siren, so she applied her brakes and stopped her car immediately. Suddenly another car, driven by the defendant, Mr. Tommy Maynard, crashed into her from behind.
>
> Michael Trumbull was a firefighter on Engine Number 9 on the day of the accident. He will tell you that the weather was clear and dry that day. He will also describe the call that his engine company received and the fact that they followed their standard procedure when they left the firehouse—flashing their lights and sounding their siren. The fire engine headed west on Alta Vista in the direction of Craycroft.

This method quickly becomes boring and hard to follow.

While the witness-by-witness approach is unlikely to result in an effective opening statement, this does not prohibit you from mentioning individual witnesses in the course of your opening. To the contrary, it is often important to inform the finder of fact of the source of a specific fact or the precise nature of some anticipated testimony. Weave the information about the witnesses into the narrative so that the witness references arise in the context of your theory of the case.

b. Use Chronology Wisely

Chronology is an obvious, natural, and often useful organizing technique for opening statements. All events in the real world, after all, occur in chronological order. Moreover, we are all used to thinking of life in chronological terms. This is why opening statements have become part of the trial: to allow lawyers to meld individual witness accounts into a single chronological narrative. Consider the following:

> The weather was clear and dry on the morning of the accident. Fire Engine Company Number 9 received a call to respond to a fire, and the crew boarded their truck and left the firehouse, headed west on Alta Vista toward Craycroft Road. In keeping with standard procedure, they sounded their siren and flashed their lights from the moment they left the station. At about that same time, the plaintiff, Lisa Gee, was driving south on Craycroft and the defendant, Tommy Maynard, was driving behind her.
>
> As Ms. Gee approached the intersection with Alta Vista, she saw and heard the firetruck, so she immediately applied her brakes. She had plenty of time to stop. The defendant, whose car was directly behind hers, didn't stop. Eventually, he slammed on his brakes, but it was too late. As hard as he hit his brakes, it did not keep him from crashing right into the plaintiff's car.

This story is far more cohesive than the witness-based account. It brings all of the vehicles together at the fateful intersection without the necessity of the jurors having to keep a running account of their whereabouts and it connects the fire engine's use of lights and siren directly to the cause of the accident.

There are, however, drawbacks to using strict chronology in telling your story. It can encourage the use of excessive detail. For instance, the fact that the plaintiff in the firetruck case left her home five minutes before the defendant left his is not worth mentioning unless it supports your theory or theme.

Chronology can also interfere with the logical exposition of your theory or theme. In the firetruck case, the plaintiff's theme is that the defendant was too rushed to be careful. This conclusion is supported by the fact that the defendant woke up late that morning as well as the fact that he called his office regarding his meeting immediately after the collision. When inserted into the story chronologically, however, the factfinder may lose these facts because they are separated by nearly an hour's worth of events. Putting these facts together maximizes their impact.

Despite the drawbacks mentioned above, the judicious use of chronology is an essential part of every opening statement. Use chronological development to explain independent events. The matter in every trial consists of a series of sub-events that fit together to comprise the entire story. You can arrange these sub-events in the order that best promotes your theory and theme. The sub-events themselves, however, have their own internal logic, which generally can be understood only when explained chronologically.

Organize your opening statement into "chunks," each of which is told chronologically. Between each chunk, insert information that helps the factfinder understand the chronological narrative. For instance, consider the question of the siren in our firetruck case. The plaintiff says there was a siren, and the defendant says there was not. Plaintiff's counsel might tell the overall story chronologically, weaving in a non-chronological "siren chunk" when it becomes relevant.

> Just as she reached the intersection, the plaintiff saw and heard an approaching firetruck. It was sounding its siren and flashing its lights. We know that the siren was operating because Lieutenant Janis Regnier, the driver of the firetruck, will testify that she always sounds the siren when she is answering a call. That is fire department policy, and Lieutenant Regnier is a decorated firefighter who has been with the department for over ten years. Perhaps, for whatever reason, the defendant didn't hear the siren, but Lieutenant Regnier will testify that she is certain that she was doing her official duty—that is, using her audio and visual alarms—on the day when the accident occurred.

Used in this manner, the information about Lieutenant Regnier corroborates and strengthens the plaintiff's theory of the case. It neither stands alone as an isolated description of the witness, nor does it interfere with the flow of the narrative. Rather, it adds support to the plaintiff's theory at the precise moment when support is likely to be most readily understood.

4. Highlight the Legal Issues

Now that you have given the factfinder your full story, briefly introduce the legal issues of the case. A statement of legal issues will put the significance of the facts into clear perspective. If you represent the plaintiff/prosecution, this is a good time to mention your burden again briefly and state that you will prove that the defendant is liable or guilty.

> The evidence you hear today will illustrate by a preponderance of the evidence that the defendant was negligent—he was too busy to be careful and so he failed to notice the firetruck, and he was driving too quickly to stop in time. You will see today that his negligence caused the collision in this case.

If you represent the defense, tell the factfinder that the other side has the burden of proof and that they will not meet that burden.

> The plaintiff has the burden of proof in this case. They must prove by a preponderance of the evidence that the defendant was negligent. The

evidence will show that the plaintiff's request for damages is unreasonable and, more importantly, that the defendant was not the cause of this collision.

5. Request a Verdict

Conclude your opening statement with a request for, or explanation of, the verdict that you will seek at the end of the trial. Make this request in general terms: "At the end of the case, we will ask you to return a verdict that the defendant was not guilty of negligence."

Summary

OPENING STATEMENT ORGANIZATION

- Begin with your theory and theme
- Introduce yourself and your client (if applicable)
- Tell the full story (avoiding a strict witness-by-witness or chronological approach)
- Highlight the legal issues
- Request a verdict

IV. Objections

Even if your mock trial competition rules allow objections during opening statements (some do not), they should be an unusual occurrence. In jury trials, the objecting attorney risks seeming rude by interrupting opposing counsel's address to the members of the jury. In bench trials, objections are even more likely to be met with annoyance. For these reasons, most attorneys try to avoid objecting during opposing counsel's opening. There are times, however, when objections are called for and should be made.

A. Raising Objections

The most common objection during an opening statement is to improper argument. Most judges will sustain this objection only when the argument is extended or over the top. An argumentative sentence or two is not likely to draw an objection and even less likely to be sustained. Drawn-out argument, however, is more vulnerable to both.

It is also objectionable to argue the law during opening statements. While some brief mention of the applicable law is unavoidable, lengthy discourse on the law, and especially any misstatement of the law, should draw an objection.

While opening statements are required to preview only the evidence that will ultimately come before the trier of fact, objections usually will not be sustained on

Chapter Fourteen

the ground that counsel is discussing inadmissible evidence. A lawyer is entitled to take a chance that the evidence will be admitted, and most judges will not rule on evidentiary objections during the opening statements.

Finally, there is no such objection as, "That is not what the evidence will show." Opposing counsel presents their case and you present yours. You naturally disagree about what the evidence will show. If counsel ultimately fails to live up to the commitments given during their opening statement, pound that point home during your final argument. For the same reason, there is also no such objection as "mischaracterizing the evidence." If a characterization amounts to argument, object to it. Otherwise, opposing counsel is free to put whatever spin they can on the evidence.

B.   *Responding to Objections*

An objection during your opening statement is distracting. Offering a lengthy argument in response to an objection is even more disruptive. The best method of handling objections during opening statements is simply to stand still (facing the jury or judge) while the objection is made and argued. Turn and respond to the objection only if the judge asks you to, and keep your argument brief.

The best response to an "argumentative" objection is to state that a witness (or several witnesses) will testify to the specific facts during the trial. For instance, say plaintiff's counsel stated during the firetruck opening: "You will learn that the defendant's first concern after the accident was his meeting and not the health of the plaintiff." If defense counsel objects to that statement as argument and the court asks for a response, the plaintiff should respond with a proffer explaining that one or more witnesses will testify to those facts. Counsel might say, "Your Honor, two witnesses will testify that immediately after the accident the defendant called his office on his cell phone before he checked on the plaintiff."

If the objection is overruled, simply pick up where you left off. If the objection is sustained, adapt your opening to the court's ruling.

Consider, for instance, what you would do if your theme "too busy to be careful" is found to be improper argument by the presiding judge. Do not ask for reconsideration or try to explain why you were not being argumentative. A small adjustment to your opening is sufficient.

> The evidence will show that the defendant was extremely busy and not careful on the morning of the accident. He was busy because he had an important meeting scheduled with a new client. He was running late for the meeting, and he wanted to get there on time. We know that he wasn't careful because he kept on driving when all of the other traffic stopped for a firetruck. The truck was flashing its lights and sounding its siren, but the defendant didn't notice it until it was too late.

Chapter Fifteen

Closing Argument

I. The Purpose of the Closing Argument

Closing argument is the advocate's only opportunity to tell the story of the case in its entirety, free from most constraining formalities. It is the moment for pure advocacy, when all of the lawyer's organizational, analytic, interpretive, and forensic skills are brought to bear on the task of persuading the trier of fact.

Closing argument is the conclusion of the battle for the factfinder's imagination. Recall that opening statement marks the beginning of the attorney's efforts to help the trier of fact construct a mental image of occurrences, locations, objects, and transactions at issue in the case. This mental image, in turn, influences the way in which the judge or jurors receive and interpret the evidence. At the close of the case, counsel returns to strengthen and explain the significance of those mental images.

Understanding this process should tell us something about closing arguments. If counsel was successful, the opening statement painted a picture that the factfinder began to accept and internalize. The witnesses, documents, and exhibits fit neatly into that picture, reinforcing the image that counsel created. At closing argument, the attorney nails down the image by pointing out the crucial details, weaving together the witnesses' accounts, and explaining the significant connections. All three aspects of the trial—opening, witness examinations, and closing—should combine to evoke a single conception of events.

This means the closing argument cannot be fully successful unless the preceding stages of the trial were also successful. The opening statement's mental image will not stay with the trier of fact unless it is sustained by evidence from the witness stand. More to the point, the closing argument must not paint a picture that is contrary to, or unsupported by, the evidence. While closing argument can and should be the capstone of a well-tried case, it is unlikely to be the saving grace of a poor one.

In mock trials, closing argument presents you with the opportunity to demonstrate that you paid close attention throughout the trial and have adapted your argument to the actual testimony and evidence admitted that day. Many students miss this opportunity—they write their closing argument in advance of the competition, memorize it, and then perform it without modification. You can give a good closing argument that way, to be sure, but not a great one.

A great mock trial closing argument incorporates the most memorable surprises or oddities that arose in the particular competition round and uses them to further persuade the factfinder. Perhaps an opposing witness was overly aggressive or defensive during cross-examination. If so, use that to argue the witness's diminished credibility. Or perhaps the witness invented facts that were arguably material and was successfully impeached by omission. Use that to assert a lack of trustworthiness. If one of your witnesses used a particularly astute description to bring to life an event in the case, use that as a persuasive tool to argue that this description of the events was true and accurate. Or maybe one of your witnesses was unfairly attacked on cross-examination, but calmly withstood the assault. Point that out to show the weakness in opposing counsel's case. Or perhaps the judge used a phrase in ruling on an objection that would serve as an effective rhetorical device when incorporated into your theme. Although mock trials can seem largely scripted, each round is bound to present participants with at least a few small nuggets they can exploit in closing to show that they were paying attention and that they can incorporate those kinds of developments into their pre-planned argument.

We recommend against reading a prepared closing argument. Instead, outline your argument and keep that outline in front of you throughout the trial. Each time something particularly memorable happens during the trial, look through your outline and figure out the best way to incorporate that event into the arguments you already planned to make. Sometimes, rather than incorporating information into an argument, you may find yourself adding new arguments into your outline. As long as the new material directly supports your theory and theme and is as strong as your planned remarks, this is a welcome development that will showcase your skill as an advocate.

Write out, however, and memorize the introduction and ending of your closing argument so you can start and end confidently. Outline the arguments you make in between to leave yourself enough flexibility to expand on some and briefly state others, depending on the events of the trial.

In sum, the closing argument must tell the whole story of the case, but it cannot tell just any story. The closing argument has to complement the portrait begun during the opening statement, and, even more important, must reflect and encompass the actual evidence presented in the case. This goal is best accomplished when you have a well-defined theory and powerful theme and you have incorporated your theory and theme into each stage of your trial. As we said at the start, great closing arguments in mock trials demonstrate that the advocate has paid close attention to what has actually occurred during the competition round.

II. The Principles of Closing Argument

The three main principles of closing argument are to use your theory and theme, to argue for a verdict in your favor based on the evidence admitted during trial, and to avoid making impermissible arguments. Each of these rules is discussed in detail below.

Remember also to use the techniques for effective communication at trial listed in Chapter Three. Especially important when giving a closing are your use of movement, hand gestures, headlines, and visual aids.

A. Use Your Theory and Theme

If nothing else, the closing argument must communicate the advocate's theory of the case. Some witnesses can be disregarded, some details can be omitted, some legal issues can be overlooked, but the theory of the case is essential.

The closing argument must illuminate your theory. Tell the jurors, or the court, why your client is entitled to a particular verdict. A simple recitation of facts is not sufficient. Rather, bring together information from the various witnesses and exhibits and persuade the listener that there can be only one result: a verdict in your client's favor.

A good trial theme provides incentive for the entry of a verdict in your client's favor. In addition to being logical and believable, a trial theme invokes shared values, civic virtues, or common motivations. The theme you stated during the opening statement and alluded to in witness examinations is hammered home in the closing argument. Again, consider the plaintiff's closing argument in the firetruck case:

> The defendant was "too busy to be careful." We know that from his actions and their consequences. But what was he busy doing? He was rushing to a meeting for the sole purpose of increasing his income. He was worrying about money, not about safety. It is true that he was late, but that was no one's fault but his own. And once he was late he was so obsessed with getting to the meeting that he threw caution out the window. He was so busy that he didn't even care to see whether the plaintiff was injured. No, that business meeting was all that mattered. Well, everyone is at risk when drivers behave that way. No one is safe on the road when people care more about their meetings than they do about the way they are driving. You cannot allow someone to think that it is all right to be "too busy to be careful."

Admittedly, the moral dimension of a traffic accident is not usually overpowering. Cases involving crimes, frauds, civil rights violations, wrongful death, child custody, reckless conduct, and even breach of contract provide more fertile ground

Chapter Fifteen

for the assertion of a moral theme. Nonetheless, you can approach even the most mundane case from the perspective of rectitude by explaining how and why your client's position makes sense for reasons other than strict legality.

B. Argue, Argue, Argue!

Recall that the cardinal rule of opening statements is that you may not argue. In closing argument, on the other hand, you may, should, and must argue if you are serious about winning your case. The gloves are off and the limitations are removed, but what precisely distinguishes argument from mere presentation of the facts? The following are some of the most useful techniques you can use during your closing argument.

1. Make Inferences and Conclusions

In closing arguments, the attorneys are free to draw and urge inferences and conclusions based upon the evidence.

For example, in the firetruck case, assume that the trial testimony showed that the defendant's parking garage is located two blocks from his office. From that known fact, it could be inferred that it would take the defendant at least five minutes to walk from the garage to his office. It could further be inferred that the defendant knew how long it would take him to reach his office. Such inferences, based upon a combination of proven fact and everyday experience, could be used to support the larger conclusions that the defendant was in a rush at the time of the accident, that he was preoccupied, or that he was trying to plan for his meeting while driving because he wouldn't have time to plan for it after he arrived at the office.

Remember as you make inferences and conclusions, however, that they will be accepted only when they are based on the facts and well-grounded in common understanding. It is not sufficient for a closing argument to draw, or even urge, inferences and conclusions; the argument must go on to explain why the desired ones are the correct ones.

2. Cluster Circumstantial Evidence and Accumulate Details

Closing argument is the time for gathering and presenting details. Although the particulars may have occurred at different times and have been testified to by several witnesses, aggregate them to make a single point in closing argument.

For instance, the plaintiff in the firetruck case will want to collect all of the details, both direct and circumstantial, that support her proposition that the defendant was preoccupied with thoughts of his important meeting.

> We know that his mind was not on his driving. Look at the details.
> He was late for work. He had an important meeting scheduled for

> 8:30 a.m., and he was still sixteen miles from downtown. He had to park his car, leave the garage, walk over two blocks to his office, and get up to the fourteenth floor. And look at what would happen if he were late. The defendant himself testified that he was meeting with a potential new client and that he hoped to land a valuable account. New clients mean advancement and raises. Losing a new client means losing money. You can't land a new client if you don't make it to the meeting. That meeting was the only thing on the defendant's mind. It was so important to him that the first thing he did after the accident was to call his office. He didn't call an ambulance, he didn't call the police, and he didn't even check to see if the other driver was injured. No, first and foremost he cared about that new client. Everything else—driving, traffic, safety—was unimportant compared to his need to get to that meeting.

Note that the details in the above passage could have come from as many as three different witnesses and that they do not strictly follow the chronology of the accident. The argument makes coordinated use of both direct evidence (the phone call after the accident) and circumstantial evidence (the distance from the garage to his office). The argument also utilizes both positive (a new client means money) and negative (he didn't call an ambulance) inferences. It is the clustering or accumulation of all of these points that gives the argument its persuasive weight.

3. Use Analogies, Allusions, and Stories

a. Analogies

An analogy explains human conduct through reference to everyday human behavior. Use an analogy to bolster a witness's testimony by comparing the witness's version of events to some widely understood experience or activity.

Suppose that the defendant in the fire engine case testified that he saw the firetruck but that he did not slow because the siren was not sounding. To show that this conduct was unreasonable, the plaintiff's attorney might compare it to playing Russian roulette with the safety of every other driver on the road.

> Just because the defendant didn't hear the siren of the firetruck doesn't mean that it wasn't sounding. You wouldn't expect someone to pick up a gun and fire it at somebody, claiming, "Well, I didn't see any bullets." Of course not. A gun is dangerous, and simple prudence means that you should always treat it as though it is loaded. Well, cars can be dangerous too. As soon as he saw the firetruck, the defendant should have recognized the possibility that traffic would slow or stop. He should have recognized the possibility that it was answering a call, whether he heard the siren or not. Continuing to drive, without at least slowing down, was the equivalent of pointing a loaded gun down the road.

Chapter Fifteen

The above excerpt takes conduct that everyone will recognize as unreasonable and explains why the defendant's conduct falls into the same category.

Analogies can support testimony as well as deride it, and they can be short as well as extended. Consider the following example from defense counsel's closing argument.

> Firetrucks use their sirens to tell traffic to stop. We have all seen fire engines on the street that weren't responding to calls. Without their sirens they are just part of traffic. If you look up into the sky and see an airplane flying by, you don't say, "I'd better take cover; it's going to crash."

While analogies can be very powerful, there is always the danger that they can be inverted and exploited by the other side. Thus, if opposing counsel still has an opportunity to argue, take care that any analogies you use are airtight.

b. Allusions

An allusion is a literary or similar reference that adds persuasive force to an argument. These references may be taken from movies, television, popular songs, fairy tales, or even advertisements. For example, defense counsel in the firetruck case might disparage the plaintiff's injury claim with a reference to the well-known fairy tale "The Princess and the Pea."

> The plaintiff claims that her life's activities are severely limited. She says that sometimes she can't even sleep. But last Labor Day, she went camping at Eagle River Falls, where she slept on the ground for four nights. Now that her case is on trial, she claims that she was in pain, but the truth is that she stayed at the campground for the whole weekend. We all know the story about the princess who could feel a pea though it was underneath a stack of mattresses. But our law doesn't allow recovery for that sort of super sensitivity. And this plaintiff, who had no hesitation about sleeping on the ground, certainly can't complain about peas under the mattress today. You can't be a backpacker when you want to and then a princess when the time comes to try for damages.

c. Stories

Stories, in the form of either hypotheticals or anecdotes, can be used effectively in closing argument. You may illustrate an argument with a hypothetical story so long as the story is based on facts that are in evidence. Again, from the plaintiff's argument in the firetruck case:

> Imagine what the defendant's morning was like. His alarm clock didn't go off. He woke up, looked at the clock, and began to panic. He

was late, and if he missed the meeting with this new client, he would lose money and damage his position with his firm. He rushed into the bathroom to shower and shave. He had no time for breakfast and no time to stop for gas. You can be sure that the defendant hurried to his car that morning and, most important, that this was not the day for a leisurely drive.

This reconstruction of the defendant's morning is hypothetical in that the details are all suppositions. It is proper argument because the entire story is derived from the defendant's own testimony.

4. Emphasize the Undisputed Facts

Undisputed facts consist of the testimony, exhibits, and other evidence that you have offered and which the other side has not controverted. The opposition's decision not to produce contrary evidence greatly enhances the value of such undisputed facts. While not quite so powerful as admissions from the other side, undisputed facts can provide a sturdy cornerstone for case theory and closing argument.

> It is undisputed that there was a firetruck at the corner of Alta Vista and Craycroft. It is undisputed that the engine was answering a call. It is undisputed that other drivers slowed down or pulled over for the firetruck. It is undisputed that Lieutenant Janis Regnier was driving the firetruck. And it is undisputed that fire department policy requires the siren to be used whenever an engine company is responding to a call. The defendant may claim that there was no siren, but he hasn't even tried to deny these uncontroverted facts.

Thus, undisputed facts are helpful not only in their own right, but also because they can be marshaled to cast light on disputed evidence.

5. Refute the Opposing Witnesses' Testimony

Opening statements and witness examinations may recite and elicit facts that are contrary to the opposition case, but closing argument can refute it directly by pointing out errors, inconsistencies, implausibilities, and contradictions. Consider this extract from the plaintiff's closing argument in the fire engine case:

> The defendant claims that he was not distracted on the morning of the accident, but that cannot be true. We know that he woke up late and had an important meeting to attend with a potential new client that morning. By the time he got ready for work and got to his car, he was already at least thirty minutes behind schedule. By the time he reached the corner of Craycroft and Alta Vista, he was still running over twenty minutes late—he still had to drive downtown, get to his garage, park his car, and proceed to his office, all in less than twenty minutes.

Chapter Fifteen

There is no plausible way for the defendant to deny that he was preoccupied and in a hurry. His mind must have been elsewhere; certainly it wasn't on his driving. Every driver saw and heard the firetruck, but not the defendant. Every driver stopped or pulled over, but not the defendant. Those were not the acts of a careful man.

One last fact shows just how absorbed the defendant was. Right after the accident, he jumped out of his car and pulled out his cell phone. He called his office. That meeting was so important to him that he didn't even check to see if the other driver was hurt. That meeting was more important to him than a possible injury. No wonder it was more important to him than safe, careful driving.

6. Tie Up Your Cross-Examinations

Use closing argument to tie up the issues that you intentionally left unaddressed during cross-examination. Recall the questions that a prudent cross-examiner avoids: never ask a witness to explain; never ask a witness to fill in a gap; never ask a witness to agree with a characterization or conclusion. If your cross-examinations were artful and effective, you should be able to spend some portion of the closing argument drawing the previously unspoken conclusions.

Likewise, capitalize on the admissions opposing witnesses made during the trial. Doing so can make for powerful arguments since the opposing party would not offer self-damaging testimony unless it was unavoidably true. The defendant in the fire engine case, for instance, makes an admission when he testifies that he was late for a meeting at the time of the accident. This fact passes every test of believability when used in the plaintiff's closing argument.

How do we know that the defendant was running late that morning? He said so himself. Just remember his words. He said, "I woke up late that morning, and I knew that I would have to hurry up to get to my meeting."

This type of argument can continue, taking advantage of points that were scored on cross-examination precisely for this purpose.

The defendant's own words also tell us how preoccupied he was. After all, it was the defendant who testified about the importance of new clients. I'm sure you remember how he answered when I asked him if new clients mean money. He said, "Yes, that's what we're in business for." And then I asked him whether this particular new client was a valuable one, and he said, "Every new client is valuable." So there he was, late for his meeting with a valuable new client, worrying about how much money he might stand to lose.

Note that for the purpose of believability analysis, admissions need not be direct concessions, nor do they need to come in the form of testimony from the actual party. Anything can be exploited as an admission so long as it was produced by the other side. A strong closing argument can therefore make use of the opposition's witness testimony, exhibits, charts or graphs, tangible objects, or even statements and promises made by opposing counsel during opening statement.

7. Argue Witness Credibility and Motive

Use closing argument to comment on, and compare, the motive and credibility of witnesses. Most mock trials involve competing renditions of past events, which the trier of fact must resolve in order to reach a verdict. Closing argument is the only time when you may directly confront the character of the witnesses and explain why some should be believed and others discounted.

Witness examinations can bring out impeaching facts, and the opening statement can use apposition to contrast the credibility of different witnesses. But only on closing argument can you make direct comparisons. Consider the question of the siren as plaintiff's counsel might argue it in the firetruck case.

> The plaintiff told you that she stopped because she saw a firetruck, which was flashing its warning lights and sounding its siren. The defendant has to concede that the truck was there, but he claims that it was not using its warning signals. Well, was there a siren or wasn't there? Who should you believe?
>
> The defendant's story just isn't credible. Everyone agrees that the firetruck entered the intersection on its way to a fire. You have even seen the transcript of the 911 call that the truck was responding to. A firetruck would have to be using its siren under those circumstances. Only the most negligent firefighter would speed toward an intersection without sounding the siren, but this truck was being driven by Lieutenant Janis Regnier, one of the most decorated firefighters on the force. Which is more likely, that Lieutenant Regnier neglected such an elementary duty or that the defendant is wrong about the siren?
>
> The plaintiff heard the siren and stopped her car. The other drivers must have heard it as well since all of the other traffic pulled over. Of course, it is possible that the defendant testified the way he did because he simply didn't hear the siren, but that is another story. Why didn't he hear the siren? Why didn't he stop his car? For the answers to those questions, we have to look at the events of his day and why he was "too busy to be careful."

Finally, motive can be argued on the basis of either proven facts or logical inferences. You may tell the factfinder why a witness would exaggerate, waffle, conceal information, quibble, or lie. The suggested reasons need not be based on outright admissions so long as they follow rationally from the testimony in the case.

Chapter Fifteen

8. Assert the Weight That Should Be Given to Evidence

Opening statement limited you to a recitation of the expected evidence. Closing argument lets you assert the weight of the evidence. Why is one version preferable to another? Why should some facts be accepted and others rejected? Why is one case stronger than the other? Consider the way in which the defense counsel in the firetruck case might argue the weight of the evidence regarding plaintiff's damages.

> The plaintiff claims extreme disability, almost all of it based on pain. But pain is an elusive concept. It cannot be seen or measured. We can, however, look at the plaintiff's activities to see the extent of her alleged disability.
>
> We know, for example, that she went camping last Labor Day at Eagle River Falls. She put all of her gear into a backpack and stayed in a tent, sleeping on the ground for four nights. Now she says that the camping trip was a mistake and that she was in agony the whole time. But you have seen the records from her doctor; she didn't visit the doctor, or even call, until over a month after the camping trip. You have also seen the records from the pharmacy; she didn't change her medication or even renew it for more than two months after the camping trip. What did she do? She took aspirin.
>
> To judge the extent of the plaintiff's alleged disability you must weigh the evidence. Evaluate the claims that she made in her testimony against the proof of her own actions and the records of her own physician and pharmacist. It is easy to claim pain, and I don't want to minimize the plaintiff's discomfort, but her own conduct makes it clear that nothing happened to limit her life's activities.

9. Comment on the Opposing Witness's Demeanor

It is fair game in closing argument to comment on a witness's negative demeanor so long as the comment is adequately based on observable fact. It is a good idea, for instance, to remark upon a witness's refusal to give a simple answer or to make an obvious concession during a cross-examination. Such witnesses are perhaps more common in mock trials because each side's witnesses are usually associated with their team. In a real trial, a recalcitrant witness would be perceived as evasive and untrustworthy. Although yours is not a real trial, your presiding judge or jury might still agree that the demeanor of the individual playing the witness role made them less than believable.

10. Confront Your Weaknesses

Use closing argument to solve problems and confront weaknesses. No matter how well the evidentiary phase of the trial proceeded, you are sure to be left with a number of difficult or troublesome issues. Address and resolve these issues in the course of closing argument.

A classic instance of such a weakness is the government's reliance on informers in drug prosecutions. Informers are assailable witnesses to begin with, and in drug cases they are often further sullied with histories of their own substance abuse. Recognizing the problems created by reliance on such witnesses, prosecutors have developed over the years an almost standardized, and extremely effective, closing argument approach. In its barest form it goes something like this:

> It is true that several of the prosecution witnesses were informers and former drug users and of course they aren't the most upstanding citizens in the world. It was not the prosecution, however, who chose them as witnesses. The defendants chose these people as witnesses when they set out to sell illegal and dangerous drugs. Who can we expect to serve as witnesses to drug deals? Drug deals take place in a shadowy world that is populated by criminals and addicts. Those were the people present for this transaction and, therefore, we had to call them to testify.

Another example of a perceived weakness in your case might be its heavy reliance on circumstantial evidence. If your opposing counsel argues this point, take time to explain the value and credibility of circumstantial evidence during your closing. This is frequently done through an analogy like this one:

> Circumstantial evidence can be just as reliable as direct evidence. For example, consider the last time it snowed while you were sleeping. There was no snow on the ground before you went to bed, but when you awoke the streets were covered in snow. Now, although you didn't actually see the snow fall, you know it had to come from the sky. That is circumstantial evidence, and just as you know it snowed even though you did not see the snow falling, you know certain events occurred in this case despite the lack of eyewitness testimony regarding those events.

11. Comment on Promises Kept and Broken

Attorneys on both sides of a case will inevitably make various promises and commitments to the factfinder during the course of the trial—usually during opening statements. Now is your chance to comment on promises made, kept, or broken. Point out the ways in which you fulfilled your commitments. Perhaps more importantly, and certainly more dramatically, underscore the ways in which the opposition failed to live up to its own promises. The most effective closing arguments are often those in which counsel is able to state that "We kept our promises and they broke theirs."

Chapter Fifteen

12. Argue Damages, Where Applicable

The trial of most civil cases can be divided into the conceptual areas of liability and damages. Although liability is the threshold issue, it is a mistake to underestimate the importance of damages. Unless the trial has been "bifurcated," meaning that liability and damages will be handled in separate stages, plaintiffs in particular should devote a significant portion of the closing argument to the development of damages.

There are two significant aspects involved in most arguments for damages: method and amount. It is important to explain precisely how damages have been (or should be) calculated. It is also usually important to request a specific amount rather than leaving the award to the factfinder's guesswork.

Some defense attorneys prefer to avoid or minimize the issue of damages, reasoning that any discussion may be seen as an implicit admission of their client's liability. Many lawyers, however, choose not to "roll the dice" on liability, concluding that a reduced damage award is the next best thing to winning the case outright. When discussing damages, defense lawyers have a choice: they may simply deny the plaintiff's damage claim, or go on to present a competing estimate. The decision will rest upon the circumstances of the particular case. If you decide to present a competing damage estimate, be absolutely sure not to say or do anything that can be interpreted as a concession of liability.

13. Apply the Law

Closing argument provides the attorney an occasion to apply the law to the facts of the case. Discussion of law is extremely limited during the opening statement and all but forbidden during witness examinations, but it is a staple of the closing argument.

If jury instructions are included in your case file, read the key portions of the instructions to the jurors and explain how the relevant law dictates a verdict for your client. If there are no jury instructions in your case file, summarize any applicable law that favors a verdict for your side. One effective way to do this is to outline the elements the plaintiff/prosecution must prove in the case and then to go through those elements individually, arguing why the prosecution did or did not prove each one.

Checklist	
IS YOUR FINAL ARGUMENT PERSUASIVE?	
☑ **Did you use your theory and theme?**	Did you invoke your theory and theme at the beginning and end of your closing argument? *If not, incorporate them now so you can take advantage of primacy and recency.*

Closing Argument

Checklist	
IS YOUR FINAL ARGUMENT PERSUASIVE?	
☑ **Did you use as many of the listed persuasive techniques as possible?**	Have you maximized the persuasive value of your arguments by carefully outlining how you will tell your story at trial? *If not, go back through the previous section and incorporate those techniques that serve your goals.*

C. Avoid Making Impermissible Arguments

The final principle of closings is to refrain from impermissible arguments.

1. Do Not Comment on Privilege

In the instances where the defendant is not called to testify during a mock trial, it is impermissible for the prosecutor in a criminal case to comment on the defendant's invocation of the privilege against self-incrimination. The prosecutor can neither point out nor ask the factfinder to draw any adverse inference from the defendant's decision not to testify or to otherwise present evidence. The law is clear that criminal defendants have an absolute right not to testify on their own behalf and have no obligation to present evidence of any kind. Even an inadvertent reference to the lack of sworn testimony from a defendant would violate the law and invite an immediate motion for a mistrial.

2. Do Not Misuse Evidence

When evidence has been admitted only for a limited or restricted use, it is improper to attempt to use it for any other purpose. Suppose, for example, that a police officer is allowed to testify that his dispatcher directed him to a local residence to investigate drug possession and the defendant is now on trial for drug trafficking. The content of the dispatcher's call, which would otherwise be hearsay, was allowed by the presiding judge to explain the officer's reason for driving to the defendant's house. Although the statement was admitted during trial, you are not free to argue in closing that, "Even the dispatcher at the police department said the defendant had drugs." That would be an improper use of the evidence. The hearsay was allowed only to show why the officer took their next step in the investigation, not as proof of drug possession.

Evidence of prior bad acts, wrongs, or crimes admitted for a purpose other than proving propensity is another good example of evidence admitted for a limited purpose. Recall the example given in Chapter Eight, Section II(E)(1), of a defendant

Chapter Fifteen

charged with burglary who was previously thrice convicted of the same offense. Although not admissible to prove propensity—e.g., that because the defendant committed burglaries before, they must be guilty of committing the charged burglary—we explained that the prior convictions could be admitted if deemed relevant to prove the defendant's knowledge, preparation, plan, or intent. In our example, there was evidence that in each of the three prior burglaries the defendant had robbed jewelry stores in the middle of the night by using a glass cutter to gain entry—the same technique used in the currently charged crime. If that evidence were admitted in your mock trial, you would most certainly want to argue its import in your closing. You must be careful, however, not to use the evidence for any purpose other than that for which it was admitted.

This can be a tricky endeavor. Certainly it would be tempting on behalf of the prosecution to point out the defendant's three prior convictions for burglary and to declare, "Based on this history, members of the jury, you already know the defendant's a burglar," or "The defendant is not just a burglar—the defendant is a professional burglar." But those claims would amount to using the evidence for a purpose beyond that which justified its admission, opening the door for defense counsel to move for a mistrial.

Avoid that scenario with the following special approach to arguing this evidence in your closing. First, when summarizing the evidence presented in support of the claims or charges at issue in your trial, do not include any mention of evidence that was admitted for a limited purpose. Completely separate such evidence from the other evidence so that you can effectively resist the temptation to use it for an improper purpose. Second, after you have summarized all the other evidence presented in support of the claim or charge, then argue the import of the evidence admitted for limited purposes and be sure to only use the evidence for the purposes for which it was admitted.

In our burglary example, the prosecution's closing argument following our advice might go like this:

> You will recall that certain evidence was admitted for limited purposes in this trial. That evidence consisted of the defendant's three prior convictions for burglary. Judge Moody is going to explain to you that that evidence can only be considered by you for the following limited purposes: as evidence of the defendant's intent, knowledge, or preparation or plan. Those are all proper purposes for you to consider the defendant's prior convictions and we submit that when you do so, you will see that it provides yet further support of the defendant's guilt in committing the crime charged.
>
> First, as to knowledge, preparation, and plan, as you heard, each of the defendant's three prior burglary offenses involved the use of a glass cutting device to gain entry to a jewelry store. There can be no

question that this defendant knows how to do that and was capable of preparing and planning to do just that. As to intent in robbing the store, you heard that in each of the defendant's prior burglaries, the defendant stole jewelry. That is powerful evidence of the intention in breaking into the Jems and Gold Corner Jewelry store on January 2nd, as charged in this case. Why else would a person go to the trouble of breaking into a jewelry store? We submit to you, members of the jury, that when considered for these limited purposes, the defendant's prior convictions show that the defendant had the know-how and the motive to commit the crime charged.

Other than reiterating or restating the above argument, make no other mention whatsoever of the defendant's prior burglary convictions.

Finally, it should go without saying that you may not use, or attempt to use, evidence that was excluded by the court. Excluded evidence is inadmissible and references to inadmissible evidence during closing argument would be cause for a mistrial.

3. Do Not Interject Your Personal Beliefs Regarding the Facts or Issues in the Case

It is improper for an attorney to assert personal knowledge of the facts in issue in a case or to state a personal opinion as to the justness of a cause, the credibility of a witness, the culpability of a civil litigant, or the guilt or innocence of an accused. Because the facts presented and parties involved in mock trials are all fictional, there is less danger than in a real case that an attorney will attempt to leverage personal credibility to win their client's case, but we nonetheless warn you that doing so is seriously improper.

4. Do Not Make Appeals to the Factfinder's Personal Interest

An appeal to the factfinder's personal interest invites the judge or jurors to decide the case on a basis other than the law and evidence. So, for instance, it is improper for defense counsel to tell the factfinder that a large verdict will raise taxes or insurance rates. Similarly, a prosecutor cannot argue that an acquittal will increase the crime rate or endanger the citizenry.

A specific form of this principle is the so-called "Golden Rule," which prohibits counsel from asking the judge or the jurors to envision themselves in the position of one of the litigants or the crime victim. The following is an excerpt from a classic forbidden argument:

> The plaintiff in this case lost his right arm in an industrial accident. You must now determine how much money is necessary to compensate him for his loss. Let me ask you this question: How much money

Chapter Fifteen

would you want if it had been your right arm? If someone offered you $1,000,000 to have your arm crushed, would you take it? Would you accept $2,000,000?

Such arguments obviously appeal to the factfinder's sympathy. They also ask the jurors to decide the case on the basis of their own self-interest, as though they were the people actually affected by the outcome of the case.

5. Do Not Make Appeals to Emotion, Sympathy, or Passion

While there is an emotional side to virtually every trial, do not use closing argument to ask the factfinder to decide the case on the basis of sympathy or passion. Impermissible appeals to passion are often found when counsel dwells upon some dramatic but barely relevant aspect of the case, such as the nature of a plaintiff's extreme injuries when only liability is at stake.

6. Do Not Misstate the Evidence

While it is permissible to draw inferences and conclusions, it is improper to intentionally misstate or mischaracterize evidence in the course of closing argument. Accordingly, defense counsel in the firetruck case could portray the plaintiff's camping trip as follows:

> The plaintiff admits that she went camping at Eagle River Falls. She did all of the things ordinary campers do. She carried a pack, she slept on the ground, she went hiking. In other words, she willingly undertook all of the strains, exertions, and activities of backpacking. No one made her take that trip; she did it for recreation. Of course, she told a different story here on the witness stand. The only possible conclusion is that she has exaggerated her claim for injuries.

To be sure, the above example is replete with characterizations, but they are fair characterizations. Even if no witness actually testified that the plaintiff went camping voluntarily, it is a reasonable inference that "no one made her take that trip."

The following argument, on the other hand, definitely appears to misstate the evidence:

> The plaintiff was an enthusiastic and carefree camper. She carried the heaviest pack in the family, and she insisted on chopping the wood and pitching the tent. She would have gone camping again the next weekend, but her family couldn't keep up with her.

These are, by and large, assertions of fact and not simply inferences. While the statement that the plaintiff was an "enthusiastic" camper might be seen as an inference, the statements concerning the "heaviest pack" and the plaintiff's desire to go

Closing Argument

camping the next weekend are clearly presented as proven facts. They may not be made in closing argument unless supported by the evidence.

7. Do Not Misstate the Law or Discourage the Jury from Following It

You may use closing argument to explain the relevant law, to discuss the jury instructions, and to apply the law to the facts of the case. You may not, however, misstate the law or argue for legal interpretations that are contrary to the court's decisions and instructions.

Thus, defense counsel in a criminal case could not argue that the factfinder must acquit the defendant "if there is any doubt whatsoever, no matter how insignificant or far-fetched it might be." By the same token, the prosecutor could not argue that a reasonable doubt only exists if the factfinder "is persuaded that there is a good chance that the defendant is not guilty." In both of these examples, the attorneys offered definitions of reasonable doubt that are not found in any court of law.

Likewise, it is improper for counsel to argue or even suggest that the jury not follow the law. The following statement, if made in closing, may be interpreted as an attempt to get the jury to nullify (i.e., not follow the law) and is therefore improper: "As jurors you are not beholden to this judge or to the government. You can do whatever you want. You need only follow your conscience." During the process of being sworn in for jury service, the members of a jury swear under oath that they will follow the law, regardless of whether they agree with it. Although juries have the power to "nullify" the law, counsel should not urge them to ignore the judge's instructions. As officers of the court, attorneys should encourage, rather than discourage, the jurors to uphold their oaths.

Summary

CLOSING ARGUMENT PROHIBITIONS:

- DO NOT comment on privilege
- DO NOT misuse evidence
- DO NOT interject your personal beliefs regarding the facts or issues in the case
- DO NOT make appeals to the factfinder's personal interest
- DO NOT make appeals to emotion, sympathy, or passion
- DO NOT misstate the facts
- DO NOT misstate the law or discourage the jury from following it

Chapter Fifteen

III. Planning Closing Arguments

A. Content

Although the facts and issues in the case determine the specific content of any closing argument, certain sorts of information should be considered for inclusion in every closing argument. You must tell a persuasive story while being mindful of the order in which each side presents its case. We address both issues below in turn.

1. Tell a Persuasive Story

Virtually every closing argument should contain all of the elements of a persuasive story. A good closing argument details the evidentiary support for your theory of the case and consistently invokes the trial theme.

We have previously discussed five substantive elements to a persuasive story. Include them all at some point in your closing argument.

Summary

A PERSUASIVE STORY . . .

- Explains all of the known facts
- Is told about people who have reasons for their actions
- Is told by credible witnesses
- Is supported by details
- Accords with common sense

---

a. Known Facts—What Happened?

A persuasive story accounts for all of the known facts; it is not premised on incomplete information, and it does not gloss over or ignore inconvenient occurrences. This is not to say that a closing argument must mention every minor detail in the case, but rather that it should, in some fashion, accommodate all of the established facts.

Assume that the firetruck case has been tried along the lines that we have discussed in previous chapters. The plaintiff has used "too busy to be careful" as a trial theme, introducing evidence of the defendant's hurried morning. Since no one disputes the details of the defendant's scheduled meeting and various travel times, these have become "known facts" in the sense that the factfinder is not likely to regard them with doubt or disbelief. Defense counsel might believe that these facts are inconsequential to the issue of liability; after all, people can be late for work and still drive carefully. Nonetheless, the defendant's closing argument should account for these facts either by refuting them or by explaining their irrelevance.

b. Reasons—Why Did It Happen?

The trial story should also explain the reasons for the actions of the parties and other witnesses. It is not enough to state that an individual did something; counsel should go on to reveal why those activities were consistent with that individual's self-interest, announced intentions, past behavior, lifestyle, or other understandable motivations.

The articulation of reasons gives logical weight to the argument and can transform it from an attorney's assertion into an acceptable statement of fact.

c. Credible Witnesses—Who Should Be Believed?

Address the credibility of witnesses during your closing argument. At a minimum, this means developing the credibility of your own witnesses in the course of establishing an affirmative case. This can usually be done subtly and indirectly, simply by providing the background information that tends to render your witnesses believable.

In cases where credibility is seriously in issue, you will need to take a more frontal approach.

d. Supportive Details—How Can We Be Sure?

As we have seen, persuasion often rests on the accumulation of supportive details. An essential task of closing argument is marshaling the details that give weight to your argument.

The inclusion or exclusion of details is a tricky problem. While the right details at the right time can add an airtight quality to your case, too many details (or their use in support of unimportant propositions) can drag a closing argument into the depths of boredom and despair. Although there is no single key to making judgments in this area, here are some guidelines.

The Basics

USING DETAILS IN CLOSING ARGUMENT

Use details when important facts are in dispute	When there is a disagreement as to an occurrence or incident, use details to support your client's version of events.
Use details when motivations are in issue	The presence (or absence) of motive can frequently be established by looking at specific facts. Explain why a witness would want to act in a certain way.

The Basics	
USING DETAILS IN CLOSING ARGUMENT	
Use details to support an interpretation of the evidence	The meaning of certain evidence is often contested even when the underlying facts are not in dispute.
Do not use details for unimportant reasons	The judge or jurors have a limited tolerance for details; every time you use a detail you diminish the effectiveness of those that follow.
Do not use details to establish uncontested facts	If a fact is uncontested, you need only state it.

e. *Common Sense—Is It Plausible?*

Perhaps the ultimate test of every closing argument is plausibility. Even if an argument accounts for the known facts, gives reasons for every action, is supported by credible witnesses, and is replete with convincing details, it still will not be accepted if it does not make sense to the factfinder. Almost every other failing can be overcome or forgiven. You cannot, however, win with an implausible argument.

It is essential, therefore, that every closing argument address the subject of common sense. Explain why your theory is realistic, using examples and analogies from everyday life. A commonsense argument can be extremely helpful, as when defense counsel argues damages in the firetruck case.

> The plaintiff claims that her life's activities have been severely limited. Now pain is a subjective thing, and no one can step inside of the plaintiff's body to see whether she is exaggerating. But we can look at her actions, and we can interpret them in the light of our own common sense. The plaintiff went camping last Labor Day at Eagle River Falls. She carried a backpack and slept on the ground for four straight nights. She could have gone home after a night or two, but she chose to stay for the entire trip. Is this the action of someone in constant pain? Is this the action of someone whose life's activities are severely limited? Can you imagine how the plaintiff might have thought about such a trip: "Well, things are difficult here at home; I guess I'll go sleep on the ground for a long weekend." I don't want to minimize the plaintiff's real injuries, but common sense certainly tells us that someone in as much pain as she claims just wouldn't go camping for four nights.

2. Use the Format of Closings to Your Advantage

Just as in real trials, mock trial closing arguments are divided into three distinct segments, presented in the following order: the plaintiff/prosecution argument in chief, the defendant's argument, and the plaintiff/prosecution rebuttal. While general principles of argument apply to all three, each segment also has its own unique set of uses, applications, and special techniques.

a. Plaintiff/Prosecution Argument in Chief

The plaintiff/prosecution must use the argument in chief to define the issues and lay out their entire theory of the case. The plaintiff's argument in chief will not be successful unless it provides the factfinder with compelling reasons to find for the plaintiff on every contested issue.

The argument in chief must be comprehensive. The plaintiff in a civil matter must prove their case by a preponderance of the evidence, and the prosecutor in a criminal case must present proof beyond a reasonable doubt.

In either situation, the burdened party must establish all of the elements of the cause of action. A civil plaintiff must establish all of the elements of the particular personal injury or contract action and a prosecutor must prove all of the elements of the charged crime. An effective way to do this is to read or publish each element for the factfinder and then summarize the key testimony presented which proved that element, and to walk systematically through until the burden has been met as to each element, placing a literal or figurative check-mark next to each as you go. Once you have summarized the evidence supporting all the elements of an offense, confidently state that you have met your burden of proof as to that charge and ask the factfinder to render a verdict of liable/guilty as to that charge. And so on until you have addressed each claim or charge the plaintiff/prosecution brought in the case.

b. Defendant's Argument

The defendant has substantially more latitude than the plaintiff in determining the content of the argument in chief. While the plaintiff/prosecution must address every element, the defendant is usually free to select only those elements or issues in which counsel has the most confidence. The defense theory, of course, must be comprehensive in the sense that it explains all of the relevant evidence, but its legal thrust may be significantly more pointed than the party carrying the burden of proof.

The defining characteristic of the defendant's argument in chief is that it is sandwiched between the two plaintiff/prosecution arguments. Defense counsel must respond to opposing counsel's argument in chief, but will not be able to respond to rebuttal.

Responding to the Plaintiff's Argument in Chief

It is essential that the defense reply directly to the plaintiff/prosecution argument in chief. After listening to the other side's prolonged criticism of the defendant,

Chapter Fifteen

the trier of fact will immediately want to know what the defendant has to say in return. This does not mean that you cannot plan a closing argument before the trial or should adopt the other side's organization and respond point by point, but you must address the major points raised by the plaintiff/prosecution.

At a minimum, the defendant should deny the specific charges leveled in opposing counsel's argument. It is a natural human response to deny unfair or untrue accusations. The factfinder will expect as much from a wrongly blamed defendant. Unless there is a good reason for doing otherwise, state the denial early in the argument.

In a more general vein, devote some time to debunking the other side's case. Even where the defense has an extremely strong affirmative case of its own, it is risky to allow the assertions of the plaintiff/prosecution to stand unrebutted. The precise handling of the various arguments will be discussed below in the section on organization.

Finally, the watchword for the defendant's argument in chief is flexibility. While the plaintiff/prosecution may have the luxury of planning every aspect of their initial closing argument beforehand, defense counsel must remain alert to new issues and nuances raised in the plaintiff's closing argument. Although you can map out much of what you will say based on the facts provided in the mock trial case file, if your opposing counsel is a skilled advocate, some of counsel's points will derive from specific testimony that was given, or specific exchanges between participants, that occurred during the mock trial round. Anticipate this by planning out and memorizing the very beginning and end of your defense closing but remaining flexible in your argument in between. Outline the general topics you want to cover and add in facts, evidence, and argument unique to your particular mock trial all the way up to and during the plaintiff/prosecution's argument in chief.

The defendant's argument is most effective to the extent that it rebuts the arguments made by opposing counsel. A particularly effective device is to use the plaintiff/prosecution theme, or an analogy counsel made during argument, against the other side by turning it around so that it is supportive of the defendant. For example, the defendant could turn around the plaintiff's theme of "too busy to be careful" and argue that because the defendant was busy, he had to be careful—that being rushed caused him to be especially watchful of what was going on around him rather than careless as the plaintiff would have the jurors believe.

Anticipating Rebuttal

The greatest difficulty for defense counsel is not being able to speak again following the plaintiff/prosecution rebuttal. The other side may comment on, criticize, or even ridicule the defendant's argument, but the defendant may not respond. Defense counsel may have perfectly good answers for everything opposing counsel says on rebuttal, but no matter.

Closing Argument

Under these circumstances, do whatever is possible to blunt the rebuttal in advance. One approach is to anticipate and reply specifically to the possible rebuttal arguments of the plaintiff/prosecution, as in this example from the defendant's argument in the firetruck case.

> This entire accident could have been avoided if the plaintiff had only pulled over instead of slamming on her brakes in the middle of the street. If she didn't cause the accident, she at least contributed to it. Now when plaintiff's counsel argues again, she may claim that there was no time to pull over. Don't believe it. There was plenty of time to pull over. Let's look at the evidence....

The danger in this approach is that you might respond to an argument that the plaintiff had not thought to make. As long as your response is stronger than the argument that could be (and, you are fairly confident, will be) made, it is fine to take this approach.

Alternatively, you can anticipate rebuttal only in the general sense, making sure to explain the phenomenon of rebuttal if your factfinder is a jury, for example:

> When I am done speaking, the plaintiff's attorney will have another opportunity to argue. That is called rebuttal. Following rebuttal, however, I will not be allowed to stand before you again. The rules of procedure allow me to speak to you only once. It is not that I don't want to speak again, or that I will have no responses to what plaintiff's counsel says, but only that I will not have the opportunity to give you my responses.
>
> I therefore have one request to make of you. When plaintiff's counsel returns to argue, please bear in mind that, whatever she says, I will not be able to answer. I think you will know from the evidence that I have answers to her rebuttal argument. So please keep what I have said in mind as you listen and please provide those answers for me.

The timing of this aspect of the argument is important. Because it relates solely to the rebuttal, it obviously is preferable to make these remarks near the end of your argument in chief. On the other hand, placing them at the very end deprives the argument of a strong finish. To keep your strong finish, discuss rebuttal as the penultimate point, saving the final moment for your most compelling substantive argument.

c. *Plaintiff/Prosecution Rebuttal*

Rebuttal is a powerful tool since it allows the plaintiff/prosecution to reply to the defendant's arguments while the defendant is forced to stand mute in response. Everyone likes to have the last word, and in trials, that right is given to the party with the burden of proof.

Chapter Fifteen

Using this powerful tool effectively is a difficult endeavor. While the plaintiff/prosecution argument in chief can be completely planned and the defendant's argument in chief can be mostly planned, rebuttal must be delivered almost extemporaneously. Preparing for rebuttal typically takes place while you listen to the defendant's argument in chief. Nonetheless, certain principles can be applied to make rebuttal more forceful and compelling.

Organize rebuttal according to your own theory of the case. Listen to the defendant's argument and match their points to your own major propositions in the case. To do this, prepare a truncated outline of the three or four most important, or hotly contested, issues in the case, leaving several blank lines under each heading. Spread these four major arguments over an entire sheet of paper, arranged in the order most advantageous to your case. As defense counsel argues, list each argument under the appropriate heading, noting how you will respond. Then deliver your rebuttal topically, without regard to the order of argument used by the defendant.

When you respond to the defendant's argument, do so affirmatively. Even when it is well organized, your rebuttal will be weak if it becomes nothing more than a series of retorts. Instead, frame every position as a constructive statement of your own theory, with the refutation of the defense being used to explain further or elaborate on the plaintiff/prosecution case. Consider this short example from the rebuttal in the fire engine case:

> I would like to talk to you again about damages. I'm sure that you remember the plaintiff's own testimony about her efforts to cope with her injuries. She has done everything possible to bring her life back to normal. She is a courageous woman who won't give up. That is why it is particularly unfair to see defense counsel trying to exploit the plaintiff's camping trip to Eagle River Falls. Of course she tried to go camping. What does the defendant want her to do, give up on life and just sit at home? Unfortunately, her efforts didn't work out. As she told you, the camping trip was pure hell. She suffered every day, and she had to stay on her back in the tent for hours at a time. Why didn't she come home early? Because she and her family had all come in the same car, and she didn't want to ruin the trip for everyone else. Sure, she tried to enjoy camping. But that only proves how brave and determined she is—it does not prove that she was not injured.

Many lawyers save a single, devastating argument for rebuttal, thinking that the argument will be even more effective if it stands unanswered. There is, no doubt, something to recommend this theory, as it deprives the defendant of all opportunity to respond. One caveat, however, is necessary. Like redirect examination, rebuttal argument is technically limited to the scope of the issues that were addressed during the defense argument. If, for whatever reason, defense counsel does not raise the "gotcha" issue, it is possible the court will sustain an objection to its coverage on rebuttal as beyond the permissible scope.

This means it is inherently risky for the plaintiff to "sandbag" by completely omitting a subject from their argument in chief. Suppose, for example, the plaintiff in the firetruck case decided to defer all discussion of damages until rebuttal, thereby precluding the defendant from replying to the plaintiff's specific arguments. Hearing no mention of damages, the defendant could decide not to address damages either. If that were to happen, some judges might refuse to allow the plaintiff to raise damages for the first time on rebuttal, which would have the effect of precluding any argument about damages during closings—a potentially devastating outcome for the plaintiff.

The rule that requires rebuttal to be within the scope of the defendant's closing argument is enforced with varying strictness by judges. It is generally safe to assume, however, that the rule will be applied more rigidly to discrete topics (such as damages) than to lines of argument (such as elaboration on a theme). Consequently, it usually is not risky to withhold the use of an analogy or story until rebuttal, thereby preventing the defendant from turning the argument around to illustrate a point of their own.

Checklist	
IS THE CONTENT OF YOUR CLOSING EFFECTIVE?	
☑ **Did you tell a persuasive story?**	Does your story include only known facts? Does your story explain the reasons why the parties acted as they did? Did you comment on the credibility of witnesses? Did you use supportive details to your advantage? Most important, does your story make absolute sense? *If not, better employ these methods to make your story more persuasive.*
☑ **Did you take the format in which closings are given into account when deciding content?**	Is your closing argued strategically based upon your opportunity to address opposing counsel's arguments? *If not, move your arguments around to make the most of the order in which closings are given.*

Chapter Fifteen

B. Organization

Construct your closing argument for maximum persuasive weight. The central thrust of the closing must always be to provide reasons—logical, moral, legal, or emotional—for the entry of a verdict in your client's favor.

1. Use Topical Organization

It is important to consider organizing your closing argument topically. Seemingly natural methods of organization, such as chronology and witness listing, will not present the evidence in its most persuasive form. Topical organization, on the other hand, allows counsel to most persuasively address the issues in the case. Topical organization can use, or combine, any of the following strategies.

a. *Issues*

One of the simplest and most effective forms of organization is to divide the case into a series of discrete factual or legal issues. Large issues, such as liability and damages, are obvious, but they are also so broad that they provide relatively little help in ordering an argument. Instead, think of issues as narrower propositions of fact or law.

In the firetruck case, for example, the plaintiff might organize the liability section of her argument according to these *factual* issues: 1) the defendant's hurried morning; 2) the siren; and 3) the events of the accident. The first section of the argument would emphasize why the defendant was inattentive; the second would explain why the other traffic stopped for the truck (and why the trier of fact should not believe the defendant's claim that there was no siren); and the third segment would describe the actual collision.

This format, as opposed to strict chronology, allows plaintiff's counsel to plan the discussions of motivation and credibility in a coherent and logical fashion. All of the considerations pointing to the defendant's preoccupation can be addressed at once, including events that occurred before (being late for the meeting) and after (calling the office without checking on the plaintiff) the accident. Similarly, the question of whether the fire engine's siren was sounding can be resolved, making it clear that it was, before discussing the collision.

b. *Elements*

A second form of topical organization revolves around elements and claims. Every legal cause or defense is composed of various discrete elements. A claim of negligence, for instance, must be supported by proof of duty, breach of duty, cause in fact, proximate cause, and damages. A plaintiff can therefore develop a closing argument by discussing the evidence as it supports each of the distinct elements of the cause of action. A defendant who needs to challenge only a single element in order to win can use the same form of organization, but can truncate it by focusing only on those elements that are truly likely to be negated.

c. Jury Instructions

If your case file includes them, you can also use the jury instructions to organize your closing argument. Use them selectively, however, both because of the time limitations in most competitions and because they can become tiresome if read in their entirety. Picking the most important instructions, develop the central points of your closing argument to address them. Thus, the plaintiff in the fire engine case might focus on the instructions dealing with due care and credibility, while the defendant might choose to utilize the instructions relating to damages.

2. Alternative Organization Methods

Although the overriding organizational method used in your closing argument should be topical, consider using chronological organization to order its discrete subparts, where helpful. On the other hand, there is little benefit to organizing your closing as a witness-by-witness account of the trial.

a. *Chronological Organization*

Chronology is the most obvious alternative structure for a closing argument. Since the events in a case manifestly occurred in a chronological order, it seems obvious to replay them in the same progression during closing argument.

While chronology certainly plays an important role in closing argument, events are unlikely to have occurred in the most persuasive possible sequence. Early events can frequently be illuminated by their subsequent consequences.

Consider, then, the following two snippets of defense argument. The first is in chronological order.

> As the firetruck approached the intersection, it flashed its lights, but it did not use its siren. The plaintiff saw the firetruck and stopped for it, but she did not have time to pull over. That is why the accident occurred. She saw the firetruck only at the last moment.

Now, the same argument presented topically.

> The plaintiff stopped her car in the middle of the street. She didn't pull over. This can only mean that the firetruck was not using its siren. Everyone knows that you must pull over as soon as you become aware of an emergency vehicle, and a siren can be heard blocks away. The location of the plaintiff's car tells us that she saw that firetruck only at the last moment.

Chapter Fifteen

While both arguments make the same point, the discussion is clearly more persuasive once it is freed of the chronological straitjacket. Moving backward and forward in time places events in the most compelling order.

Chronology is, of course, unavoidable in the structure of a closing argument. There will come a time, or several times, in every argument when key occurrences will have to be time-ordered. Indeed, the precise sequence of events can often be the central issue in a case. But do not rely on chronology as your primary organizational device. Instead, think of the case as consisting of a series of discrete sub-stories. Each sub-story can be set out in chronological order while maintaining an overall format of topical organization.

b. Witness Listing

Some lawyers persist in presenting closing argument as a series of witness descriptions and accounts, essentially recapitulating the testimony of each person who took the stand. This approach diminishes the argument's logical coherence and force. Where topical organization focuses on the importance of issues and chronological organization focuses on real-life sequences of events, witness listing depends on nothing more than the serendipity of what each witness said. It is a lazy, and usually ineffective, method of organization.

This does not mean that you avoid mentioning witnesses. You will often need to compare witness accounts in the course of a closing argument: to demonstrate the consistency of your own witnesses as opposed to the contradictions among the opposition's witnesses; to dwell on the integrity and credibility of your witnesses; or to point out the bias and self-interest of opposing witnesses. All of this can be accomplished, and accomplished better, through topical organization.

3. Whatever Your Format, Follow These Guidelines

Whatever organizational method you employ, follow these important principles.

a. Start Strong and End Strong

Primacy and recency apply with full force to the closing argument. Closing argument gives you a limited window in which to attempt to shape the factfinder's mental image of the acts, events, and circumstances at issue in the case. Eliminate anything that bores the judge or jurors, or that distracts from the task at hand. Devote your prime time—the very beginning and the very end of the argument—to the most important considerations in the case.

The strength of a starting point can be measured against standards such as theory value, thematic value, dramatic impact, or undeniability. What is the central proposition of your client's theory? What aspect of the evidence best evokes your

Closing Argument

theme? What is the most emotional or memorable factor in the case? What is the opposing party's greatest concession?

In the fire engine case, plaintiff's counsel might begin the closing argument with a compelling restatement of her theory.

> The plaintiff was driving safely in the southbound lane of Craycroft Road. A firetruck approached the intersection from the east, flashing its lights and sounding its siren. As the law requires and as every driver understands, she stopped her car. All of the other traffic stopped as well, with one exception. The defendant kept his foot on the accelerator until it was too late, causing him to crash his car right into the backside of the plaintiff's automobile.

Alternatively, plaintiff's counsel could start with her theme.

> This accident happened because the defendant was too busy to be careful. He was so preoccupied with his thoughts of a new client that he failed to notice what every other driver on the road saw and heard. He was so late and so rushed and so distracted that he paid no attention to the traffic all around him. He was in such a hurry to get to his office that the firetruck's emergency lights and sirens had no impact on him at all. He was so busy that getting to work became more important than ordinary caution. And make no mistake—ordinary caution would have been enough to avoid this accident completely.

Dramatic impact also works.

> In a single instant, the defendant's carelessness changed the plaintiff's life forever. In one moment, she went from being an ordinary, healthy, active individual to being a person who cannot go camping, lift a child, or even prepare a meal without pain.

As does undeniability.

> The one thing the defendant cannot deny is that he failed to stop for a fire engine. There is no doubt that the firetruck was there. There is no doubt that it was answering a call. There is no doubt that the other cars stopped. And there is no doubt that the defendant kept driving right into the back of the plaintiff's automobile.

Focus the opening salvo of your closing argument on making the trier of fact *want* to decide the case in your favor.

Employ the last few minutes of your closing argument for the same function, either summarizing the theory, utilizing the theme, driving home the strongest evidence, or painting the most compelling picture. Ending on a strong and memorable note is essential for the defendant, who cannot argue again following the plaintiff's rebuttal.

Chapter Fifteen

b. Argue Your Affirmative Case First

Most closing arguments consist of two distinct components: developing the affirmative case and debunking the opposing party's claims and/or defenses. It is generally preferable to build up your own case first before debunking the opposition's.

As plaintiff/prosecution in particular, resist the temptation to begin by criticizing the defense case. No matter how weak or ridiculous the defenses, it is best to begin with the strong points of your own case. You bear the burden of proof and cannot win without establishing all of the elements of your affirmative case. Refuting the defense is fruitless if you cannot prove your own case first.

The defendant has more latitude. The factfinder is unlikely to draw any adverse inference should you begin by refuting the plaintiff/prosecution's case. Factfinders will, in fact, be waiting to hear the defendant's denial. Unless there is an obvious reason not to, begin by denying the claims of the plaintiff/prosecution. After all, the natural response of an innocent person accused of wrongdoing is denial.

Once you assert a strong denial, support it, if possible, by developing an affirmative case. Explain why the defendant is right before explaining why the plaintiff is wrong.

Finally, devote a substantial portion of your closing argument to the weaknesses in the opposition case. Make notes during the plaintiff/prosecution's closing, and create a closing that parallels your opponent's presentation, picking it apart at every possible step.

Using this format, the defendant's argument in the firetruck case might—in extremely skeletal form—proceed as follows:

> The defendant was not the cause of this accident. It was the plaintiff's fault. The defendant was driving safely and carefully; well within the speed limit. The fire engine was not sounding its siren, but as soon as he saw it, he hit his brakes and started to pull over. Unfortunately, the plaintiff chose to stop dead in the middle of the road instead of pulling over to the side of the road as the traffic laws require.

The real argument, of course, would be far longer, but the organization of the above paragraph holds true. Counsel began with a denial, demonstrated that the defendant's actions were reasonable, and went on to explain the plaintiff's own negligence.

c. Embrace or Displace the Burden of Proof

If you represent the prosecution in a criminal matter, you have no other choice than to embrace your burden of proof. The less you address it, the more likely the trier of fact is to question whether you have met it. Remind the factfinder that you have the burden, acknowledge that you are required to prove each element of your case beyond a reasonable doubt, and confidently state that you have met your burden.

The plaintiff in a civil case must also embrace the burden, with one proviso. Given that the burden in civil cases is the lesser requirement of proof by a preponderance of the evidence, explain to the jury what that means. (There is no need to give this explanation to a judge during a bench trial.) For example, you might say:

> We have met our burden of proof by a preponderance of the evidence. Remember that this is not a criminal case and the plaintiff does not have to prove its case beyond a reasonable doubt. Instead, we need only prove to you that it is more likely than not that the defendant is liable. That means that we need only tip the scales of justice one small fraction to prevail—if you find that it is fifty-one percent likely that the defendant is liable and forty-nine percent likely that the plaintiff is not, you must find in favor of my client.

When defending criminal cases, emphasize the fact that the prosecution has the burden of proof and that the defendant is presumed innocent by law and has no obligation to put forth any testimony or evidence whatsoever. When the defendant does testify, consider reminding the jurors that the defendant did not have to take the stand but chose to so that the jurors could hear directly from the defendant that they did not commit the crime charged.

Unlike criminal proceedings, civil matters require the defendant to proceed with mild caution when raising the burden of proof. It should be raised, to be sure. But, because it is a relatively low requirement to meet, the defendant is best off stopping with the recitation that "The plaintiff has the burden to prove their case by a preponderance of the evidence." Many lawyers state the term ominously and place emphasis on the word "preponderance," hoping to make the plaintiff's burden sound heavy.

d. Address Witness Credibility Throughout

As discussed above, reciting the trial testimony witness by witness is a useless endeavor. Likewise, there is little value in addressing the credibility of each witness in turn. Instead, weave discussion of the witnesses, and their relative credibility, into the fabric of the story you tell during your closing.

In most cases, discuss witnesses only at the point that they become important to the theory of the case. So, for example, the credibility of the defendant in the firetruck case should not form a separate section of the plaintiff's argument. Plaintiff gains little value from a freestanding attack on the defendant's credibility; it will seem like just that, an attack. On the other hand, the factfinder will be most receptive to a credibility argument at a moment when its significance is apparent.

Chapter Fifteen

> Let us turn to the question of the siren. There is no doubt that a fire engine's siren is a signal that traffic must stop. Ignoring a siren is definite negligence. The defendant claims that there was no siren, but he cannot be believed. He has too much at stake in this case, and he knows that the siren is a vital piece of evidence against him. And remember that Lieutenant Janis Regnier testified that she always used her siren when answering a call. She has no stake in this case and no reason to tell you anything but the truth. So it comes down to this: either you believe the defendant or you believe Lieutenant Regnier.

While the defendant might be unsavory and Lieutenant Regnier upstanding, it makes no sense to discuss their character traits in the abstract. By weaving the witnesses into the story, however, counsel can make full use of their disparate believability.

e. **Argue Damages**

The timing of when to argue damages in civil cases presents a special problem, especially in the context of cases involving torts. Where your mock trial covers both liability and damages in a tort case, argue liability before proceeding to damages. Particularly where the damages are great or ongoing, the trier of fact will be more inclined to accept the plaintiff's argument once convinced the defendant is liable for those damages. The desire to award damages flows naturally from a conclusion of liability. The converse, however, is not true. Proof of damages does not necessarily imply that the defendant was at fault.

For the same reason, defendants are often advised to address damages first, if at all. It is discordant to argue, "The defendant was not at fault, but even if he was, the damages were not so great as the plaintiff claims." Any discussion of damages that follows may be taken as a concession of liability.

Of course, you might have a mock trial based primarily, if not exclusively, on the issue of damages. In these cases, damages form the first, last, and most important part of the argument.

Summary
FINAL ARGUMENT STRUCTURE
• Use topical organization whenever possible • Use chronological and witness-by-witness organization sparingly • Use jury instructions (if allowed) • Start strong and end strong • Argue your affirmative case first

Closing Argument

> **Summary**
> **FINAL ARGUMENT STRUCTURE**
> - Tie up cross-examination
> - Embrace or displace the burden of proof
> - Address witness credibility throughout
> - Argue damages (if applicable)

IV. Objections

Some mock trial competitions do not permit objections during closing arguments. If allowed, objections are still unusual during closings. It is common courtesy to allow opposing counsel to speak uninterrupted. This does not mean, of course, that improper arguments should be tolerated.

A. Raising Objections

If opposing counsel makes an improper argument (as discussed above in Section II(C)), do not hesitate to object.

Objections during closing argument follow the same general pattern as objections during witness examinations. Stand and state succinctly the ground for the objection. There is usually no need to present argument unless requested by the court.

It is unethical to raise objections during your opponent's closing argument simply for the purpose of interfering or breaking up its flow. The mock trial judge will not take kindly to such behavior.

B. Responding to Objections

The best response to an objection is often no response. An objection disrupts the flow of closing argument, and an extended colloquy with the court only prolongs the interruption. A dignified silence allows the court to rule and impresses the judge or jurors with the rudeness of the interruption. Even more effective is keeping silent without turning your gaze away from the factfinder.

Once the court rules, whether favorably or unfavorably, simply proceed by adapting your argument to the court's ruling.

C. Asking for a Cautionary Instruction

In jury trials, when an objection to a closing argument has been sustained, the judge will usually caution the jurors to disregard the offending remarks. If the court

Chapter Fifteen

does not give such an instruction on its own motion, objecting counsel should ask for one. To do so, simply wait for the court's ruling and then politely say, "We ask that the jury be instructed to disregard that statement, Your Honor." Doing so allows the jury to see that opposing counsel has made an improper argument, which can affect their credibility and thus their persuasiveness.

In extreme cases, and especially where a cautionary instruction may only exacerbate the situation, a motion for a mistrial may be appropriate when allowed by your competition rules. To avoid letting the jurors know you are moving for a mistrial, you can simply state, "I have a motion to make and ask to be heard at sidebar," or "Your Honor, I'd like to make a motion outside the presence of the jury." Then, when it is safe to do so, explain why the offending argument has cost your client a fair trial and ask the court to declare a mistrial.

Appendix

OBJECTIONS FOR YOUR TRIAL BINDER	
Ambiguous, Vague, Unintelligible Argumentative Asked and Answered Beyond the Scope (redirect examination only) Compound Question Improper Lay Opinion Improper Character Evidence Irrelevant Lack of Foundation Leading (direct or redirect examination only) (Calls for) Narrative Answer Nonresponsive (cross-examination only) (Calls for) Speculation	**Hearsay** <u>Non-Hearsay Statements:</u> • Admission of Party Opponent • Prior Inconsistent Statement • Statements Not Offered for Their Truth <u>Hearsay Exceptions:</u> • Business Record • Excited Utterance • Present Sense Impression • Public Record/Vital Statistic • Recorded Recollection • State of Mind • Statement Made for Medical Diagnosis <u>Exceptions that only apply if the declarant is unavailable to testify as a witness at the trial:</u> • Former Testimony (when offered against the eliciting party) • Dying Declaration • Statement Against Interest

APPENDIX

INDEX

A

Admissibility
    Facts, 2IID
    Foundation
        Conditional, 8IC4
        Specificity, 8IB3

Admissions of party
    Hearsay, 8IIF1
    Hearsay exception, 8IVE3

Affirmative defenses
    Criminal cases, 1IB2

Allusions
    Closing argument, 15IIB3b

Analogies
    Closing argument, 15IIB3a

Apposition
    Communication, verbal, 3IIIH

Argumentative questions
    Objections, 13IVA4

B

Bench trial
    Jury trial or, treatment as, 4IA

Body movement
    Nonverbal communication, 3IID

Burden of proof
    Civil cases, 1IA2
    Closing argument, 15IIIB3c
    Criminal cases, 1IB1

Business records
    Hearsay exception, 8IVE1

C

Casefiles
    Anatomy of, 1IV

Case law
    Generally, 1IC
    Applicable, 2IIA

Cause of action
    Civil cases, 1IA1

Chain of custody
    Exhibits, 8IVA2

Character evidence (*See* Evidence)

Charts
    Demonstrative evidence, 8IVC1

Circumstantial evidence
    Authorship or origin, 8IVD1b
    Closing argument, 15IIB2
    Cross-examination, 9IIIB1d

Civil cases
    Generally, 1IA
    Burden of proof, 1IA2
    Cause of action, 1IA1
    Damages, 1IA3

Closing argument
    Affirmative case first, arguing, 15IIIB3b
    Allusions, 15IIB3b
    Alternative organization methods, 15IIIB2
    Analogies, 15IIB3a
    Burden of proof, 15IIIB3c
    Chronological organization, 15IIIB2a
    Circumstantial evidence, 15IIB2
    Common sense, 15IIIA1e
    Content, 15IIIA
    Cross-examinations, tying up, 15IIB6
    Damages, arguing, 15IIB12; 15IIIB3e
    Defendant's argument, 15IIIA2b
    Details
        Accumulating, 15IIB2
        Supportive, 15IIIA1d
    Elements, 15IIIB1b
    Emotion, sympathy, or passion, making appeals to, 15IIC5

Ending strong, 15IIIB3a
Evidence
    Misstating, 15IIC6
    Misusing, 15IIC2
Format to advantage, using, 15IIIA2
Impermissible arguments, avoiding, 15IIC
Inferences and conclusions, making, 15IIB1
Issues, 15IIIB1a
Jury instructions, 15IIIB1c
Known facts, 15IIIA1a
Law, applying, 15IIB13
Misstating law or discouraging jury from using it, 15IIC7
Objections
    Generally, 15IV
    Cautionary instruction, asking for, 15IVC
    Raising, 15IVA
    Responding to, 15IVB
Opposing witnesses
    Demeanor, commenting on, 15IIB9
    Refuting testimony, 15IIB5
Organization, 15IIIB
Personal beliefs, interjecting, 15IIC3
Personal interest of fact-finder, making appeals to, 15IIC4
Persuasive story, telling, 15IIIA1
Plaintiff/prosecution argument in chief
    Generally, 15IIIA2a
    Rebuttal, anticipating, 15IIIA2bii
    Responding to, 15IIIA2bi
Plaintiff/prosecution rebuttal, 15IIIA2c
Planning, 2IVA
Plausibility, 15IIIA1e
Privilege, commenting on, 15IIC1
Promises kept and broken, commenting, 15IIB11
Purpose of, 15I
Reasons, 15IIIA1b
Rules of, 15II
Starting strong, 15IIIB3a
Stories, 15IIB3c
Theme of case, using, 15IIA
Theory of case, using, 15IIA
Topical organization, 15IIIB1
Undisputed facts, emphasizing, 15IIB4
Weaknesses, confronting own, 15IIB10
Weight given to evidence, asserting, 15IIB8
Witness
    Believing, 15IIIA1c
    Credibility, 15IIB7; 15IIIB3d
    Demeanor, commenting on, 15IIB9
    Listing, 15IIIB2b
    Motive, 15IIB7
    Refuting testimony, 15IIB5

Communication
Confidence, 3IA
Effective, importance of, 3I
Integrity, 3IB
Nonverbal
    Body movement, 3IID
    Eye contact, 3IIC
    Reliance on notes, minimizing, 3IIE
    Role, staying in, 3IIA
    Witnesses, upstaging, 3IIB
Verbal
    Apposition, using, 3IIIH
    Descriptive language and legalese
        Judge as fact-finder, 3IIIC2
        Jury as fact-finder, 3IIIC1
    Duration, 3IIIE
    Enumeration, using, 3IIIJ
    Headlines, using, 3IIII
    Judge, respecting, 3IIIA
    Nouns and verbs instead of adjectives, using, 3IIIG
    Overly thankful, 3IIIK
    Powerful speech, using, 3IIIB
    Primacy and recency, using, 3IIID
    Reflective questioning, 3IIIF
    Repetition, 3IIIE
    Witnesses' answers, responding to, 3IIIL

Compound questions
Objections, 13IVA2

Confidence
Communication, effective, 3IA

Controversy
Planning for, 4IIC

Conversations
In-person, 8IIB1
Telephone, 8IIB2

Courtroom
Format of, 1III
Moving around, 4IC

Criminal cases
Generally, 1IB

Affirmative defenses, 1IB2
Aggravating and mitigating factors, 1IB2
Burden of proof, 1IB1

Cross-examination
Affirmative information, 9IIIB2b
Already know answers, asking questions to which, 9IIC
Arguing with witness, 9IID
Brevity, 9IIB
Challenging information, 9IIIB2d
Circumstantial evidence, 9IIIB1d
Closing argument, tying up during, 15IIB6
Content, 9IIIA
Control, staying in, 9IF
Correcting problem yourself, 9IIF1
Damage done on direct, repair or minimize, 9IA
Details first, 9IIIB1c
Detract from opponent's case, 9IC
Discredit witness or another witness, 9IE
Enhancing case, 9IB
Ethics of, 9IV
Exhibits, lay foundation for, 9ID
Expert (*See* Expert testimony)
Expert Witnesses (*See* Expert witnesses)
Fair questions, 9IID2
Format, classic, 9IIIB2
Foundation, 8IC3
Friendly information, 9IIIB2a
Hostile information, 9IIIB2e
Judge's help, 9IIF2
Leading questions, 9IIA
Objections, 9IID
Organization, 9IIIB
Planning, 2IVC; 9III
Purpose of, 9I
Questions, preparing, 9IIIA2
Recross-examination, 11II
Responsive answer, 9IIF
Rules of, 9II
Short questions, 9IID1
Starting strong, 9IIIB1a
Tips for organizing, 9IIIB1
Topical organization, 9IIIB1b
Ultimate question, 9IIE
Uncontrovertible information, 9IIIB2c
Usable universe, determining, 9IIIA1
Zinger, saving, 9IIIB1e

D

Damages
Civil cases, 1IA3
Closing argument, arguing during, 15IIB12; 15IIB3e
Cross-examination, 9IA

Demonstrations
Conducting, 3IVC

Demonstrative evidence
Charts, 8IVC1
Diagrams, 8IVC1
Exhibits, 8IIIB2
Maps, 8IVC1
Plan to use, informing court on, 4IIB

Diagrams
Demonstrative evidence, 8IVC1

Direct examinations
Affirm before refuting, 7IIIB6
Attention of trier of fact, holding, 7IF
Clincher, ending with, 7IIIB8
Content of
  Generally, 7IIIA
  Exclude in, 7IIIA2
  Include in, 7IIIA1
Credibility of witnesses, 7IE
Disputed facts, 7IC
Ethics of
  Objectionable questions, asking, 7IVA
  Unreasonable inferences, 7IVB
Expert witnesses, 12III
Identification of defendant, 7IIE
Ignoring rules, 7IIIB9
Interrupting action, 7IIIB5
"Narrative" responses, 7IIB
Nonleading questions, 7IIIA
Nonopinion rule, 7IIC
Objectionable questions, asking, 7IVA
Organization, 7IIIB
Overall, 7IIIB1a
Planning, 2IVB; 7III
Point of, getting to, 7IIIB3
Recollection of witness, 7IID
Role of, 7I
Rules of, 7II
Sting, drawing, 7IIIB7
Stipulations, 7IIF
Story, telling, 7IIIB4
Sub-examinations, 7IIIB1b

Index

Theory of case, setting forth, 7IA
Topical organization, 7IIIB2
Undisputed facts, 7IB

Documentary evidence
Authentication, 8IVD1
Circumstantial evidence, 8IVD1b
Exhibits, 8IIIB3
Handwriting, 8IVD1a
Mailing or transmission, 8IVD1c
Signature, 8IVD1a
Transmission or mailing, 8IVD1c

Duration
Communication, verbal, 3IIIE

Dying declaration
Hearsay, 8IIF5

E

Enumeration
Communication, verbal, 3IIIJ

Ethics
Generally, 13III
Cross-examination, 9IV
Direct examination
  Objectionable questions, 7IVA
  Unreasonable inferences, 7IVB
Objectionable questions
  Asking, 13IIIA
  Making, 13IIIB

Evidence
Character
  Crime, conviction of, 6VA
  Objections, 13IVB4
  Untruthfulness, 6VB
Circumstantial (*See* Circumstantial evidence)
Closing argument
  Misstating, 15IIC6
  Misuse during, 15IIC2
Crime, conviction of, 6VA
Documentary (*See* Documentary evidence)
Exhibits (*See* Exhibits)
Foundation (*See* Foundation)
Hearsay, 6IV
Opening statement, 14IB
Personal knowledge, lack of, 6III
Prejudice, unfair, 6II
Relevance, 6I

Speculation, 6III
Untruthfulness, 6VB

Excited utterances
Hearsay, 8IIF3

Exhibits
Authenticity, establishing, 8IVA1
Chain of custody, 8IVA2
Cross-examination to lay foundation for, 9ID
Demonstrative evidence, 8IIIB2
Documentary evidence, 8IIIB3
Foundation for, laying, 7ICD
Identification, mark for, 8IIIC1
Illustrative aids, 8IVC2
Offering at trial, 8IIIC
Offering into evidence, 8IIIC6
Opposing counsel, identify for, 8IIIC2
Photographs, 8IVB
Publication of, 8IIIC7a
Real or tangible evidence, 8IIIB1; 8IVA
Role of, 8IIIA
Specific foundations for, 8IV
Sufficiency, 8IIIC5
Use of, 3IVA
Using, 8IIIC7b
Witness
  Identifying exhibit, 8IIIC4
  Showing to, 8IIIC3

Expert testimony
Affirming, 12IVB1
Areas of agreement, 12IVB2
Areas of expertise, 12IIA
Assumptions, 12IIIB4b; 12IVE1
Credentials
  Generally, 12IVA2
  Challenging, 12IVA
  Contrast, 12IVA2c
  Missing, 12IVA2b
Cross-examination
  Generally, 12IV
  Affirming, 12IVB1
  Areas of agreement, 12IVB2
  Assumptions, 12IVE1
  Challenging credentials, 12IVA
  Contrast credentials, 12IVA2c
  Credentials, 12IVA2
  Favorable information, 12IVB
  Fees, 12IVC1
  Impartiality of witness, 12IVC
  Missing credentials, 12IVA2b

318

Omissions, 12IVD
Opposing party's conduct,
 criticizing, 12IVB3
Positional bias, 12IVC3
Relationship with participants,
 12IVC2
Scope of expertise, 12IVA2a
Technique or theory, 12IVF
Uncertainty, 12IVE2
Voir dire, 12IVA1
Data, explaining, 12IIIB4a
 Direct examination, 12III
 Favorable information, 12IVB
 Foreshadow, 12IIIB1
 Impartiality
  Generally, 12IVC
  Fees, 12IVC1
  Positional bias, 12IVC3
  Relationship with participants,
   12IVC2
 Internal summaries, 12IIIA3a
 Introducing witness, 12IIIB1
 Narratives, 12IIIA3
 Omissions, 12IVD
 Opinion
  Generally, 12IIIB3a; 12IIIB4
  Bases for, 12IIC
  Scope of, 12IIB
 Opposing party's conduct,
  criticizing, 12IVB3
 Organizing, 12IIIB
 Plain language, 12IIIA2
 Planning, 12IIIA
 Purpose of, 12I
 Qualifications, 12IIIB2; 12IIIB2b
 Scope of expertise, 12IVA2a
 Technical requirements,
  12IIIB2a
 Technique or theory, 12IVF
 Tendering witness, 12IIIB2c
 Theory
  Determining, 12IIIA1
  Differentiation, 12IIIB5
  Eliciting, 12IIIB3b
 Uncertainty, 12IVE2
 Visual aids, 12IIIA3b
 Voir dire, 12IVA1

Effective witnesses
 Direct and cross-examination, techniques
  for handling
  Advocates and, 5IIIG

Assumptions, premises, or
 predicates separately,
 addressing internal, 5IIIC
Care listening and pause before
 answering, 5IIIA
Compound, 5IIIB2
Fight and, 5IIIF
Hearsay, calls for, 5IIIB5
Inferences, reasonable, 5IIII
Listen for clues within objections,
 5IIIB
Precise questions, answering, 5IIID
Referring documents, 5IIIE
Relevance, 5IIIB4
Speculation, calls for, 5IIIB3
Steady explanation, 5IIIH
Vague, 5IIIB1
Importance of, 5I
Key qualities of
 Believability and credibility, 5IIB
 Confident and, 5IIB
 Describing key facts, 5IIA3
 Forgetting important fact, 5IIA2
 Interest and, 5IIC
 Preparation, 5IIA
 Taking note for any conflicts, 5IIA1

Eye contact
 Nonverbal communication, 3IIC

F

Favorable facts
 Identifying, 2IIC

Fees
 Expert testimony, 12IVC1

Foundation
 Admissibility
  Conditional, 8IC4
  Specific, 8IB3
 Authenticity, 8IB2
 Character, 8IIE
 Components of, 8IB
 Crimes or past misconduct, other, 8IIE1
 Cross-examination, 8IC3
 Documentary evidence (*See*
  Documentary evidence)
 Evidence, testimonial
  Habit, 8IID
  Identification, prior, 8IIC
  In-person conversations, 8IIB1

Index

    Personal knowledge, 8IIA
    Routine, 8IID
    Telephone conversations, 8IIB2
Exhibits (*See* Exhibits)
Habit, 8IID
Hearsay statements (*See* Hearsay)
Identification, prior, 8IIC
In-person conversations, 8IIB1
Personal knowledge, 8IIA
Relevance, 8IB1
Reputation, 8IIE
Requirement of, 8IA
Routine, 8IID
Telephone conversations, 8IIB2
Untruthfulness, reputation for, 8IIE2
Witnesses
    Multiple, 8IC2
    Single, 8IC1

H

Handwriting
    Documentary evidence, 8IVD1a
Headlines
    Communication, verbal, 3IIII
Hearsay
    Admissions of party, 8IIF1
    Business records, 8IVE1
    Dying declaration, 8IIF5
    Evidence, 6IV
    Exceptions
        Generally, 8IVD; 13IVB1b
        Business records, 8IVE1
        Party admissions, 8IVE3
        Public records, 8IVE2
    Excited utterance, 8IIF3
    Objections, 13IVB1
    Party admissions, 8IVE3
    Present sense impression, 8IIF2
    Public records, 8IVE2
    Statements, 8IIF; 13IVB1a
    State of mind, 8IIF4
"Housekeeping" matters
    Generally, 4I

I

Impeachment
    Case-specific motive, 10IIIC2

    Character of witness, 10IIIC1
    Confront witness, 10IIIB3
    Conviction of crime, 10IIIC1a
    Favorable information, 10IID
    Impaired perception or recollection, 10IIIC1c
    Inconsistencies, actual, 10IIB
    Multiple, 10IIE
    Omission, 10IIIB
    Opportunity to tell full story, accreditation of prior, 10IIIA2; 10IIIB2
    Past untruthfulness and other bad acts, 10IIIC1b
    Prior inconsistent statements, 10IIIA
    Prior statement, confront, 10IIIA3
    Recommit witness, 10IIIA1; 10IIIB1
    Role of, 10I
    Rules of, 10II
    Significant matters, 10IIA
    Success before beginning, 10IIC
    Timing of, 10IIF
Integrity
    Communication, effective, 3IB

J

Judge
    Cross-examination, 9IIF2
    Objections (*See* Objections)
    Verbal communication with
        Descriptive and legalese, 3IIIC2
        Showing respect, 3IIIA
Jury
    Verbal communication with, descriptive and legalese, 3IIIC1
Jury instructions
    Closing argument, 15IIIB1c
Jury trial
    Bench trial or, treatment as, 4IA
    Objections, requesting sidebar during, 13IIC
    Stipulations aloud, reading, 4IE

L

Leading questions
    Cross-examination, 9IIA
    Objections, 13IVA1

M

Mail
  Documentary evidence, 8IVD1c
Maps
  Demonstrative evidence, 8IVC1
Motions in limine
  Generally, 4III

N

Narratives
  Direct examination, 7IIB
  Expert witnesses, 11IIIA3
  Objections, 13IVA5
Nonleading questions
  Direct examination, 7IIA
Nonopinion rule
  Direct examinations, 7IIC
Notes
  Reliance on, minimizing, 3IIE

O

Objections
  Appropriate, raising, 13IID
  Argumentative question, 13IVA4
  Arguments to judge, directing, 13IIB
  Asked and answered, 13IVA6
  Authenticity, 13IVB7
  Carefulness, 13IIA
  Character evidence, 13IVB4
  Closing argument (*See* Closing argument)
  Common, 13IV
  Compound question, 13IVA2
  Conviction of crime, 13IVB4a
  Cross-examination, 9IID
  Direct examinations, 7IVA
  Facts not in evidence, assuming, 13IVA7
  Grounds for, 13IID2
  Hearsay, 13IVB1
  Irrelevant, 13IVB2
  Judge, directing arguments to, 13IIB
  Judge's consideration of, pausing for, 13IID3
  Judge's ruling, following up, 13IIG
  Jury trials, requesting sidebars in, 13IIC
  Lack of foundation, 13IVB8
  Lay opinion, improper, 13IVB6
  Leading question, 13IVA1
  Narratives, 13IVA5
  Nonresponsive answers, 13IVA8
  Nonsubstantive, 13IA
  Objectionable questions
    Asking, 7IVA; 13IIIA
    Making, 13IIIB
  Opening statement
    Raising during, 14IVA
    Responding during, 14IVB
  Overruled, 13IIG1
  Personal knowledge, lack of, 13IVB5
  Planning, 2IVD
  Prejudice, unfair, 13IVB3
  Purpose of, 13I
  Repeated, 13IID5a
  Reputation, 13IVB4c
  Responding to
    Conditional offer, 13IIF3b
    Court, 13IID4
    Cure when possible, 13IIF4
    Limited admissibility, 13IIF3a
    Request to heard, 13IIF2
    Specificity, 13IIF3
    Waiting for judge's cue, 13IIF1
  Rules of, 13II
  Sidebar conference, 4IB; 13IIC
  Speculation, 13IVB5
  Standing up while, 13IID1
  Substantive, 13IB; 13IVB
  Sustained, 13IIG2
  "Tactical", making, 13IIIC
  Theory of case, reevaluating, 13IIH
  Timing, 13IIE
  Untruthfulness, 13IVB4b
  Vague question, 13IVA3
  Voir dire, requesting, 13IID5b

Opening statement
  Action or key events, 14IIIA2b
  Advocate for client, 14IC
  Anticipated evidence, explaining, 14IB
  Argumentative, 14IIA2
  Chronology, using, 14IIIB3b
  Commenting on law, 14IIB
  Content, 14IIIA
  Contrast facts persuasively, 14IID
  Defendant's, 14IIIA3b
  Defining argument, 14IIA1
  Introductions, 14IIIB2
  Key events or action, 14IIIA2b
  Legal issues, highlighting, 14IIIB4
  Moment, grabbing, 14IA

Necessary facts, 14IIIA2
Objections
    Raising, 14IVA
    Responding to, 14IVB
Ordering of facts persuasively, 14IID
Organization, 14IIIB
Physical scene, 14IIIA2a
Plaintiff/prosecution, 14IIIA3a
Planning, 2IVA; 14III
Provable facts, 14IIIA1
Purpose of, 14I
Reference to other side's case, 14IIIA3
Rules of, 14II
Theme of case, 14IIC2; 14IIIB1
Theory of case, 14IIC1; 14IIIB1
Transactions and agreements, 14IIIA2c
Verdict, requesting, 14IIIB5
Witness-by-witness approach, avoiding, 14IIIB3a

Order of trial
Generally, 1II

P

Photographs
Exhibits, 8IVB

Preliminary matters
Generally, 4I

Present sense impression
Hearsay, 8IIF2

Pretrial notice
Providing, 4IIA

Primacy and recency
Communication, verbal, 3IIID

Prior inconsistent statements
Impeachment, 10IIIA

Public records
Hearsay exception, 8IVE2

R

Real evidence
Exhibits, 8IIIB1; 8IVA

Recross-examination
Generally, 11II

Redirect examinations
Conducting, 11IE

Planning, 11IC
Purpose of, 11IA
Rules of, 11IB
Waiving, 11ID

Reflective questioning
Communication, verbal, 3IIIF

Repetition
Communication, verbal, 3IIIE

Reputation
Foundation, 8IIE
Objections, 13IVB4c
Untruthfulness, 8IIE2

Responses
Planning, 2IVD

S

Sidebar conference
Jury trials, objections during, 13IIC
Objections, 4IB

Signature
Documentary evidence, 8IVD1a

State of mind
Hearsay, 8IIF4

Statutes
Applicable, 2IIA

Stipulations
Direct examinations, 7IIF
Jury trial, reading aloud at, 4IE

Surprises
Planning for, 4IIC

T

Telephone conversations
Foundation, 8IIB2

Theme of case
Closing argument, 15IIA
Developing, 2IIIB2
Opening statement, 14IIC2; 14IIIB1

Theory of case
Closing argument, 15IIA
Developing, 2IIIB1
Direct examination, setting forth during, 7IA

Opening statement, 14IIC1; 14IIIB1
Reevaluating, 13IIH

Trial
Key facts for, compiling summary of, 2IIE
Law, understanding, 1I
Order of, 1II

Trial binder
Organizing, 2I

Trial story
Developing, 2III
Possibilities for, consider, 2IIIA
Returning to, 2IIIB3

U

Unfavorable facts
Identifying, 2IIC

Unreasonable inferences
Direct examinations, 7IVB

V

Vague questions
Objections, 13IVA3

Visual aids
Creating, 3IVB
Expert testimony, 11IIIA5

Voirdire
Cross-examination of expert's credentials, 11IVA1
Objection requesting, 13IID5b

W

Waiver
Redirect examinations, 11ID

Witnesses
Answers of, responding to, 3IIIL
Closing argument (*See* Closing argument)
Cross-examination (*See* Cross-examination)
Direct examination (*See* Direct examinations)
Exhibits
  Identifying, 8IIIC4
  Showing, 8IIIC3
Expert (*See* Expert testimony; Expert Witnesses)
Helpful, determining, 2IIB
Impeachment (*See* Impeachment)
Key favorable and unfavorable facts, identifying, 2IIC
Multiple, 8IC2
Nonverbal communication with
  Eye contact, 3IIC
  Upstaging, 3IIB
Opening statement, 14IIIB3a
Permission prior to approaching, seeking, 4ID
Single, using, 8IC1

www.ingramcontent.com/pod-product-compliance
Lightning Source LLC
LaVergne TN
LVHW061727060925
820435LV00019B/166